# Welcome to the *EVERYTHING*® series!

These handy, accessible books give you all you need to tackle a difficult project, gain a new hobby, comprehend a fascinating topic, prepare for an exam, or even brush up on something you learned back in school but have since forgotten.

You can read an *EVERYTHING*® book from cover-to-cover or just pick out the information you want from our four useful boxes: e-facts, e-ssentials, e-alerts, and e-questions. We literally give you everything you need to know on the subject, but throw in a lot of fun stuff along the way, too.

We now have well over 100 *EVERYTHING*® books in print, spanning such wide-ranging topics as weddings, pregnancy, wine, learning guitar, one-pot cooking, managing people, and so much more. When you're done reading them all, you can finally say you know *EVERYTHING*®!

**FACTS**
Important sound bytes
of information

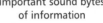
**SSENTIALS**
Quick handy tips

**ALERT**
Urgent warnings

**QUESTIONS?**
Solutions to
common problems

# THE

# EVERYTHING®

# DIABETES COOKBOOK

300 creative and healthy recipes
that put the fun back into cooking

Pamela Rice Hahn
Foreword by Sally Kattau, R.D., L.D., C.D.E.

Adams Media Corporation
Avon, Massachusetts

EDITORIAL
Publishing Director: Gary M. Krebs
Managing Editor: Kate McBride
Copy Chief: Laura MacLaughlin
Acquisitions Editor: Bethany Brown
Development Editor: Christel A. Shea
Production Editor: Khrysti Nazzaro

PRODUCTION
Production Director: Susan Beale
Production Manager: Michelle Roy Kelly
Series Designers: Daria Perreault, Colleen Cunningham
Layout and Graphics: Colleen Cunningham,
Rachael Eiben, Michelle Roy Kelly, Daria Perreault

An Everything® Series Book.
Everything® and everything.com® are registered trademarks of F+W Publications, Inc.

Published by Adams Media, an F+W Publications Company
57 Littlefield Street, Avon, MA 02322 U.S.A.
*www.adamsmedia.com*
ISBN 13: 978-1-58062-691-0
ISBN 10: 1-58062-691-2
Printed in the United States of America.

J I H G

**Library of Congress Cataloging-in-Publication Data**
Hahn, Pamela Rice.
The everything diabetes cookbook : 300 creative and healthy recipes
that put the fun back into cooking / Pamela Rice Hahn
p.    cm. -- (An everything series book)
Includes bibliographical references. ISBN 1-58062-691-2
1. Diabetes–Diet therapy–Recipes. II. Title. III. Everything series.
RC662 .H33 2002
641.5′6314–dc21            2002008442

**Recipes that include smoked ingredients or sausage may be high in sodium.
Consult with your doctor and use in moderation.**

Information in the Nutritional Analyses was generated by the NutriBase 2001 software program.

Many of the designations used by manufacturers and sellers to distinguish their products are claimed as trademarks. Where those designations appear in this book and Adams Media was aware of a trademark claim, the designations have been printed in initial capital letters.

This publication is designed to provide accurate and authoritative information with regard to the subject matter covered. It is sold with the understanding that the publisher is not engaged in rendering legal, accounting, or other professional advice. If legal advice or other expert assistance is required, the services of a competent professional person should be sought.
                —From a *Declaration of Principles* jointly adopted by a Committee of the
            American Bar Association and a Committee of Publishers and Associations

Illustrations by Barry Littmann. Illustration on page 3 by Eulala Conner.

*This book is available at quantity discounts for bulk purchases.*
*For information, call 1-800-289-0963.*

**Visit the entire Everything® series at everything.com**

# Contents

ACKNOWLEDGMENTS . . . . . . . . . . . . . . . . . . . . . . . . . . . . . . . . . . . . . . vi

FOREWORD . . . . . . . . . . . . . . . . . . . . . . . . . . . . . . . . . . . . . . . . . . . . . vii

INTRODUCTION . . . . . . . . . . . . . . . . . . . . . . . . . . . . . . . . . . . . . . . . . . ix

CHAPTER 1 *Managing Diabetes* . . . . . . . . . . . . . . . . . . . . . . . . . . . 1

CHAPTER 2 *Salsas, Sauces, Shortcuts, and Spices* . . . . . . . . . . . 29

CHAPTER 3 *Appetizers* . . . . . . . . . . . . . . . . . . . . . . . . . . . . . . . . . 51

CHAPTER 4 *Breakfast and Brunch* . . . . . . . . . . . . . . . . . . . . . . . . 65

CHAPTER 5 *A Bounty of Breads* . . . . . . . . . . . . . . . . . . . . . . . . . . 73

CHAPTER 6 *Main Dishes and Casseroles* . . . . . . . . . . . . . . . . . . . 85

CHAPTER 7 *Poultry* . . . . . . . . . . . . . . . . . . . . . . . . . . . . . . . . . . . 103

CHAPTER 8 *Seafood* . . . . . . . . . . . . . . . . . . . . . . . . . . . . . . . . . . . 123

CHAPTER 9 *Meats* . . . . . . . . . . . . . . . . . . . . . . . . . . . . . . . . . . . . 145

CHAPTER 10 *Pasta and Pizza* . . . . . . . . . . . . . . . . . . . . . . . . . . . 169

CHAPTER 11 *Soups and Stews* . . . . . . . . . . . . . . . . . . . . . . . . . . 181

CHAPTER 12 *Side Salads* . . . . . . . . . . . . . . . . . . . . . . . . . . . . . . 195

CHAPTER 13 *Vegetables and Side Dishes* . . . . . . . . . . . . . . . . . 213

CHAPTER 14 *Desserts* . . . . . . . . . . . . . . . . . . . . . . . . . . . . . . . . . 225

CHAPTER 15 *Snacks and Beverages* . . . . . . . . . . . . . . . . . . . . . . 249

APPENDIX A *Resources* . . . . . . . . . . . . . . . . . . . . . . . . . . . . . . . . 271

INDEX . . . . . . . . . . . . . . . . . . . . . . . . . . . . . . . . . . . . . . . . . . . . . . . . 295

To all my visitors at *CookingWithPam.com*

# Acknowledgments

Thank you . . .

For their help and support, I would like to thank everyone at Adams Media. For all of their hard work and perseverance, I would like to thank my agent Sheree Bykofsky and her associate Janet Rosen. Special thanks also go to my daughter Lara Sutton and the other joys in my life: Taylor, Charlie, and Courtney; Andrew, Tony, Dennis, and Ann Rice; my parents and the siblings; my photographer friend who makes house calls Bill Grunden; computer guru buddy Don Lachey; the most helpful and friendliest realtor in the world Doris Meinerding; and my online friends: David Hebert, Eric J. Ehlers, Jodi Cornelius, Catherine Misener, Richard Mann, the elusive Bishop Ra Fiki, and all the Authors on the Undernet regulars.

Special thanks to Barbara Pearl, M.S., R.D.,
for her technical review of the book.

# Foreword

The best way for the person with diabetes to stay healthy is to control blood sugars within the normal limits in the morning and at bedtime, and keep them under 140 one and a half to two hours after each meal. Evidence suggests that these new lower standards are the way to prevent complications such as the loss of vision or the loss of kidney function.

The food consumed makes a major difference in a person's ability to control blood sugars. The total carbohydrate is important on a daily basis, and distributing this carbohydrate evenly between meals greatly helps maintain the correct level of blood sugar throughout the day. Skipping or eliminating meals does not help control weight or blood sugar.

The person who has diabetes has much more flexibility in meal planning today than in years past. He or she, by today's standards, is educated to select food items based on carbohydrate and fat content. Carbohydrates affect blood sugar the most, and fat adds major calories.

Fat, because it has more than twice the calories of protein or carbohydrates, is a major contributor to excess weight, and weight is a major factor in the development of type 2 diabetes. There is also an extremely close relationship between diabetes and heart disease, so controlling sodium content is also advisable.

The recipes in this book control sodium, fat, and "carbs," and give information as to the content of each in the recipes. When the diabetic food plan is followed, the person with diabetes, and his or her family, will develop very healthy, balanced eating habits. This food plan is meant to be a lifestyle, not a "diet" that is followed for a few weeks or months. Therefore, the more variety and the more choices that are made available, the better the plan.

Recipes are important tools for creating a diet with variety. A creative selection of healthy recipes give the person with diabetes choices and options just like the rest of us.

Sally Kattau, R.D., L.D., C.D.E.

# Introduction

Knowledge is the first step to controlling blood glucose levels. Use that knowledge to form a plan of action and then put that plan into play. The following is not meant to be the only resource you will need on diabetes. It is merely an overview, and, hopefully, a springboard, giving you a place to start in gathering more information.

## Diabetes Mellitus

Our bodies make the foods we eat into glucose. Insulin is what is needed to take that glucose into the cells where it can be used as energy.

When a person has diabetes, either the body does not make enough insulin or the cells are unable to use the insulin that is there. Doctors do not yet understand an exact cause of diabetes nor is there a cure. However, doctors do know that genetics, obesity, and lack of exercise do play a role in contracting diabetes.

Fortunately, much is known about how to control diabetes, so those affected by the disease can live long and healthy lives. Unfortunately, the complications of not maintaining good control of blood glucose levels are also well documented, and affect nearly every vital system in the body.

It does not take a diabetic long to figure out that blood glucose readings can vary greatly, depending on when the test is performed and how well he or she has stuck to the prescribed diet on that particular day. Don't be tempted to cheat on your diet and "just be good" when you have a doctor's appointment. That is where glycated hemoglobin comes into play. A glycated hemoglobin test, often known as Hemoglobin A1C, can give an average reading for the past three to four months. Hemoglobin is the oxygen-carrying substance in red blood cells. Glucose binds (or glycates) to the hemoglobin and stays there for the life of the red blood cell. That is how your doctor can know if you have been cheating even if your blood glucose levels are wonderful in the office.

# Be Informed and Educated

You need to know the type of diabetes you or your loved one has. The treatments vary considerably for each type.

## Type 1 Diabetes

Type 1 diabetes is also known as juvenile-onset diabetes or insulin-dependent diabetes mellitus (IDDM). As the latter title suggests, this is the type of diabetes that requires insulin in order for the patient to survive. The beta cells in the pancreas produce no insulin. Those people affected by this type of the disease must receive insulin injections either by self-injection or insulin pump.

With type 1 diabetes, it is important to monitor the blood glucose levels not only to keep the level from going too high (hyperglycemia) but also to keep the level from going too low (hypoglycemia). Hypoglycemia, also known as an insulin reaction, is the result of too much insulin in the blood stream. This can happen if a planned meal is delayed or if there has been increased physical activity. Basically, this occurs any time nearly all of the glucose has been taken from the blood stream into the cells to be used for energy and there is still some insulin from the last injection floating around. For this reason, it is very important to know the peak and duration times for the type of insulin that you use.

Symptoms of hypoglycemia include, but are not limited to, shakiness, dizziness, sweating, hunger, pale skin color, and disorientation. If these symptoms occur, test your blood sugar immediately. If the glucose level is indeed low, consume approximately ½ cup of fruit juice, five to six Life Savers, or the same calorie equivalent.

The best way to avoid a hypoglycemic reaction is to maintain good control of blood glucose levels. An injection called glucagon is available from a doctor for those diabetics prone to severe hypoglycemic reactions. Glucagon is synthetic glucose that can be injected much like insulin. A close friend or loved one should be trained to administer the injection if needed.

One word of caution: People often go overboard when treating a hypoglycemic reaction. An entire king-sized candy bar is not needed.

Consuming excessive calories will send the blood glucose level too high, continuing the cat and mouse cycle of trying to maintain healthy levels.

## Type 2 Diabetes

Type 2 diabetes is also known as non-insulin-dependant diabetes mellitus (NIDDM). With type 2 diabetes, the beta cells in the pancreas still produce insulin, but not in adequate enough amounts for the body to use it properly.

Type 2 diabetes is the most common form of diabetes. It is generally diagnosed in mid to late adulthood, and is the type that is most likely to be related to lifestyle. The onset of type 2 diabetes is generally not as dramatic as with type 1.

The good news is that type 2 diabetes often does not require any form of medical intervention. It can often be controlled with diet, exercise, and weight loss. Notice the prior sentence did not say "cured." Maintaining the new lifestyle will be a lifelong commitment, but at least it may not require expensive medications.

If you and your health care provider are not able to see that you maintain healthy glucose levels with diet and exercise alone, oral medications may be required. Insulin is also used with oral medications or by itself if the condition warrants. (Refer back to the type 1 diabetes section for special considerations on insulin use.)

Extremes in glucose levels are not as much of a concern with type 2 diabetes, but it is important to know the medications you are taking and what some of the possible side effects could be.

## Gestational Diabetes

Gestational diabetes is a diabetic condition that occurs during pregnancy. It is more closely related to type 2 diabetes in that the body still makes insulin, but is not able to maintain healthy glucose levels due to contra-insulin hormones released by the placenta. Usually, blood sugar levels will remain within normal limits until about the twenty-fourth week of gestation.

Gestational diabetes can often be controlled by diet and exercise alone. However, if extra means are needed, oral medications cannot be used. Insulin is the only way to maintain glucose levels in this case. Some studies have been done with a family of diabetic medications called glyburides, but these have not yet been approved for use during pregnancy. The gestational diabetic mother is at risk for any of the complications related to diabetes if her blood glucose levels are not kept under control. The most common side effect is elevated blood pressure, which can lead to a dangerous condition known as eclampsia. (Eclampsia is the most severe condition of pregnancy-induced hypertension [PIH]; it can involve seizures and dangerously high blood pressures that can cause maternal stroke or death, and fetal death.)

In most cases, the condition leaves after the infant, and more specifically, the placenta, have been delivered. Some studies have shown, however, that one-third to one-fourth of women who have gestational diabetes will develop type 2 diabetes within ten years.

As mentioned earlier, gestational diabetes usually doesn't occur until after the twenty-fourth week of pregnancy. Most birth defects originate in the first trimester, so this is not generally a concern with the later onset of gestational diabetes. The major concerns with gestational diabetes are macrosomia and hypoglycemia of the infant after delivery.

Macrosomia simply means "large body." The fetus gets its nutrients from the mother's blood via the placenta. If the mother has high blood glucose levels, the fetus will produce more insulin in response. The excess glucose in the fetus is turned into fat, and the fetus may grow too large to be delivered vaginally.

Hypoglycemia may occur after delivery if the mother's blood glucose levels have been high. The infant is used to producing high levels of insulin and will continue to do so after delivery. Without the excess glucose to use up, the infant's blood sugar drops. The infant then has to be given extra glucose either by oral feedings or intravenously.

Both of these complications for the developing fetus and complications for the mother can be avoided if blood glucose levels are kept under tight control.

Diet control is a vital aspect for the management of all types of diabetes at all stages. Making a lifelong commitment to eat a healthy diet literally is a life or death decision for the diabetic.

Larisa D. Sutton, R.N., B.S.N.

## CHAPTER 1
# *Managing Diabetes*

Changing your lifestyle after years of habit and routine is rarely easy, but you're taking the first big step—congratulations! As you make small changes to what you eat, when you eat, and what you do in between, you'll realize that you can have some control over your diabetes. Work closely with your doctor, and even a dietitian, to set guidelines and goals for delicious meals and healthful living.

# Daily Steps to Managing Diabetes

Dietary changes required for managing your health may seem intimidating at first; however, the eating habits that control your diabetes are really just the same as any other plan for a better diet. In the long run, it'll be easier to maintain near-normal blood glucose levels if you think of your diet modifications as realistic goals rather than inflexible rules and regulations. With help and advice from your dietitian, adapt these suggestions so that they work for you and your lifestyle:

- Maintain regular eating habits.
- Incorporate snacks into your daily eating plans.
- Try new foods.
- Eat a variety of foods.
- Make healthy food choices.
- Drink more water.

When you skip meals, you're just asking for trouble. Maintaining the regular eating times (*when* you eat) is as important as controlling *what* you eat. Your dietary objective is to sustain healthy blood glucose levels. You can't do that if you indulge one minute, and try starving yourself later to compensate. It just doesn't work that way.

## Old Myths, New Ideas

Trying new foods helps, too—if you do so in a systematic way. If you're used to a huge bowl of rich ice cream every night, switching to a fat-free choice will probably leave you (and your tummy) feeling disappointed. Gradually adjusting your diet works much better for most people.

Registered dietitian Sally Kattau says she recommends that her clients begin by eating one-third less than what they're used to. "I tell them to fill up their plates like they usually do, then scrape a third of it off the plate." She says that that technique along with a commitment to learn healthier cooking techniques and make wiser food choices is much easier—and less expensive—than thinking you must go out and buy all sorts of new, so-called diabetic cooking ingredients.

# Meeting Your Dietary Needs

Everybody has the same food needs, regardless of whether they have diabetes. The diabetes food guide pyramid has only two major differences from the USDA Food Guide Pyramid: starchy vegetables like green peas, corn, and potatoes are in the Grains/Beans and Starchy Vegetables group, and cheese is in the Meat and Others group.

USDA Food
Guide
Pyramid

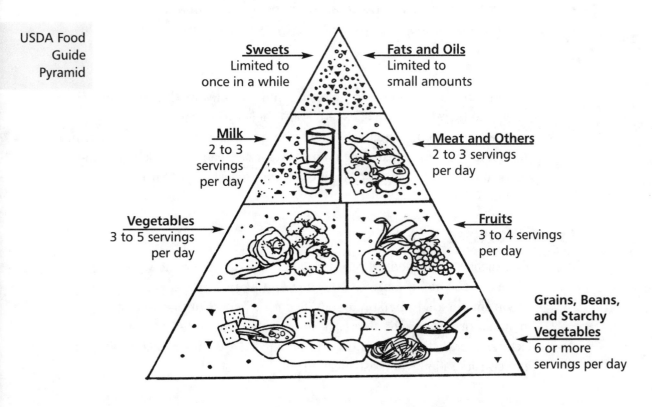

**Sweets**
Limited to
once in a while

**Fats and Oils**
Limited to
small amounts

**Milk**
2 to 3
servings
per day

**Meat and Others**
2 to 3 servings
per day

**Vegetables**
3 to 5 servings
per day

**Fruits**
3 to 4 servings
per day

**Grains, Beans,
and Starchy
Vegetables**
6 or more
servings per day

Keep a food journal for a day or two, and then compare the number of servings you eat to the number recommended by the diabetes food guide pyramid. This will show whether or not you are eating too much or too little of any of the food groups. It also gives you a realistic record of what to discuss with your dietitian, something that's especially important if you're experiencing fluctuations in your blood glucose levels.

If you're honest with yourself, you already know how to make healthier food choices. The easiest one is cutting the fat in your diet. Another is to add more fiber. (The recipes in this book will show you how!) Analyzing your food journal and discussing those results with your dietitian will determine what foods you need to increase or reduce in your diet.

> Forget what you've heard about between-meal snacks. As long as you choose snack foods wisely, they can be an important part of a healthy diet.

Drinking more water also helps in a number of ways. It helps you feel fuller, and therefore more satisfied. It also helps you maintain regularity, especially when combined with more fiber in your diet. (In fact, introducing more fiber and not consuming enough water can cause constipation. Fiber needs the help of water to pass through your digestive system.)

## Diet Versus Lifestyle

Your dietitian and medical provider will help you determine what other changes you should make to your diet and lifestyle. Healthy food choices vary from person to person, depending on whether or not you need to maintain or lose weight, decrease your cholesterol levels, and other factors. Your dietitian will show you how to take your personal food goals into consideration when establishing your meal plan.

> Try to keep your food journal consistently. You need to be honest with your dietitian (and yourself!) about what you're eating, if only to help understand your current eating habits relative to your long-term health.

Don't think you need to make massive changes all at once. In fact, that can also have a negative effect. It's harder to determine which foods adversely alter your blood glucose levels if you can't pinpoint which food was new to your diet. Gradual changes will mean you take longer to accomplish your goals, but for those gradual changes stand a better chance of becoming permanent ones because you'll be learning how to incorporate the foods you like so that they fit your lifestyle.

# Control What You Can

So far there isn't a cure for diabetes, which is why it's important that you learn how to manage what you can on your own. Successful diabetes management is the best way for you to feel your best on a daily basis while also preventing long-term complications. Diabetes management involves three things:

1. food
2. exercise
3. medication

This is a cookbook, so the emphasis here is on making your food choices and learning how best to prepare those foods. In simple terms, food raises your blood glucose level; exercise and medication lower it. Your choices need to achieve the balance that keeps your blood glucose level as close to normal as possible. As always, check with your dietitian and medical provider for advice on what roles those three factors will play in your lifestyle.

## Tips for Dining Out

All sorts of things can sabotage a meal plan. These pitfalls can be especially common when you eat away from home, and often encounter things like:

- Delay in eating time
- Hidden fats
- Impatient people behind you in line
- Massive-sized portions
- Tempting cafeteria dessert displays

- Uncertainty about food preparation methods and ingredients
- Vending machine temptations

Delays can wreak havoc with your best-laid meal plans, and, if your blood glucose gets low because of eating delays, your health will suffer as well.

## Keep Your Body's Schedule

When you know there will be a delay (like when you normally have lunch at noon but know it will be at least an hour later than that when you eat), consider doing a food plan reversal: Eat your next snack at your usual meal time and eat your meal instead of the later snack.

Not all delays are scheduled, however. Because it's impossible to know in advance when some delays can occur, always carry some form of easy-to-eat carbohydrate with you. You can carry crackers, dried fruit, or pretzels in a purse or attaché. Delays can happen in traffic as well as in restaurants. Get in the habit of being prepared for almost any eventuality.

**FACTS**

You benefit by eating breakfast. Breakfast provides the energy necessary to have a productive morning, which is what, after all, starts off and sets the tone for your day. This is especially true for the diabetic. Without breakfast, blood sugar levels can dip drastically low.

If you eat out often, learn about the healthy selections on your favorite restaurant menus. Knowing what you'll order in advance will help you avoid unwise decisions made in haste because you don't want to hold up the line. Conscious food choices are especially important at fast-food restaurants, where the standard fare is fried and high in sodium.

Your best choices at fast-food restaurants are:

- Broiled or grilled chicken or fish sandwiches
- Pizza or sandwiches with vegetables
- Plain hamburger or roast beef sandwiches
- Salad bar offerings—as long as you avoid mayonnaise-based pasta salads or fatty toppings like cheese or bacon
- Sandwiches on whole-wheat breads without dressing or sauces

When you are eating at a restaurant that serves huge portions and are dining with a friend, you can overcome the temptation to eat too much if you agree to split the entrée. Ask for an extra plate so you can divide the main course once it arrives. Get your own salad, and remember to stick with a dressing that's low in fat.

*The American Diabetes Association Guide to Healthy Restaurant Eating* by Hope S. Warshaw has nutrition information for more than 2,500 menu items from more than fifty popular American restaurant chains.

If you're dining alone, avoid the temptation of overeating by asking for a "doggie bag" when the meal is served. Divide the food between the plate and the carryout container. Treat your meal like it's a two-for-the-price-of-one selection.

If you aren't able to select low- or no-fat salad dressings when eating out, Michelle Jones, from ✐ *www.cookinglow-fat.com* recommends ordering your dressing on the side. Dip the end of your fork into the dressing before picking up the salad—every bite will still taste good and you'll be surprised how much dressing will be left-over when you're done!

# Consumption of Alcohol

Managing diabetes is, in large part, managing your entire lifestyle. That does not mean, however, that you cannot still enjoy many things in moderation, including alcohol.

Barring other physical conditions or medical restrictions, most diabetics can consume alcohol—in moderation. Moderation is usually defined as two drinks a day for men and one drink a day for women. A drink is a 5-ounce glass of wine, a 12-ounce light beer, or 1½ ounces of 80-proof distilled spirits. One alcoholic beverage most often is counted as 2 Fat Exchanges.

As always, check with your dietitian before making any adjustments to your food plan so that you'll know how best to calculate the exchanges in your diet. Also confirm that none of your medications require that you avoid alcohol.

Although it's easy to monitor your alcohol consumption of beverages, the alcohol in cooked foods, sauces, or desserts is a little harder to judge. Based on information published by the U.S. Department of Agriculture, the alcohol content in cooked foods is:

| PREPARATION METHOD | | PERCENT OF ALCOHOL RETAINED |
|---|---|---|
| Added to boiling liquid, then removed from heat | | 85% |
| Flamed | | 75% |
| No heat, stored overnight | | 70% |
| Baked 25 minutes, alcohol not stirred into mixture | | 45% |
| Baked and simmered with alcohol stirred into mixture: | | |
| | 15 minutes | 40% |
| | 30 minutes | 35% |
| | 1 hour | 25% |
| | 1½ hours | 20% |
| | 2 hours | 10% |
| | 2½ hours | 5% |

If you prefer not to cook with alcohol, here are other substitution suggestions:

**BRANDY:** Substitute a small amount of brandy extract or pure vanilla extract and appropriate amount of water.

**COFFEE LIQUEUR:** Substitute double-strength espresso, or instant coffee made with four to six times the amount of coffee normally used.

**ORANGE LIQUEUR** (such as Grand Marnier): Substitute an equivalent amount of frozen orange juice concentrate plus some grated orange zest.

**RUM:** Substitute a small amount of rum extract or pure vanilla extract and appropriate amount of water.

**COOKING WINE:**

    **SAVORY DISHES:** For 1 cup of wine, substitute 7/8 cup of fat-free low-sodium chicken, beef, or vegetable broth, apple juice, white grape juice, or tomato juice mixed with $\frac{1}{8}$ cup (2 tablespoons) of fresh lemon juice or vinegar.

    **DESSERTS:** Substitute fruit juice with a dash of balsamic vinegar for the wine.

The purpose of cooking with alcohol is to add flavor, and these substitutions are effective whether you have dietary restrictions or not. Feel free to experiment with whatever combination will suit your purposes—and your tastes.

**E**SSENTIALS

For many, diet is a dirty word. If you're in that camp, then use the term eating habits—it sounds less like punishment, and more like a way of life. If you're diabetic, then you know: It is a way of life.

# Nutrition at a Glance: A Primer

We are what we eat! Recent research indicates that many serious diseases in addition to diabetes—heart disease, certain cancers, and high blood pressure—are diet-related. The typical American diet contains far more fat than is healthy, and surprisingly, about twice the amount of necessary protein.

Transition to healthier foods sensibly so you can adjust to new tastes. If you've always eaten regular ice cream, you won't be satisfied switching to fat free or ice milk immediately. Instead, switch to smaller servings of sherbet—or a sorbet.

Remember that learning food facts shouldn't be an intimidating process. Make one change at a time by switching to skim milk or eating more vegetables, for example. When one change becomes a part of your daily eating habits, make another change. Eventually these changes will reflect improved blood glucose control, cholesterol levels, weight, and overall health.

## Proteins

Proteins are the "building blocks" of the body, which uses them for growth, maintenance, and rebuilding cells. The most concentrated sources of protein are animal products. Animal proteins, such as meat, fish, eggs, and milk contain the nine essential amino acids that proteins can provide, and are called *complete proteins*.

Vegetable proteins are present in nuts, seeds, whole grains, and legumes. However, all vegetable proteins—with the exception of soy—are incomplete. If animal sources of protein are not included in the diet, vegetable proteins must be combined carefully to supply the body with essential amino acids.

## Carbohydrates

Carbohydrates provide most of the body's energy. Simple carbohydrates are sweet and include all kinds of sugars. Complex carbohydrates include grain products, and some fruits and vegetables like beans and potatoes. Because complex carbohydrates must be split apart before the body can absorb them, they take longer to burn. Therefore, they supply energy over a longer period of time than simple carbohydrates do.

FACTS

According to the May 2000 issue of the *New England Journal of Medicine*, studies seem to indicate that the fiber from 48 grams of fruits and vegetables in your diet may be an effective way to reduce blood glucose levels by as much as 10 percent.

Complex carbohydrates also contain vitamins, minerals, and dietary fiber (or as it used to be called, "roughage"). Fiber is the part of a plant that cannot be digested by humans. Water-insoluble fiber (found in fruits, vegetables, and grains) stimulates and regulates the digestive tract when combined with appropriate amounts of liquids. (Remember to drink plenty of water every day!) Water-soluble fiber, present in fruits, vegetables, oat bran, and beans, are also beneficial to diabetics, as they may slow the absorption of sugar into the blood stream and reduce blood cholesterol levels.

## Fats

Although they have a deservedly bad reputation, fats are also necessary to good health when consumed in appropriate amounts. Fats provide the body insulation, cushioning, and energy reserves, and they allow the body to use fat-soluble vitamins. In addition, fats make the body feel full or satisfied after eating.

## Recipe Comparison

The ratio for fat to acid in salad dressing is usually three parts fat (usually vegetable oil) and one part acid (usually vinegar or lemon juice). When you consider that one teaspoon of oil is one Fat Exchange, you can appreciate the importance of reducing the amount of oil in salad dressing. For example, a simple oil-and-vinegar salad dressing has the following nutritional analysis (Breakdown A):

| Nutritional Analysis: | |
| --- | --- |
| Calories: | 90.03 |
| Protein: | 0.00 g |
| Carbohydrate: | 0.22 g |
| Fat: | 10.13 g |
| Sat. Fat: | 1.37 |
| Cholesterol: | 0.00 mg |
| Sodium: | 0.04 mg |
| Fiber: | 0.00 g |
| PCF Ratio: | 0-1-99 |
| **Exchange Approx.:** | |
| 2 Fats | |

BREAKDOWN A

| Nutritional Analysis: | |
| --- | --- |
| Calories: | 35.82 |
| Protein: | 0.57 g |
| Carbohydrate: | 0.43 g |
| Fat: | 3.69 g |
| Sat. Fat: | 0.50 g |
| Cholesterol: | 0.00 mg |
| Sodium: | 0.61 mg |
| Fiber: | 0.03 g |
| PCF Ratio: | 6-5-89 |
| **Exchange Approx.:** | |
| 1 Fat | |

BREAKDOWN B

In comparison, Breakdown B analyzes a recipe that replaces a third of the oil with two parts tofu.

Adding tofu to a salad dressing is an easy way to reduce the fat. Tofu absorbs the flavors of the ingredients it's blended with, so chances are you won't even notice the difference.

You can use tofu to help cut the fat and calories in your favorite commercial salad dressings, too. First try mixing equal parts of silken or other softer forms of tofu and salad dressing. Refrigerate overnight. If the flavor isn't strong enough for your tastes, add additional salad dressing—just don't go beyond two parts salad dressing to one part tofu. Adjust Exchange Approximations according to the ratios used.

QUESTIONS?

**What is a PCF Ratio?**
The PCF Ratio represents the relationship between the percentage of proteins, carbohydrates, and fats within a food.

### Fat Facts

All fats are not created equally. It seems that every few months, you hear about new theories on fat, and what's good or bad for you and your body. Consider the following points, and remember that moderation and common sense are still your best guides.

UNSATURATED FATS (fat from most vegetables) are better for your body than are saturated fats (animal fats).

COCONUT AND PALM OIL are saturated fats and are used in most bakery and processed snack foods.

ALL OILS are 100 percent fat, as are butter and margarine.

A LOW-FAT FOOD is defined as containing 3 grams of fat or less per serving.

A NONFAT FOOD may not be completely free of fat; a nonfat food is defined as one containing less than half a gram of fat per serving.

Your body produces CHOLESTEROL from the fatty acids in vegetables, seeds, and nuts. Because this healthy form of cholesterol is the basis for all sex hormones, cutting all fat from your diet can drastically decrease your libido, which is another important reason for you to include healthy fats in your diet.

Both your doctor and your dietitian will help you determine not only which fats are best for you, but also the best way for you to incorporate them into your ever-improving eating habits.

## Cholesterol

Cholesterol itself is not a fat, but a substance that is present in some fats. Cholesterol is necessary for proper functioning of nerves and hormones, but the human liver can manufacture all the cholesterol the body needs. A high level of cholesterol in the blood is known to be related to cardiovascular disease; however, dietary cholesterol may not necessarily contribute to those higher levels.

**QUESTIONS?**

**Do eggs have a lot of cholesterol?**
Although the cholesterol content of eggs is high, research indicates that eating foods containing saturated fat is far more likely to raise a person's blood cholesterol level than eating foods containing cholesterol. Still, people with high cholesterol should probably only consume one to two eggs per week; others should limit themselves to three to four per week.

Fats contain both saturated and unsaturated essential fatty acids. Saturated fats not only contain dietary cholesterol but also encourage the body to produce more than it needs. All animal fat is saturated fat. Two plant fats—coconut and palm oils—are also heavily saturated. Both are used extensively in processed and packaged bakery products, sweets, snacks, and other junk food. To break it down further:

UNSATURATED FATS, which include most vegetable fats, are believed to reduce blood cholesterol levels when they replace saturated fat in the diet.

MONOUNSATURATED FATS include fish oils and olive, canola, and peanut oils.

**POLYUNSATURATED FATS** include tuna, salmon, sunflower, corn, and sesame oils.

**PARTIALLY HYDROGENATED VEGETABLE OILS** (although unsaturated) contain trans fatty acids, which research has shown raises blood cholesterol. Partially hydrogenated vegetable oils are used in most shortenings and margarines.

Even if your dietitian hasn't placed restrictions on your cholesterol intake, most recommendations are that daily cholesterol intake should be 300 milligrams or less.

## Sodium

Although sodium does not affect blood glucose levels, it can alter your blood pressure. Elevated or erratic blood pressure is an important consideration when you consider that diabetics have an increased risk of heart disease. The recommended sodium intake for healthy adults is 2,400 to 3,000 milligrams per day. If you already have high blood pressure, you probably need to consume far less than that. (In fact, your body only needs about 500 milligrams per day.)

- Fat and salt can be entirely left out of recipes for casseroles, soups, and stews.
- Use herb blends to season foods instead of salt.
- Salt can be reduced 25 to 50 percent in recipes for baked goods made without yeast.
- Kosher salt and sea salt are alternate choices for table salt; it takes less kosher salt to equal the same "salty" taste and even less sea salt to achieve the same results. As always, consult your dietitian or doctor before introducing sea salt into your diet if you've been told to avoid salt altogether.
- Dried kelp or seaweed can be ground in the coffee grinder as a fine powder and used as a substitute for salt.

Just like fat, salt makes food taste good. Therefore, be especially cautious with restaurant foods, which are usually very high in sodium. If the menu doesn't specifically indicate which selections are "healthy," don't be afraid to make some special requests.

# Dietary Considerations

The nutrition labels that now appear on most food packages show how much protein, carbohydrate, and fat a serving contains in gram weight. Keep in mind that the serving on the food label may not be the same as the serving size in your food plan.

A healthy food plan should include a diet that is:

- High in grains, vegetables, and fruits
- Low in fat, saturated fat, and cholesterol
- Moderate in all forms of sugar and salt
- A balanced variety of foods

Remember that these changes are all linked to your lifestyle modifications. It can be difficult to change the food itself while keeping everything else the same. Instead, try healthier foods in new recipes, make shopping for fresh fruits or vegetables a mini-event, and do more cooking at home, which will save you money, too!

## Label Considerations

Unless you understand what they're really telling you, nutrition information on foods you purchase might not give you the information you need. Keep these things in mind when you check product labels:

PERCENTAGE (%) DAILY ALLOWANCE or VALUE indicates how much of a specific nutrient a serving of food contains compared to a 2,000-calorie diet.

**REDUCED** means that the product has been nutritionally altered so that it now contains 25 percent less of a specific nutrient such as fat, calories, sugar, or sodium.

**FREE** means that the product contains none or almost none of the specified nutrient; sugar-free foods have less than half a gram of sugars per serving, which doesn't necessarily mean they're carbohydrate free.

**QUESTIONS?**

**How free is sugar-free?**
Most dietitians recommend that you compare the total carbo-hydrate content of a sugar-free food with that of the standard product. If there is a big difference in carbohydrate content between the products, buy the sugar-free food. If there is little difference in the total grams of carbohydrate between them, choose the product you prefer based on price and taste.

Foods with **NO SUGAR ADDED** do not have any form of sugar added during processing or packaging, and do not contain high-sugar ingredients; these foods may still be high in carbohydrate, so be sure to check the label.

**FAT-FREE** foods are often higher in carbohydrate than the foods they replace, so they are not necessarily a better choice than the standard product.

In most nutritional analysis information, the grams of sugar and fiber are counted as part of the grams of total carbohydrate. For a more accurate estimate of the carbohydrate content, if a food has 5 grams or more fiber in a serving, subtract the fiber grams from the total grams of carbohydrate.

## Sugary Stuff

Sugar in your diet adds empty calories that, if you eat more than you need, cause you to gain weight. Diabetics already need to guard against the risk of obesity, because the disease itself carries with it an increased risk of heart disease, high blood pressure, and some forms of cancer—health conditions often also affecting the obese. If you are diabetic, you have additional concerns: the sugar in your diet increases your blood glucose to unhealthy levels.

Once you and your dietitian determine the amount of sugars you can include in your food plan, tracking those sugars is not an easy task. It's difficult to identify "added sugar" in foods because the new food label lumps all sugars (disaccharides) together, so there's no label distinction between milk sugar (lactose), fruit sugar (fructose), and granulated sugar (sucrose).

**FACTS**

Carbohydrates, including sugars, are your body's main source of energy. The food we eat can contain naturally occurring sugars, like those in fruits and dairy products; and added sugars, such as refined sugar, and corn syrup solids (to name just a few). The body converts the sugar and other carbohydrates you eat into the sugar you find in your blood (glucose).

A good rule to follow is that if you include any foods in your diet that contain added sugars, choose foods that also contain nutrients like vitamins, minerals, or fiber. Limit foods like candy, high-sugar jam or jelly, regular soda, and syrup. Instead, get most of your carbohydrates (sugars) from starchy foods such as high-fiber bread and other grain products, fruit and fruit juice, pasta, starchy vegetables, and rice. These foods have enough complex carbohydrates, minerals, fiber, and vitamins to be considered "nutrient dense."

# Tips on Modifying Your Recipes and Diet

If you are a moderately capable and creative cook, you may have spent your time in the kitchen doing things based on instinct and years of experience. Your challenge is to take a step back and relearn how to cook in a way that suits your new lifestyle.

## Cut the Sugar

Sugar is, in essence, an "empty" calorie; it has no measurable nutritional value; it's simply a flavor enhancer. Like any seasoning, sugar isn't meant to overpower the flavors of the dish; it's there to punch 'em up a bit.

- Honey can replace sugar if you make some recipe adjustments. Use ½ cup of honey to replace 1 cup of sugar; in some cases, you may need to reduce the liquid by ¼ cup for each ½ cup of honey you add to the recipe. (Using all honey isn't always an exact science, so you'll need to experiment.)
- Use artificial sweeteners if you can tolerate chemical substitutes, and your dietitian approves them.
- Use fruit canned in water or fruit juice.
- Reduce a recipe's sugar by as much as 25 to 50 percent when possible. Try this the next time you're converting one of your favorite recipes: Use the next lowest measuring cup. For example, when a recipe calls for ½ cup of sugar, use the ⅓ cup instead.

Although it may take awhile, once you get used to eating healthier foods in compliance with your food plan, you'll eventually get to where you notice the natural sweetness in food and won't want too much sugar obscuring that taste!

## Cut the Fat

A diet high in saturated fat restricts the blood vessels and lowers the amount of healthy cholesterol (HDL) in the bloodstream. Healthy fats, such as fish or walnut oil, may have the opposite effect. That's why it's important to not only limit the amount of fat in your diet, but to also use healthier unsaturated fat as often as possible.

**SSENTIALS** Get the benefit of fat flavor without lots of saturated fat calories— just a small amount of butter to a nonfat sauce or gravy at the end of the cooking time. The French term for this is *monter*—using butter to "finish off" a sauce.

So, is it possible to lose the fat but keep the flavor? Yes, if you do so within reason. Part of that "within reason" involves removing as much of the *other* fat in the diet as possible. That way, you only occasionally "introduce" fat for flavor, which marks the difference between a healthy diet, and one too high in fat. Here are some easy ways to cut the bad fat from your diet:

- Bake, boil, broil, grill, roast, simmer, or steam rather than frying with added fat.
- Before you use the drippings from roasted meat or poultry to make soup stock or gravies, first chill them in the refrigerator. As it cools, the fat rises to the top; once chilled, the fat will harden, which makes it easy to remove.
- Do not add bread crumbs, coating mixes, fat, or flour, unless you do so following specific lower-fat preparation suggestions in this book.
- Fool the eye with pretty plate presentations; slicing meat on the diagonal and fanning it out on the plate makes it look like there's more there.
- Use a roasting rack, or elevate meatloaf or a roast on pieces of celery. The celery raises the meat up out of the fat, which then drains away. Discard the celery when done.
- Lower oven temperatures (325 to 350 degrees) allow more fat to drain out of cooking meat.
- Marinate, baste, or sauté foods with lemon, lime, or tomato juice, wine, or fat-free broth instead of butter or oil.
- Steam vegetables like onions first; you'll need less fat to sauté them.

- Stretch ground meat by adding finely chopped vegetables, or tofu, to the mixture.
- Use arrowroot, cornstarch, or potato flour to thicken defatted pan drippings to make low-fat gravy, or sauce to use in soup or stew.
- Weigh meat after removing bones and fat, and then again after cooking. As a general rule, four ounces of raw meat will weigh three ounces after it's cooked. By checking the cooked weight, you'll be confirming that you're accounting for the correct food exchange amounts.

Nutritional Analysis and Exchange Approximations for the recipes in this book follow the "worst case scenario" method. In other words, maximum cooked weight was assumed. In most cases, the cooked results may be lower than what's given in a recipe, but you can't count on that.

Many recipes can accommodate about a 50 percent reduction in fat, although you may need to replace that fat with additional liquid in recipes for cakes, quick breads, and muffins to maintain the proper batter consistency. For example, if a recipe calls for ½ cup of oil and ½ cup of skim milk, try using ¼ cup of oil and increase the milk to ¾ cup.

In moist baked goods, you can usually replace half or all of the oil with nonfat plain yogurt, applesauce, plum pulp, or mashed bananas. (If you want to use fruit to replace the fat in more tender baked goods, it helps if you use cake flour or other lower-gluten flour instead of all-purpose flour.)

Small changes—giving up fat where you'll miss it the least—make it possible for you to enjoy fat where it counts: in the flavor.

## Frying Foods

Fried foods are the biggest pitfall for people who must monitor (and reduce) their fat intake. There are times, however, when you do need to fry foods. That's when it's important for you to understand the different oils, and why some are better for you than others.

Canola, peanut, and olive oil are all oils that allow for higher cooking temperatures before they'll burn. Because of the high omega-3 fatty acid content of canola oil, many nutritionists prefer this oil. Some chefs also like canola oil because it supposedly imparts very little flavor to the food; others experience an unpleasant aftertaste from it.

A lifestyle change doesn't have to mean total abstinence. If you plan your diet wisely, you don't have to give up your favorite foods completely; you just have to accept that you won't eat them as often.

If you find that you occasionally crave French fries or other fried dishes—and using the baked method to prepare them just won't do, it's much healthier to make them at home because then you control all of the ingredients.

Olive oil is a good choice, and because it can be heated to 375 degrees, very little oil is absorbed by the food. Olive oil also lasts much longer before it becomes "fatigued." This can be a way for you to self-restrict your decisions about what you'll fry.

## Add in Fiber

Fiber is found in plant foods, including dried beans and peas, fruit pulp (not the juice), vegetables, and whole grain breads and cereals. It's recommended that you include 20 to 35 grams of fiber a day to your diet. If that is considerably more than you usually eat, increase the amount slowly. Be sure that you also increase the amount of water that you drink.

When practical (as with muffin recipes), consider using two tablespoons of wheat germ or bran in place of an equal amount of a recipe's dry mixture.

You can also add ¼ cup nonfat dry milk (or other dry "milk" powder, such as Ener-G NutQuik or Ener-G SoyQuik) to the recipe.

Add more beans to your diet, and eat more whole-grain bread. Studies show that dietary fiber seems to be responsible for slower digestion and absorption of the carbohydrates in whole grains than those in low-fiber, refined grain products. This slower absorption is why whole grains help control blood sugar and insulin levels in people with diabetes. Whole grains are also usually higher in vitamins $B_6$ and E, as well as minerals such as magnesium, selenium, and zinc.

In most baked goods, you can substitute oat bran for one-fourth of the flour. When cooking rice, prepare brown rice instead of white and serve stir-fry dishes over whole-grain pasta.

## Cut the Sodium

Much like sugar, sodium seems to appear in your diet, even when you don't think you're using it. Salting your food at the table is certainly the first habit you need to break, but pay special attention to the salt (or high-sodium products) you use while you're cooking.

- Do not add salt to the water when you cook pasta or other foods.
- Increase your use of herbs and spices in place of salt.
- Reduce the salt in olives by blanching them briefly in a small pan of boiling water, then transferring them to an ice water bath to stop the cooking process. (Repeat this process two or three times.)
- Rinse canned, salt-added foods like tuna or vegetables with water.
- Whenever possible, use fresh foods instead of canned or processed goods.

Often the smallest changes have the greatest effects. By reducing the salt in your cooking process, you're not only taking care of your health— you're also reducing the sodium intake of those you're feeding.

## Creative Cooking

One of the biggest myths about low- or no-fat cooking is that the food has no flavor. As you experiment with different foods, consider experimenting with different cooking methods! Stir-fry and steaming are both healthier alternatives to baking or boiling; they are lower fat, and they also preserve foods' nutritional value.

## Steaming Facts

Steaming food in a basket over simmering water preserves natural flavor and nutritional value. Adding herbs to the steaming water or using broth instead of water boosts the flavor without adding any fat. Use caution when removing the lid from your steamer, as the steam is very hot. Tip the lid away from you to let the first billow of steam escape before removing the lid completely.

## Stir-Fry Tips

If you have a wok, use it! If you don't, however, any large skillet will work. Nonstick skillets are usually the best for stir-fry, because they require less oil or nonstick spray than other cookware.

- Have everything ready—chop and measure all of your ingredients in advance. Have the finishing sauce mixed so it's ready when you are, too. It helps to have all ingredients close at hand, lined up in the order you'll need them.
- Cut vegetables in small, uniform-sized pieces and meats in paper-thin slices so they only need a brief and equal time to cook. Only cook meat until it turns color—brown for red meats, opaque for poultry and fish—and vegetables until crisp-tender.
- If you use oil when you stir-fry, choose one with a high "smoke point," like peanut, canola, or olive oil. Better still, avoid using oil altogether! Stir-fry the meat first, then remove it and place it in the warm oven. Use the meat juices for stir-frying the remaining ingredients. Add the meat back into the dish when you're ready to complete the recipe.

Stir-frying lets you create fast and healthy dishes from fresh meat, seafood, and vegetables. Team your stir-fry with brown rice, for a complete and filling meal.

## Microwaving Tips

Microwave cooking is an efficient way to prepare food with little or no fat. Just keep these things in mind:

- Arrange food so that the thinnest part of the food is in the center of the microwave and the thickest part is toward the outside. Whenever possible, fold under the thin edges of fish or chicken breast fillets, and other tapered food, to create more uniformly sized pieces of food.
- Be careful not to overcook food. Check it at the minimum time, and continue to cook in fifteen-second increments, if needed. Food prepared in the microwave continues to cook, regardless of whether it's left in the microwave or removed, so another option is to allow the food to rest for a minute before resuming the fifteen-second cooking increments. If, after setting, the food is not done, nuke it some more.
- To ensure that food cooks evenly, always stir or rearrange the food at the midway point. Similarly, stir soup or other liquid dishes before, during, and after heating.
- Vegetables taken directly from the freezer to the microwave will often steam properly without the addition of water. Check at the halfway point to be sure. Fresh vegetables usually only need a tablespoon or two. Again, check at the halfway point and add more, if necessary. Although adding water near the end of the cooking time will "refresh" vegetables that seem too dry, there isn't a "cure" for vegetables that are mushy because of too much liquid.

The best thing about microwave cooking, of course, is the speed with which you can heat or reheat small portions of food. Following the preceding tips will help you cook your food evenly, without overcooking in hot spots, or drying out fresh foods.

# Gluten-Free Suggestions

The condition that prevents the body from properly metabolizing gluten (the protein in grain that increases its ability to react with leavening agents, like yeast, and "rise") results in an autoimmune disorder known as celiac disease (CD). Left untreated, CD can damage the small intestine and interfere with adequate absorption of nutrients from food. Over time, this disruption to the digestion can cause someone with CD to become malnourished regardless of what he or she eats. When gluten is removed from the diet, the body is usually able to heal itself; however, this healing time can take anywhere from three months to up to two years, depending on the age of the person with CD.

According to doctors at the Medical College of Wisconsin, almost 5 percent of children with insulin-dependent type I diabetes also exhibit symptoms of CD. Adults with CD also have a higher than average incidence of developing type II diabetes (Source: Eileen Early, "Researchers Recommend Testing Diabetic Children for Celiac Disease," *HealthLINK* [December, 2001]: at *http://healthlink.mcw.edu*).

Even if you don't suffer from CD, adding gluten-free grains to your diet is another way to introduce variety; most gluten-free grains are often higher in protein and other nutrients than all-purpose wheat flour. (For somebody with CD, there are good grain proteins and bad ones: for them, the good ones can be found in gluten-free grains; the bad ones are in grains with gluten.)

Nongluten grains are:

- corn
- millet
- milo (also called *sorghum* or *jowar*)
- rice
- teff
- wild rice

For comprehensive information on other nongrain and gluten-free flours, search online for "gluten-free." Several Web sites have links for purchasing gluten-free goods, as well as additional information on other special diets.

To make gluten-free all-purpose flour, keep the following mixture on hand: 4 cups brown rice flour, 1½ cups sweet rice flour, 1 cup tapioca starch flour, 1 cup Rice Polish, and 1 tablespoon guar gum. Mix all ingredients well and store in an airtight container in a cool place.

Gluten-free substitutions for all-purpose wheat flour vary depending upon which alternate flour you've chosen. Most gluten-free cookbooks will give you not only the amounts for their recipes; they will also provide background information on how cooking with gluten-free flours is a wholly different baking experience.

# CHAPTER 2

# Salsas, Sauces, Shortcuts, and Spices

| | |
|---|---|
| Toasted Sesame Seeds | 30 |
| Asian Gingered Almonds | 30 |
| Almond Spread | 31 |
| Horseradish Mustard | 31 |
| Piccalilli | 32 |
| Pepper and Corn Relish | 33 |
| Cranberry-Raisin Chutney | 33 |
| Fruit Salsa | 34 |
| Marmalade–Black Bean Salsa | 34 |
| Strawberry Spoon Sweet | 35 |
| Pineapple-Chili Salsa | 35 |
| Salsa with a Kick | 36 |
| Avocado-Corn Salsa | 36 |
| Plum Sauce | 37 |
| Roasted Red Pepper and Plum Sauce | 38 |
| Homemade Worcestershire Sauce | 40 |
| Pesto Sauce | 41 |
| Gingered Peach Sauce | 42 |
| Mock Cream | 42 |
| Mock White Sauce | 43 |
| Fat-Free Roux | 44 |
| Madeira Sauce | 45 |
| Mock Béchamel Sauce | 46 |
| Mock Cauliflower Sauce | 47 |

# Toasted Sesame Seeds

| Yields ½ cup Serving size: 1 tsp. |
| --- |

**Nutritional Analysis (per serving):**

| | |
| --- | --- |
| Calories: | 15.12 |
| Protein: | 0.45 g |
| Carbohydrate: | 0.69 g |
| Fat: | 1.28 g |
| Sat. Fat: | 0.18 g |
| Cholesterol: | 0.00 mg |
| Sodium: | 25.60 mg |
| Fiber: | 0.45 g |
| PCF Ratio: | 11-17-72 |

**Exchange Approx.:**
½ Fat

*½ cup white sesame seeds*        *¼ teaspoon sea salt (optional)*

1. Add the sesame seeds to a nonstick skillet over low heat. Toast until golden, shaking the pan or stirring the mixture frequently so that the seeds toast evenly. (The seeds will swell slightly during the toasting process.) When the aroma of the sesame seeds becomes evident and they've reached a light brown color, remove from the heat and pour into a bowl. Add the sea salt and mix well. Set aside and allow to cool.
2. Once cooled, grind using a mortar and pestle or blender, and season to taste. Store in an airtight container.

### Toasting Frenzy
*Many nuts, including pine nuts, almonds, and even sunflower seeds toast well. Simply follow the recipe for Toasted Sesame Seeds. Store them, whole or ground, in an airtight container.*

# Asian Gingered Almonds

| Yields 1 cup Serving size: 1 tbs. |
| --- |

**Nutritional Analysis (per serving):**

| | |
| --- | --- |
| Calories: | 58.03 |
| Protein: | 2.16 g |
| Carbohydrate: | 1.92 g |
| Fat: | 5.07 g |
| Sat. Fat: | 0.65 g |
| Cholesterol: | 1.29 mg |
| Sodium: | 43.89 mg |
| Fiber: | 0.96 g |
| PCF Ratio: | 14-12-74 |

**Exchange Approx.:**
1½ Fats

*2 teaspoons unsalted butter*       *1 teaspoon ground ginger*
*1 tablespoon Bragg's Liquid Aminos*       *1 cup slivered almonds*

1. Preheat oven to 350 degrees. In a microwave-safe bowl, mix the butter, Bragg's Liquid Aminos, and ginger. Microwave on high for 30 seconds, or until the butter is melted; blend well.
2. Spread the almonds on a shallow baking sheet treated with nonstick spray. Bake for 12 to 15 minutes or until light gold, stirring occasionally.
3. Pour the seasoned butter over the almonds, and stir to mix. Bake an additional 5 minutes. Store in airtight containers in cool place.

### Good Fat!
*Almonds and many other nuts fall within the "good fats" category because they are low in unhealthy, saturated fats.*

# Almond Spread

¼ cup ground, raw almonds
2 teaspoons honey

4 teaspoons water
Pinch of salt (optional)

In a blender, combine all ingredients and process until smooth.

## Toasted Almond Seasoning

*Add an extra flavor dimension to salads, rice dishes, or vegetables by sprinkling some toasted almonds over the top of the dish. Toast ½ cup ground raw almonds in a nonstick skillet over low heat, stirring frequently until they are a light brown color. Store the cooled almonds in an airtight container in a cool, dry place. This low-sodium substitute has only 16 calories per teaspoon, a PCF Ratio of 14-12-74, and counts as a ½ Fat Exchange Approximation.*

**Yields ½ cup**
**Serving size: 1 tbs.**

**Nutritional Analysis**
**(per serving, without salt):**

| | |
|---|---|
| Calories: | 29.97 |
| Protein: | 0.85 g |
| Carbohydrate: | 2.70 g |
| Fat: | 2.00 g |
| Sat. Fat: | 0.15 g |
| Cholesterol: | 0.00 mg |
| Sodium: | 0.13 mg |
| Fiber: | 0.47 g |
| PCF Ratio: | 11-34-56 |

**Exchange Approx.:**
½ Fat

# Horseradish Mustard

¼ cup dry mustard
2½ tablespoons prepared
　horseradish
1 teaspoon sea salt
¼ cup white wine vinegar

1 tablespoon olive oil
Cayenne pepper to taste
　(optional)

Combine the ingredients in a food processor or blender and process until smooth. Pour into a decorative jar and store in the refrigerator.

## The Vinegar-Oil Balancing Act

*The easiest way to tame too much vinegar is to add some vegetable oil. Because oil adds fat, the better alternative is to start with less vinegar and add it gradually to the recipe until you arrive at a flavor you prefer.*

**Yields ¾ cup**
**Serving size: 1 tsp.**

**Nutritional Analysis**
**(per serving):**

| | |
|---|---|
| Calories: | 9.89 |
| Protein: | 0.32 g |
| Carbohydrate: | 0.65 g |
| Fat: | 0.74 g |
| Sat. Fat: | 0.07 g |
| Cholesterol: | 0.00 mg |
| Sodium: | 67.94 mg |
| Fiber: | 0.22 g |
| PCF Ratio: | 12-25-63 |

**Exchange Approx.:**
1 Free Condiment

# Piccalilli

| Yields 2 quarts Serving size: 2 tbs. | |
| --- | --- |
| **Nutritional Analysis (per serving, without salt):** | |
| Calories: | 13.15 |
| Protein: | 0.15 g |
| Carbohydrate: | 3.40 g |
| Fat: | 0.02 g |
| Sat. Fat: | 0.00 g |
| Cholesterol: | 0.00 mg |
| Sodium: | 1.37 mg |
| Fiber: | 0.21 g |
| PCF Ratio: | 4-94-1 |
| **Exchange Approx.:** (per ⅛-c. serving): ½ Misc. Carb. | |

*1 cup chopped green tomatoes*
*1½ cups chopped cabbage*
*1 cup white onions*
*1 cup chopped cauliflower*
*1 cup chopped cucumber*
*½ cup chopped red pepper*
*½ cup chopped green pepper*
*¼ cup pickling salt*
*1½ cups apple cider **or** white vinegar*

*¾ cup sugar*
*½ teaspoon turmeric*
*1 teaspoon ginger*
*1½ teaspoons dried mustard*
*1½ teaspoons mustard seed*
*1 teaspoon celery seed*
*Sachet of pickling spices*
*Pickled whole onions to taste (optional)*

1. Dice the vegetables and layer them in a bowl with the pickling salt. Store in the refrigerator overnight to remove moisture from the vegetables.
2. Drain and rinse the vegetables. (Rinsing will remove much of the salt; however, if sodium is a concern, you can omit it altogether.)
3. To make the marinade, combine the vinegar, sugar, turmeric, ginger, dried mustard, mustard seed, celery seed, and pickling spice sachet in a large, noncorrosive stockpot. Bring ingredients to a boil, and boil for 2 minutes. Add the vegetables to the stockpot and boil for an additional 10 minutes.
4. Remove the pickling spice sachet and add the pickled onions, if you are using them; boil for another 2 minutes.
5. Remove from heat and allow to cool. Pack the vegetables in jars, then fill with the pickling liquid until the vegetables are covered. Store the covered glass jars in the refrigerator. Serve chilled as a relish or on deli sandwiches.

## Comparative Analysis

*Omitting both sugar and pickling salt makes this recipe even better for you with a third of the calories, less than half the carbohydrates, and a PCF Ratio of 12-84-4. The Exchange Approximations is ½ Free Vegetable.*

# Pepper and Corn Relish

4 banana **or** jalapeño peppers
⅓ cup frozen corn, thawed
⅓ cup chopped red onion
⅛ teaspoon ground coriander

2 teaspoons lime juice
Freshly ground black pepper
   to taste

Seed and chop the peppers, and in a bowl, toss with the remaining ingredients. Relish can be served immediately, or chilled and served the next day. For a colorful, mild relish, use a combination of 2 tablespoons of chopped green bell pepper and an equal amount of chopped red pepper in place of the jalapeño peppers.

| Serves 4 |  |
| --- | --- |
| **Nutritional Analysis (per serving):** | |
| Calories: | 39.33 |
| Protein: | 1.64 g |
| Carbohydrate: | 9.00 g |
| Fat: | 0.40 g |
| Sat. Fat: | 0.06 g |
| Cholesterol: | 0.00 mg |
| Sodium: | 6.57 mg |
| Fiber: | 2.09 g |
| PCF Ratio: | 14-78-8 |
| **Exchange Approx.:** | |
| ½ Starch | |

# Cranberry-Raisin Chutney

1 cup diced onions
1 cup diced peeled apples
1 cup diced bananas
1 cup diced peaches
¼ cup raisins
¼ cup dry white wine

¼ cup American Spoon Foods
   Dried Cranberries
¼ cup apple cider vinegar
1 teaspoon brown sugar
Sea salt and freshly ground black
   pepper to taste (optional)

In a large saucepan, combine all the ingredients. Cook over low heat for about 1 hour, stirring occasionally. Cool completely. Can be kept for a week in the refrigerator or in the freezer for 3 months, or canned using the same sterilizing method you'd use to can mincemeat.

TIP: *This chutney is also good if you substitute other dried fruit for the raisins or cranberries, such as using the dried Fancy Fruit Mix (strawberries, blueberries, cranberries, sweet cherries, and tart cherries) from Nutty Guys (✑www.nuttyguys.com).*

| Yields about 3 cups Serving size: 1 tbs. | |
| --- | --- |
| **Nutritional Analysis (per serving, without salt):** | |
| Calories: | 14.04 |
| Protein: | 0.14 g |
| Carbohydrate: | 3.38 g |
| Fat: | 0.05 g |
| Sat. Fat: | 0.01 g |
| Cholesterol: | 0.00 mg |
| Sodium: | 0.34 mg |
| Fiber: | 0.38 g |
| PCF Ratio: | 4-93-3 |
| **Exchange Approx.:** | |
| 1 Free Condiment | |

# Fruit Salsa

<table>
<tr><td colspan="2">Yields about 2 cups<br>Serving size: 2 tbs.</td></tr>
<tr><td colspan="2">Nutritional Analysis<br>(per serving):</td></tr>
<tr><td>Calories:</td><td>23.56</td></tr>
<tr><td>Protein:</td><td>0.42 g</td></tr>
<tr><td>Carbohydrate:</td><td>5.94 g</td></tr>
<tr><td>Fat:</td><td>0.1 g</td></tr>
<tr><td>Sat. Fat:</td><td>0.02 g</td></tr>
<tr><td>Cholesterol:</td><td>0.00 mg</td></tr>
<tr><td>Sodium:</td><td>4.68 mg</td></tr>
<tr><td>Fiber:</td><td>1.02 g</td></tr>
<tr><td>PCF Ratio:</td><td>6-90-4</td></tr>
<tr><td colspan="2">Exchange Approx.:<br>½ Fruit</td></tr>
</table>

½ of a cantaloupe
1 jalapeño **or** banana pepper
1 cup blackberries
1 small red **or** green bell
  pepper
1 medium-sized red onion

1 tablespoon lemon juice
Optional seasonings to taste:
  Parsley
  Cilantro
  Sea salt
  Cayenne pepper

Place all the ingredients in a food processor and process until well mixed. Do not over process; you want the salsa to remain somewhat chunky.

### Salsa Status

*Salsa is now the number 1 condiment in America. (Source: Food Finds, ✐www.foodtv.com)*

# Marmalade—Black Bean Salsa

<table>
<tr><td colspan="2">Yields about 1⅛ cup<br>Serving size: 1 tbs.</td></tr>
<tr><td colspan="2">Nutritional Analysis<br>(per serving):</td></tr>
<tr><td>Calories:</td><td>13.98</td></tr>
<tr><td>Protein:</td><td>0.72 g</td></tr>
<tr><td>Carbohydrate:</td><td>2.78 g</td></tr>
<tr><td>Fat:</td><td>0.06 g</td></tr>
<tr><td>Sat. Fat:</td><td>0.015 g</td></tr>
<tr><td>Cholesterol:</td><td>0.00 mg</td></tr>
<tr><td>Sodium:</td><td>0.27 mg</td></tr>
<tr><td>Fiber:</td><td>0.71 g</td></tr>
<tr><td>PCF Ratio:</td><td>20-77-3</td></tr>
<tr><td colspan="2">Exchange Approx.:<br>1 Free Condiment</td></tr>
</table>

1 tablespoon Smucker's Low-Sugar
  Sweet Orange Marmalade
½ cup chopped roasted red
  pepper (for roasting instructions, see "Roasted Red (or
  Other) Peppers" on page 39)
2 cloves roasted garlic
  (see "Dry-Roasted Garlic"
  on page 54 for roasting
  instructions)

½ cup cooked black beans
1 teaspoon key lime **or** fresh
  lime juice
Optional seasonings to taste:
  Sea salt
  Freshly ground black pepper
  Cilantro
  Parsley

Place all the ingredients in a food processor and process until well mixed. Do not over process; you want the salsa to remain somewhat chunky.

## Strawberry Spoon Sweet

6 cups small, hulled strawberries
¾ cup sugar

½ cup dry red wine
5–7 fresh thyme sprigs

Combine all the ingredients in a large bowl. Microwave uncovered on high for 3 to 5 minutes, or until the liquid is thick enough to heavily coat a spoon. Remove and discard the thyme sprigs. Let cool, then refrigerate for several hours to set before serving. This recipe keeps for several months in the refrigerator.

| Yields: 1 quart Serving size: 2 tbs. | |
| --- | --- |
| **Nutritional Analysis (per serving)** | |
| Calories: | 41.22 |
| Protein: | 0.28 g |
| Carbohydrate: | 9.49 g |
| Fat: | 0.16 g |
| Sat. Fat: | 0.01 g |
| Cholesterol: | 0.00 mg |
| Sodium: | 0.75 mg |
| Fiber: | 1.02 g |
| PCF Ratio: | 3-94-4 |
| **Exchange Approx.:** ½ Fruit, ¼ Misc. Carb. | |

## Pineapple-Chili Salsa

½ cup unsweetened, diced pineapple
½ cup roughly chopped papaya, peach, **or** mango
1 small poblano chili pepper
¼ cup chopped red bell pepper

¼ cup chopped yellow bell pepper
1 tablespoon fresh key lime **or** fresh lime juice
¼ cup chopped red onion

Combine all the ingredients in a bowl and toss to mix.

| Serves 4 | |
| --- | --- |
| **Nutritional Analysis (per serving):** | |
| Calories: | 28.76 |
| Protein: | 0.64 g |
| Carbohydrate: | 7.13 g |
| Fat: | 0.17 g |
| Sat. Fat: | 0.02 g |
| Cholesterol: | 0.00 mg |
| Sodium: | 2.07 mg |
| Fiber: | 1.14 g |
| PCF Ratio: | 8-87-5 |
| **Exchange Approx.:** ½ Fruit | |

# Salsa with a Kick

| Yields about 2 cups Serving size: 1 tbs. |
| --- |

| Nutritional Analysis (per serving): | |
| --- | --- |
| Calories: | 5.06 |
| Protein: | 0.20 g |
| Carbohydrate: | 0.94 g |
| Fat: | 0.14 g |
| Sat. Fat: | 0.02 g |
| Cholesterol: | 0.00 mg |
| Sodium: | 1.75 mg |
| Fiber: | 0.26 g |
| PCF Ratio: | 14-65-21 |

**Exchange Approx.:**
3 tbs. = 1 Free Condiment

2 teaspoons ground flaxseed
4 medium tomatoes, chopped
1 clove garlic, chopped
½ of a small onion
½ tablespoon cider vinegar
¼ teaspoon Tabasco sauce
⅛ teaspoon ground cayenne pepper
1 tablespoon chopped fresh coriander

Place all the ingredients in a blender or food processor; process briefly, until blended but not smooth.

# Avocado-Corn Salsa

| Serves 4 |
| --- |

| Nutritional Analysis (per serving): | |
| --- | --- |
| Calories: | 132.73 |
| Protein: | 2.49 g |
| Carbohydrate: | 13.56 g |
| Fat: | 9.22 g |
| Sat. Fat: | 1.43 g |
| Cholesterol: | 0.00 mg |
| Sodium: | 9.61 mg |
| Fiber: | 3.99 g |
| PCF Ratio: | 7-37-56s |

**Exchange Approx.:**
½ Starch/Vegetable,
2 Fats

1 cup corn kernels, blanched fresh **or** thawed frozen
1 small banana pepper, seeded and chopped
¼ cup diced red radishes
⅛ cup thinly sliced green onion
1 avocado, diced
1 tablespoon lime juice
½ teaspoon white wine vinegar
1 teaspoon extra-virgin olive oil
¼ teaspoon dried oregano
Dash of ground cumin
Dash of Tabasco sauce
Freshly ground black pepper (optional)

Combine the corn, banana pepper, radish, and green onion in a medium bowl. In another bowl, combine half of the diced avocado and the lime juice, and stir to thoroughly coat. In a blender, combine the other half of the avocado, the vinegar, oil, oregano, cumin, and Tabasco. Process until smooth, then pour it over the corn mixture and stir. Add the avocado mixture. Serve immediately.

# Plum Sauce

1 cup Smucker's Plum Jam
2 teaspoons grated lemon zest
1 tablespoon lemon juice
1 tablespoon rice wine vinegar
½ teaspoon ground ginger
½ teaspoon crushed anise
  seeds

¼ teaspoon dry mustard
¼ teaspoon ground cinnamon
⅛ teaspoon ground cloves
⅛ teaspoon hot pepper sauce

| Yields 1¼ cups Serving size: 1 tbs. | |
|---|---|
| **Nutritional Analysis (per serving):** | |
| Calories: | 28.74 |
| Protein: | 0.01 g |
| Carbohydrate: | 7.51 g |
| Fat: | 0.00 g |
| Sat. Fat: | 0 g |
| Cholesterol: | 0.00 mg |
| Sodium: | 0.03 mg |
| Fiber: | 0.02 g |
| PCF Ratio: | 0-100-0 |
| **Exchange Approx.:** ½ Fruit | |

Heat the plum jam in a small saucepan over medium heat until melted. Stir in remaining ingredients. Bring the mixture to a boil, lower the heat, and simmer for 1 minute, stirring constantly. Use the cooled sauce as a meat seasoning, or as a dip for eggrolls.

## Dipping Sauce

*Whisk together: 1 tablespoon rice wine vinegar, 2½ teaspoons water, 2 teaspoons sesame oil, 2 teaspoons minced scallions or green onions, and ⅛ teaspoon sugar. Use with pot stickers, steamed dumplings, or egg rolls. A 2-teaspoon serving has: Calories: 21.40; Protein: 0.02 g; Carbohydrate: 0.43 g; Fat: 2.27 g; Sat. Fat: 0.32 g; Cholesterol: 0.00 mg; Sodium: 0.21 mg; Fiber: 0.03 g; PCF Ratio: 0-8-92. Exchange Approximations: ½ Fat.*

# Roasted Red Pepper and Plum Sauce

| Yields 2 cups |
| :---: |
| Serving size: 1 tbs. |

| Nutritional Analysis (per serving): | |
| :--- | ---: |
| Calories: | 38 |
| Protein: | less than 1 g |
| Carbohydrate: | 9.5 g |
| Fat: | less than 1 g |
| Sat. Fat: | 0 g |
| Cholesterol: | 0.00 mg |
| Sodium: | 76 mg |
| Fiber: | 0.5 g |
| PCF Ratio: | 3-95-2 |

**Exchange Approx.:**
½ Misc. Carb.

1 large roasted red pepper (pulp only) (see page 39)
½ pound apricots, quartered and pitted
¾ pound plums, quartered and pitted
1⅓ cups apple cider vinegar
⅔ cup water
⅓ cup white sugar
½ cup brown sugar
2 tablespoons corn syrup
2 tablespoons fresh grated ginger
1 teaspoon salt
1 tablespoon toasted mustard seeds
4 scallions, chopped (white part only)
1 teaspoon minced garlic
½ teaspoon ground cinnamon

1. Place all the ingredients together in a large pot and bring to a boil. Reduce heat and simmer, covered, for 30 minutes.
2. Uncover and simmer for another hour. Place in a blender or food processor and process to desired consistency. Can be stored in refrigerator for 4 to 6 weeks.

### Speedy Sauce

*In a hurry? You can make an individual "1 Fruit"-choice plum sauce by mixing 1 tablespoon of Smucker's Plum Jam, ⅛ teaspoon white wine vinegar **or** rice wine vinegar, ⅛ teaspoon Bragg's Liquid Aminos **or** low-sodium soy sauce, and some seasonings (such as a pinch of dried onion, minced garlic, ground ginger, allspice, and cayenne **or** crushed red pepper flakes). Mix together the ingredients in a microwave-safe cup and heat until mixture comes to a boil. Add pinch of cornstarch and whisk until it stops boiling, then serve.*

# Roasted Red (or Other) Peppers

THE TRADITIONAL METHOD of roasting a red pepper is to use a long-handled fork to hold the pepper over the open flame of a gas burner until it's charred. Of course, there are a variety of other methods as well.

- Place the pepper on a rack set over an electric burner and turn it occasionally, until the skin is blackened. This should take about 4 to 6 minutes.
- You can also put the pepper over direct heat on a preheated grill. Use tongs to turn the pepper occasionally.
- Another method is to broil the pepper on a broiler rack about 2 inches from the heat, turning the pepper every five minutes. Total broiling time will be about 15 to 20 minutes, or until the skins are blistered and charred.
- You can also roast a pepper by placing it on a baking sheet treated with nonstick spray and baking it in a 400-degree oven for 20 to 30 minutes. (The skin of the pepper will not get as dark using this method.)

The key to peeling the peppers is letting them sit in their steam in a closed container until they are cool. Seal the peppers in either a brown paper bag, a plastic bag, or a bowl covered with plastic wrap. Once the peppers are cool, the skin will rub or peel off easily. Keep the pepper whole to peel it, then cut off the top and discard the seeds and rib membrane.

Store roasted peppers in a plastic bag in the refrigerator for a few days. To preserve them for a week, cover the roasted pepper completely with extra-virgin olive oil and refrigerate in an airtight container. Be sure to account for any oil that remains on the roasted pepper when you use it. You can use the oil, too! It absorbs some of the pepper's flavor, and is a delicious addition to salad dressings. ∾

# Homemade Worcestershire Sauce

| Yields 1 cup<br>Serving size: 1 tbs. | |
|---|---|
| **Nutritional Analysis<br>(per serving):** | |
| Calories: | 14.31 |
| Protein: | 0.11 g |
| Carbohydrate: | 4.12 g |
| Fat: | 0.01 g |
| Sat. Fat: | 0.00 g |
| Cholesterol: | 0.00 mg |
| Sodium: | 14.79 mg |
| Fiber: | 0.05 g |
| PCF Ratio: | 3-97-0 |
| **Exchange Approx.:**<br>1 Free Condiment | |

1½ cups cider vinegar
¼ cup Smucker's Plum Jam
1 tablespoon blackstrap
   molasses
1 clove garlic, crushed
⅛ teaspoon chili powder
⅛ teaspoon ground cloves
Pinch of cayenne pepper
¼ cup chopped onion

½ teaspoon ground allspice
⅛ teaspoon dry mustard
1 teaspoon Bragg's Liquid
   Aminos

Combine all the ingredients in large saucepan. Stir over heat until the mixture boils. Lower the heat and simmer uncovered for 1 hour, stirring occasionally. Store in a covered jar in the refrigerator.

### Mock Hollandaise Sauce

*Mix ⅛ cup yogurt with 1 teaspoon lemon juice, and serve with Eggs Benedict Redux (see page 69). The Nutritional Analysis for a 2-tablespoon serving is: Calories: 17.03; Protein: 1.64 g; Carbohydrate: 2.61 g; Fat: 0.05 g; Sat. Fat: 0.03 g; Cholesterol: 0.51 mg; Sodium: 21.66 mg; Fiber: 0.02 g; PCF Ratio: 38-60-3. Exchange Approximations: 1 Free.*

# Pesto Sauce

3/4 cup pine nuts

4 cups tightly packed basil
   leaves

1/2 cup freshly grated Parmesan
   cheese

3 large garlic cloves, minced

1/4 teaspoon salt

1 teaspoon freshly ground
   black pepper

1/2 cup extra-virgin olive oil

**Yields about 3 cups
Serving size: 1 tbs.**

**Nutritional Analysis
(per serving):**

| | |
|---|---|
| Calories: | 36.61 |
| Protein: | 0.93 g |
| Carbohydrate: | 0.55 g |
| Fat: | 3.58 g |
| Sat. Fat: | 0.62 g |
| Cholesterol: | 0.60 mg |
| Sodium: | 14.39 mg |
| Fiber: | 0.24 g |
| PCF Ratio: | 10-6-85 |

**Exchange Approx.:**
1 Fat

1. Preheat oven to 350 degrees. Spread the pine nuts on a baking sheet and bake for about 5 minutes; stir the nuts. Continue to bake until the nuts are golden brown and highly aromatic, stirring occasionally. Let the nuts cool completely, then chop finely.

2. Fill a medium-sized heavy saucepan halfway with water. Place over medium heat and bring the water to a boil. Next to the pot, place a large bowl filled with water and ice. Using tongs, dip a few of the basil leaves into the boiling water, blanch for 3 seconds, then quickly remove them from the boiling water and place them in the ice water. Repeat process until all of the basil has been blanched, adding ice to the water as needed. Drain the basil in a colander and pat dry with a towel.

3. In a blender or food processor, combine the basil, pine nuts, cheese, garlic, salt, pepper, and all but 1 tablespoon of the olive oil; process until the pesto is smooth and uniform. Pour the pesto into an airtight container and add the remaining olive oil to the top to act as a protective barrier. Pesto can be stored in the refrigerator for up to 5 days.

4. To freeze pesto, place it in a tightly sealed container. To freeze small amounts of pesto to use in recipes, pour the pesto into ice cube trays and freeze until solid. Once it's frozen, you can remove the pesto cubes and place them in sealed freezer bags.

## Preserving Fresh Basil

*If you have a large crop of fresh basil, blanch and freeze it in ice cubes for easy-to-use portions. Follow the instructions for blanching the basil in the Pesto Sauce recipe on this page.*

# Gingered Peach Sauce

| Serves 4 | |
|---|---|
| **Nutritional Analysis (per serving):** | |
| Calories: | 53.57 |
| Protein: | 0.56 g |
| Carbohydrate: | 4.97 g |
| Fat: | 2.29 g |
| Sat. Fat: | 0.31 g |
| Cholesterol: | 0.00 mg |
| Sodium: | 56.58 mg |
| Fiber: | 0.45 g |
| PCF Ratio: | 5-47-48 |
| **Exchange Approx.:** | |
| ½ Fat, | |
| 1 Fruit | |

2 teaspoons olive oil
1 tablespoon chopped shallot
2 teaspoons grated fresh ginger
⅓ cup dry white wine
1 small peach, peeled and diced
1 tablespoon frozen unsweetened orange juice concentrate
1 teaspoon Bragg's Liquid Aminos
½ teaspoon cornstarch

1. Heat the olive oil in a nonstick skillet over medium heat and sauté the shallot and ginger. Add the wine and simmer until reduced by half. Add the diced peach, orange juice concentrate, and Bragg's Liquid Aminos; return to a simmer, stirring occasionally.
2. In a separate container, mix the cornstarch with a tablespoon of the sauce; stir to create a *slurry*, mixing well to remove any lumps. Add the slurry to the sauce and simmer until the mixture thickens. Transfer the mixture to a blender or food processor and process until smooth.

# Mock Cream

| Yields 1¼ cups | |
|---|---|
| **Nutritional Analysis (per recipe):** | |
| Calories: | 146.61 |
| Protein: | 14.32 g |
| Carbohydrate: | 20.75 g |
| Fat: | 0.56 g |
| Sat. Fat: | 0.37 g |
| Cholesterol: | 7.96 mg |
| Sodium: | 220.73 mg |
| Fiber: | 0.00 g |
| PCF Ratio: | 39-57-3 |
| **Exchange Approx.:** | |
| 1½ Skim Milks | |

1 cup skim milk                    ¼ cup nonfat dry milk

Process the ingredients in a blender until mixed., and use as a substitute for heavy cream.

### Comparative Analysis

*Using 1¼ cups heavy cream would give you the following breakdown: Calories: 515.02; Protein: 3.06 g; Carbohydrate: 4.17 g; Fat: 55.27 g; Sat. Fat: 34.40 g; Cholesterol: 204.79 mg; Sodium: 56.16 mg; Fiber: 0.00 g; PCF Ratio: 2-3-95. Exchange Approximations: 11 Fat.*

# Mock White Sauce

1  tablespoon unsalted butter
1  tablespoon flour
¼ teaspoon sea salt
Pinch of white pepper

1 cup Mock Cream (see recipe
   on page 42)

| Yields about 1 cup |
| :--: |
| **Serving size: ½ cup** |

| Nutritional Analysis (per recipe): ||
| :-- | --: |
| Calories: | 60.74 |
| Protein: | 3.10 g |
| Carbohydrate: | 5.64 g |
| Fat: | 3.01 g |
| Sat. Fat: | 1.87 g |
| Cholesterol: | 9.36 mg |
| Sodium: | 189.77 mg |
| Fiber: | 0.05 g |
| PCF Ratio: | 20-36-44 |

**Exchange Approx.:**
½ Fat,
½ Skim Milk

1. In a medium-sized, heavy nonstick saucepan, melt the butter over very low heat. The butter should gently melt; you do not want it to bubble and turn brown. While the butter is melting, mix together the flour, salt, and white pepper in a small bowl.
2. Once the butter is melted, add the flour mixture to the butter and stir constantly. (A heat-safe, flat-bottom spoon safe for nonstick pans works well for this.) Once the mixture thickens and starts to bubble, slowly pour in some of the Mock Cream. Stir until it's blended in with the roux. Add a little more of the Mock Cream and stir until blended. Add the remaining Mock Cream and continue cooking, stirring constantly to make sure the sauce doesn't stick to the bottom of the pan. Once the sauce begins to steam and appears it's just about to boil, reduce the heat and simmer until the sauce thickens, or about 3 minutes.

### Mock Sour Cream

*In a blender, combine: ⅛ cup nonfat yogurt, ¼ cup nonfat cottage cheese, and ½ teaspoon vinegar. If you prefer a more sour taste, add another ½ teaspoon of vinegar. The type of vinegar you use will affect the taste as well. Apple cider vinegar tends to be more sour than white wine vinegar, for example. The Nutritional Analysis for each tablespoon is: Calories: 7.81; Protein: 1.31 g; Carbohydrate: 0.50 g; Fat: 0.03 g; Sat. Fat: 0.02 g; Cholesterol: 0.49 mg; Sodium: 4.40 mg; Fiber: 0.00 g; PCF Ratio: 70-26-4. Exchange Approximations: ½ Free*

# Fat-Free Roux

| Yields enough to thicken 1 cup of liquid Serving size: ¼ cup |
| :---: |

| Nutritional Analysis (per serving, Roux only): ||
| :--- | ---: |
| Calories: | 12.78 |
| Protein: | 0.02 g |
| Carbohydrate: | 1.93 g |
| Fat: | 0.00 g |
| Sat. Fat: | 0.00 g |
| Cholesterol: | 0.00 mg |
| Sodium: | 0.77 mg |
| Fiber: | 0.02 g |
| PCF Ratio: | 1-99-0 |
| Exchange Approx.: 1 Free ||

1  tablespoon cornstarch          2  tablespoons wine

1. Make this roux with red wine for a defatted beef broth gravy. Use white wine if you plan to use it for chicken or seafood gravy or sauce. Whisk ingredients together until well-blended, making sure there are no lumps.
2. To use as a thickener for 1 cup of broth, heat the broth until it reaches a boil. Slowly whisk the cornstarch-wine mixture into the broth and return to a boil, then reduce heat; simmer, stirring constantly, until the mixture thickens enough to coat the back of a spoon. (A gravy or sauce made in this manner will thicken more as it cools. It's important to bring a cornstarch slurry to a boil; this helps it thicken and removes the "starchy" taste.)

### Flavor Facts
*Regardless of the thickener you use to make gravy, be sure to strain the pan drippings to remove as much residue fat as possible. That way you'll save the juice—and flavor—of the meat.*

# Madeira Sauce

2 teaspoons olive oil

1 clove garlic, crushed

1 tablespoon chopped shallot

1 teaspoon unsalted tomato
paste

⅓ cup Madeira

1 tablespoon lemon juice

2 teaspoons Mock Cream
(see page 42)

¼ cup shellfish, vegetable, **or**
chicken broth

2 teaspoons unsalted butter

Salt and freshly ground black
pepper (optional)

| Serves 4 | |
|---|---|
| **Nutritional Analysis (per serving):** | |
| Calories: | 56.01 |
| Protein: | 0.23 g |
| Carbohydrate: | 1.60 g |
| Fat: | 4.18 g |
| Sat. Fat: | 1.50 g |
| Cholesterol: | 5.18 mg |
| Sodium: | 2.91 mg |
| Fiber: | 0.09 g |
| PCF Ratio: | 2-14-84 |
| **Exchange Approx.:** | |
| 1 Fat, ½ Vegetable | |

Heat the olive oil in a nonstick saucepan over medium heat. Add the garlic and shallot, and sauté until translucent. Add the tomato paste and sauté for 30 seconds, stirring as needed. Add the Madeira, broth, lemon juice, Mock Cream, and simmer until the mixture is reduced by half. Whisk in the butter to form an emulsion. Optional: Strain the sauce and season with salt and pepper.

TIP: *Keep the sauce warm until needed, being careful not to let it boil or become too cold after the butter has been added.*

# Mock Béchamel Sauce

| Yields 1 cup |
|---|
| **Serving size: ¼ cup** |

| Nutritional Analysis (per serving): | |
|---|---|
| Calories: | 53.07 |
| Protein: | 4.25 g |
| Carbohydrate: | 4.28 g |
| Fat: | 2.17 g |
| Sat. Fat: | 1.01 g |
| Cholesterol: | 50.93 mg |
| Sodium: | 57.99 mg |
| Fiber: | 0.00 g |
| PCF Ratio: | 32-32-36 |

**Exchange Approx.:**
½ Fat,
½ Skim Milk

1 egg
1 cup Mock Cream
  (see page 42)

1 teaspoon unsalted butter

1. In a quart-size or larger microwave-safe bowl, whisk the egg into the Mock Cream until it's well blended. Microwave on high for 1 minute. Whisk the mixture again. Microwave on high for 30 seconds and then whisk the mixture again. Microwave on high for another 30 seconds, then whisk again. (Strain the mixture if there appears to be any cooked egg solids; this seldom occurs if the mixture is whisked at the intervals specified.)
2. Allow the mixture to cool slightly, then whisk in the butter.

# Mock Cauliflower Sauce

2 cups cauliflower
¼ cup diced Spanish onion
1 tablespoon dry white wine
⅛ cup (2 tablespoons) Mock
    Cream (see page 42)
1 clove roasted garlic
    (for roasting instructions,

see "Dry-Roasted Garlic"
on page 54) **or** ½ clove
crushed garlic
Freshly ground white pepper
    to taste

| Serves 4 | |
|---|---|
| **Nutritional Analysis (per serving):** | |
| Calories: | 27.18 |
| Protein: | 1.73 g |
| Carbohydrate: | 4.68 g |
| Fat: | 0.32 g |
| Sat. Fat: | 0.06 g |
| Cholesterol: | 0.20 mg |
| Sodium: | 15.51 mg |
| Fiber: | 1.87 g |
| PCF Ratio: | 24-66-10 |
| **Exchange Approx.:** | |
| 1 Vegetable | |

1. Add the cauliflower, onion, garlic, and white wine to a microwave-safe bowl. Cover and microwave on high for 5 minutes, or until the cauliflower is tender and the onions are transparent. (Microwave on high for additional 1-minute intervals, if necessary.)
2. Pour the vegetable-wine mixture into a blender or food processor container, being careful not to burn yourself on the steam. Season with the white pepper, add the Mock Cream, and process until smooth.

**TIP:** *If you use frozen cauliflower to make Mock Cauliflower Sauce, be sure to thaw and drain it first. Otherwise, there will be too much moisture and the resulting sauce will be too thin.*

# Spices

## Herbal and Other Seasoning Mixtures

*Using herbs is a delicious way to season dishes and cut the amount of salt needed for flavor, too. Although fresh herbs need to be used immediately; dried herb mixtures can be prepared in advance and stored in an airtight container.*

*The easiest way to dry fresh herbs is to put the baking sheet in an oven at 200- to 225-degrees for 1 hour. Blends made from whole seeds or leaves usually need to be coarsely ground in a spice grinder or small food processor prior to using.*

## Spice Facts

*As a general rule, nuts, seeds, and roots are spices; leafy plants are herbs.*

### Barbecue Blend

4 tablespoons dried basil
4 tablespoons dried rubbed sage
4 tablespoons dried thyme
4 teaspoons cracked black pepper
4 teaspoons dried savory
1 teaspoon dried lemon peel

### Caribbean Blend

1 tablespoon curry powder
1 tablespoon ground cumin
1 tablespoon ground allspice
1 tablespoon ground ginger
1 teaspoon ground cayenne pepper

### Cajun Blend

2 tablespoons paprika
1½ tablespoons garlic powder
1 tablespoon onion powder
½ tablespoon black pepper
2 teaspoons cayenne pepper
2 teaspoons dried oregano
2 teaspoons dried thyme

### Country Blend

5 teaspoons dried thyme
4 teaspoons dried basil
4 teaspoons dried chervil
4 teaspoons dried tarragon

# Spices

## Fish and Seafood Herbs

5 teaspoons dried basil
5 teaspoons crushed fennel seed
4 teaspoons dried parsley
1 teaspoon dried lemon peel

## French Blend

1 tablespoon crushed dried tarragon
1 tablespoon crushed dried chervil
1 tablespoon onion powder

## Herbes de Provence

4 teaspoons dried oregano
2 teaspoons dried basil
2 teaspoons dried sweet marjoram
2 teaspoons dried thyme
1 teaspoon dried mint
1 teaspoon dried rosemary
1 teaspoon dried sage leaves
1 teaspoon fennel seed
1 teaspoon dried lavender (optional)

## Italian Blend

1 tablespoon crushed dried basil
1 tablespoon crushed dried thyme
1 tablespoon crushed dried oregano
2 tablespoons garlic powder

## Mediterranean Blend

1 tablespoon dried sun-dried tomatoes
1 tablespoon dried basil
1 teaspoon dried oregano
1 teaspoon dried thyme
1 tablespoon garlic powder

**TIP** If you don't have a food processor, you can freeze the sun-dried tomatoes so they will be easier to crush; however, that adds moisture to the herb blend, so it can't be stored.

## Middle Eastern Blend

1 tablespoon ground coriander
1 tablespoon ground cumin
1 tablespoon turmeric
1 teaspoon ground cinnamon
1 teaspoon crushed dried mint

# Spices

## Old Bay Seasoning

1 tablespoon celery seed
1 tablespoon whole black peppercorns
6 bay leaves
½ teaspoon whole cardamom
½ teaspoon mustard seed
4 whole cloves
1 teaspoon sweet Hungarian paprika
¼ teaspoon mace

## Pacific Rim

1 tablespoon Chinese five-spice powder
1 tablespoon paprika
1 tablespoon ground ginger
1 teaspoon black pepper

## Sonoran Blend

1 tablespoon ground chili powder
1 tablespoon black pepper
1 tablespoon crushed dried oregano
1 tablespoon crushed dried thyme
1 tablespoon crushed dried coriander
1 tablespoon garlic powder

## Stuffing Blend

6 tablespoons dried rubbed sage
3 tablespoons dried sweet marjoram
2 tablespoons dried parsley
4 teaspoons dried celery flakes

## Texas Seasoning

3 tablespoons dried cilantro
2 tablespoons dried oregano
4 teaspoons dried thyme
2 tablespoons pure good-quality chili
   powder
2 tablespoons freshly ground black
   pepper
2 tablespoons ground cumin
2 small crushed dried chili peppers
1 teaspoon garlic powder

CHAPTER 3
# *Appetizers*

| | |
|---|---|
| Cucumber Slices with Smoked Salmon Cream | 52 |
| Flaxseed Oil–Fortified Salsa Dip | 53 |
| Lemon Tahini Vegetable Dip | 53 |
| Garlic and Feta Cheese Dip | 54 |
| Spicy Almond Dip | 55 |
| Cinnamon Nut Butter | 55 |
| Onion Dip | 56 |
| French Onion Soup Dip | 56 |
| Horseradish Dip | 57 |
| Bean Dip | 57 |
| Garbanzo Dip | 58 |
| Herbed Cheese Spread | 58 |
| Zesty Almond Spread | 59 |
| Almond Honey Mustard | 59 |
| Smoked Mussel Spread | 60 |
| Easy Olive Spread | 61 |
| Mushroom Caviar | 62 |
| Gluten-Free Sesame Seed Crackers | 63 |

# Cucumber Slices
# with Smoked Salmon Cream

| Yields about ½ cup<br>Serving size: 1 tsp. | |
|---|---|
| **Nutritional Analysis<br>(per serving):** | |
| Calories: | 27.39 |
| Protein: | 1.18 g |
| Carbohydrate: | 0.53 g |
| Fat: | 2.32 g |
| Sat. Fat: | 1.40 g |
| Cholesterol: | 7.10 mg |
| Sodium: | 50.23 mg |
| Fiber: | 0.07 g |
| PCF Ratio: | 17-8-75 |
| **Exchange Approx.:** | |
| ½ Fat | |

2–3 cucumbers

1 ounce Ducktrap River
  smoked salmon

8 ounces Neufchatel cheese,
  room temperature

½ tablespoon lemon juice

½ teaspoon freshly ground
  pepper

Dried dill (optional)

1. Cut the cucumbers into slices about ¼-inch thick. Place the slices on paper towels to drain while you prepare the salmon cream.
2. Combine the smoked salmon, Neufchatel cheese, lemon juice, and pepper in a food processor; blend until smooth.
3. Fit a pastry bag with your choice of tip, and spoon the salmon cream into the bag. Pipe 1 teaspoon of the salmon cream atop each cucumber slice. Garnish with dried dill, if desired.

### Comparative Analysis

*If you choose to use cream cheese instead of Neufchâtel, the Nutritional Analysis will be: Calories: 35.48; Protein: 0.96 g; Carbohydrate: 0.50 g; Fat: 3.36 g; Sat. Fat: 2.05 g; Cholesterol: 10.15 mg; Sodium: 40.81 mg; Fiber: 0.07 g; PCF Ratio: 11-6-84. Exchange Approximations: 1 Fat.*

# Flaxseed Oil–Fortified Salsa Dip

⅛ cup flaxseed oil
½ cup mild salsa
1 teaspoon freeze-dried chives

1 teaspoon dried basil
Pinch of sea salt
¼ cup chopped onion

Blend all the ingredients together in food processor or blender for a smooth dip; otherwise, mix thoroughly with a fork.

### ℰ Preventative Measures

*Whole ground flaxseed is rich in phytoestrogens (the plant substances that mimic the female sex hormone estrogen) in even greater quantities than in soy, so it's now also considered another possible way to help prevent breast cancer in postmenopausal women. Flaxseed also has omega-3 and -6 essential fatty acids, both of which are known for their health benefits. (Source: WebMDHealth,* ✐ http://my.webmd.com)

| Yields about 1 cup Serving size: 1 tbs. | |
|---|---|
| **Nutritional Analysis (per serving):** | |
| Calories: | 18.12 |
| Protein: | 0.21 g |
| Carbohydrate: | 0.75 g |
| Fat: | 1.50 g |
| Sat. Fat: | 0.13 g |
| Cholesterol: | 0.00 mg |
| Sodium: | 48.53 mg |
| Fiber: | 0.24 g |
| PCF Ratio: | 5-17-78 |
| **Exchange Approx.:** 3 servings = 1 Fat | |

# Lemon Tahini Vegetable Dip

1 cup sesame seeds
¼ cup lemon juice
1 cup water
2 tablespoons ground flaxseed

1 teaspoon garlic powder
⅛ teaspoon cider vinegar
1 teaspoon sea salt

Put all the ingredients in a food processor and blend until smooth.

| Yields about 5 cups Serving size: 1 tbs. | |
|---|---|
| **Nutritional Analysis (per serving):** | |
| Calories: | 26.27 |
| Protein: | 1.15 g |
| Carbohydrate: | 0.76 g |
| Fat: | 2.32 g |
| Sat. Fat: | 0.31 g |
| Cholesterol: | 0.00 mg |
| Sodium: | 61.41 mg |
| Fiber: | 0.63 g |
| PCF Ratio: | 16-11-73 |
| **Exchange Approx.:** ½ Fat | |

# Garlic and Feta Cheese Dip

## Yields 1 ½ cups
## Serving size: 1 tbs.

### Nutritional Analysis
### (per serving):

| | |
|---|---|
| Calories: | 11.48 |
| Protein: | 0.28 g |
| Carbohydrate: | 0.29 g |
| Fat: | 1.04 g |
| Sat. Fat: | 0.54 g |
| Cholesterol: | 0.00 mg |
| Sodium: | 22.09 mg |
| Fiber: | 0.00 g |
| PCF Ratio: | 9-10-80 |

### Exchange Approx.:
1 Free

½ cup feta cheese, crumbled
4 ounces softened cream cheese
¼ cup Hellmann's or Best
   Foods Real Mayonnaise
1 clove dry-roasted garlic
   (see "Dry Roasted Garlic"
   on this page)
¼ teaspoon dried basil

¼ teaspoon dried cilantro
   **or** oregano
⅛ teaspoon dried dill
⅛ teaspoon dried thyme

In a food processor, combine all the ingredients and process until thoroughly mixed. Cover and chill until ready to serve with assorted vegetables. This dip is somewhat high in fat if you use regular cream cheese, whereas nonfat cream cheese would lower the total fat in this recipe by 38 grams. People on a salt-restricted diet need to check with their dietitians about using nonfat cream cheese because it's much higher in sodium.

### Dry-Roasted Garlic

*Roasted garlic is delicious spread on toasted baguette slices, but is also flavorful in some of the salad dressings and other recipes in this book. The traditional method calls for roasting a full head of garlic in olive oil. Dry roasting works just as well and doesn't add fat.*

*Preheat oven to 350 degrees and lightly spray a small, covered baking dish with nonstick spray. Slice off ½ inch from the top of each garlic head and rub off any loose skins, being careful not to separate the cloves. Place the garlic in baking dish, cut-side up (if roasting more than 1 head of garlic, arrange them in the dish so that they don't touch). Cover and bake until the garlic cloves are very tender when pierced, about 30 to 45 minutes. Roasted garlic heads will keep in the refrigerator for 2 or 3 days.*

# Spicy Almond Dip

¼ cup ground, raw almonds
2 teaspoons Worcestershire
  sauce (see recipe for
  Homemade Worcestershire
  on page 40)
½ teaspoon honey
½ teaspoon chili powder

1 teaspoon poppy seeds
½ teaspoon onion powder
⅛ cup water
Pinch of black pepper

Put all the ingredients in a food processor and blend until smooth.

| Yields about ½ cup Serving size: 1 tbs. | |
| --- | --- |
| **Nutritional Analysis (per serving):** | |
| Calories: | 22.57 |
| Protein: | 0.73 g |
| Carbohydrate: | 1.47 g |
| Fat: | 1.69 g |
| Sat. Fat: | 0.14 g |
| Cholesterol: | 0.00 mg |
| Sodium: | 18.08 mg |
| Fiber: | 0.45 g |
| PCF Ratio: | 12-25-63 |
| **Exchange Approx.:** ½ Fat | |

# Cinnamon Nut Butter

¼ cup sesame seeds
¼ cup ground almonds
¼ cup sunflower seeds
1 tablespoon honey
½ teaspoon cinnamon

Pinch of cocoa (optional)
Pinch of sea salt (optional)

Put all the ingredients in a food processor and blend to desired consistency, scraping down the sides of the bowl as necessary. Serve with toast points, crackers, or celery sticks. Refrigerate any leftovers.

| Yields ¾ cup Serving size: 1 tsp. | |
| --- | --- |
| **Nutritional Analysis (per serving):** | |
| Calories: | 17.10 |
| Protein: | 0.55 g |
| Carbohydrate: | 1.06 g |
| Fat: | 1.33 g |
| Sat. Fat: | 0.15 g |
| Cholesterol: | 0.00 mg |
| Sodium: | 0.18 mg |
| Fiber: | 0.32 g |
| PCF Ratio: | 12-23-65 |
| **Exchange Approx.:** ½ Fat | |

# Onion Dip

| Yields 1½ cups Serving size: 1 tbs. |
| --- |

| Nutritional Analysis (per serving, without salt): | |
| --- | --- |
| Calories: | 12.07 |
| Protein: | 0.60 g |
| Carbohydrate: | 1.15 g |
| Fat: | 0.59 g |
| Sat. Fat: | 0.09 g |
| Cholesterol: | 0.17 mg |
| Sodium: | 7.38 mg |
| Fiber: | 0.08 g |
| PCF Ratio: | 19-38-43 |

| Exchange Approx.: |
| --- |
| 1 Free Condiment |

1 cup nonfat yogurt
1 tablespoon olive oil
½ cup water
1 teaspoon lemon juice
1 teaspoon cider vinegar

1 medium-sized sweet onion, chopped
Sea salt to taste (optional)
Lemon pepper to taste (optional)

Combine all the ingredients in a food processor and pulse to desired consistency. Refrigerate for 1 hour to allow the flavors to merge, then serve.

### Quick Thickener

*If your dip or spread is too runny, stir in ¼ teaspoon of potato flour. Let it set for 1 or 2 minutes, then add more flour if necessary. The addition of potato flour won't make a significant change to the flavor or Exchange Approximations.*

# French Onion Soup Dip

| Yields about 1¾ cups Serving size: 1 tbs. |
| --- |

| Nutritional Analysis (per serving): | |
| --- | --- |
| Calories: | 6.92 |
| Protein: | 1.04 g |
| Carbohydrate: | 0.48 g |
| Fat: | 0.08 g |
| Sat. Fat: | 0.05 g |
| Cholesterol: | 0.48 mg |
| Sodium: | 10.79 mg |
| Fiber: | 0.05 g |
| PCF Ratio: | 61-28-11 |

| Exchange Approx.: |
| --- |
| 1 Free Condiment |

1 cup chopped sweet onion
1 tablespoon Parmesan cheese
1 cup nonfat cottage cheese

2 tablespoons reduced (double-strength) beef broth (see "Know Your Terms" on page 104)

1. Put the onion and beef broth in a microwave-safe dish. Cover and microwave on high for 1 minute; stir. Continue to microwave on high for 30-second intervals until the onion is transparent. Stir in Parmesan cheese. Set aside and allow to cool.
2. In a blender, process the cottage cheese until smooth. Mix the cottage cheese into the onion mixture. Serve warm or refrigerate until needed and serve cold.

### Guilt-Free Flavors

*Adjust the flavor of dips or spreads without adding calories by adding onion or garlic powder or your choice of herbs.*

# Horseradish Dip

1 cup nonfat cottage cheese
1 tablespoon olive oil
½ cup nonfat plain yogurt
3 tablespoons prepared
   horseradish
1 teaspoon lemon juice

Optional seasonings to taste:
   Onion powder to taste
   Pinch of cumin
   Sea salt
   Pinch of ginger

Combine all the ingredients in a blender or food processor and process until smooth.

**Yields 1¾ cups**
**Serving size: 1 tbs.**

| Nutritional Analysis (per serving): | |
| --- | --- |
| Calories: | 11.72 |
| Protein: | 1.15 g |
| Carbohydrate: | 0.60 g |
| Fat: | 0.52 g |
| Sat. Fat: | 0.09 g |
| Cholesterol: | 0.00 mg |
| Sodium: | 8.81 mg |
| Fiber: | 0.05 g |
| PCF Ratio: | 39-21-40 |

**Exchange Approx.:**
1 Free Condiment

# Bean Dip

½ cup cooked pinto
   (**or** other) beans
1 tablespoon Bragg's Liquid
   Aminos
3 tablespoons cider vinegar
1 teaspoon honey
¼ teaspoon dried basil

¼ teaspoon dried parsley
1 stalk celery, diced
¼ cup chopped green onion
½ cup alfalfa sprouts, lightly
   chopped
1 medium tomato, diced

Add the beans, Liquid Aminos, cider vinegar, honey, and dried herbs to a blender, and process until smooth. Stir in remaining ingredients.

## Low-Sodium Substitutions

*Bragg's Liquid Aminos is a lower-sodium substitution for soy sauce. Because Bragg's isn't a fermented product, many people who can't tolerate soy can use it.*

**Yields about 2 cups**
**Serving size: 1 tbs.**

| Nutritional Analysis (per serving): | |
| --- | --- |
| Calories: | 6.76 |
| Protein: | 0.39 g |
| Carbohydrate: | 1.36 g |
| Fat: | 0.03 g |
| Sat. Fat: | 0.01 g |
| Cholesterol: | 0.00 mg |
| Sodium: | 23.01 mg |
| Fiber: | 0.34 g |
| PCF Ratio: | 22-75-4 |

**Exchange Approx.:**
½ Free Condiment

# Garbanzo Dip

| Yields about 2 cups |
| :---: |
| Serving size: 1 tbs. |

| Nutritional Analysis (per serving): | |
| :--- | ---: |
| Calories: | 25.44 |
| Protein: | 1.64 g |
| Carbohydrate: | 4.79 g |
| Fat: | 0.06 g |
| Sat. Fat: | 0.02 g |
| Cholesterol: | 0.00 mg |
| Sodium: | 1.04 mg |
| Fiber: | 1.06 g |
| PCF Ratio: | 25-73-2 |

**Exchange Approx.:**
½ Very-Lean Meat

3 cups cooked garbanzo
   (**or** other) white beans
½ teaspoon ground cumin
1 tablespoon lemon juice
1 tablespoon parsley flakes

¼ teaspoon dried basil
1 teaspoon onion powder
¼ teaspoon garlic powder
1 tablespoon honey

Combine all the ingredients in a food processor or blender and process until smooth. Add a teaspoon of water or bean broth if you need to thin the dip.

# Herbed Cheese Spread

| Yields about 1 cup |
| :---: |
| Serving size: 1 tbs. |

| Nutritional Analysis (per serving): | |
| :--- | ---: |
| Calories: | 20.06 |
| Protein: | 1.34 g |
| Carbohydrate: | 0.32 g |
| Fat: | 1.50 g |
| Sat. Fat: | 0.94 g |
| Cholesterol: | 5.06 mg |
| Sodium: | 25.79 mg |
| Fiber: | 0.03 g |
| PCF Ratio: | 27-6-67 |

**Exchange Approx.:**
¼ Skim Milk
or 1 Free Condiment

2 teaspoons chopped fresh
   parsley leaves
2 teaspoons chopped fresh chives
1 teaspoon chopped fresh thyme
½ cup nonfat cottage cheese

½ teaspoon freshly ground
   black pepper
4 ounces Neufchâtel cheese,
   at room temperature

Place the herbs in a food processor and pulse until chopped. Add the cheeses and process until smooth.

### Toasted Nut Garnish

*Herbed Cheese Spread is good on Garlic Toast (see page 175) sprinkled with a few toasted pine nuts, sunflower or sesame seeds, or other chopped nuts. Toast the nuts in a small skillet in a single layer. Over low heat, toast until lightly golden, stirring often to prevent burning. This takes 3 or 4 minutes. Cool on paper towels.*

# Zesty Almond Spread

30 unsalted almonds
2 teaspoons honey
1 teaspoon chili powder

¼ teaspoon garlic powder
Pinch of sea salt (optional)

Place all the ingredients in a food processor or blender and process to desired consistency.

| Yields about ¼ cup Serving size: 1 tbs. | |
| --- | --- |
| **Nutritional Analysis (per serving, without salt):** | |
| Calories: | 50.13 |
| Protein: | 1.54 g |
| Carbohydrate: | 3.73 g |
| Fat: | 3.65 g |
| Sat. Fat: | 0.28 g |
| Cholesterol: | 0.00 mg |
| Sodium: | 0.18 mg |
| Fiber: | 0.86 g |
| PCF Ratio: | 11-28-61 |
| **Exchange Approx.:** 1 Fat | |

# Almond Honey Mustard

¼ cup unsalted almond butter
2 teaspoons mustard
1 teaspoon honey
2 tablespoons lemon juice

½ teaspoon garlic powder
Pinch of cumin (optional)
Pinch of sea salt (optional)

Add all the ingredients to a food processor or blender and process until smooth.

| Yields about ½ cup Serving size: 1 tsp. | |
| --- | --- |
| **Nutritional Analysis (per serving, without salt):** | |
| Calories: | 20.53 |
| Protein: | 0.47 g |
| Carbohydrate: | 1.07 g |
| Fat: | 1.77 g |
| Sat. Fat: | 0.17 g |
| Cholesterol: | 0.00 mg |
| Sodium: | 5.69 mg |
| Fiber: | 0.13 g |
| PCF Ratio: | 9-19-72 |
| **Exchange Approx.:** ½ Fat | |

# Smoked Mussel Spread

| Yields 4¼ cup |
| :---: |
| **Serving size: 1 tbs.** |

| Nutritional Analysis (per serving): | |
| :--- | ---: |
| Calories: | 20.51 |
| Protein: | 1.21 g |
| Carbohydrate: | 0.78 g |
| Fat: | 1.40 g |
| Sat. Fat: | 0.77 g |
| Cholesterol: | 5.36 mg |
| Sodium: | 29.90 mg |
| Fiber: | 0.02 g |
| PCF Ratio: | 24-15-61 |

**Exchange Approx.:**
½ Fat

*4 ounces cream cheese*
*1 cup nonfat plain yogurt*
*½ cup nonfat cottage cheese*
*2 ounces Ducktrap River*
   *smoked mussels*

*¼ cup chopped onion*
   *or scallion*
*1 teaspoon dried dill*
*1 teaspoon dried parsley*

Place all the ingredients in a food processor or blender and process until smooth. Chill for at least 2 hours or overnight before serving. This spread also works well made with smoked oysters, shrimp, or turkey. Serve on crackers or cracker-sized bread rounds.

### Conservative Exchanges

*Keep in mind that whenever Exchange Approximations are given in this book, it's always with an "err on the side of caution" philosophy, so the numbers are rounded up.*

# Easy Olive Spread

1 cup black olives
3 cloves garlic
1 tablespoon fresh Italian
 flat-leaf parsley
1 tablespoon fresh basil
2 teaspoons minced lemon zest
Freshly ground black pepper
 to taste
½ cup nonfat cottage cheese

2 tablespoons cream cheese
1 tablespoon Hellmann's or Best
 Foods Real Mayonnaise

| Yields about 3 cups Serving size: 1 tbs. | |
|---|---|
| **Nutritional Analysis (per serving):** | |
| Calories: | 15.01 |
| Protein: | 0.67 g |
| Carbohydrate: | 0.74 g |
| Fat: | 1.11 g |
| Sat. Fat: | 0.30 g |
| Cholesterol: | 1.28 mg |
| Sodium: | 56.20 mg |
| Fiber: | 0.21 g |
| PCF Ratio: | 17-19-64 |
| **Exchange Approx.:** 1 Free Condiment | |

1. Combine the olives, garlic, herbs, and spices in a food processor and pulse until chopped. Transfer to a bowl and set aside.
2. Add the cottage cheese, cream cheese, and mayonnaise to the blender or food processor and process until smooth. Fold the cheese mixture into the chopped olive mixture.

## Delicious Substitutions
Substitute marinated mushrooms or artichoke hearts for the olives in the Easy Olive Spread recipe.

# Mushroom Caviar

| Yields about 3 cups |
|---|
| Serving size: 1 tbs. |

| Nutritional Analysis (per serving): | |
|---|---|
| Calories: | 8.77 |
| Protein: | 0.25 g |
| Carbohydrate: | 0.77 g |
| Fat: | 0.61 g |
| Sat. Fat: | 0.08 g |
| Cholesterol: | 0.00 mg |
| Sodium: | 0.43 mg |
| Fiber: | 0.25 g |
| PCF Ratio: | 11-32-57 |

**Exchange Approx.:**
1 Free Condiment

1½ cups portobello mushrooms
1½ cups white button mushrooms
¼ cup chopped scallions
4 cloves dry-roasted garlic
  (see "Dry-Roasted Garlic" on
  page 54)
1 teaspoon fresh lemon juice
½ teaspoon balsamic vinegar

1 tablespoon extra-virgin olive oil
½ teaspoon fresh, chopped
  thyme (optional)
Sea salt and freshly ground
  black pepper to taste
  (optional)

1. Cut the portobello mushrooms into ¼-inch cubes. Cut the white button mushrooms into halves or quarters. (The mushroom pieces should be roughly uniform in size.) Place the mushrooms and chopped scallion in a microwave-safe bowl; cover, and microwave on high for 1 minute. Rotate the bowl. Microwave for 30-second intervals until tender.
2. Transfer the scallions and mushrooms to a food processor. (Reserve any liquid to use for thinning the "caviar," if necessary.) Pulse the food processor several times to chop the mixture, scraping down the sides of the bowl as needed. Add the remaining ingredients and pulse until mixed. Place in a small crock or serving bowl, and serve warm.

**TIP:** *Refrigerated leftovers will last a few days. Spread on toasted bread and pop under the broiler for 1 or 2 minutes for tasty mushroom-garlic toast.*

### Pseudo-Sauté

*When onions and scallions are sautéed in butter or oil, they go through a caramelization process that doesn't occur when they're steamed. To create this flavor without increasing the fat in a recipe, transfer steamed vegetables to a nonstick wok or skillet (coated with nonstick spray, or a small portion of the oil called for in the recipe) and sauté until the extra moisture evaporates.*

# Gluten-Free Sesame Seed Crackers

1½ cups spelt flour
1 cup sesame seeds
¼ cup arrowroot
1 tablespoons olive **or**
    vegetable oil
3 tablespoons nonfat yogurt
¼ cup nonfat dry milk
½ teaspoon Ener-G
    nonaluminum baking powder

½ cup water
⅔ teaspoon sea salt (optional)

| Yields 36 crackers Serving size: 1 cracker | |
|---|---|
| **Nutritional Analysis (per serving):** | |
| Calories: | 49.85 |
| Protein: | 1.98 g |
| Carbohydrate: | 5.01 g |
| Fat: | 2.71 g |
| Sat. Fat: | 0.37 g |
| Cholesterol: | 0.10 mg |
| Sodium: | 4.94 mg |
| Fiber: | 0.64 g |
| PCF Ratio: | 15-38-47 |
| **Exchange Approx.:** ½ Starch | |

1. Preheat oven to 400 degrees. Mix together all ingredients, then add the water, a little at a time, to form a soft doughlike consistency. Be careful not to work the dough too much; you do not want to knead spelt flour.

2. On a floured surface, use a rolling pin to roll the dough until it's ⅛-inch thick. Use a cookie cutter to cut it into shapes and place them on a cookie sheet treated with nonstick spray. (Or use a pizza cutter to crosscut the dough into square- or rectangular-shaped crackers.) Prick each cracker with a fork. Bake for about 12 minutes or until golden brown. Store cooled crackers in an airtight container.

# CHAPTER 4
# Breakfast and Brunch

| | |
|---|---|
| Egg White Pancakes | 66 |
| Buckwheat Pancakes | 66 |
| Berry Puff Pancakes | 67 |
| Buttermilk Pancakes | 68 |
| Sweet Potato Flour Crêpes | 68 |
| Eggs Benedict Redux | 69 |
| Fruit Smoothie | 69 |
| Tofu Smoothie | 70 |
| Overnight Oatmeal | 70 |
| Egg Clouds on Toast | 71 |

# Egg White Pancakes

| Serves 2 | |
| --- | --- |

**Nutritional Analysis
(per serving):**

| | |
| --- | --- |
| Calories: | 197.11 |
| Protein: | 13.62 g |
| Carbohydrate: | 30.53 g |
| Fat: | 2.69 g |
| Sat. Fat: | 0.47 g |
| Cholesterol: | 0.00 mg |
| Sodium: | 120.33 mg |
| Fiber: | 4.13 g |
| PCF Ratio: | 27-61-12 |

**Exchange Approx.:**
1 Free Sweet,
1 Lean Meat,
1½ Breads

*4 egg whites*
*½ cup oatmeal*
*4 teaspoons reduced-calorie **or***
*   low-sugar strawberry jam*

*1 teaspoon powdered sugar*

Put all the ingredients in a blender and process until smooth. Preheat a nonstick pan treated with cooking spray over medium heat. Pour half of the mixture into the pan and cook for 4 to 5 minutes. Flip the pancake and cook until the inside of the cake is cooked. Repeat using remaining batter for second pancake. Dust each pancake with the powdered sugar, if using.

## Creative Toppings

*Experiment with toast and pancake toppings. Try a tablespoon of raisins, almonds, apples, bananas, berries, nut butters (limit these to 1 teaspoon per serving), peanuts, pears, walnuts, or wheat germ.*

# Buckwheat Pancakes

| Serves 2 | |
| --- | --- |

**Nutritional Analysis
(per serving):**

| | |
| --- | --- |
| Calories: | 220.00 |
| Protein: | 11.00 g |
| Carbohydrate: | 44.00 g |
| Fat: | 1.00 g |
| Sat. Fat: | 0.00 g |
| Cholesterol: | 1.00 mg |
| Sodium: | 200.00 mg |
| Fiber: | 5.00 g |
| PCF Ratio: | 76-19-5 |

**Exchange Approx.:**
2 Breads,
½ Skim Milk,
½ Fruit

*1 cup whole-wheat flour*
*½ cup buckwheat flour*
*1½ teaspoons baking powder*

*2 egg whites*
*¼ cup apple juice concentrate*
*1¼ to 1½ cups skim milk*

1. Sift the flours and baking powder together. Combine the egg whites, apple juice concentrate, and 1¼ cups of the skim milk. Add the milk mixture to the dry ingredients and mix well, but do not overmix. Add the remaining milk if necessary to reach the desired consistency.
2. Cook the pancakes in a nonstick skillet or on a griddle treated with nonstick spray over medium heat.

# Berry Puff Pancakes

2 large whole eggs
1 large egg white
½ cup skim milk
½ cup all-purpose flour
1 tablespoon granulated sugar
⅛ teaspoon sea salt
1 tablespoon powdered sugar

2 cups of fresh berries, such as
  raspberries, blackberries,
  boysenberries, blueberries,
  strawberries, or a combination

| Serves 6 | |
|---|---|
| **Nutritional Analysis (per serving):** | |
| Calories: | 110 |
| Protein: | 5 g |
| Carbohydrate: | 36.75 g |
| Fat: | 2 g |
| Sat. Fat: | 1 g |
| Cholesterol: | 71 mg |
| Sodium: | 89 mg |
| Fiber: | 3 g |
| PCF Ratio: | 65-18-17 |
| **Exchange Approx.:** 1 Bread, ½ Fruit | |

1. Preheat oven to 450 degrees. Treat a 10-inch ovenproof skillet or deep pie pan with nonstick spray. Once the oven is heated, place the pan in the oven for a few minutes to get it hot.
2. Add the eggs and egg white to a medium bowl and beat until mixed. Whisk in the milk. Slowly whisk in the flour, sugar, and salt.
3. Remove the preheated pan from the oven and pour the batter into it. Bake for 15 minutes. Reduce the heat to 350 degrees and bake for an additional 10 minutes, or until the batter is puffed and brown. Remove from the oven and slide the puffed pancake onto a serving plate. Cover the pancake with the fruit and sift the powdered sugar over the top. Cut into 6 equal wedges and serve.

## Syrup Substitutes

Spreading 2 teaspoons of your favorite Smucker's Low Sugar jam or jelly on a waffle or pancake not only gives you a sweet topping, it can be one of your Free Exchange List choices for the day.

# Buttermilk Pancakes

| Serves 2 | |
|---|---|

**Nutritional Analysis (per serving):**

| | |
|---|---|
| Calories: | 143.32 |
| Protein: | 5.72 g |
| Carbohydrate: | 25.87 g |
| Fat: | 1.60 g |
| Sat. Fat: | 0.51 g |
| Cholesterol: | 49.00 mg |
| Sodium: | 110.52 mg |
| Fiber: | 0.86 g |
| PCF Ratio: | 16-74-10 |

**Exchange Approx.:**
1½ Breads

*1 cup all-purpose flour*
*2 tablespoons nonfat buttermilk powder*
*¼ teaspoon baking soda*
*½ teaspoon low-salt baking powder*
*1 cup water*

1. Blend together all the ingredients, adding more water if necessary, to get the batter consistency you desire.
2. Pour a quarter of the batter into a nonstick skillet or a skillet treated with nonstick cooking spray. Cook over medium heat until bubbles appear on the top half of the pancake. Flip and continue cooking until the center of pancake is done. Repeat process with remaining batter.

### Nut Butter Batter

*For a change of pace, try adding 1 Exchange amount per serving of nut butter to pancake batter and then use jelly or jam instead of syrup.*

# Sweet Potato Flour Crêpes

| Yields 10 crepes Serving size: 1 crepe | |
|---|---|

**Nutritional Analysis (per serving):**

| | |
|---|---|
| Calories: | 67 |
| Protein: | 2.79 g |
| Carbohydrate: | 11 g |
| Fat: | 1.1 g |
| Sat. Fat: | 0.35 G |
| Cholesterol: | 37.92 mg |
| Sodium: | 41.54 mg |
| Fiber: | 0.28 g |
| PCF Ratio: | 17-68-15 |

**Exchange Approx.:**
1 Bread/Starch

*2 eggs*
*¾ cup Ener-G sweet potato flour*
*½ teaspoon vanilla*
*1 cup skim milk*
*1 tablespoon nonfat dry milk*
*Pinch of sea salt*

1. Put all the ingredients in a blender or food processor and process until the mixture is the consistency of cream.
2. To prepare the crêpes, treat an 8-inch nonstick skillet heated over medium heat with nonstick spray. Pour about 2 tablespoons of the crêpe batter into the hot pan, tilting in a circular motion until the batter spreads evenly over the pan. Cook the crêpe until the outer edges just begin to brown and loosen from the pan. Flip the crêpe to the other side and cook about 30 seconds. Using a thin spatula, lift the crêpe from the pan and place on warm plate. Continue until all the crêpes are done.

# Eggs Benedict Redux

1 (2-ounce) slice reduced-calorie
   oat bran bread
1 egg
1 ounce Ducktrap River
   smoked salmon

2 tablespoons nonfat plain
   yogurt
1 teaspoon fresh lemon juice

Toast the bread and poach the egg. Place the salmon over the top of the toasted bread. Top the salmon with the poached egg. Stir the lemon juice into the yogurt and spoon that mixture over the top of the egg; serve immediately.

| Serves 1 |
|---|
| **Nutritional Analysis (per serving):** |

| | |
|---|---|
| Calories: | 317.66 |
| Protein: | 18.26 g |
| Carbohydrate: | 36.75 g |
| Fat: | 11.20 g |
| Sat. Fat: | 3.33 g |
| Cholesterol: | 195.27 mg |
| Sodium: | 698.20 mg |
| Fiber: | 2.00 g |
| PCF Ratio: | 23-46-31 |

**Exchange Approx.:**
1 Lean Meat,
1 Medium-Fat Meat, 2 Breads,
1 Free Condiment

# Fruit Smoothie

1 cup skim milk
2 Exchange servings of any
   diced fruit

1 tablespoon honey
4 teaspoons toasted wheat germ
6 large ice cubes

Put all the ingredients into a blender or food processor and process until thick and smooth!

## Batch 'Em

*Make large batches of smoothies so you can keep single servings in the freezer. Get out a serving as you begin to get ready for your day. This should give the smoothie time to thaw enough for you to stir it when you're ready to have breakfast.*

| Serves 1 |
|---|
| **Nutritional Analysis (per serving):** |

The Nutritional Analysis and Fruit Exchange for this recipe will depend on your choice of fruit. Otherwise, allow ½ Skim Milk Exchange and ½ Misc. Food Exchange. The wheat germ adds fiber, but at less than 20 calories a serving, it can count as 1 Free Exchange.

| Serves 1 | |
|---|---|
| **Nutritional Analysis (per serving):** | |
| Calories: | 287.79 |
| Protein: | 19.83 g |
| Carbohydrate: | 35.01 g |
| Fat: | 10.96 g |
| Sat. Fat: | 1.60 g |
| Cholesterol: | 0.00 mg |
| Sodium: | 18.58 mg |
| Fiber: | 8.90 g |
| PCF Ratio: | 25-44-31 |

**Exchange Approx.:**
1 Meat Substitute,
2 Fruits

# Tofu Smoothie

1 1/3 cups frozen unsweetened          1/2 cup (4 ounces) silken tofu
  strawberries
1/2 of a banana

In a food processor or blender, process all the ingredients until smooth. Add a little chilled water for thinner smoothies if desired.

| Serves 4 | |
|---|---|
| **Nutritional Analysis (per serving):** | |
| Calories: | 220.76 |
| Protein: | 8.77 g |
| Carbohydrate: | 42.19 g |
| Fat: | 2.88 g |
| Sat. Fat: | 0.53 g |
| Cholesterol: | 0.80 mg |
| Sodium: | 25.07 mg |
| Fiber: | 6.00 g |
| PCF Ratio: | 15-73-11 |

**Exchange Approx.:**
1 Fruit,
1 Bread,
1/2 Skim Milk

# Overnight Oatmeal

1 cup steel-cut oats          4 cups water
14 dried apricot halves       1/2 cup Mock Cream
1 dried fig                     (see page 42)
2 tablespoons golden raisins

Add all the ingredients to a slow cooker with a ceramic interior, and set to low heat. Cover and cook overnight (for 8 to 9 hours).

# Egg Clouds on Toast

2 egg whites
½ teaspoon sugar
1 tablespoon frozen apple juice
   concentrate

1 cup water
1 slice reduced-calorie oat bran
   bread, lightly toasted

1. In a copper bowl, beat the egg whites until they thicken. Add the sugar, and continue to beat until stiff peaks form.
2. In a small saucepan, heat the water and apple juice over medium heat until it just begins to boil; reduce heat and allow mixture to simmer. Drop the egg whites by the teaspoonful into the simmering water. Simmer for 3 minutes, then turn the egg white "clouds" over and simmer for an additional 3 minutes.
3. Ladle the "clouds" over the bread and serve immediately.

**TIP:** *Additional serving suggestions: Spread 1 teaspoon of low-sugar or all-fruit spread on the toast ( ½ Fruit Exchange) before you ladle on the "clouds." Or, for cinnamon French-style toast, sprinkle ¼ teaspoon cinnamon and ½ teaspoon powdered sugar (less than 10 calories) over the top of the clouds.*

| Serves 1 | |
|---|---|
| **Nutritional Analysis (per serving):** | |
| Calories: | 56.68 |
| Protein: | 4.42 g |
| Carbohydrate: | 9.28 g |
| Fat: | 0.43 g |
| Sat. Fat: | 0.07 g |
| Cholesterol: | 0.00 mg |
| Sodium: | 101.18 mg |
| Fiber: | 0.00 g |
| PCF Ratio: | 30-63-7 |

**Exchange Approx.:**
½ Very Lean Fat Meat,
½ Bread

# CHAPTER 5

# A Bounty of Breads

| | |
|---|---|
| Basic White Bread | 74 |
| Cinnamon Raisin Bread | 75 |
| Whole-Wheat Bread | 76 |
| Bread Machine White Bread | 77 |
| Honey Oat Bran Bread | 77 |
| 7-Grain Bread | 78 |
| Cheddar Cornbread | 78 |
| Cottage Cheese Bread | 79 |
| Hawaiian-Style Bread | 80 |
| Milk Biscuits | 81 |
| Angelic Buttermilk Batter Biscuits | 82 |
| Zucchini Bread | 83 |
| Orange Date Bread | 84 |

# Basic White Bread

**Yields 2 large loaves**
**Serving size: 1 slice**

| Nutritional Analysis (per serving): | |
| --- | --- |
| Calories: | 76.86 |
| Protein: | 2.00 g |
| Carbohydrate: | 15.00 g |
| Fat: | 0.83 g |
| Sat. Fat: | 0.21 g |
| Cholesterol: | 0.00 mg |
| Sodium: | 174.88 mg |
| Fiber: | 0.54 g |
| PCF Ratio: | 11-79-10 |

**Exchange Approx.:**
1 Bread/Starch

5½–6 cups flour
1 package (2½ teaspoons)
   active dry yeast
¼ cup warm water
2 tablespoons sugar

1¾ cups warm potato water
   **or** plain water
2 tablespoons shortening
1 tablespoon sea salt

1. Place about a third of the flour in a large bowl and set aside. Mix the yeast with the ¼ cup warm water in another bowl, stirring well. Add the sugar and potato water to the yeast; add that mixture to the flour in the bowl and stir well. Set aside for 5 minutes to allow the yeast to "proof."
2. Stir the mixture and cut in the shortening using a pastry blender or your hands. Stir in the salt and as much of the remaining flour as possible. The dough has enough flour when it's still somewhat sticky to the touch, yet pulls away from the side of the bowl as it's stirred. Turn the dough onto a lightly floured work surface. Knead for 8 to 10 minutes until smooth and elastic, adding flour as necessary. The dough will take on an almost "glossy" appearance once it's been kneaded sufficiently.
3. Transfer the dough to a bowl treated with nonstick spray. Cover with a damp cloth and place in a warm, draft-free area. Allow to rise until double in volume, about 1 to 1½ hours.
4. Punch the dough down and let it rise a second time until almost doubled in bulk.
5. Treat two 9" × 5" bread pans with nonstick spray. Punch the dough down again and divide into 2 loaves. Shape the loaves and place in the prepared bread pans. Cover and let rise until almost doubled.
6. Preheat oven to 350 degrees. Bake for 20 to 30 minutes, or until golden brown. Remove bread from pans and allow to cool on a rack.

## Bread Basics

*Always place bread pans and muffin tins in the center of the oven to allow proper heat circulation.*

# Cinnamon Raisin Bread

*Basic White Bread recipe*          *1 cup raisins*

1. Toss the raisins with 1 tablespoon of flour to coat them; shake off excess. When stirring in the bulk of the flour, add the raisins (Step 2 of Basic White Bread).
2. While following steps 3–4 for Basic White Bread, mix together ⅓ cup sugar and 2½ teaspoons cinnamon in a separate bowl. Divide the dough in half (Step 5 of Basic White Bread). Using a rolling pin, roll each half into a rectangular shape about ½-inch thick. Use a pastry brush to brush each rectangle with enough water to dampen the dough. Divide the cinnamon-sugar mixture into 2 equal portions. Sprinkle across the dampened surface of the dough.
3. Starting at a long end of the rectangle, use your fingers to roll the dough. Place it in a 9" × 5" loaf pan, tucking under then ends of the dough. Repeat with the second rectangle of dough. Allow to rise until doubled in bulk, and bake according to the instructions for Basic White Bread.

**Yields 2 large loaves**
**Serving size: 1 slice**

**Nutritional Analysis (per serving):**

| | |
|---|---|
| Calories: | 94.56 |
| Protein: | 2.13 g |
| Carbohydrate: | 19.65 g |
| Fat: | 0.85 g |
| Sat. Fat: | 0.22 g |
| Cholesterol: | 0.00 mg |
| Sodium: | 175.37 mg |
| Fiber: | 0.77 g |
| PCF Ratio: | 9-83-8 |

**Exchange Approx.:**
1 Bread/Starch;
½ Fruit

### Any Way You Slice It . . .

*It's usually easier to slice a loaf of homemade bread into 10 thicker slices than into 20 thinner ones. To arrive at 1 serving, either cut each thick slice in half or remove the crusts. (Be sure to reserve the crusts for use in other recipes.)*

# Whole-Wheat Bread

| Yields 2 loaves Serving size: 1 slice | |
|---|---|
| **Nutritional Analysis (per serving):** | |
| Calories: | 86.42 |
| Protein: | 2.27 g |
| Carbohydrate: | 17.06 g |
| Fat: | 1.23 g |
| Sat. Fat: | 0.32 g |
| Cholesterol: | 0.00 mg |
| Sodium: | 118.08 mg |
| Fiber: | 1.39 g |
| PCF Ratio: | 10-77-13 |
| **Exchange Approx.:** | |
| 1 Bread/Starch | |

1 package (2½ teaspoons) active dry yeast
2 cups warm water
3 cups unbleached all-purpose **or** bread flour
2 tablespoons sugar
½ cup hot water
2 teaspoons salt
½ cup brown sugar
3 tablespoons shortening
3 cups whole-wheat flour

1. Add the yeast to the 2 cups warm water. Stir in the all-purpose flour and sugar. Beat the mixture until smooth, either by hand or with a mixer. Set the mixture in a warm place to "proof" until it becomes foamy and bubbly (up to 1 hour).
2. Combine the ½ cup hot water, the salt, brown sugar, and shortening; stir. Allow to cool to lukewarm. (Stirring the sugar until it's dissolved should be sufficient to cool the water; test to be sure, as adding liquid that's too warm can "kill" the yeast.) Add to the bubbly flour mixture (the "sponge"). Stir in the whole-wheat flour and beat until smooth, but *do not knead*.
3. Divide the dough into 2 lightly greased pans, cover, and set in a warm place until doubled in size. Preheat oven to 350 degrees and bake for 50 minutes.

### History Lesson
*The sponge process of making bread was more popular years ago, when foodstuffs were less processed and the quality of yeast was less reliable. The yeast works in a batter and the dough rises only once. The sponge process produces a loaf that is lighter but coarser grained.*

## Bread Machine White Bread

1¼ cups skim milk
2 tablespoons nonfat milk
   powder
1 tablespoon olive **or** canola oil
1 teaspoon sea salt
1 tablespoon granulated sugar

4 cups unbleached all-purpose
  **or** bread flour
1 package (2½ teaspoons)
  active dry yeast

Add the ingredients to your bread machine in the order recommended by the manufacturer, being careful that the yeast doesn't come in contact with the salt.

| Yields 1 large loaf<br>Serving size: 1 slice | |
| --- | --- |
| **Nutritional Analysis<br>(per serving):** | |
| Calories: | 89.44 |
| Protein: | 2.82 g |
| Carbohydrate: | 17.34 g |
| Fat: | 0.81 g |
| Sat. Fat: | 0.13 g |
| Cholesterol: | 0.30 mg |
| Sodium: | 106.01 mg |
| Fiber: | 0.62 g |
| PCF Ratio: | 13-79-8 |
| **Exchange Approx.:**<br>1 Bread/Starch | |

## Honey Oat Bran Bread

1¼ cups skim milk
2 tablespoons nonfat buttermilk
   powder
1 tablespoon olive **or** canola oil
1 medium egg
1 cup oat bran
1 teaspoon sea salt
½ cup whole-wheat flour

2½ cups unbleached all-purpose
  **or** bread flour
1 tablespoon honey
1 package (2½ teaspoons)
  active dry yeast

Use the light-crust setting on your bread machine, and add the ingredients to your bread machine in the order recommended by the manufacturer. Be careful that the yeast doesn't come in contact with the salt.

| Yields 1 large loaf<br>Serving size: 1 slice | |
| --- | --- |
| **Nutritional Analysis<br>(per serving):** | |
| Calories: | 85.78 |
| Protein: | 3.22 g |
| Carbohydrate: | 15.59 g |
| Fat: | 1.25 g |
| Sat. Fat: | 0.24 g |
| Cholesterol: | 8.40 mg |
| Sodium: | 109.31 mg |
| Fiber: | 1.20 g |
| PCF Ratio: | 15-72-13 |
| **Exchange Approx.:**<br>1 Bread/Starch | |

# 7-Grain Bread

| Yield: 1 large loaf Serving size: 1 slice | |
|---|---|
| **Nutritional Analysis (per serving):** | |
| Calories: | 82.47 |
| Protein: | 3.02 g |
| Carbohydrate: | 15.30 g |
| Fat: | 1.14 g |
| Sat. Fat: | 0.21 g |
| Cholesterol: | 8.09 mg |
| Sodium: | 108.42 mg |
| Fiber: | 1.22 g |
| PCF Ratio: | 14-73-12 |
| **Exchange Approx.:** 1 Bread/Starch | |

1¼ cups skim milk
2 tablespoons nonfat milk powder
1 tablespoon olive **or** canola oil
¾ cup dry 7-grain cereal
½ cup oat bran
1 teaspoon sea salt

2¼ cups unbleached all-purpose **or** bread flour
½ cup whole-wheat flour
1 tablespoon honey
1 package (2½ teaspoons) dry yeast

Add the ingredients to your bread machine in the order recommended by the manufacturer, being careful that the yeast doesn't come in contact with the salt. Bake on whole-wheat bread setting.

### Lactose-Free Bread
*When cooking for someone who is lactose intolerant, substitute equal amounts of water or soy milk for any milk called for in bread recipes.*

# Cheddar Cornbread

| Yields 1 large loaf Serving size: 1 slice | |
|---|---|
| **Nutritional Analysis (per serving):** | |
| Calories: | 101.84 |
| Protein: | 3.20 g |
| Carbohydrate: | 15.93 g |
| Fat: | 2.72 g |
| Sat. Fat: | 1.60 g |
| Cholesterol: | 7.42 mg |
| Sodium: | 172.32 mg |
| Fiber: | 0.84 g |
| PCF Ratio: | 13-63-24 |
| **Exchange Approx.:** 1 Bread/Starch, ½ Fat | |

1¼ cup water
1 tablespoon honey
3 tablespoons butter
¼ cup nonfat milk powder
1 package (2½ teaspoons) active dry yeast

2½ cups unbleached all-purpose **or** bread flour
1 cup yellow cornmeal
1½ teaspoons sea salt
⅔ cup grated Cheddar cheese

Use the light-crust setting, and add all the ingredients **except** the cheese in the order suggested by your bread machine manual. Process on the basic bread cycle according to the manufacturer's directions. At the beeper (or at the end of the first kneading), add the cheese.

# Cottage Cheese Bread

¼ cup water
1 cup nonfat cottage cheese
2 tablespoons butter
1 egg
1 tablespoon sugar
¼ teaspoon baking soda
1 teaspoon salt

3 cups unbleached all-purpose
  **or** bread flour
1 package (2½ teaspoons)
  active dry yeast

Add the ingredients to your bread machine in the order recommended by the manufacturer, being careful that the yeast doesn't come in contact with the salt. Check the bread machine at the "beep" to make sure the dough is pulling away from the sides of the pan and forming a ball. Add water or flour, if needed. (Note: You do not want the dough to be overly dry.) Bake at the white bread setting, light crust.

## Why Breads Need Salt

*Salt is only used in bread to enhance the flavor. If salt comes directly in contact with the yeast before the yeast has had a chance to begin to work, it can hinder the action of the yeast. Keep that in mind when you add ingredients to your bread machine.*

| Yields 1 large loaf Serving size: 1 slice | |
|---|---|
| **Nutritional Analysis (per serving):** | |
| Calories: | 76.09 |
| Protein: | 3.01 g |
| Carbohydrate: | 12.69 g |
| Fat: | 1.33 g |
| Sat. Fat: | 0.70 g |
| Cholesterol: | 10.78 mg |
| Sodium: | 113.68 mg |
| Fiber: | 0.48 g |
| PCF Ratio: | 16-68-16 |
| **Exchange Approx.:** 1 Bread/Starch | |

# Hawaiian-Style Bread

| Yields 1 large loaf, 24 slices |
|---|
| **Serving size: 1 slice** |

| Nutritional Analysis (per serving): | |
|---|---|
| Calories: | 89.15 |
| Protein: | 2.41 g |
| Carbohydrate: | 16.64 g |
| Fat: | 1.33 g |
| Sat. Fat: | 0.69 g |
| Cholesterol: | 10.50 mg |
| Sodium: | 103.25 mg |
| Fiber: | 0.55 g |
| PCF Ratio: | 11-75-14 |

**Exchange Approx.:**
1 Bread/Starch

1 egg
½ cup pineapple juice
   (**or** ⅛ cup frozen pineapple
   juice concentrate and
   ³/₈ cup water)
¾ cup water
2 tablespoons butter
1 teaspoon vanilla
½ teaspoon dried ginger
1 teaspoon salt

1½ cups unbleached bread flour
2⅛ cups unbleached
   all-purpose flour
¼ cup sugar
2 tablespoons nonfat milk
   powder
1 package (2½ teaspoons)
   active dry yeast

Unless the instructions for your bread machine differ, add the ingredients in the order listed here. Use the light-crust setting.

## Tools of the Trade

*Nonstick pans with a dark surface absorb too much heat, which causes breads to burn. Chicago Metallic makes muffin, mini-muffin, and other bread pans with a lighter-colored, Silverstone nonstick coating that are much better suited for baking.*

# Milk Biscuits

3 cups unbleached all-purpose
   flour
1 teaspoon salt
1½ teaspoons baking soda
1 tablespoon cream of tartar
1 teaspoon baking powder

½ cup butter
1⅓ cups milk

| Yields 24 biscuits Serving size: 1 biscuit | |
|---|---|
| **Nutritional Analysis (per serving):** | |
| Calories: | 98.47 |
| Protein: | 2.19 g |
| Carbohydrate: | 12.96 g |
| Fat: | 4.15 g |
| Sat. Fat: | 2.51 g |
| Cholesterol: | 10.9 mg |
| Sodium: | 204.87 mg |
| Fiber: | 0.01 g |
| PCF Ratio: | 9-53-38 |
| **Exchange Approx.:** 1 Bread/Starch; ½ Fat | |

1. Preheat oven to 400 degrees. For quick mixing, use a food processor. Just add all of the ingredients at once and pulse until just blended. Be careful not to overprocess, as the rolls won't be as light.
2. To mix by hand, sift together the dry ingredients. Cut in the butter using a pastry blender or fork until the mixture resembles coarse crumbs. Add the milk and stir until the mixture pulls away from the sides of the bowl.
3. Use 1 heaping tablespoon for each biscuit, dropping the dough onto greased baking sheets. (You can also try pan liners, such as parchment.) Bake until golden brown, about 20 to 30 minutes. Despite the downside of all the butter, the upside to all the butter is that these biscuits are so rich you won't even notice that they don't contain any sugar. Consult your dietitian, however, if you are on a diet to control your cholesterol.

## Healthy Substitutions
*You can substitute ¼ cup nonfat yogurt for half of the butter in this recipe.*

# Angelic Buttermilk Batter Biscuits

| Yields 24 biscuits<br>Serving size: 1 biscuit | |
|---|---|
| **Nutritional Analysis<br>(per serving):** | |
| Calories: | 74.45 |
| Protein: | 1.97 g |
| Carbohydrate: | 11.81 g |
| Fat: | 2.12 g |
| Sat Fat: | 1.25 g |
| Cholesterol: | 5.78 mg |
| Sodium: | 55.33 mg |
| Fiber: | 0.46 g |
| PCF Ratio: | 11-64-26 |
| **Exchange Approx.:**<br>1 Bread/Starch | |

3 tablespoons nonfat buttermilk powder

2 tablespoons granulated sugar

¾ cup warm water

2½ cups unbleached all-purpose flour

1 tablespoon active dry yeast

½ teaspoon sea salt

½ teaspoon baking powder

¼ cup unsalted butter

¼ cup nonfat plain yogurt

1. Put the buttermilk powder, sugar, and warm water in food processor and process until mixed. Sprinkle the yeast over the buttermilk-sugar mixture and pulse once or twice to mix. Allow the mixture to sit at room temperature for about 5 minutes, or until the yeast begins to bubble. Add all the remaining ingredients to the food processor and pulse until mixed, being careful not to overprocess the dough.
2. Preheat oven to 400 degrees and drop 1 heaping teaspoon per biscuit onto a baking sheet treated with nonstick spray. Set the tray in a warm place and allow the biscuits to rise for about 15 minutes. Bake the biscuits for 12 to 15 minutes.

 **Why Breads Need Sugar**

*Bread recipes need sugar or sweetener, like honey, to "feed" the yeast. This helps the yeast work, which in turn helps the bread rise.*

# Zucchini Bread

3 eggs
1½ cups sugar
1 cup nonfat plain yogurt
1 tablespoon vanilla
2 cups, loosely packed, grated,
    unpeeled zucchini
2 cups unbleached all-purpose
    flour

2 teaspoons baking soda
½ teaspoon baking powder
1 teaspoon sea salt
1½ teaspoons cinnamon
1 cup chopped walnuts

### Yields 2 large loaves
### Serving size: 1 slice

**Nutritional Analysis (per serving):**

| | |
|---|---|
| Calories: | 130.61 |
| Protein: | 3.38 g |
| Carbohydrate: | 23.15 g |
| Fat: | 2.89 g |
| Sat. Fat: | 0.42 g |
| Cholesterol: | 23.73 mg |
| Sodium: | 232.21 mg |
| Fiber: | 0.82 g |
| PCF Ratio: | 10-70-20 |

**Exchange Approx.:**
1 Bread/Starch;
1 Carb./Sugar

1. Preheat oven to 350 degrees. Treat two 9-inch loaf pans with nonstick spray. In a large bowl, beat the eggs until frothy. Beat in the sugar, yogurt, and vanilla until thick and lemon-colored. Stir in the zucchini.
2. Sift together the flour, baking soda, baking powder, salt, and cinnamon. Stir dry ingredients into the zucchini batter. Fold in the nuts.
3. Pour the mixture into the prepared pans. Bake for 40 minutes, or until the center springs back when lightly touched. Allow to cool for 10 minutes before turning out onto a wire rack.

### Are Your Eyes Bigger Than Your Stomach?

*Use miniloaf pans. It's much easier to arrive at the number of servings in the form of a full slice when you use smaller loaf pans. There's a psychological advantage to getting a full, rather than a half slice.*

# Orange Date Bread

**Yields 2 large loaves**
**Serving size: 1 slice**

### Nutritional Analysis (per serving):

| | |
|---|---|
| Calories: | 79.03 |
| Protein: | 1.92 g |
| Carbohydrate: | 16.33 g |
| Fat: | 0.95 g |
| Sat. Fat: | 0.14 g |
| Cholesterol: | 7.98 mg |
| Sodium: | 130.23 mg |
| Fiber: | 1.12 g |
| PCF Ratio: | 9-80-10 |

**Exchange Approx.:**
1 Bread/Starch

2 tablespoons frozen orange
  juice concentrate
2 tablespoons orange zest
¾ cup pitted, chopped dates
½ cup brown sugar
¼ cup granulated sugar
1 cup plain nonfat yogurt
1 egg
1¼ cups all-purpose flour
¾ cup whole-wheat flour

1 teaspoon baking soda
1 teaspoon baking powder
½ teaspoon salt
1 tablespoons vegetable oil
1 teaspoon vanilla extract

1. Preheat oven to 350 degrees. Spray 4 mini-loaf pans with nonfat cooking spray. In a food processor, process the orange juice concentrate, orange zest, dates, sugars, yogurt, and egg until mixed. (This will cut the dates into smaller pieces, too.) Add the remaining ingredients and pulse until mixed, scraping down the side of the bowl if necessary.
2. Divide the mixture between the 4 pans. Spread the mixture so each pan has an even layer. Bake until a toothpick inserted into the center of a loaf comes out clean, about 15 to 20 minutes. Cool the bread in the pans on a wire rack for 10 minutes. Remove the bread to the rack and cool to room temperature.

# CHAPTER 6

# Main Dishes and Casseroles

| | |
|---|---|
| Condensed Cream of Mushroom Soup | 87 |
| Condensed Cream of Chicken Soup, Minor's Base Method | 88 |
| Condensed Cream of Celery Soup | 89 |
| Condensed Cream of Potato Soup | 89 |
| Condensed Tomato Soup | 90 |
| Condensed Cheese Soup | 91 |
| Soup Preparation Method I: Stovetop | 92 |
| Soup Preparation Method II: Microwave | 92 |
| Soup Preparation III: Extra-Rich Creamed Soup | 93 |
| Traditional Stovetop Tuna-Noodle Casserole | 94 |
| Chicken and Mushroom Rice Casserole | 95 |
| Italian Ground Turkey Casserole | 96 |
| Aloha Ham Microwave Casserole | 97 |
| Shrimp Microwave Casserole | 98 |
| Single-Serving Beef (Almost) Stroganoff | 99 |
| Single-Serving Smoked Turkey Casserole | 100 |
| Single-Serving Salmon Scramble | 100 |
| Single-Serving Unstuffed Cabbage and Green Peppers | 101 |

# Condensed Soup Primer

Condensed soups are the most popular ingredient shortcut in most casseroles. Your choice of which condensed soup to use can greatly affect the calorie and fat content of your dish.

For example, the average 10.75-ounce can of commercial cream of mushroom soup has the following nutritional breakdown: Calories: 314.15; Protein: 4.91 g; Carbohydrate: 22.57 g; Fat: 23.09 g; Sat. Fat g: 6.25; Cholesterol: 3.05 mg; Sodium: 2110.60 mg; Fiber: 0.91 g; PCF Ratio: 6-28-65.

Now, Exchange Approximations (for homemade or canned condensed soups) will depend on the serving size and soup preparation method. You may use skim milk, soy milk, or water, or you may use nonfat dry milk and butter, which will have an obvious effect on the Nutritional Analysis. Even so, these homemade recipes are better for you than store brands.

On the surface, 314 calories for canned cream soup doesn't seem too bad when you consider that the one can of soup will probably yield at least four servings. However, when you consider the PCF Ratio (65 percent of calories are from fat!) and the sodium content, a less healthy picture emerges.

For further comparison, commercial cream of celery soup has around 220 calories, cheese soup has 378, chicken mushroom has 332, cream of chicken has 284, and tomato soup has 207.

**QUESTIONS?**

**How can I reduce the sodium in soup?**
Switching to low-sodium condensed soup isn't always the answer. To compensate for the lack of salt and to enhance the flavor, manufacturers often increase the amount of sugar in the soup. Read product labels carefully.

Many of the recipes in this chapter use simplified condensed soup that you can make at home. These condensed soup recipes are not seasoned—instead, seasoning suggestions are made in the casserole recipes. "Salt and pepper to taste" is also assumed in all recipes, noting that salt will be determined by your own dietary restrictions.

# Condensed Cream of Mushroom Soup

½ cup water
⅛ cup Ener-G potato flour
¾ cup finely chopped fresh
    mushrooms

Optional ingredients:
    1 teaspoon chopped onion
    1 tablespoon of chopped
        celery

| Yields equivalent of 1 (10.75-ounce) can | |
| --- | --- |
| **Nutritional Analysis (per recipe):** | |
| Calories: | 92.46 |
| Protein: | 3.07 g |
| Carbohydrate: | 20.63 g |
| Fat: | 0.44 g |
| Sat. Fat: | 0.07 g |
| Cholesterol: | 0.00 mg |
| Sodium: | 12.56 mg |
| Fiber: | 2.90 g |
| PCF Ratio: | 12-84-4 |

**Exchange Approx.:**
will depend on the serving size and soup preparation method.

1. In a microwave-safe, covered container, microwave the chopped mushrooms (and the onion and celery, if using) for 2 minutes, or until tender. (About ¾ cup of chopped mushrooms will yield a half cup of steamed ones.) Reserve any resulting liquid from the steamed mushrooms, and then add enough water to equal 1 cup.
2. Place all the ingredients in a blender and process. The thickness of this soup concentrate will vary according to how much moisture remains in the mushrooms. If necessary, add 1–2 tablespoons of water to achieve a paste. Low-sodium, canned mushrooms work in this recipe, but the Nutritional Analysis assumes that fresh mushrooms are used. Adjust the sodium content accordingly.

## Potato Flour Substitute?

*Instant mashed potatoes can replace potato flour; however, the amount needed will vary according to the brand of potatoes. Also, you'll need to consider other factors such as added fats and hydrogenated oils.*

# Condensed Cream of Chicken Soup, Minor's Base Method

| Yields equivalent of 1 (10.75-ounce) can | |
|---|---|
| **Nutritional Analysis (per recipe):** | |
| Calories: | 157.80 |
| Protein: | 3.66 g |
| Carbohydrate: | 35.13 g |
| Fat: | 0.54 g |
| Sat. Fat: | 0.14 g |
| Cholesterol: | 0.90 mg |
| Sodium: | 162 mg |
| Fiber: | 2.36 g |
| PCF Ratio: | 9-88-3 |

**Exchange Approx.:**
will depend on the serving size and soup preparation method.

1 cup water
3/4 teaspoon Minor's Low-Sodium Chicken Base

1/4 cup Ener-G potato flour

Place all the ingredients in a blender and process until well blended. As you can tell from the Nutritional Analysis of this recipe, this condensed soup made using Minor's Low-Sodium Chicken Broth Base has only a third of the fat of the previous recipe, and the total calories are less, too. The biggest difference is in the amount of sodium; this version has only a fifth (20 percent) of the sodium that is in the recipe using canned broth.

## Condensed Cream of Chicken Soup

*For the equivalent of 1 (10.75-ounce) can of condensed chicken soup, blend 1 cup reduced fat canned chicken broth with 1/4 cup Ener-G potato flour. The recipe will last, refrigerated, for 3 days. The Nutritional Analysis for the entire recipe is: Calories: 181.20; Protein: 7.61 g; Carbohydrate: 34.14 g; Fat: 1.50 g; Sat. Fat: 0.42 g; Cholesterol: 0.00 mg; Sodium: 785.20 mg; Fiber: 2.36 g; PCF Ratio: 17-76-7. Exchange Approximations will depend on the serving size and soup preparation method.*

# Condensed Cream of Celery Soup

*½ cup water*
*⅛ cup Ener-G potato flour*

*½ cup steamed, chopped
celery*

1. In a microwave-safe, covered container, microwave the chopped celery for 2 minutes, or until tender. Do not drain off any of the resulting liquid. If necessary, add enough water to bring the steamed celery and liquid to 1 cup total.
2. Place all the ingredients in a blender and process. Use immediately, or store in a covered container in the refrigerator for use within 3 days. The thickness of this concentrate will depend upon how much moisture remains in the celery; add 1–2 tablespoons of water, if necessary, to achieve a paste.

| Yields equivalent of 1 (10.75-ounce) can | |
| --- | --- |
| **Nutritional Analysis (per recipe):** | |
| Calories: | 84.90 |
| Protein: | 2.00 g |
| Carbohydrate: | 19.62 g |
| Fat: | 0.19 g |
| Sat. Fat: | 0.05 g |
| Cholesterol: | 0.00 mg |
| Sodium: | 79.25 mg |
| Fiber: | 2.38 g |
| PCF Ratio: | 9-89-2 |
| **Exchange Approx.:** will depend on the serving size and soup preparation method. | |

# Condensed Cream of Potato Soup

*½ cup peeled, diced potatoes*
*½ cup water*

*1 tablespoon Ener-G potato
flour*

1. Place the potatoes and water in a covered, microwave-safe bowl and microwave on high for 4 to 5 minutes, until the potatoes are fork-tender.
2. Pour the potatoes and water into a blender, being careful of the steam. Remove the vent from the blender lid and process until smooth. Add the Ener-G potato flour 1 teaspoon at a time while the blender is running.

**TIP:** *The Nutritional Analysis for this recipe assumes you'll use the entire tablespoon of Ener-G potato flour; however, the amount needed will depend on the amount of starch in the potatoes you use. For example, new potatoes will require more Ener-G potato flour than will larger, Idaho-style potatoes.*

| Yields equivalent of 1 (10.75-ounce) can | |
| --- | --- |
| **Nutritional Analysis (per recipe):** | |
| Calories: | 102.78 |
| Protein: | 2.02 g |
| Carbohydrate: | 23.92 g |
| Fat: | 0.11 g |
| Sat. Fat: | 0.03 g |
| Cholesterol: | 0.00 mg |
| Sodium: | 9.40 mg |
| Fiber: | 1.99 g |
| PCF Ratio: | 8-91-1 |
| **Exchange Approx.:** will depend on the serving size and soup preparation method. | |

# Condensed Tomato Soup

*1 cup peeled, chopped tomato,
    with the juice*
*¼ teaspoon baking soda*

*Additional tomato juices
    (if necessary)*
*⅛ cup Ener-G potato flour*

Place the tomato in a microwave-safe bowl and microwave on high for 2 to 3 minutes, until the tomato is cooked. Add additional tomato juices if necessary to bring the mixture back up to 1 cup. Add the baking soda and vigorously stir until the bubbling stops. Pour the cooked tomato mixture into a blender; add the potato flour, 1 tablespoon at a time, processing until well blended.

**TIP:** *The Nutritional Analysis for this recipe assumes you use 2 tablespoons (⅛ cup) of potato flour; however, the amount needed will depend on the ratio of tomato pulp to juice. The juicier the cooked tomatoes, the more potato flour required.*

### Direct Preparation
*If you'll be making the soup immediately after you prepare the condensed soup recipe, you can simply add your choice of the additional 1 cup of liquid (such as skim milk, soy milk, or water) to the blender and use that method to mix the milk and soup concentrate together. Pour the combined mixture into your pan or microwave-safe dish.*

# Condensed Cheese Soup

½ cup water
⅛ cup Ener-G potato flour
¼ cup nonfat cottage cheese

2 ounces American, Cheddar,
 **or** Colby Cheese, shredded
 (to yield ½ cup)

This replacement for canned, condensed cheese soup is perfect in casserole recipes. Place the water, potato flour, and cottage cheese in a blender and process until well blended. Stir in the shredded cheese. The cheese will melt as the casserole is baked, prepared in the microwave, or cooked on the stovetop, according to recipe instructions.

## Be Aware of Your Exchanges

*When using any of the suggested soup preparation methods, you'll need to add the appropriate Exchange Approximations for each serving amount (usually ¼ of the total) of whatever condensed soup you make. For example, broth-based soups like chicken and cream of mushroom or celery would be a Free Exchange. The cream of potato soup would add 1 Carbohydrate/Starch.*

| Yields equivalent of 1 (10.75-ounce) can | |
|---|---|
| **Nutritional Analysis (per recipe):** | |
| Calories: | 314.95 |
| Protein: | 20.20 g |
| Carbohydrate: | 18.19 g |
| Fat: | 17.94 g |
| Sat. Fat: | 11.28 g |
| Cholesterol: | 55.95 mg |
| Sodium: | 384.19 mg |
| Fiber: | 1.18 g |
| PCF Ratio: | 26-23-51 |

**Exchange Approx.:**
will depend on the serving size and soup preparation method.

| Serves 4 |
| --- |

| Nutritional Analysis (per serving, skim milk): | |
| --- | --- |
| Additional Calories: | 21.44 |
| Protein: | 2.09 g |
| Carbohydrate: | 2.97 g |
| Fat: | 0.11 g |
| Sat. Fat: | 0.07 g |
| Cholesterol: | 1.23 mg |
| Sodium: | 31.85 mg |
| Fiber: | 0.00 g |
| PCF Ratio: | 39-56-5 |

**Exchange Approx.:**
1 Low-Fat Milk for entire pot of soup; divide accordingly per serving

# Soup Preparation Method I: Stovetop

To use any of the homemade condensed soup recipes as soup, add 1 cup of skim milk (or soy milk or water) to a pan. Stir using a spoon or whisk to blend. Cook over medium heat until mixture begins to simmer. Season according to taste.

| Serves 4 |
| --- |

| Nutritional Analysis (per serving, skim milk): | |
| --- | --- |
| Additional Calories: | 21.44 |
| Protein: | 2.09 g |
| Carbohydrate: | 2.97 g |
| Fat: | 0.11 g |
| Sat. Fat: | 0.07 g |
| Cholesterol: | 1.23 mg |
| Sodium: | 31.85 mg |
| Fiber: | 0.00 g |
| PCF Ratio: | 39-56-5 |

**Exchange Approx.:**
1 Low-Fat Milk for entire pot of soup; divide accordingly per serving

# Soup Preparation Method II: Microwave

Add your choice of condensed soup and 1 cup of skim milk (or soy milk or water) to a 2-quart microwave-safe dish with a cover. Stir using a spoon or whisk to blend. Microwave, covered, on high for 1 to 3 minutes, until soup is hot. Do not boil.

# Soup Preparation III: Extra-Rich Creamed Soup

*1 cup skim milk*  
*¼ cup nonfat milk powder*

*4 teaspoons unsalted butter*

| Serves 4 |
|---|
| **Nutritional Analysis (per serving):** |
| Additional Calories: 70.57 |
| Protein: 3.62 g |
| Carbohydrate: 5.19 g |
| Fat: 3.98 g |
| Sat. Fat: 2.48 g |
| Cholesterol: 12.35 mg |
| Sodium: 55.69 mg |
| Fiber: 0.00 g |
| PCF Ratio: 20-29-50 |
| **Exchange Approx.:** 1 Milk, 1 Fat for entire pot of soup; divide accordingly per serving |

In a saucepan, whisk together the skim milk, milk powder, and your choice of 1 recipe of condensed soup; warm on medium-low heat. Add the butter 1 teaspoon at a time, allowing each teaspoon to melt and stirring to fully incorporate it into the mixture before adding more. Heat to serving temperature, stirring constantly; do not allow the mixture to boil. The butter in this extra-rich version will affect its fat content, so check with your dietitian to determine whether it's okay to make your soup this way.

## ℭ Condensed Soup Casserole Guidelines

*The casseroles in this section use the condensed soup recipes in this chapter. If you substitute canned, condensed soup, be sure to adjust the Exchange Approximations when necessary.*

# Traditional Stovetop
# Tuna-Noodle Casserole

| Serves 4 | |
|---|---|
| **Nutritional Analysis (per serving):** | |
| Calories: | 244.69 |
| Protein: | 19.78 g |
| Carbohydrate: | 32.74 g |
| Fat: | 4.25 g |
| Sat. Fat: | 1.85 g |
| Cholesterol: | 46.08 mg |
| Sodium: | 240.76 mg |
| Fiber: | 3.71 g |
| PCF Ratio: | 32-53-15 |
| **Exchange Approx.:** 1½ Breads, 1 Vegetable, 1 Medium Fat Meat | |

*2 cups cooked egg noodles*
*1 recipe Condensed Cream*
   *of Mushroom Soup*
   *(see page 87)*
*1 teaspoon steamed, chopped*
   *onion*
*1 tablespoon steamed, chopped*
   *celery*
*½ cup skim milk*

*1 ounce American, Cheddar,*
   ***or** Colby cheese, shredded*
   *(to yield ¼ cup)*
*1 cup frozen mixed peas and*
   *carrots*
*1 cup steamed, sliced fresh*
   *mushrooms*
*1 can water-packed tuna,*
   *drained*

Cook the egg noodles according to package directions. Drain and return to pan. Add all the ingredients to the pan; stir to blend. Cook over medium heat, stirring occasionally, until the cheese is melted. (1⅓ cups of dried egg noodles will yield 2 cups of cooked egg noodles. The Nutritional Analysis for this recipe assumes that the egg noodles were cooked without salt.)

### Extra-Rich Stovetop Tuna-Noodle Casserole
*Add 1 medium egg (beaten) and 1 tablespoon mayonnaise to give this casserole the taste of rich, homemade egg noodles, while—at 21 percent of total calories—still maintaining a good fat ratio. It's still less than 300 calories per serving, too! The per-serving Nutritional Analysis is: Calories: 275.40; Protein: 21.18 g; Carbohydrate: 33.75 g; Fat: 6.58 g; Sat. Fat: 2.37 g; Cholesterol: 93.78 mg; Sodium: 280.75 mg; Fiber: 3.71 g; PCF Ratio: 30-48-21. Exchange Approximations: 1½ Bread, 1 Vegetable, 1 Meat, 1 Medium Meat Fat.*

# Chicken and Mushroom Rice Casserole

*1 recipe Condensed Cream
  of Chicken Soup
  (see page 88)*
*1 cup diced chicken breast*
*1 large onion, chopped*
*½ cup chopped celery*
*1 cup uncooked rice
  (not instant rice)*
*Freshly ground black pepper
  to taste (optional)*

*1 teaspoon dried Herbes de
  Provence blend
  (see page 48), optional*
*2 cups boiling water*
*2½ cups chopped broccoli
  flowerets*
*1 cup sliced fresh mushrooms*

| Serves 8 | |
| --- | --- |
| **Nutritional Analysis (per serving):** | |
| Calories: | 164.73 |
| Protein: | 9.47 g |
| Carbohydrate: | 29.53 g |
| Fat: | 1.11 g |
| Sat. Fat: | 0.27 g |
| Cholesterol: | 14.99 mg |
| Sodium: | 41.29 mg |
| Fiber: | 3.08 g |
| PCF Ratio: | 23-71-6 |

**Exchange Approx.:**
1 Very Lean Meat,
1 Bread/Starch,
1 Vegetable

1. Preheat oven to 350 degrees. In a 4-quart casserole dish (large enough to prevent boil-overs in the oven) that's been treated with nonstick spray, combine the condensed soup, chicken breast, celery, rice, and seasonings; mix well. Pour the boiling water over the top of the mixture, and bake, covered, for 30 minutes.

2. Stir the casserole, adding the broccoli and mushrooms, replace the cover, and return to the oven to bake for an additional 20 to 30 minutes, or until the celery is tender and the rice has absorbed all the liquid.

# Italian Ground Turkey Casserole

| Serves 8 | |
|---|---|
| **Nutritional Analysis (per serving):** | |
| Calories: | 297.73 |
| Protein: | 28.98 g |
| Carbohydrate: | 23.36 g |
| Fat: | 12.17 g |
| Sat. Fat: | 5.62 g |
| Cholesterol: | 66.57 mg |
| Sodium: | 461.57 mg |
| Fiber: | 4.51 g |
| PCF Ratio: | 36-29-34 |

**Exchange Approx.:**
3 Medium Fat Meats,
2 Vegetables,
¼ Bread

*1 pound ground turkey **or**
    turkey sausage*
*1 large onion, chopped*
*2 cups sliced fresh mushrooms*
*1 teaspoon minced garlic*
*1 teaspoon dried basil*
*¼ teaspoon dried oregano*
*½ teaspoon dried parsley*
*6 cups shredded cabbage*
*2 cups nonfat cottage cheese*
*⅛ cup Ener-G potato flour*

*4 ounces Parmesan cheese,
    grated (to yield 1 cup)*
*4 ounces part-skim mozzarella
    cheese, grated (to yield 1 cup)*
*1 recipe Condensed Tomato
    Soup (see page 90)*
*1 (6-ounce) can salt-free tomato
    paste*
*1 (16-ounce) can salt-free diced
    tomatoes*

1. Place the ground turkey in a large, covered skillet over medium-low heat and allow it to steam, being careful not to brown the meat. Drain off the grease and use paper towels to blot the meat to absorb any excess fat from the turkey. Add the onion, mushrooms, minced garlic, and herbs, and toss lightly. Return the cover to the skillet and steam the vegetables until they are tender, about 3 minutes. Set aside.

2. Put the shredded cabbage in a large, covered microwave-safe dish and steam until the cabbage is crisp-tender, about 5 minutes. (If your microwave doesn't have a carousel, turn the dish about halfway through the cooking time.) Drain the cabbage in a colander, being careful not to burn yourself from the steam. Press out any excess moisture.

3. Mix the cottage cheese, potato flour, and half of the Parmesan and mozzarella cheeses together. (Note: The potato flour acts as a bonding agent to keep the whey from separating from the cottage cheese. The tradition method of doing this is to add egg, but potato flour accomplishes the same thing without adding fat.) Add the condensed tomato soup, tomato paste, and canned tomatoes to the meat mixture and stir well.

4. Preheat oven to 350 degrees. Coat a deep rectangular baking dish or roasting pan with nonstick spray. Spoon a third of the meat mixture

*(continued)*

into the bottom of the pan. Top with half of the cooked cabbage. Add another third of the meat mixture. Top that with the cottage cheese mixture, and the rest of the cabbage. Add the remaining meat mixture and sprinkle the top of the casserole with the remaining Parmesan and mozzarella cheeses.

5. Bake for 45 minutes, or until the casserole is heated through and the cheeses on top are melted and bubbling.

### Base Basics

*An easy way to add rich flavor to the condensed soup or casserole recipes without adding extra calories is to use ⅛ to ¼ teaspoon of other Minor's bases, like Roasted Mirepoix, Onion, or Garlic.*

## Aloha Ham Microwave Casserole

1⅓ cups cooked rice
1 medium onion, chopped
1 recipe Condensed Cream of
  Celery Soup (see page 89)
1 (8-ounce) can pineapple
  chunks

¼ cup water
1 teaspoon brown sugar
½ pound (8 ounces) sliced
  lean baked **or** boiled ham
Sliced green onions, for garnish
  (optional)

| Serves 4 | |
| --- | --- |
| **Nutritional Analysis (per serving):** | |
| Calories: | 207.53 |
| Protein: | 13.56 g |
| Carbohydrate: | 32.14 g |
| Fat: | 2.69 g |
| Sat. Fat: | 0.91 g |
| Cholesterol: | 25.53 mg |
| Sodium: | 741.59 mg |
| Fiber: | 1.59 g |
| PCF Ratio: | 26-62-12 |

**Exchange Approx.:**
1 Lean Meat,
1 Bread/Starch,
1 Fruit

1. Cook the rice according to package directions. Put the rice in a casserole dish and set aside. Place the chopped onion in a microwave-safe, covered bowl and microwave on high until tender, about 1 minute. Add the soup, pineapple with juice, water, and brown sugar to the onion. Heat, covered, on high until the mixture begins to boil, about 1 minute. Stir mixture until the brown sugar is dissolved.

2. Pour half of the soup mixture over the rice. Arrange the ham slices on top of the rice and pour the remaining soup mixture over it. Cover loosely with plastic wrap or a paper towel (to prevent splatters in the microwave) and heat on high until the rice is reheated and ham is warm, about 1 minute. (If you are on a sodium-restricted diet, consider substituting chicken or turkey breast for the ham.)

# Shrimp Microwave Casserole

**Serves 4**

**Nutritional Analysis
(per serving):**

| | |
|---|---|
| Calories: | 195.53 |
| Protein: | 17.35 g |
| Carbohydrate: | 27.23 g |
| Fat: | 1.92 g |
| Sat. Fat: | 0.48 g |
| Cholesterol: | 130.93 mg |
| Sodium: | 290.35 mg |
| Fiber: | 1.89 g |
| PCF Ratio: | 35-56-9 |

**Exchange Approx.:**
1 Starch,
1 Vegetable,
1 Medium Fat Meat

1⅓ uncooked egg noodles (to yield 4½ (½-cup) servings)
1 cup chopped green onion
1 cup chopped green pepper
1 cup sliced mushrooms
1 recipe Condensed Cream of Celery Soup (see page 89)
1 teaspoon Worcestershire sauce (see recipe for Homemade Worcestershire on page 40)
4 drops Tabasco (optional)
¼ cup diced canned pimientos
½ cup pitted, chopped ripe olives
½ cup skimmed milk
½ pound (8 ounces) cooked, deveined, shelled shrimp

1. Cook the egg noodles according to package directions and keep warm. Place the green onion and green pepper in a covered, microwave-safe dish and microwave on high for 1 minute. Add the mushroom slices and microwave for another minute, or until all the vegetables are tender.
2. Add the soup, Worcestershire sauce, Tabasco (if using), pimiento, ripe olives, and milk, and stir well. Microwave covered for 1 to 2 minutes until the mixture is hot and bubbly.
3. Add the cooked shrimp and noodles and stir to mix; microwave for another 30 seconds to 1 minute, or until the mixture is hot.

# Single-Serving Beef (Almost) Stroganoff

1 tablespoon steamed or low-fat sautéed diced celery

1 teaspoon diced onion, steamed or low-fat sautéed

½ cup sliced mushrooms, steamed or low-fat sautéed

1 cup shredded, unseasoned cabbage, steamed

½ cup cooked egg noodles

¼ cup nonfat cottage cheese

1 teaspoon finely grated Parmesan cheese

½ teaspoon Ener-G potato flour

1 clove roasted garlic (for roasting instructions, see "Dry-Roasted Garlic" on page 54)

1 tablespoon nonfat yogurt **or** nonfat sour cream

1 ounce lean roast beef, pulled or cubed

⅛ teaspoon nutmeg

| Serves 1 | |
| --- | --- |
| **Nutritional Analysis (per serving):** | |
| Calories: | 286.03 |
| Protein: | 24.09 g |
| Carbohydrate: | 36.67 g |
| Fat: | 5.49 g |
| Sat. Fat: | 1.72 g |
| Cholesterol: | 52.75 mg |
| Sodium: | 104.94 mg |
| Fiber: | 6.42 g |
| PCF Ratio: | 33-50-17 |

**Exchange Approx.:**
1 Very Lean Meat,
1 Lean Meat, 1 Free,
1 Vegetable, 1 Starch

1. Toss the celery, onion, mushrooms, cabbage, and noodles together in a microwave-safe, covered serving dish.
2. Put the cheeses, roasted garlic, potato flour, and yogurt (**or** sour cream) in a blender and process until smooth. Lightly mix the cheese sauce with the vegetables, then top the vegetables with the roast beef and sprinkle the nutmeg over the top of the dish. Microwave, covered, on high for 1 to 2 minutes, or until heated through.

## Single-Serving Smoked Turkey Casserole

| Serves 1 | |
|---|---|
| **Nutritional Analysis (per serving):** | |
| Calories: | 220.64 |
| Protein: | 17.66 g |
| Carbohydrate: | 27.33 g |
| Fat: | 4.80 g |
| Sat. Fat: | 1.60 g |
| Cholesterol: | 46.30 mg |
| Sodium: | 363.12 mg |
| Fiber: | 2.91 g |
| PCF Ratio: | 32-49-19 |

**Exchange Approx.:**
2 Lean Meats,
1 Starch,
1 Vegetable

1 tablespoon steamed or low-fat sautéed diced celery
1 teaspoon diced onion, steamed or low-fat sautéed
1 tablespoon diced green pepper, steamed or low-fat sautéed
½ cup sliced mushrooms, steamed or low-fat sautéed

1 ounce smoked turkey, diced or thinly sliced
¼ cup nonfat cottage cheese
1 teaspoon finely grated Parmesan cheese
½ teaspoon Ener-G potato flour
½ cup cooked egg noodles

In a covered, microwave-safe bowl, combine all the ingredients and microwave on high for 1 to 2 minutes, or until heated through.

## Single-Serving Salmon Scramble

| Serves 1 | |
|---|---|
| **Nutritional Analysis (per serving):** | |
| Calories: | 222.19 |
| Protein: | 21.90 g |
| Carbohydrate: | 12.26 g |
| Fat: | 10.26 g |
| Sat Fat: | 2.55 g |
| Cholesterol: | 0.00 mg |
| Sodium: | 420.97 mg |
| Fiber: | 4.98 g |
| PCF Ratio: | 38-21-40 |

**Exchange Approx.:**
2 Lean Meats,
1 Medium-Fat Meat,
½ Bread, 1 Vegetable

1 cup chopped broccoli (fresh or frozen)
1 medium egg
½ teaspoon Hellmann's or Best Foods tartar sauce

1½ teaspoons yellow cornmeal
2 Keebler low-salt soda crackers, crumbled
2 ounces canned salmon, drained

1. In a microwave-safe covered bowl, steam the broccoli for 5 minutes, or until tender. Drain any moisture from the broccoli; add it to a non-stick skillet treated with nonstick spray, and dry-sauté it to remove any excess moisture.
2. In another bowl, beat the egg and mix in the tartar sauce, cornmeal, cracker crumbs, and salmon. Pour the salmon mixture over the broccoli and toss to mix. Cook over medium-low heat until the egg is done, stirring the mixture occasionally with a spatula.

# Single-Serving Unstuffed Cabbage and Green Peppers

3 ounces uncooked Laura's
   Lean Beef ground round
⅛ teaspoon dried oregano
¼ teaspoon minced, dried
   garlic (**or** ½ clove minced
   fresh garlic)
¼ teaspoon dried parsley
Dash of dried ginger
Dash of dried mustard
2 tablespoons chopped celery

2 tablespoons chopped onion
1 cup chopped green pepper
½ cup steamed cabbage,
   shredded or rough chopped
1 medium peeled, chopped
   tomato
¼ teaspoon dried basil

| Serves 1 | |
| --- | --- |
| **Nutritional Analysis (per serving):** | |
| Calories: | 206.65 |
| Protein: | 16.44 g |
| Carbohydrate: | 14.43 g |
| Fat: | 10.03 g |
| Sat. Fat: | 3.71 g |
| Cholesterol: | 46.47 mg |
| Sodium: | 54.86 mg |
| Fiber: | 4.11 g |
| PCF Ratio: | 31-27-42 |

**Exchange Approx.:**
2 Lean Meats,
2 Vegetables,
1 Free

1. In a microwave-safe, covered dish, microwave the ground round, oregano, garlic, parsley, ginger, mustard, celery, onion, and green pepper for 2 minutes. Stir the mixture, being careful not to burn yourself on the steam. Microwave on high for another 2 to 3 minutes, or until the meat is no longer pink. Drain any fat residue or dab the beef mixture with a paper towel.

2. Heat the steamed cabbage in the microwave on high for 30 seconds to 1 minute to warm it to serving temperature. Toss the chopped, raw tomato with the ground round mixture and spoon it over the warmed cabbage. Sprinkle the dried basil over the top of the dish and serve. (If you serve this dish over ½ cup cooked rice instead of cabbage, add 1 Starch Exchange.)

# CHAPTER 7

# Poultry

| | |
|---|---|
| Chicken Broth: Easy Slow-Cooker Method | 104 |
| Oven-Fried Chicken Thighs | 105 |
| Another Healthy "Fried" Chicken | 106 |
| Buttermilk Ranch Chicken Salad | 107 |
| Molded Chicken Salad | 108 |
| Herbed Chicken and Brown Rice Dinner | 109 |
| Walnut Chicken with Plum Sauce | 109 |
| Easy Chicken Paprikash | 110 |
| Chicken and Broccoli Casserole | 111 |
| Chicken à la King | 111 |
| Chicken and Green Bean Stovetop Casserole | 112 |
| Chicken Pasta with Herb Sauce | 113 |
| Chicken Thighs Cacciatore | 114 |
| Thanksgiving Feast: Turkey Casserole in a Pumpkin | 115 |
| Stovetop Grilled Turkey Breast | 116 |
| Turkey Mushroom Burgers | 117 |
| Cranberry-Turkey Sausage | 118 |
| Pineapple–Black Bean Sauce | 119 |
| Christmas Colors with Yogurt Sauce | 120 |
| Honey and Cider Glaze for Baked Chicken | 121 |

# Chicken Broth: Easy Slow-Cooker Method

| Yield about 4 cups |
|---|
| Serving size: ½ cup |

| Nutritional Analysis (per serving): | |
|---|---|
| Calories: | 67.19 |
| Protein: | 8.62 g |
| Carbohydrate: | 0.00 g |
| Fat: | 3.37 g |
| Sat. Fat: | 0.88 g |
| Cholesterol: | 23.53 mg |
| Sodium: | 22.11 mg |
| Fiber: | 0.00 g |
| PCF Ratio: | 53-0-47 |

**Exchange Approx.:**
½ Very Lean Meat,
½ Lean Meat

1 small onion, chopped
2 carrots, peeled and chopped
2 celery stalks and leaves, chopped
1 bay leaf
4 sprigs parsley

6 black peppercorns
¼ cup dry white wine
2 pounds chicken pieces,
    skin removed
4½ cups water

1. Add all ingredients **except** the water to the slow cooker. The chicken pieces and vegetables should be loosely layered and fill no more than ³/₄ of the slow cooker. Add enough water to just cover the ingredients, and cover the slow cooker. Use the high setting until the mixture almost reaches a boil, then reduce heat to low. Allow to simmer overnight or up to 16 hours, checking occasionally and adding more water, if necessary.
2. Remove the chicken pieces and drain on paper towels to absorb any fat. Allow to cool, then remove the meat from the bones. Strain the vegetables from the broth and discard. (You don't want to eat vegetables cooked directly with the chicken because they will have absorbed too much of the residue fat.) Put the broth in a covered container and refrigerate for several hours or overnight, allowing the fat to congeal on top of the broth. Remove the hardened fat and discard.
3. To separate the broth into small amounts for use when you steam vegetables or potatoes, fill up an ice cube tray with stock. Let freeze, then remove the cubes from the tray and store in a labeled freezer bag. (Note the size of the ice cubes. Common ice cube trays allow for ⅛ cup or 2 tablespoons of liquid per section.)

**TIP:** *The broth will be richer than what most recipes call for, so unless you need "reduced" broth, thin the broth with water as needed. Assuming you remove the fat from the broth, the Exchange Approximation for it will be a Free Exchange.*

### Know Your Terms
*Reducing broth is the act of boiling it to decrease the amount of water, so you're left with a richer broth. Boiling nonfat, canned chicken broth won't reduce as a homemade broth would.*

# Oven-Fried Chicken Thighs

| | Serves 4 |

4 chicken thighs, skin removed
1 tablespoon unbleached, white
   all-purpose flour
1 large egg white
½ teaspoon sea salt
1 tablespoon rice flour

½ teaspoon olive oil (optional;
   see the "with olive oil"
   Comparison Analysis)
1 tablespoon cornmeal

1. Preheat oven to 350 degrees. Rinse and dry the chicken thighs. Put the white flour on a plate. In a small, shallow bowl, whip the egg white together with the sea salt; add the olive oil, if using, and mix well. Put the rice flour and cornmeal on another plate and mix them together. Place a rack on a baking sheet and spray both with nonstick cooking spray.

2. Roll each chicken thigh in the white flour, dip it into the egg mixture, and then roll it in the rice flour mixture. Place the chicken thighs on the rack so that they aren't touching. Bake for 35 to 45 minutes, until the meat juices run clear.

**TIP:** *Boneless, skinless chicken breast strips will work, although the meat tends to be drier. Allow 1 Very Lean Meat Exchange List choice for each 1-ounce serving.*

**Nutritional Analysis**
**(per serving, no oil):**

| | |
|---|---|
| Calories: | 73.53 |
| Protein: | 9.46 g |
| Carbohydrate: | 4.65 g |
| Fat: | 1.69 g |
| Sat. Fat: | 0.42 g |
| Cholesterol: | 34.03 mg |
| Sodium: | 331.03 mg |
| Fiber: | 0.06 g |
| PCF Ratio: | 53-26-21 |

**Exchange Approx.:**
2 Very Lean Meats

ɷ

**Comparison Analysis**
**(with olive oil)**

| | |
|---|---|
| Calories: | 78.53 |
| Protein: | 9.46 g |
| Carbohydrate: | 4.65 g |
| Fat: | 2.27 g |
| Sat. Fat: | 0.50 g |
| Cholesterol: | 34.03 mg |
| Sodium: | 331.03 mg |
| Fiber: | 0.06 g |
| PCF Ratio: | 49-24-27 |

**Exchange Approx.:**
2 Lean Meats

# Another Healthy "Fried" Chicken

| Serves 4 |
| :---: |

| Nutritional Analysis (per serving): | |
| :--- | ---: |
| Calories: | 117.85 |
| Protein: | 18.56 g |
| Carbohydrate: | 5.23 g |
| Fat: | 1.99 g |
| Sat. Fat: | 0.55 g |
| Cholesterol: | 44.22 mg |
| Sodium: | 90.63 mg |
| Fiber: | 0.14 g |
| PCF Ratio: | 66-18-16 |

**Exchange Approx.:**
2 Very Lean Meats,
½ Starch

*10 ounces raw boneless, skinless chicken breasts (fat trimmed off)*
*½ cup nonfat plain yogurt*
*½ cup bread crumbs*
*1 teaspoon garlic powder*
*1 teaspoon paprika*
*¼ teaspoon dried thyme*

1. Preheat oven to 350 degrees and prepare a baking pan with nonstick cooking spray. Cut the chicken breast into 4 equal pieces and marinate it in the yogurt for several minutes.
2. Mix together the bread crumbs, garlic, paprika, and thyme; dredge the chicken in the crumb mixture, and arrange on prepared pan. Bake for 20 minutes. To give the chicken a deep golden color, place the pan under the broiler for the last 5 minutes of cooking. Watch closely to ensure the chicken "crust" doesn't burn.

### Chicken Fat Facts

*When faced with the decision of whether to have chicken with or without the skin, consider that ½ pound of skinless chicken breast has 9 grams of fat; a ½ pound with the skin on has 38 grams!*

# Buttermilk Ranch Chicken Salad

1 tablespoon Hellmann's or
    Best Foods Real Mayonnaise

3 tablespoons nonfat plain
    yogurt

½ cup nonfat cottage cheese

½ teaspoon cider vinegar

1 teaspoon brown sugar

1 teaspoon Dijon mustard

½ cup buttermilk

2 tablespoons dried parsley

1 clove garlic, minced

2 tablespoons grated Parmesan
    cheese

¼ teaspoon sea salt (optional)

¼ teaspoon freshly ground
    pepper (optional)

1 cup chopped, cooked chicken
    breast

½ cup sliced cucumber

½ cup chopped celery

½ cup sliced carrots

4 cups salad greens

½ cup red onion slices

Fresh parsley for garnish
    (optional)

| Serves 4 | |
|---|---|
| **Nutritional Analysis (per serving):** | |
| Calories: | 146.64 |
| Protein: | 17.97 g |
| Carbohydrate: | 10.63 g |
| Fat: | 3.68 g |
| Sat. Fat: | 1.24 g |
| Cholesterol: | 32.54 mg |
| Sodium: | 183.64 mg |
| Fiber: | 1.77 g |
| PCF Ratio: | 49-29-22 |

**Exchange Approx.:**
2 Very Lean Meats,
½ Vegetable,
1 Free Vegetable, ½ Skim Milk

1. In a blender or food processor, combine the mayonnaise, yogurt, cottage cheese, vinegar, brown sugar, mustard, buttermilk, parsley, garlic, and cheese; if you're using them, add the salt and pepper at this time, too. Process until smooth. Pour this dressing over the chicken, cucumber, celery, and carrots. Chill for at least 2 hours.
2. To serve, arrange 1 cup of the salad greens on each of 4 serving plates. Top each salad with an equal amount of the chicken salad. Garnish with the red onion slices and fresh parsley, if desired.

## Get More Mileage from Your Meals

*Leftover Chicken Salad makes great sandwiches. Put it and lots of lettuce between two slices of bread for a quick lunch. The lettuce helps keep the bread from getting soggy if you're preparing the sandwich "to go."*

# Molded Chicken Salad

| Serves 12 | |
|---|---|
| **Nutritional Analysis (per serving):** | |
| Calories: | 203.74 |
| Protein: | 20.98 g |
| Carbohydrate: | 5.20 g |
| Fat: | 10.60 g |
| Sat. Fat: | 3.94 g |
| Cholesterol: | 58.40 mg |
| Sodium: | 172.94 mg |
| Fiber: | 0.36 g |
| PCF Ratio: | 42-10-48 |

**Exchange Approx.:**
1 Very Lean Meat,
1 Lean Meat, 1½ Fats,
½ Skim Milk

½ cup nonfat plain yogurt
2 envelopes unflavored gelatin
¼ cup boiling water
1 teaspoon cider vinegar
1 teaspoon Dijon mustard
1 teaspoon brown sugar
1 tablespoon Hellmann's or
   Best Foods Real Mayonnaise
½ cup nonfat cottage cheese
4 ounces cream cheese
1 teaspoon celery seed

½ cup chopped dill pickle
¼ cup chopped green onion
   (scallions)
1 recipe Condensed Cream of
   Chicken Soup (see page 98)
1½ pounds (24 ounces)
   cooked, chopped chicken

1. Put the yogurt in a blender or food processor and sprinkle the gelatin on top; let stand for 2 minutes to soften the gelatin.
2. Add the boiling water and process until the gelatin is dissolved. Add the remaining ingredients except for the chicken and process until smooth. Fold in the chopped chicken, and taste for seasonings. Herbs like chopped chives, a little more cider vinegar, or ground black pepper won't affect Exchange Approximations.
3. Pour into a mold or terrine treated with nonstick spray and chill until firm.

# Herbed Chicken and Brown Rice Dinner

1 tablespoon canola oil
4 (4-ounce) boneless chicken
    breast pieces, skin removed
¾ teaspoon garlic powder
¾ teaspoon dried rosemary
⅓ cup water
1 (10.5-ounce) can low-fat,
    reduced-sodium chicken broth
2 cups uncooked instant brown
    rice

1. Heat the oil in large nonstick skillet on medium-high. Add the chicken and sprinkle with half of the garlic powder and crushed rosemary. Cover, and cook for 4 minutes on each side, or until cooked through. Remove the chicken from the skillet and set aside.
2. Add the broth and water to the skillet, stir to deglaze the pan, and bring to a boil. Stir in the rice and the remaining garlic powder and rosemary. Top with the chicken and cover. Cook on low heat for 5 minutes. Remove from the heat and let stand, covered, for 5 minutes.

**Serves 4**

**Nutritional Analysis (per serving):**

| | |
|---|---|
| Calories: | 300.49 |
| Protein: | 32.85 g |
| Carbohydrate: | 26.03 g |
| Fat: | 6.19 g |
| Sat Fat: | 0.27 g |
| Cholesterol: | 75 mg |
| Sodium: | 111.81 mg |
| Fiber: | 0.15 g |
| PCF Ratio: | 45-36-19 |

**Exchange Approx.:**
1½ Starches,
2 Very Lean Meats,
2 Lean Meats

# Walnut Chicken with Plum Sauce

¾ pound (12 ounces) raw bone-
    less, skinless chicken breast
1 teaspoon sherry
1 egg white
2 teaspoons peanut oil
2 drops toasted sesame oil
    (optional)
⅓ cup ground walnuts

1. Preheat oven to 350 degrees. Cut the chicken into bite-sized pieces, sprinkle with the sherry, and set aside.
2. In a small bowl, beat the egg white and oils until frothy. Fold the chicken pieces into the egg mixture, then roll them, individually, in chopped walnuts. Arrange the chicken pieces on a baking sheet treated with nonstick cooking spray. Bake for 10 to 15 minutes, or until the walnuts are lightly browned and the chicken juices run clear. (The walnuts make the fat ratio of this dish high, so serve it with steamed vegetables and rice to bring the ratios into balance.)

**Serves 4**

**Nutritional Analysis (per serving):**

| | |
|---|---|
| Calories: | 158.65 |
| Protein: | 18.27 g |
| Carbohydrate: | 1.01 g |
| Fat: | 8.86 g |
| Sat. Fat: | 1.42 g |
| Cholesterol: | 43.66 mg |
| Sodium: | 50.75 mg |
| Fiber: | 0.45 g |
| PCF Ratio: | 47-3-51 |

**Exchange Approx.:**
2 Very Lean Meats,
1½ Fats

# Easy Chicken Paprikash

| Serves 4 |
| :---: |

**Nutritional Analysis
(per serving, using equal
amounts of light and
dark meat chicken):**

| | |
| :--- | ---: |
| Calories: | 376.34 |
| Protein: | 21.58 g |
| Carbohydrate: | 58.44 g |
| Fat: | 6.42 g |
| Sat. Fat: | 1.54 g |
| Cholesterol: | 77.68 mg |
| Sodium: | 135.15 mg |
| Fiber: | 4.22 g |
| PCF Ratio: | 23-62-15 |

**Exchange Approx.:**
½ Very Lean Meat,
½ Lean Meat, 2½ Starches,
1 Vegetable, 1 Skim Milk

1 recipe Condensed Cream of
  Chicken Soup (see page 88)
½ cup skim milk
2 teaspoon paprika
⅛ teaspoon ground red pepper
  (optional)
¼ pound (4 ounces) chopped
  cooked, boneless skinless
  chicken

1½ cups sliced steamed
  mushrooms
½ cup diced steamed onion
½ cup nonfat plain yogurt
4 cups cooked medium-sized
  egg noodles

1. In a saucepan, combine the soup, skim milk, paprika, and pepper
   (if using); whisk until well mixed. Bring to a boil over medium heat,
   stirring occasionally. Reduce the heat to low and stir in the chicken,
   mushrooms, and onion; cook until the chicken and vegetables are
   heated through. Stir in the yogurt.
2. To serve, put 1 cup of warm, cooked noodles on each of 4 plates.
   Top each portion of noodles with an equal amount of the chicken
   mixture. Garnish by sprinkling with additional paprika, if desired.

### For Best Results . . .

*Mock condensed soup recipes are used in the dishes in this
book so that you know the accurate Nutritional Analysis information. In all cases, you can substitute commercial canned, condensed
soups; however, be sure to use the lower fat and sodium content
varieties.*

# Chicken and Broccoli Casserole

2 cups broccoli
½ pound (8 ounces) cooked, chopped chicken
½ cup skim milk
⅛ cup (2 tablespoons) Hellmann's or Best Foods Real Mayonnaise
¼ teaspoon curry powder

1 recipe Condensed Cream of Chicken Soup (see page 88)
1 tablespoon lemon juice
½ cup (2 ounces) grated Cheddar cheese
½ cup bread crumbs
1 teaspoon melted butter
1 teaspoon olive oil

Preheat oven to 350 degrees. Treat an 11" × 7" casserole dish with nonstick spray. Steam the broccoli until tender; drain. Spread out the chicken on the bottom of the dish and cover it with the broccoli. Combine the milk, mayonnaise, soup, curry powder, and lemon juice; pour over broccoli. Mix together the cheese, bread crumbs, butter, and oil; sprinkle over the top of the casserole. Bake for 30 minutes.

| Serves 4 | |
| --- | --- |
| **Nutritional Analysis (per serving):** | |
| Calories: | 327.80 |
| Protein: | 25.65 g |
| Carbohydrate: | 19.54 g |
| Fat: | 16.65 g |
| Sat. Fat: | 5.99 g |
| Cholesterol: | 67.27 mg |
| Sodium: | 253.82 mg |
| Fiber: | 3.01 g |
| PCF Ratio: | 31-24-45 |

**Exchange Approx.:**
1 Very Lean Meat, 1 Lean Meat, ½ High-Fat Meat, 1 Fat, 1 Vegetable, 1 Skim Milk, ½ Starch

# Chicken à la King

1 recipe Condensed Cream of Chicken Soup (see page 88)
¼ cup skim milk
½ teaspoon Worcestershire sauce (see recipe for Homemade on page 40)
1 tablespoon Hellmann's or Best Foods Real Mayonnaise
¼ teaspoon ground black pepper

2 cups frozen mix of peas and pearl onions, thawed
1 cup frozen sliced carrots, thawed
1 cup sliced mushrooms, steamed
½ pound (8 ounces) cooked, chopped chicken
4 slices whole-wheat bread, toasted

Combine the soup, milk, Worcestershire, mayonnaise, and pepper in a saucepan and bring to a boil. Reduce heat and add the peas and pearl onions, carrots, mushrooms, and chicken. Simmer until the vegetables and chicken are heated through. Serve over toast.

| Serves 4 | |
| --- | --- |
| **Nutritional Analysis (per serving):** | |
| Calories: | 335.40 |
| Protein: | 25.47 g |
| Carbohydrate: | 37.79 g |
| Fat: | 9.78 g |
| Sat. Fat: | 2.32 g |
| Cholesterol: | 48.55 mg |
| Sodium: | 298.87 mg |
| Fiber: | 6.99 g |
| PCF Ratio: | 30-44-26 |

**Exchange Approx.:**
2 Lean Meats, 1 Vegetable, 1 Starch, 1 Skim Milk

# Chicken and Green Bean Stovetop Casserole

| Serves 4 |
| --- |

| Nutritional Analysis (per serving): | |
| --- | --- |
| Calories: | 305.29 |
| Protein: | 22.85 g |
| Carbohydrate: | 35.59 g |
| Fat: | 8.31 g |
| Sat. Fat: | 2.06 g |
| Cholesterol: | 47.91 mg |
| Sodium: | 101.20 mg |
| Fiber: | 5.56 g |
| PCF Ratio: | 30-46-24 |

**Exchange Approx.:**
1 Very Lean Meat,
1 Lean Meat, 1 Vegetable,
1 Starch, 1 Skim Milk

1 recipe Condensed Cream of Chicken Soup (see page 88)
¼ cup skim milk
2 teaspoons Worcestershire sauce (see recipe for Homemade on page 40)
1 teaspoon Hellmann's or Best Foods Real Mayonnaise
½ teaspoon onion powder
¼ teaspoon garlic powder
¼ teaspoon ground black pepper
1 (4-ounce) can sliced water chestnuts, drained
2½ cups frozen green beans, thawed
1 cup sliced mushrooms, steamed
½ pound (8 ounces) cooked, chopped chicken
1⅓ cups cooked brown, long-grain rice

Combine the soup, milk, Worcestershire, mayonnaise, onion and garlic powder, and pepper in a saucepan and bring to a boil. Reduce heat and add the water chestnuts, green beans, mushrooms, and chicken. Simmer until vegetables and chicken are heated through. Serve over rice.

## Veggie Filler

*Steamed mushrooms are a low-calorie way to add flavor to a dish and "stretch" the meat. If you don't like mushrooms, you can substitute an equal amount of other low-calorie steamed vegetables like red and green peppers and not significantly affect the total calories in the recipe.*

# Chicken Pasta with Herb Sauce

1 recipe Condensed Cream of
   Chicken Soup (see page 88)
¼ cup skim milk
½ teaspoon Worcestershire
   sauce (see recipe for
   Homemade on page 40)
1 teaspoon Hellmann's or Best
   Foods Real Mayonnaise
¼ cup grated Parmesan cheese
¼ chili powder
½ teaspoon garlic powder
¼ teaspoon dried rosemary

¼ teaspoon dried thyme
¼ teaspoon dried marjoram
1 cup sliced mushrooms,
   steamed
½ pound (8 ounces) cooked,
   chopped chicken
4 cups cooked pasta
Freshly ground black pepper
   (optional)

| Serves 4 | |
|---|---|
| **Nutritional Analysis** **(per serving):** | |
| Calories: | 392.57 |
| Protein: | 26.22 g |
| Carbohydrate: | 51.62 g |
| Fat: | 8.43 g |
| Sat. Fat: | 2.03 g |
| Cholesterol: | 47.91 mg |
| Sodium: | 71.24 mg |
| Fiber: | 3.83 g |
| PCF Ratio: | 27-53-20 |

**Exchange Approx.:**
2 Lean Meats,
3 Starches,
½ Skim Milk

Combine the soup, milk, Worcestershire, mayonnaise, and cheese
in a saucepan and bring to a boil. Reduce heat and add the chili
powder, garlic powder, rosemary, thyme, and marjoram; stir well.
Add the mushrooms and chicken and simmer until heated through.
Serve over pasta, and top with freshly ground pepper, if desired.

# Chicken Thighs Cacciatore

| | |
|---|---|
| **Serves 4** | |

**Nutritional Analysis (per serving):**

| | |
|---|---|
| Calories: | 369.73 |
| Protein: | 18.79 g |
| Carbohydrate: | 48.19 g |
| Fat: | 9.27 g |
| Sat. Fat: | 2.43 g |
| Cholesterol: | 38.95 mg |
| Sodium: | 165.80 mg |
| Fiber: | 3.81 g |
| PCF Ratio: | 21-55-24 |

**Exchange Approx.:**
1½ Lean Meats,
2½ Starches,
1 Fat, 1 Vegetable

2 teaspoons olive oil
½ cup chopped onion
2 cloves garlic, minced
4 chicken thighs, skin removed
½ cup dry red wine
1 (14½-oz.) can unsalted diced
   tomatoes, undrained
1 teaspoon dried parsley
½ teaspoon dried oregano
¼ teaspoon pepper
⅛ teaspoon sugar
¼ cup grated Parmesan cheese
4 cups cooked spaghetti
2 teaspoons extra-virgin olive oil

1. Heat a deep, nonstick skillet over medium-high heat and add the 2 teaspoons of olive oil. Add the onion and sauté until transparent. Add the garlic and chicken thighs; sauté for 3 minutes on each side, or until lightly browned.

2. Remove the thighs from the pan and add the wine, the tomatoes and their juices, parsley, oregano, pepper, and sugar. Stir well, and bring to a boil. Add the chicken back to the pan and sprinkle the Parmesan cheese over the top of the chicken and sauce. Cover, reduce heat, and simmer for 10 minutes. Uncover and simmer 10 more minutes.

3. To serve, put 1 cup of cooked pasta on each of 4 plates. Top each pasta serving with a chicken thigh and then divide the sauce between the dishes. Drizzle ½ teaspoon of extra-virgin olive oil over the top of each dish, and serve.

**TIP:** *To add even more flavor to this recipe, substitute beef broth for half of the red wine.*

### For Cheese Lovers!

*Indulge your love of extra cheese and still have a main dish that's under 400 calories. Prepare the Chicken Thighs Cacciatore according to the recipe instructions. Top each portion with 1 table-spoon freshly grated Parmesan cheese. With the cheese, the analysis is: Calories: 398.22; Protein: 21.39 g; Carbohydrate: 48.43 g; Fat: 11.15 g; Sat. Fat: 3.62 g; Cholesterol: 43.87 mg; Sodium: 282.14 mg; Fiber: 3.81 g; PCF Ratio: 23-51-26. Exchange Approximations: 2 Lean Meats, 2½ Starches, 1 Fat, 1 Vegetable.*

# Thanksgiving Feast:
# Turkey Casserole in a Pumpkin

4 small pumpkins

1 recipe Condensed Cream of
   Chicken Soup (see page 88)

1 cup skim milk

1 cup low-fat, reduced-sodium
   chicken broth

1 tablespoon, plus 1 teaspoon
   butter

½ cup steamed, diced celery

1 cup steamed, diced onion

1 cup steamed, sliced mushrooms slices

1 tablespoon cognac (optional)

Parsley, thyme, and sage to
   taste (optional)

1⅓ cups cubed red potatoes,
   steamed

½ pound (8 ounces) steamed,
   chopped oysters

¼ pound (4 ounces) shredded
   cooked turkey

8 slices day-old bread, torn
   into cubes

2 eggs, beaten

| Serves 4 | |
|---|---|
| **Nutritional Analysis (per serving):** | |
| Calories: | 484.56 |
| Protein: | 30.24 g |
| Carbohydrate: | 64.11 g |
| Fat: | 12.98 g |
| Sat. Fat: | 4.74 g |
| Cholesterol: | 186.11 mg |
| Sodium: | 277.67 mg |
| Fiber: | 9.30 g |
| PCF Ratio: | 24-52-24 |

**Exchange Approx.:**
2 Lean Meats,
1 Medium-Fat Meat, 1 Fat,
1 Vegetable, 2 Starches,
1 Skim Milk

1. Preheat oven to 375 degrees. Clean the pumpkins, cut off tops, and scrape out the seeds. Put on baking sheet and cover with foil or parchment paper. Bake for 30 minutes, or until the inside flesh is somewhat tender but the pumpkins still retain their shapes.

2. While the pumpkins bake, prepare the dressing-style casserole by combining the soup, milk, broth, and butter in a saucepan; stir well to mix and bring to a boil over medium heat. Lower the heat and add the celery, onion, mushrooms, and the cognac and seasonings, if using. Simmer for 3 minutes. Remove from heat and allow to cool slightly.

3. In a large bowl, add the potatoes, oysters, turkey, and bread cubes, and toss to mix.

4. Gradually add the eggs to the soup mixture, whisking the mixture constantly; pour the mixture over the potatoes, meat, and bread cubes. Mix well to coat the bread evenly. Divide the resulting mixture into the four pumpkins. Reduce oven temperature to 350 degrees, and bake for 30 to 40 minutes, or until the casserole is firm. (The Analysis for this recipe assumes you'll use pumpkins that will yield ¾ cup of cooked pumpkin each.)

# Stovetop Grilled Turkey Breast

| Serves 4 |  |
| --- | --- |
| **Nutritional Analysis (per serving):** | |
| Calories: | 206.55 |
| Protein: | 30.80 g |
| Carbohydrate: | 1.65 g |
| Fat: | 7.64 g |
| Sat. Fat: | 1.63 g |
| Cholesterol: | 85.05 mg |
| Sodium: | 67.78 mg |
| Fiber: | 0.03 g |
| PCF Ratio: | 62-3-35 |

**Exchange Approx.:**
4 Very Lean Meats,
½ Fat

*1 teaspoon cider vinegar*
*1 teaspoon garlic powder*
*1 teaspoon Dijon mustard*
*1 teaspoon brown sugar*
*¼ teaspoon black pepper*
*2 teaspoons olive oil*
*4 (4-ounce) turkey breast cutlets*

1. In a medium bowl, combine the cider vinegar, garlic powder, mustard, brown sugar, and black pepper. Slowly whisk in the olive oil to thoroughly combine and make a thin paste.
2. Rinse the turkey cutlets and dry thoroughly on paper towels. If necessary to ensure a uniform thickness of the cutlets, put them between sheets of plastic wrap and pound to flatten them.
3. Pour the paste into a heavy-duty (freezer-style) resealable plastic bag. Add the turkey cutlets, moving them around in the mixture to coat all sides. Seal the bag, carefully squeezing out as much air as possible. Refrigerate to allow the turkey to marinate for at least 1 hour, or as long as overnight.
4. Place a nonstick, hard anodized stovetop grill pan over high heat. When the pan is heated thoroughly, add the cutlets. (Depending on the amount of marinade you prefer to leave on the cutlets, you may want to use a splatter screen to prevent a mess on your stovetop.) Lower the heat to medium-high. Cook the cutlets for 3 minutes on 1 side. Use tongs to turn the cutlets and cook for another 3 minutes, or until the juices run clean.

**TIP:** *Cutlets prepared this way tend to cook faster than they do on an outdoor grill. If using an indoor grill that cooks both sides at once, like the George Foreman or Hamilton Beach models, allow 4 to 5 minutes total cooking time. You can also use a well-seasoned, cast iron skillet instead of a grill pan; however, you may need to introduce more oil to the pan to prevent the cutlets from sticking. Cooking time will be the same as with a grill pan. Be sure to adjust the Fat Exchange, if necessary.*

# Turkey Mushroom Burgers

1 pound turkey breast
1 pound fresh button mush-
    rooms
1 tablespoon olive oil
1 teaspoon butter
1 clove garlic, minced
1 tablespoon chopped green
    onion
¼ teaspoon dried thyme

¼ teaspoon dried oregano
¼ teaspoon freshly ground
    black pepper
Cayenne pepper **or** dried red
    pepper flakes to taste
    (optional)

| Yields 8 large burgers | |
|---|---|
| **Nutritional Analysis (per serving):** | |
| Calories: | 100.14 |
| Protein: | 15.09 g |
| Carbohydrate: | 2.55 g |
| Fat: | 3.30 g |
| Sat. Fat: | 0.85 g |
| Cholesterol: | 34.18 mg |
| Sodium: | 36.45 mg |
| Fiber: | 0.71 g |
| PCF Ratio: | 60-10-30 |

**Exchange Approx.:**
1 Lean Meat,
1 Vegetable,
½ Fat

1. Cut the turkey into even pieces about 1-inch square. Place the turkey cubes in the freezer for 10 minutes, or long enough to allow the turkey to become somewhat firm.
2. In a covered, microwave-safe container, microwave the mushrooms on high for 3 to 4 minutes, or until they begin to soften and sweat. Set aside to cool slightly.
3. Process the turkey in a food processor until ground, scraping down the sides of the bowl as necessary. Add the oil, butter, garlic, onion, and mushrooms (and any resulting liquid from the mushrooms) and process until the mushrooms are ground, again scraping down the sides of the bowl as necessary. Add the remaining ingredients and pulse until mixed. Shape into 8 equal-sized patties. Cooking times will vary according to the method used and how thick you form the burgers.

# Cranberry-Turkey Sausage

| Serves 8 |
| --- |

| Nutritional Analysis (per serving): | |
| --- | --- |
| Calories: | 107.40 |
| Protein: | 13.95 g |
| Carbohydrate: | 4.76 g |
| Fat: | 3.31 g |
| Sat. Fat: | 0.86 g |
| Cholesterol: | 34.18 mg |
| Sodium: | 59.48 mg |
| Fiber: | 0.30 g |
| PCF Ratio: | 53-18-28 |

| Exchange Approx.: |
| --- |
| 1 Lean Meat, |
| ½ Fruit, |
| ½ Fat |

1 pound raw turkey breast
¼ cup Cranberry-Raisin Chutney (see page 33)
¼ cup low-fat, reduced-sodium chicken broth
1 tablespoon green onion
¼ cup cornmeal
1 teaspoon dried rosemary
½ teaspoon ground black pepper
1 tablespoon olive oil
1 teaspoon butter

1. Cut the turkey into even pieces about 1-inch square. Place the turkey cubes in the freezer for 10 minutes, or long enough to allow the turkey to become somewhat firm. Process the turkey in a food processor until ground, scraping down the sides of the bowl as necessary.
2. Add the remaining ingredients and pulse until well blended. Form into 8 patties and "fry" in a nonstick skillet over medium heat, allowing about 4 minutes per side, or until juices run clear. (Alternatively, you can cook the patties on a lidded, indoor grill; allow about 4 minutes total, or until juices run clear.)

TIP: *To substitute cooked turkey, add 1 Lean Meat Exchange per serving. Add water 1 tablespoon at a time if the mixture is too dry.*

## Poultry Sauces and Toppings

*It's easy to prepare quick and healthy meals if you keep skinless, boneless chicken or turkey in the freezer. If you use an indoor grill, you don't even need to thaw them first. In fact, you can prepare most of the sauces and toppings in this section in the time it takes for the chicken or turkey to cook.*

# Pineapple–Black Bean Sauce

1 red pepper, sliced
¼ cup sliced green onions
   (white and green parts)
3 cloves garlic, minced
1–2 jalapeño peppers, seeded
   and minced
2 teaspoons curry powder
2 teaspoons minced ginger root
1½ cups chicken broth
   (see page 104)
2 cups cubed pineapple

½ cup Cranberry-Raisin Chutney
   (see page 33)
2 tablespoons, firmly packed,
   light brown sugar
2 tablespoons cornstarch
¼ cup cold water
2 cups cooked black beans

| Serves 6 | |
| --- | --- |
| **Nutritional Analysis (per serving):** | |
| Calories: | 166.11 |
| Protein: | 6.80 g |
| Carbohydrate: | 34.19 g |
| Fat: | 0.87 g |
| Sat. Fat: | 0.19 g |
| Cholesterol: | 0.00 mg |
| Sodium: | 216.69 mg |
| Fiber: | 4.08 g |
| PCF Ratio: | 16-80-5 |

**Exchange Approx.:**
1 Starch,
1 Fruit,
1 Vegetable

1. Treat a nonstick skillet with nonstick cooking spray. Heat over medium heat until hot. Sauté the red pepper, onions, garlic, jalapeño, curry powder, and ginger until the onions are tender, about 5 minutes.
2. Stir in the chicken broth, pineapple, chutney, and brown sugar, and bring to a boil. Mix together the cornstarch and cold water, and whisk it into the pineapple mixture. Boil, stirring constantly, until thickened, about 1 minute.
3. Stir in the black beans and continue to cook over medium heat until the beans are warmed, about 2 to 3 minutes. To serve, spoon the pineapple-bean sauce over chicken and serve with rice.

## Proper Meat Handling

*Be sure to wash any utensil that comes in contact with raw chicken in hot soapy water and rinse well. This includes washing any utensils each time after they're used to baste a grilling, roasting, or baking chicken.*

# Christmas Colors with Yogurt Sauce

| Yields 2 cups |
|---|
| Serving size: ½ cup |

| Nutritional Analysis (per serving): | |
|---|---|
| Calories: | 97.05 |
| Protein: | 7.22 g |
| Carbohydrate: | 14.24 g |
| Fat: | 1.43 g |
| Sat. Fat: | 0.30 g |
| Cholesterol: | 2.03 mg |
| Sodium: | 211.99 mg |
| Fiber: | 0.78 g |
| PCF Ratio: | 29-58-13 |

**Exchange Approx.:**
½ Skim Milk,
1 Vegetable, ½ Fat

1 teaspoon olive oil
1 chopped, roasted **or** steamed
  red pepper (for roasting
  instructions, see "Roasted
  Red (and Other) Peppers,"
  page 39)
1 chopped, roasted **or** steamed
  green pepper
1 cup chopped onion, steamed
2 cups nonfat plain yogurt
Sea salt and freshly ground
  pepper to taste (optional)

Add the olive oil to a preheated nonstick skillet and sauté the peppers and onion until they're heated through. Add the yogurt and slowly bring it up to temperature, being careful not to boil it. Season with salt and pepper, if desired.

# Honey and Cider Glaze
# for Baked Chicken

3 tablespoons cider **or** apple
   juice
½ teaspoon honey
1 teaspoon lemon juice

1 teaspoon Bragg's Liquid
   Aminos
½ teaspoon lemon zest

| Serves 4 |  |
| --- | --- |
| **Nutritional Analysis**<br>**(per serving, glaze only):** | |
| Calories: | 9.56 |
| Protein: | 0.23 g |
| Carbohydrate: | 2.28 g |
| Fat: | 0.01 g |
| Sat. Fat: | 0.00 g |
| Cholesterol: | 0.00 mg |
| Sodium: | 55.41 mg |
| Fiber: | 0.04 g |
| PCF Ratio: | 9-90-1 |

**Exchange Approx.:**
1 Free Condiment

1  Preheat oven to 375 degrees. Combine all the ingredients in a microwave safe bowl. Microwave on high for 30 seconds. Stir until the honey is dissolved.

2. To use the glaze, arrange 4 boneless chicken pieces with the skin removed on a rack placed in a roasting pan or broiling pan. Brush or spoon 1 teaspoon of glaze over the top of each piece. Baste halfway through the cooking time, and again, 5 minutes before the chicken is done. Allow the chicken to set for 5 minutes before serving.

### Spice Tea Chicken Marinade

*Steep 4 Orange or Lemon Spice tea bags in 2 cups boiling water for 4 minutes. Dissolve 1 teaspoon honey into the tea, pour it over 4 chicken pieces, and marinate for 30 minutes. Occasionally turn and baste any exposed portions of chicken. Pour the tea into the roasting pan to provide moisture—discard it after cooking.*

*Nutritional Analysis for 1 (of 4) serving: Calories: 7.69; Protein: 0.01 g; Carbohydrate: 1.92 g; Fat: 0.00 g; Sat. Fat: 0.01 g; Cholesterol: 0.00 mg; Sodium: 2.44 mg; Fiber: 0.00 g; PCF Ratio: 0-100-0. Exchange Approximations: ½ Free Condiment*

# CHAPTER 8
# *Seafood*

| | |
|---|---|
| Fish Stock | 124 |
| Asian-Style Fish Cakes | 125 |
| Slow-Roasted Salmon | 126 |
| Salmon Patties | 126 |
| Crab Cakes with Sesame Crust | 127 |
| Creamy Shrimp Pie with Rice Crust | 128 |
| Mock Sour Cream Baked Catfish | 129 |
| Baked Bread Crumb–Crusted Fish with Lemon | 130 |
| Baked Red Snapper Almandine | 131 |
| A Taste of Italy Baked Fish | 131 |
| Baked Snapper with Orange-Rice Dressing | 132 |
| Crunchy "Fried" Catfish Fillets | 133 |
| Baked Orange Roughy with Spicy Plum Sauce | 134 |
| Sweet Onion–Baked Yellowtail Snapper | 135 |
| Stir-Fried Ginger Scallops with Vegetables | 136 |
| Scallops and Shrimp with White Bean Sauce | 137 |
| Smoked Mussels and Pasta | 138 |
| Pasta and Smoked Trout with Lemon Pesto | 139 |
| Smoked Mussels Cream Sauce with Pasta | 140 |
| Smoked Mussels Scramble | 141 |
| Smoked Salmon Cream Sauce | 142 |
| Smoked Shrimp Sandwich Filling | 142 |
| Smoked Shrimp and Cheese Quesadillas | 143 |
| Fish Pie | 144 |

# Fish Stock

4 cups fish heads, bones,
  and trimmings
  (approx. 1 pound)
2 stalks celery and leaves,
  chopped
1 onion, chopped
1 carrot, peeled and chopped

1 bay leaf
4 sprigs fresh parsley
Sea salt and pepper to taste
  (optional)

1. Use your own fish trimmings (saved in bag in the freezer), or ask the butcher at your local fish market or supermarket for fish trimmings. Wash the trimmings well.
2. In a stockpot, combine all the ingredients and add enough water to cover everything by an inch or so. Bring to a boil over high heat, then reduce heat to low. Skim off the foam that rises to the top. Cover and simmer for 20 minutes.
3. Remove from the heat and strain through a sieve, discarding all solids. Refrigerate or freeze.

**TIP:** *To make stock from shellfish, simply substitute shrimp, crab, or lobster shells for the fish heads and bones.*

## Proper Fish Handling
*Always wash your hands after handling raw fish, and wash all surfaces and utensils that the raw fish touched.*

# Asian-Style Fish Cakes

1 pound catfish fillet
2 green onions, minced
1 banana pepper, cored,
    seeded, and chopped
2 cloves garlic, minced
1 tablespoon grated or minced
    ginger
1 tablespoon Bragg's Liquid
    Aminos
1 tablespoon lemon juice

1 teaspoon lemon zest
Optional seasonings to taste:
    Old Bay Seasoning
        (see page 48)
    Rice flour
    Olive **or** peanut oil

| Serves 8 | |
| --- | --- |
| **Nutritional Analysis (per serving):** | |
| Calories: | 65.98 |
| Protein: | 11.02 g |
| Carbohydrate: | 1.22 g |
| Fat: | 1.66 g |
| Sat. Fat: | 0.43 g |
| Cholesterol: | 40.80 mg |
| Sodium: | 112.44 mg |
| Fiber: | 0.36 mg |
| PCF Ratio: | 69-8-23 |
| **Exchange Approx.:** 1 Lean Meat, 1 Free Condiment | |

1. Preheat oven to 375 degrees. Cut the fish into 1-inch pieces and combine with the green onions, banana pepper, garlic, ginger, Bragg's Liquid Aminos, lemon juice, and lemon zest in a food processor. Process until chopped and mixed. (You do not want to purée this mixture; it should be a rough chop.) Add the Old Bay Seasoning, if using, and stir to mix.
2. Form the fish mixture into patties of about 2 tablespoons each; you should have 16 patties total. Place the patties on a baking sheet treated with nonstick cooking spray, and bake for 12 to 15 minutes, or until crisp. (Alternatively, you can fry these in a nonstick pan for about 4 minutes on each side.)

TIP: *For crunchy fish cakes, coat each side in the rice flour and then lightly spritz the top of the patties with the olive or peanut oil before baking as directed.*

## Not All Weeds Are Bad
*Seaweed is an important ingredient in many processed foods, such as commercial ice cream and other foods that contain carrageenan, a thickener found in several kinds of seaweed.*

# Slow-Roasted Salmon

**Serves 4**

**Nutritional Analysis (per serving):**

| | |
|---|---|
| Calories: | 256.96 |
| Protein: | 25.44 g |
| Carbohydrate: | 0.52 g |
| Fat: | 16.34 g |
| Sat. Fat: | 3.16 g |
| Cholesterol: | 71.40 mg |
| Sodium: | 69.49 mg |
| Fiber: | 0.30 g |
| PCF Ratio: | 41-1-59 |

**Exchange Approx.:**
4 Lean Meats,
½ Fat

*4 (5-ounce) salmon fillets with
 skin, at room temperature
2 teaspoons extra-virgin olive oil
1 cup finely minced fresh chives*

*Sea or kosher salt and
 freshly ground white
 pepper to taste (optional)
Sage sprigs, for garnish*

Preheat oven to 250 degrees. Rub ½ teaspoon of the olive oil into the flesh side of each salmon fillet. Completely cover the fillets with the chives and gently press them into the flesh. Season with salt and white pepper, if desired. Place the fillets skin-side down on a nonstick, oven-safe skillet or a foil-lined cookie sheet treated with nonstick spray, and roast for 25 minutes.

# Salmon Patties

**Serves 5**

**Nutritional Analysis (per serving):**

| | |
|---|---|
| Calories: | 168.05 |
| Protein: | 17.17 g |
| Carbohydrate: | 3.19 g |
| Fat: | 9.18 g |
| Sat. Fat: | 1.92 g |
| Cholesterol: | 70.20 mg |
| Sodium: | 92.31 mg |
| Fiber: | 0.13 g |
| PCF Ratio: | 42-8-50 |

**Exchange Approx.:**
2 Lean Meats,
½ Fat,
½ Starch

*2 cups flaked cooked salmon
 (no salt added)
6 crushed soda crackers
1 egg
½ cup skim milk
1 small onion, chopped*

*1 tablespoon chopped fresh
 parsley
1 tablespoon unbleached
 all-purpose flour
1 tablespoon olive oil
Ener-G flour (optional)*

1. Place the salmon in a bowl and flake with a fork. Add the crushed crackers, egg, milk, onion, parsley, and flour; mix well. Gently form into 5 patties.
2. Heat the oil in a nonstick skillet over medium heat. (Optional: Lightly dust the patties with some Ener-G rice flour for crispier patties.) Fry on both sides until browned, about 5 minutes per side.

# Crab Cakes with Sesame Crust

1 pound (16 ounces) lump
    crabmeat
1 egg
1 tablespoon minced fresh ginger
1 small scallion, finely chopped
1 tablespoon dry sherry
1 tablespoon freshly squeezed
    lemon juice
6 tablespoons Hellmann's or
    Best Foods Real Mayonnaise

Sea salt and freshly ground
    white pepper to taste
    (optional)
Old Bay Seasoning (see page
    48) to taste (optional)
¼ cup lightly toasted sesame
    seeds

| Serves 5 | |
| --- | --- |
| **Nutritional Analysis (per serving):** | |
| Calories: | 107.69 |
| Protein: | 9.04 g |
| Carbohydrate: | 2.93 g |
| Fat: | 6.45 g |
| Sat. Fat: | 1.05 g |
| Cholesterol: | 45.46 mg |
| Sodium: | 170.88 mg |
| Fiber: | 0.60 g |
| PCF Ratio: | 34-11-55 |
| **Exchange Approx.:** | |
| 1 Very Lean Meat, 1½ Fats | |

1. Preheat oven to 375 degrees. In a large bowl, mix together the crab, egg, ginger, scallion, sherry, lemon juice, mayonnaise, and the seasonings, if using.
2. Form the mixture into 10 equal cakes. Spread the sesame seeds over a sheet pan and dip both sides of the cakes to coat them. Arrange the crab cakes on a baking sheet treated with nonstick spray. Typical baking time is 8 to 10 minutes (depending on how thick you make the cakes).

## So, What Is Aquaculture?

*"Aquaculture produces about 17 percent of the world's seafood. . . . Seaweed cultivation ranks first in volume, followed by carp, and blue mussels. In the U.S., catfish is the predominant farmed species, followed by trout, salmon, and shellfish." (Source: Ducktrap River Fish Farm's Aquaculture FAQ page at ⬡www.ducktrap.com)*

# Creamy Shrimp Pie with Rice Crust

| Serves 4 | |
|---|---|
| **Nutritional Analysis (per serving):** | |
| Calories: | 273.12 |
| Protein: | 26.24 g |
| Carbohydrate: | 26.80 g |
| Fat: | 6.39 g |
| Sat. Fat: | 2.39 g |
| Cholesterol: | 180.04 mg |
| Sodium: | 172.34 mg |
| Fiber: | 1.69 g |
| PCF Ratio: | 39-40-21 |

**Exchange Approx.:**
2 Very Lean Meats,
2 Starches,
1 Fat

1⅓ cups cooked white rice
2 teaspoons dried parsley
2 tablespoons grated onion
1 teaspoon olive oil
1 tablespoon butter
1 clove garlic, crushed
1 pound shrimp, peeled and deveined

1 recipe Condensed Cream of Mushroom Soup (see page 89)
1 teaspoon lemon juice
1 cup sliced mushrooms, steamed

1. Preheat oven to 350 degrees. Combine the cooked rice, parsley, and onion; mix well. Use the olive oil to coat a 10-inch pie plate. Press the rice mixture evenly around the sides and bottom. This works best if the rice is moist; if necessary, add 1 teaspoon of water.

2. Melt the butter in a deep, nonstick skillet over medium heat and sauté the garlic. Add the shrimp and cook, stirring frequently, until pink, about 5 minutes. Add the soup and lemon juice to the skillet. Stir until smooth and thoroughly heated. (If the soup seems too thick, add some water, 1 teaspoon at a time.) Stir the mushrooms into the soup mixture, then pour it over the rice "crust." Bake for 30 minutes, or until lightly browned on top. Serve hot.

## Fat-Free Flavor

*To add the flavor of sautéed mushrooms or onions without the added fat of butter or oil, roast or grill them first. Simply spread them on a baking sheet treated with nonstick spray. Roasting them for 5 minutes in a 350-degree oven will be sufficient if the vegetables are sliced, and will not add additional cooking time to the recipe.*

# Mock Sour Cream Baked Catfish

*1 pound (16 ounces) catfish
    fillets*
*2 teaspoons Hellmann's or
    Best Foods Real Mayonnaise*
*2 teaspoons all-purpose flour*
*½ cup plain nonfat yogurt*
*½ teaspoon white wine vinegar*
*4 teaspoons chopped pimiento-
    stuffed green olives*
*½ teaspoon ground celery seed*
*¼ teaspoon paprika*

*¼ teaspoon freshly ground
    white **or** black pepper*
*¼ teaspoon thyme*
*1 teaspoon fresh dill (or a
    pinch of dried dill per fillet)*
*1 lemon, cut into 4 wedges
    (optional)*
*Fresh chopped **or** dried parsley
    (optional)*

| Serves 4 | |
|---|---|
| **Nutritional Analysis (per serving):** | |
| Calories: | 170.59 |
| Protein: | 17.80 g |
| Carbohydrate: | 1.79 g |
| Fat: | 9.73 g |
| Sat. Fat: | 2.17 g |
| Cholesterol: | 53.90 mg |
| Sodium: | 101.93 mg |
| Fiber: | 0.12 g |
| PCF Ratio: | 43-4-53 |
| **Exchange Approx.:** 3 Lean Meats | |

1. Preheat oven to 350 degrees. Prepare a baking dish by spraying it with nonstick spray. Rinse the fillets in water and then dry between layers of paper towels. Arrange the fillets in the baking dish.
2. In a small bowl, combine the mayonnaise, flour, yogurt, vinegar, olives, celery seed, paprika, pepper, and thyme; spread the mixture over the fish and sprinkle with dill. Bake for 15 minutes, or until the fish flakes when touched with a fork. Garnish with lemon wedges and parsley, if desired.

# Baked Bread Crumb–
# Crusted Fish with Lemon

| Serves 6 |
| :---: |

| **Nutritional Analysis (per serving, without salt):** | |
| :--- | ---: |
| Calories: | 137.36 |
| Protein: | 24.18 g |
| Carbohydrate: | 4.87 g |
| Fat: | 2.78 g |
| Sat. Fat: | 0.39 g |
| Cholesterol: | 36.29 mg |
| Sodium: | 73.38 mg |
| Fiber: | 1.74 g |
| PCF Ratio: | 68-14-18 |

**Exchange Approx.:**
2 Very Lean Meats,
½ Starch,
½ Free Condiment

*2 large lemons*
*1½ pounds (24 ounces) halibut*
  *fillets*
*¼ cup dried bread crumbs*

*Sea or kosher salt and freshly*
  *ground white or black*
  *pepper to taste (optional)*

1. Preheat oven to 375 degrees. Wash 1 lemon and cut it into thin slices. Grate 1 tablespoon of zest from the second lemon, then juice it. Combine the grated zest and bread crumbs in a small bowl and stir to mix; set aside.
2. Put the lemon juice in a shallow dish, and arrange the lemon slices in the bottom of a baking dish treated with nonstick spray. Dip the fish pieces in the lemon juice and set them on the lemon slices in the baking dish. Sprinkle the bread crumb mixture evenly over the fish pieces, along with the salt and pepper, if using, and bake until the crumbs are lightly browned and the fish is just opaque, 10 to 15 minutes. (Baking time will depend on the thickness of the fish.) Serve immediately, using the lemon slices as garnish.

### Lemon Infusion
*Mildly flavored fish, such as catfish, cod, halibut, orange roughy, rockfish, and snapper, benefit from the distinctive flavor of lemon. Adding slices of lemon to the top of the fish allows the flavor to infuse into the fish.*

# Baked Red Snapper Almandine

1 pound (16 ounces) red
   snapper fillets
Sea **or** kosher salt and freshly
   ground white **or** black pepper
   to taste (optional)

4 teaspoons all-purpose flour
2 teaspoons olive oil
2 tablespoons ground raw almonds
2 teaspoons unsalted butter
1 tablespoon lemon juice

1. Preheat oven to 375 degrees. Rinse the red snapper fillets and dry between layers of paper towels. Season with salt and pepper, if using. Sprinkle the fillets with the flour, front and back.
2. In an ovenproof nonstick skillet, sauté the fillets in the olive oil until they are nicely browned on both sides. Combine the ground almonds and butter in a microwave-safe dish and microwave on high for 30 seconds, or until the butter is melted; stir to combine. Pour the almond-butter mixture and the lemon juice over the fillets. Bake for 3 to 5 minutes, or until the almonds are nicely browned.

**Serves 4**

**Nutritional Analysis
(per serving, without salt):**

| | |
|---|---|
| Calories: | 177.78 |
| Protein: | 24.18 g |
| Carbohydrate: | 2.90 g |
| Fat: | 7.22 g |
| Sat. Fat: | 1.94 g |
| Cholesterol: | 47.11 mg |
| Sodium: | 72.91 mg |
| Fiber: | 0.44 g |
| PCF Ratio: | 56-7-37 |

**Exchange Approx.:**
3 Lean Meats

# A Taste of Italy Baked Fish

1 pound (16 ounces) cod fillets
1 (14½-ounce) can stewed
   tomatoes
¼ teaspoon dried minced onion
½ teaspoon dried minced garlic
¼ teaspoon dried basil

¼ teaspoon dried parsley
⅛ teaspoon dried oregano
⅛ teaspoon sugar
1 tablespoon grated Parmesan
   cheese

1. Preheat oven to 375 degrees. Rinse the cod with cold water and pat dry with paper towels.
2. In a 2- to 3-quart baking pan or casserole treated with nonstick cooking spray, combine all the ingredients except the fish, and mix. Arrange the fillets over the tomato mixture, folding thin tail ends under; spoon some of the tomato mixture over the fillets. For fillets about 1 inch thick, bake uncovered for 20 to 25 minutes, or until the fish is opaque and flaky.

**Serves 4**

**Nutritional Analysis
(per serving):**

| | |
|---|---|
| Calories: | 127.91 |
| Protein: | 21.68 g |
| Carbohydrate: | 7.15 g |
| Fat: | 1.27 g |
| Sat. Fat: | 0.41 g |
| Cholesterol: | 49.72 mg |
| Sodium: | 311.59 mg |
| Fiber: | 1.03 g |
| PCF Ratio: | 68-23-9 |

**Exchange Approx.:**
2½ Very Lean Meats,
1½ Vegetables

# Baked Snapper
# with Orange-Rice Dressing

| Serves 4 |
| :---: |

| Nutritional Analysis (per serving, without salt): | |
| :--- | :--- |
| Calories: | 256.69 |
| Protein: | 26.03 g |
| Carbohydrate: | 25.12 g |
| Fat: | 5.19 g |
| Sat. Fat: | 1.68 g |
| Cholesterol: | 47.11 mg |
| Sodium: | 82.51 mg |
| Fiber: | 1.00 g |
| PCF Ratio: | 41-40-19 |

**Exchange Approx.:**
2 Lean Meats,
½ Fruit, ½ Fat,
1 Starch

¼ cup chopped celery
½ cup chopped onion
½ cup orange juice
1 tablespoon lemon juice
1 teaspoon grated orange zest
1⅓ cups cooked rice
1 pound (16 ounces) red
    snapper fillets

Sea **or** kosher salt and freshly
    ground white **or** black
    pepper to taste (optional)
2 tablespoons ground raw
    almonds
2 teaspoons unsalted butter

1. Preheat oven to 350 degrees. In a microwave-safe bowl, mix the celery and onion with the juices and orange zest; microwave on high for 2 minutes, or until the mixture comes to a boil. Add the rice and stir to moisten, adding some water 1 tablespoon at a time if necessary to thoroughly coat the rice. Cover and let stand for 5 minutes.

2. Rinse the fillets and pat dry between paper towels. Prepare a baking dish with nonstick spray. Spread the rice mixture in the dish and arrange the fillets on top. Season the fillets with salt and pepper, if using. Combine the butter and almonds in a microwave-safe bowl and microwave on high for 30 seconds, or until the butter is melted. Stir and spoon over the top of the fillets. Cover and bake for 10 minutes. Remove the cover and bake for another 5 to 10 minutes, or until the fish flakes easily when tested with a fork and the almonds are lightly browned.

# Crunchy "Fried" Catfish Fillets

*1 egg white (from a large egg), at room temperature*
*¼ cup bread crumbs*
*¼ cup enriched white cornmeal*
*1 teaspoon grated lemon zest*
*½ teaspoon crushed dried basil*
*¼ cup all-purpose flour*

*⅛ teaspoon kosher **or** sea salt (optional)*
*¼ teaspoon lemon pepper*
*1 pound (16 ounces) farm-raised catfish fillets*

| Serves 4 | |
| --- | --- |
| **Nutritional Analysis (per serving, without salt):** | |
| Calories: | 243.57 |
| Protein: | 20.91 g |
| Carbohydrate: | 17.58 g |
| Fat: | 9.20 g |
| Sat. Fat: | 2.12 g |
| Cholesterol: | 53.27 mg |
| Sodium: | 248.46 mg |
| Fiber: | 1.11 g |
| PCF Ratio: | 35-30-35 |
| **Exchange Approx.:** 3 Lean Meats, 1 Starch | |

1. Preheat oven to 450 degrees and treat a shallow baking pan with non-stick spray. Rinse the catfish fillets and dry them between layers of paper towels.
2. In a shallow dish, beat the egg white until frothy. In another dish, combine the bread crumbs, cornmeal, lemon zest, and basil. In a third dish, combine the flour, salt (if using), and lemon pepper.
3. Dip the fish into the flour mixture to coat 1 side of each fillet. Shake off any excess flour mixture, then dip the flour-covered side of the fillet into the egg white. Next, coat the covered side of the fillet with the breadcrumb mixture. Arrange the prepared fillets side by side, coated sides up on the prepared baking pan. Tuck in any thin edges. Bake for 6 to 12 minutes, or until the fish flakes easily with a fork.

### Zesty Crunch
*Grated lemon or lime zest is a great way to give added citrus flavor to a crunchy bread crumb topping for fish.*

# Baked Orange Roughy
# with Spicy Plum Sauce

| Serves 4 | |
| --- | --- |
| **Nutritional Analysis (per serving):** | |
| Calories: | 221.31 |
| Protein: | 18.60 g |
| Carbohydrate: | 30.62 g |
| Fat: | 2.60 g |
| Sat. Fat: | 0.30 g |
| Cholesterol: | 22.67 mg |
| Sodium: | 101.04 mg |
| Fiber: | 2.04 g |
| PCF Ratio: | 34-56-11 |

**Exchange Approx.:**
2 Very Lean Meats,
1 Fruit,
1 Starch

1 pound (16 ounces) orange
 roughy fillets
1 teaspoon paprika
1 bay leaf
1 clove garlic, crushed
1 apple, peeled, cored, and cubed
1 teaspoon grated fresh ginger
1 small red **or** Spanish onion,
 chopped
1 teaspoon olive oil

¼ cup Plum Sauce
 (see page 37)
¼ teaspoon Chinese five-spice
 powder
1 teaspoon frozen unsweetened
 apple juice concentrate
½ teaspoon Bragg's Liquid
 Aminos
¼ teaspoon blackstrap molasses
1⅓ cup cooked brown rice

1. Preheat oven to 400 degrees. Treat a baking dish with nonstick spray. Rinse the orange roughy and pat dry between paper towels. Rub both sides of the fish with the paprika, then set them in the prepared dish.
2. In a covered, microwave-safe bowl, mix the bay leaf, garlic, apple, ginger and onion in the oil and microwave on high for 3 minutes, or until the apple is tender and the onion is transparent. Stir, discard the bay leaf, and top the fillets with the apple mixture. Bake uncovered for 15 to 18 minutes, or until the fish is opaque.
3. While the fish bakes, add the plum sauce to a microwave-safe bowl. Add the 5-spice powder, apple juice concentrate, Liquid Aminos, and molasses. Microwave on high for 30 seconds, stir, add a little water if needed to thin mixture, and then microwave another 15 seconds. Cover until ready to serve. If necessary, bring back to temperature by microwaving the mixture for another 15 seconds just prior to serving.
4. To serve, equally divide the cooked rice among 4 serving plates. Top each with an equal amount of the baked fish mixture and plum sauce mixture, drizzling the sauce atop the fish.

# Sweet Onion–Baked Yellowtail Snapper

2 cups sliced Vidalia onions
1 tablespoon balsamic vinegar
2 teaspoons brown sugar
4 teaspoons olive oil
1 pound (16 ounces) skinless
  yellowtail snapper fillets

Sea salt and freshly ground
  white **or** black pepper to
  taste (optional)

| Serves 4 | |
|---|---|
| **Nutritional Analysis (per serving, no salt):** | |
| Calories: | 188.57 |
| Protein: | 24.67 g |
| Carbohydrate: | 13.11 g |
| Fat: | 3.97 g |
| Sat. Fat: | 0.66 g |
| Cholesterol: | 41.93 mg |
| Sodium: | 76.62 mg |
| Fiber: | 1.47 g |
| PCF Ratio: | 53-28-19 |

**Exchange Approx.:**
1 Lean Meat,
2 Very Lean Meats
1 Vegetable, ½ Starch

1. In a covered, microwave-safe dish, microwave the onion on high for 5 minutes, or until it is transparent. Carefully remove the cover and stir in the vinegar and brown sugar. Cover and allow to set for several minutes so the onion absorbs the flavors.
2. Heat a nonstick pan on medium-high and add the olive oil. Transfer the steamed onion mixture to the pan and sauté until browned but not crisp. (Be careful as the onions will burn easily because of the brown sugar; if the onion browns too quickly, lower the heat and add a few tablespoons of water.) Cook until all liquid has evaporated from the pan, stirring often. The onions should have a shiny and dark caramelized color. (This can be prepared 2 to 3 days in advance; store tightly covered in the refrigerator.)
3. Preheat oven to 375 degrees. Rinse the snapper fillets in cold water and dry between paper towels. Arrange the fillets on a baking sheet treated with nonstick spray. Spoon the caramelized onions over the tops of the fillets, pressing it to form a light "crust" over the top of the fish. Bake for 12 to 15 minutes, or until the fish flakes easily with a fork. Serve immediately with Madeira sauce divided on 4 plates with the fish placed on top.

# Stir-Fried Ginger Scallops
## with Vegetables

### Serves 4

### Nutritional Analysis
### (per serving):

| | |
|---|---|
| Calories: | 145.43 |
| Protein: | 22.26 g |
| Carbohydrate: | 8.35 g |
| Fat: | 2.68 g |
| Sat. Fat: | 0.37 g |
| Cholesterol: | 37.40 mg |
| Sodium: | 372.92 mg |
| Fiber: | 2.33 g |
| PCF Ratio: | 61-23-16 |

### Exchange Approx.:
3 Very Lean Meats,
½ Vegetable

1 pound (16 ounces) scallops
1 teaspoon peanut **or** sesame oil
1 tablespoon chopped fresh ginger
2 cloves garlic, minced
1 teaspoon rice wine vinegar
2 teaspoons Bragg's Liquid Aminos
½ cup low-fat, reduced-sodium chicken broth
2 cups broccoli florets
4 scallions, thinly sliced (optional)
1 teaspoon cornstarch
¼ teaspoon toasted sesame oil

1. Rinse the scallops and pat them dry between layers of paper towels. If necessary, slice the scallops so they're a uniform size. Set aside.
2. Add the peanut oil to a heated nonstick deep skillet or wok. Sauté the ginger and garlic for 1 to 2 minutes, being careful that the ginger doesn't burn. Add the vinegar, Liquid Aminos, and broth, and bring to a boil. Remove from heat.
3. Place the broccoli in a large, covered microwave-safe dish and pour the chicken broth mixture over the top. Microwave on high for 3 to 5 minutes, depending on how you prefer your vegetables cooked. (Keep in mind that the vegetables will continue to steam for a minute or so if the cover remains on the dish.)
4. Heat the skillet or wok over medium-high temperature. Add the scallops and sauté for 1 minute on each side. (Do the scallops in batches if necessary. Be careful not to overcook the scallops.) Remove the scallops from pan when done and set aside. Drain off (but *do not discard*) the liquid from the broccoli; return the liquid to the bowl and transfer the broccoli to the heated skillet or wok. Stir-fry the vegetables to bring them up to serving temperature.
5. In the meantime, in a small cup or bowl, add enough water to the cornstarch to make a slurry, or roux. Whisk the slurry into the reserved broccoli liquid; microwave on high for 1 minute. Add the toasted sesame oil to the broth mixture, then whisk again. Pour the thickened broth mixture over the broccoli and toss to mix. Add the scallops back to the broccoli mixture and stir-fry over medium heat to return the scallops to serving temperature. Serve over rice or pasta, and adjust Exchange Approximations accordingly.

# Scallops and Shrimp with White Bean Sauce

½ cup finely chopped onion, steamed

2 cloves garlic, minced

2 teaspoons olive oil, divided

¼ cup dry white wine

¼ cup, tightly packed, fresh parsley leaves

¼ cup, tightly packed, fresh basil leaves

1 ⅓ cups canned cannellini (white) beans, drained and rinsed

¼ cup low-fat, reduced-sodium chicken broth

½ pound (8 ounces) shrimp, shelled and deveined

½ pound (8 ounces) scallops

| Serves 4 | |
|---|---|
| **Nutritional Analysis (per serving):** | |
| Calories: | 231.32 |
| Protein: | 26.93 g |
| Carbohydrate: | 18.38 g |
| Fat: | 4.17 g |
| Sat. Fat: | 0.66 g |
| Cholesterol: | 104.83 mg |
| Sodium: | 217.26 mg |
| Fiber: | 6.48 g |
| PCF Ratio: | 49-34-17 |

**Exchange Approx.:**
3 Very Lean Meats,
½ Fat, 1 Starch,
½ Vegetable

1. In a nonstick saucepan, sauté the onion and garlic in 1 teaspoon of the oil over moderately low heat until the onion is soft. Add the wine and simmer the mixture until the wine is reduced by half. Add the parsley, basil, ⅓ cup of the beans, and the chicken broth; simmer the mixture, stirring constantly, for 1 minute.

2. Transfer the bean mixture to a blender or food processor and purée it. Pour the purée back into the saucepan and add the remaining beans; simmer for 2 minutes.

3. In a nonstick skillet, heat the remaining 1 teaspoon of oil over moderately high heat until it is hot but not smoking. Sauté the shrimp for 2 minutes on each side, or until they are cooked through. Using a slotted spoon, transfer the shrimp to a plate and cover to keep warm. Add the scallops to the skillet and sauté them for 1 minute on each side, or until they are cooked through. To serve, divide the bean sauce between 4 shallow bowls and arrange the shellfish over the top.

# Smoked Mussels and Pasta

| Serves 4 |
| :---: |

**Nutritional Analysis (per serving):**

| | |
| :--- | ---: |
| Calories: | 205.64 |
| Protein: | 10.18 g |
| Carbohydrate: | 22.57 g |
| Fat: | 8.01 g |
| Sat. Fat: | 1.81 g |
| Cholesterol: | 31.23 mg |
| Sodium: | 371.25 mg |
| Fiber: | 1.26 g |
| PCF Ratio: | 20-44-35 |

**Exchange Approx.:**
1 Carb./Starch,
1 Lean Meat, ½ Fat,
½ Skim Milk

*1⅓ cups uncooked pasta (to yield 2 cups cooked pasta)*
*½ cup chopped leek*
*4 ounces Ducktrap River smoked mussels, drained of all excess oil*
*⅛ teaspoon cayenne pepper*
*½ teaspoon dried oregano*
*¼ cup nonfat cottage cheese*
*⅛ cup nonfat plain yogurt*
*2 teaspoons grated Parmesan cheese*
*2 teaspoons extra-virgin olive oil*
*Cracked black pepper to taste*

1. Cook the pasta according to package directions; drain and set aside. In a covered, microwave-safe bowl, microwave the leek on high for 2 to 3 minutes, or until limp and translucent. Add the mussels and cayenne pepper to the leeks; stir. Cover and microwave on high for 30 seconds to heat the mussels.
2. In a blender, combine the oregano, cottage cheese, yogurt, and Parmesan cheese; process until smooth. Combine the cottage cheese and mussel mixtures, and microwave on high until warm, about 30 seconds. Toss the pasta with the olive oil, then stir in the mussel mixture. Divide into 4 portions and serve immediately, topped with cracked pepper.

### Savory Smoke
*Smoked meats impart a strong, pleasant flavor to dishes, so you can use less meat to achieve a rich taste.*

# Pasta and Smoked Trout
# with Lemon Pesto

2 cloves garlic

2 cups fresh basil leaves,
   tightly packed

⅛ cup pine nuts, toasted (see
   page 30)

2 teaspoons fresh lemon juice

2 teaspoons water

4 teaspoons extra-virgin olive oil

4 tablespoons grated Parmesan
   cheese, divided

1⅓ cups uncooked linguini **or**
   other pasta (to yield
   2 cups cooked pasta)

2 ounces Ducktrap River whole,
   boneless smoked trout

Freshly ground black pepper to
   taste

| Serves 4 |  |
|---|---|
| **Nutritional Analysis (per serving):** |  |
| Calories: | 209.29 |
| Protein: | 10.29 g |
| Carbohydrate: | 23.49 g |
| Fat: | 8.33 g |
| Sat. Fat: | 1.34 g |
| Cholesterol: | 3.75 mg |
| Sodium: | 151.45 mg |
| Fiber: | 1.43 g |
| PCF Ratio: | 20-45-36 |

**Exchange Approx.:**
1 Fat,
1½ Lean Meats,
1 Carb./Starch

1. Put the garlic in food processor and pulse until finely chopped. Add the basil, pine nuts, lemon juice, and water; process until just puréed. (Note: You can substitute fresh parsley for the basil; supplement the flavor by adding some dried basil, too, if you do.) Add the olive oil and 3 tablespoons of the Parmesan cheese; pulse until the pesto is smooth, occasionally scraping down the side of the bowl, if necessary. Set aside.

2. Cook the pasta according to package directions, and while it is cooking, flake the smoked trout. When the pasta is cooked, pulse the pesto to ensure it has remained blended, and toss the pesto and trout with the pasta. Sprinkle the remaining grated Parmesan cheese on top of each serving. (Although this recipe uses heart-healthy extra-virgin olive oil, it is a little higher in fat but still low in calories. Consult your dietitian if you have any question as to whether you should include this recipe in your meal plans.)

# Smoked Mussels Cream Sauce with Pasta

**Serves 4**

**Nutritional Analysis**
**(per serving, without flour):**

| | |
|---|---|
| Calories: | 311.88 |
| Protein: | 22.23 g |
| Carbohydrate: | 27.91 g |
| Fat: | 10.30 g |
| Sat. Fat: | 3.06 g |
| Cholesterol: | 39.88 mg |
| Sodium: | 362.01 mg |
| Fiber: | 3.00 g |
| PCF Ratio: | 30-38-32 |

**Exchange Approx.:**
2 Very Lean Meats,
1 Lean Meat, 1 Fat,
1½ Carbs./Starches

*2 teaspoons unsalted butter*
*2 cloves garlic, crushed*
*½ cup sliced leeks **or** green onions*
*½ cup dry white wine*
*2 cups steamed sliced mushrooms*
*1⅓ cups uncooked pasta (to yield 2 cups cooked)*
*2 cups nonfat cottage cheese*
*1 teaspoon potato flour (optional)*

*4 ounces Ducktrap River smoked mussels, drained of any oil*
*2 teaspoons extra-virgin olive oil*
*Parsley to taste (optional)*
*Tarragon to taste (optional)*
*Cracked black **or** white pepper to taste (optional)*

1. Melt the butter in a deep nonstick skillet. Add the garlic and leeks (***or*** green onions) and sauté just until transparent. Add the wine and bring to a boil; cook until reduced by half. Add the mushrooms and toss in the wine mixture. Start preparing the pasta according to package directions.
2. In a blender or food processor, purée the cottage cheese. Add it to the wine-mushroom mixture and bring to serving temperature over low heat, being careful that the mixture doesn't boil. If the mixture seems too wet (if you didn't reduce the wine enough, for example), sprinkle potato flour over the mixture, stir until blended, and cook until thickened.
3. Add the mussels to the cottage cheese mixture just prior to serving, stirring well to bring the mussels to serving temperature. Serve over the drained cooked pasta, tossed with the olive oil and the herbs, if using. Top with cracked pepper.

# Smoked Mussels Scramble

4 smoked mussels (1 ounce)
1 egg
1 tablespoon unbleached all-
purpose flour
1 tablespoon cornmeal
1 tablespoon rice flour
1 tablespoon diced, sautéed
celery
1 tablespoon diced, sautéed
green pepper

2 tablespoons diced, sautéed
onion
6 ounces (2 small) diced,
boiled potatoes
Rice flour (optional)

| Serves 4 | |
| --- | --- |
| **Nutritional Analysis (per serving):** | |
| Calories: | 92.57 |
| Protein: | 4.27 g |
| Carbohydrate: | 13.37 g |
| Fat: | 2.53 g |
| Sat. Fat: | 0.69 |
| Cholesterol: | 54.21 mg |
| Sodium: | 108.03 mg |
| Fiber: | 1.93 g |
| PCF Ratio: | 18-57-24 |

**Exchange Approx.:**
1 Starch,
½ Very Lean Meat

In a bowl, combine all the ingredients. "Fry" in a nonstick skillet sprayed with olive oil nonstick spray. You can prepare the scramble loose, or in patties.

**TIP:** *For patties, shape into balls, roll in rice flour (for extra crispness), place in skillet, and flatten with the back of a spatula. Because this is a very moist mixture, be sure to wet your hands before you shape it into balls.*

## Know Your Ingredients
*Because smoked meats are also often high in sodium, most recipes in this book state the brand used so that the sodium counts given in the Nutritional Analysis are accurate. If you substitute another brand, consult the label and adjust the nutritional values, if necessary.*

# Smoked Salmon Cream Sauce

| Serves 4 | |
|---|---|
| **Nutritional Analysis (per serving, sauce only):** | |
| Calories: | 143.28 |
| Protein: | 18.04 g |
| Carbohydrate: | 1.34 g |
| Fat: | 6.72 g |
| Sat. Fat: | 2.64 g |
| Cholesterol: | 15.03 mg |
| Sodium: | 354.54 mg |
| Fiber: | 0.00 g |
| PCF Ratio: | 52-4-44 |

**Exchange Approx.:**
3 Very Lean Meats,
½ Fat

2 teaspoons butter
4 ounces Ducktrap River
  smoked salmon
2 cups nonfat cottage cheese

Ground nutmeg (optional)
Freshly ground white **or** black
  pepper (optional)

Melt the butter in a nonstick skillet. Cut the smoked salmon into julienne strips, and sauté in the butter until heated through. In a blender or food processor, blend the cottage cheese until smooth. Stir the puréed cottage cheese into the sautéed salmon and heat on low until the cottage cheese is brought to serving temperature. Spoon the sauce over 4 servings of cooked pasta or toast. Top with the nutmeg and pepper, if desired.

# Smoked Shrimp Sandwich Filling

| Serves 4 | |
|---|---|
| **Nutritional Analysis (per serving, filling only):** | |
| Calories: | 103.64 |
| Protein: | 9.17 g |
| Carbohydrate: | 3.14 g |
| Fat: | 5.49 g |
| Sat. Fat: | 2.99 g |
| Cholesterol: | 78.30 mg |
| Sodium: | 341.56 mg |
| Fiber: | 0.53 g |
| PCF Ratio: | 37-13-50 |

**Exchange Approx.:**
1½ Lean Meats,
1 Vegetable

1 large roasted red pepper,
  chopped
⅛ cup (2 tablespoons) dry
  white wine
⅛ teaspoon granulated sugar
1 cup thinly sliced red onion

1 clove garlic, crushed
4 ounces Ducktrap River
  smoked shrimp
2 ounces fontina cheese
Mayonnaise (optional)

Combine the wine and sugar in a nonstick skillet and bring to a boil. Add the roasted red pepper (see "Roasted Red (or Other) Peppers," page 39), red onion, and garlic. Continue to boil, stirring frequently, until the wine is absorbed by the peppers and the onion is transparent. Turn off the heat and stir the shrimp and cheese into the sauce until well mixed and the cheese is melted. Serve immediately on French bread. (It's good if you first spread the bread with a very thin layer of mayonnaise and adjust the Exchange Approximations accordingly.)

# Smoked Shrimp and Cheese Quesadillas

4 (8-inch) flour tortillas
4 teaspoons olive oil
2 ounces part-skim mozzarella
    **or** other mild cheese (such
    as fontina or baby swiss)
    **or** go wild and use goat
    cheese
1 jalapeño **or** banana pepper,
    finely chopped

2 cloves garlic, crushed
4 ounces Ducktrap River
    smoked shrimp
1 cup thinly sliced red onion
½ cup roughly chopped fresh
    cilantro

| Serves 4 | |
| --- | --- |
| **Nutritional Analysis (per serving):** | |
| Calories: | 271.82 |
| Protein: | 11.47 g |
| Carbohydrate: | 31.53 g |
| Fat: | 11.05 g |
| Sat. Fat: | 3.15 g |
| Cholesterol: | 38.58 mg |
| Sodium: | 428.14 mg |
| Fiber: | 2.72 g |
| PCF Ratio: | 17-46-37 |

**Exchange Approx.:**
1 Carb./Starch,
1½ Lean Meats,
1 Fat, ½ Vegetable

1. Preheat oven to 375 degrees. Lightly brush 1 side of each tortilla with some of the olive oil. Mix the cheese, pepper, and garlic with the remaining olive oil. Spread ¼ of the cheese mixture in the center of the oiled half of each tortilla. Top with the shrimp, red onion, and cilantro. Fold the tortilla in half to cover over the ingredients.
2. Place the tortillas in a baking pan treated with nonstick spray. Bake for 3 to 5 minutes, or until nicely browned and the cheese is melted. Serve with your choice of tomato salsa.

## Cut Added Sodium

*Reduce some of the sodium content (salty flavor) from smoked seafood like mussels or shrimp by rinsing them in a little water.*

# Fish Pie

1 cup Mock Cream
(see page 42)
¼ cup grated, low-salt Cheddar
cheese
1 tablespoon grated Parmesan
cheese
¼ cup red **or** sweet onion,
steamed
¼ cup lemon juice
1 teaspoon stone-ground mustard
1 teaspoon dried parsley
½ cup sliced carrot, steamed
1 cup, tightly packed, spinach
2 ounces Ducktrap River smoked
trout, cut into small pieces

1 pound (16 ounces) skinless cod
fillets, cut into 1-inch cubes
1 hard-boiled egg, grated or
finely chopped
¾ pound (12 ounces) potatoes,
boiled (without salt) and diced
2 teaspoons extra-virgin olive oil
Optional seasonings to taste:
Sea **or** kosher salt and freshly
ground black pepper
Ground nutmeg

1. Preheat oven to 450 degrees. In a nonstick saucepan, heat the Mock
Cream and bring it to a boil. Remove from the heat and add the
cheeses, onion, lemon juice, mustard, parsley, and carrots. Press the
steamed spinach between layers of paper towels to remove any
excess moisture.
2. Mix together the spinach, smoked trout, cod, and egg; put into a
baking dish treated with nonstick spray. Pour the cheese mixture over
the fish mixture.
3. In a food processor, combine the steamed potatoes, olive oil, and seasonings (if using), and pulse until the potatoes are coarsely mashed.
Spread the potatoes over the top of the fish mixture. Bake for 25 to
30 minutes, or until the potatoes are golden.

| | |
|---|---|
| Beef Broth: Easy Slow-Cooker Method | 146 |
| Stovetop Grilled Beef Loin | 147 |
| The Ultimate Grilled Cheeseburger Sandwich | 148 |
| Kovbasa (Ukrainian Kielbasa) | 149 |
| Kielbasa | 149 |
| Italian Sausage | 150 |
| Italian Sweet Fennel Sausage | 151 |
| Mock Chorizo 1 | 152 |
| Mock Chorizo 2 | 153 |
| Mock Chorizo Moussaka | 154 |
| Rich Sausage Gravy | 155 |
| Slow-Cooker Pork with Plum Sauce | 156 |
| Warm Pork Salad | 156 |
| Cinnamon Grilled Pork Tenderloin | 157 |
| Fruited Pork Loin Roast Casserole | 158 |
| White Wine and Lemon Pork Roast | 159 |
| Pecan-Crusted Roast Pork Loin | 160 |
| Main Dish Pork and Beans | 161 |
| Ham and Artichoke Hearts Scalloped Potatoes | 162 |
| Slow-Cooked Venison | 163 |
| Slow-Cooker Venison BBQ | 164 |
| Venison with Dried Cranberry Vinegar Sauce | 165 |
| Easy Venison Stovetop Casserole | 166 |
| Venison Liverwurst | 167 |

# Beef Broth: Easy Slow-Cooker Method

| Yields about |
| :---: |
| **3 cups broth** |
| **Serving size: ½ cup** |

| Nutritional Analysis (per serving): | |
| :--- | ---: |
| Calories: | 57.52 |
| Protein: | 8.95 g |
| Carbohydrate: | 0.00 g |
| Fat: | 2.15 g |
| Sat. Fat: | 0.73 g |
| Cholesterol: | 27.20 mg |
| Sodium: | 14.45 mg |
| Fiber: | 0.00 g |
| PCF Ratio: | 65-0-35 |

| Exchange Approx.: |
| :---: |
| 1 Lean Meat |

1 pound lean round steak
1 onion, chopped
2 carrots, peeled and chopped
2 celery stalks and leaves, chopped
1 bay leaf

4 sprigs parsley
6 black peppercorns
¼ cup dry white wine
4½ cups water

1. Cut the beef into several pieces and add it to the slow cooker with all of the other ingredients. Use the high setting until the mixture reaches a boil, then reduce the heat to low. Allow to simmer, covered, overnight, or up to 16 hours.

2. Remove beef and drain on paper towels to absorb any fat. Strain the broth, discarding the meat and vegetables. (You don't want to eat vegetables cooked directly with the beef because they will have absorbed too much of the residue fat.) Put the broth in a covered container and refrigerate for several hours or overnight; this allows time for the fat to congeal on top of the broth. Remove the hardened fat and discard. (When you remove the fat from the broth, the Exchange Approximation for it will be a Free Exchange.)

**TIP:** *Broth will keep in the refrigerator for a few days. Freeze any that you won't use within that time.*

### Trade Secrets

*Some chefs swear that a hearty beef broth requires oven-roasted bones. Place bones on a roasting tray and bake them in a 425-degree oven for 30 to 60 minutes. Blot the fat from the bones before adding them to the rest of the broth ingredients. You may need to reduce the amount of water in your slow cooker, which will produce a more concentrated broth.*

# Stovetop Grilled Beef Loin

1 Laura's Lean Beef tenderloin
    fillet, no more than 1 inch
    thick
½ teaspoon paprika
1½ teaspoons garlic powder
⅛ teaspoon cracked black
    pepper
¼ teaspoon onion powder

Pinch to ⅛ teaspoon cayenne
    pepper (according to taste)
⅛ teaspoon dried oregano
⅛ teaspoon dried thyme
½ teaspoon brown sugar
½ teaspoon olive oil

**Yields 1 (5-ounce) loin
Serving size: 1 ounce**

| Nutritional Analysis (per serving): | |
| --- | --- |
| Calories: | 42.13 |
| Protein: | 6.00 g |
| Carbohydrate: | 0.56 g |
| Fat: | 1.69 g |
| Sat. Fat: | 0.58 g |
| Cholesterol: | 16.25 mg |
| Sodium: | 11.47 mg |
| Fiber: | 0.00 g |
| PCF Ratio: | 58-5-37 |

**Exchange Approx.:**
1 Lean Meat

1. Remove the loin from the refrigerator 30 minutes before you plan to prepare it to allow it to come to room temperature. Pat the meat dry with paper towels.
2. Mix together all the dry ingredients. Rub ¼ teaspoon of the olive oil on each side of the fillet. (The olive oil is used in this recipe to help the "rub" adhere to the meat and to aid in the caramelization process.) Divide the seasoning mixture and rub it into each oiled side.
3. Heat a grill pan on high for 1 or 2 minutes until the pan is sizzling hot. Place the beef fillet in the pan, reduce the heat to medium-high, and cook for 3 minutes. Use tongs to turn the fillet. (Be careful not to pierce the meat.) Cook for another 2 minutes for medium or 3 for well done.
4. Remove from heat and let the meat "rest" in the pan for at least 5 minutes, allowing the juices to redistribute throughout the meat and complete the cooking process—which makes for a juicier fillet.

## Weights and Measures: Before and After

*Exchanges are based on cooking weight of meats; however, in the case of lean pork loin trimmed of all fat, very little weight is lost during the cooking process. Therefore, the amounts given for raw pork loin in the recipes equal the cooked weights. If you find your cooking method causes more variation in weight, adjust accordingly.*

# The Ultimate Grilled Cheeseburger Sandwich

| Serves 4 |
| --- |

| Nutritional Analysis (per serving): | |
| --- | --- |
| Calories: | 261.97 |
| Protein: | 16.94 g |
| Carbohydrate: | 15.39 g |
| Fat: | 14.54 g |
| Sat. Fat: | 5.40 g |
| Cholesterol: | 60.19 mg |
| Sodium: | 186.96 mg |
| Fiber: | 1.22 g |
| PCF Ratio: | 26-24-50 |

**Exchange Approx.:**
2 Lean Meats,
1 Fat,
1 Bread/Starch

1 tablespoon olive oil
1 teaspoon butter
2 thick slices of 7-grain bread
 (see page 78)
1 ounce Cheddar cheese
½ pound (8 ounces) ground round
Fresh minced garlic to taste

Balsamic vinegar to taste
Worcestershire sauce
 (see Homemade recipe,
 page 40) to taste
Toppings of your choice, such as
 stone-ground mustard, mayonnaise, and so on

1. Preheat your indoor grill. Combine the olive oil and butter, then use half of the mixture to "butter" 1 side of each slice of bread. Place the Cheddar cheese on the unbuttered side of 1 slice of bread and top with the other slice, buttered side up.
2. Combine the ground round with the Worcestershire sauce, garlic, and balsamic vinegar, if using. Shape the ground round into a large, rectangular patty, a little larger than a slice of the bread. Grill the patty and then the cheese sandwich. (If you are using a large indoor grill, position the hamburger at the lower end, near the area where the fat drains; grill the cheese sandwich at the higher end.)
3. Once the cheese sandwich is done, separate the slices of bread, being careful not to burn yourself on the cheese. Top 1 slice with the hamburger and add your choice of condiments and fixin's.

TIP: *Allow for your choice of condiments and side dishes when you calculate additional Exchange Approximations, fats, and calories. For lean, organic (and delicious!) beef, check out Laura's Lean Beef. For information, go to ✐www.laurasleanbeef.com.*

### The Olive Oil Factor

*Once you've used an olive oil and butter mixture to "butter" the bread for a toasted or grilled sandwich, you'll never want to use just plain butter again! The olive oil helps make the bread crunchier and imparts a subtle taste difference to the sandwich as well.*

# Kovbasa (Ukrainian Kielbasa)

1 pound (16 ounces) pork shoulder
½ pound (8 ounces) beef chuck
1 teaspoon freshly ground black
   pepper
½ teaspoon ground allspice

1 teaspoon garlic powder
1 teaspoon peperivka (spiced
   whiskey; see step 1 following)
Kosher **or** sea salt to taste
   (optional)

1. To prepare the peperivka, put 1 teaspoon of bourbon in a microwave-safe bowl and add a pinch of dried red pepper flakes. Microwave on high for 15 seconds, or until the mixture is hot. Set aside to cool.
2. Remove all the fat from the meat. Cut the meat into cubes, put them in a food processor and grind to desired consistency. Add all the remaining ingredients, including the cooled peperivka, and mix until well blended. The traditional preparation method calls for putting the sausage mixture in casings; however, it works equally well when broiled or grilled as fresh sausage patties.

**Yields 1½ pounds**
**(24 ounces)**
**Serving size: 1 ounce**

**Nutritional Analysis**
**(per serving):**

| | |
|---|---|
| Calories: | 70.18 |
| Protein: | 7.99 g |
| Carbohydrate: | 0.00 g |
| Fat: | 3.95 g |
| Sat. Fat: | 1.50 g |
| Cholesterol: | 24.56 mg |
| Sodium: | 15.02 mg |
| Fiber: | 0.00 g |
| PCF Ratio: | 47-0-53 |

**Exchange Approx.:**
1 Medium-Fat Meat

# Kielbasa

1 pound (16 ounces) pork
   shoulder
½ pound (8 ounces) beef chuck
2 teaspoons minced garlic
1 tablespoon brown sugar
1 teaspoon freshly ground
   black pepper

½ teaspoon ground allspice
1 teaspoon fresh marjoram
Sea **or** kosher salt (optional)

Remove all fat from the meat. Cut the meat into cubes, put them in a food processor, and grind to desired consistency. Add the remaining ingredients and mix until well blended. You can put the sausage mixture in casings, but it works equally well broiled or grilled as patties.

**Yields 1½ pounds**
**(24 ounces)**
**Serving size: 1 ounce**

**Nutritional Analysis**
**(per serving, without salt):**

| | |
|---|---|
| Calories: | 72.21 |
| Protein: | 8.00 g |
| Carbohydrate: | 0.64 g |
| Fat: | 3.95 g |
| Sat. Fat: | 1.50 g |
| Cholesterol: | 24.56 mg |
| Sodium: | 15.28 mg |
| Fiber: | 0.00 g |
| PCF Ratio: | 46-4-51 |

**Exchange Approx.:**
1 Medium-Fat Meat

# Italian Sausage

**Yields about 2 pounds**
(32 ounces)
**Serving size: 1 ounce**

**Nutritional Analysis**
**(per serving, without salt):**

| | |
|---|---|
| Calories: | 67.72 |
| Protein: | 7.72 g |
| Carbohydrate: | 0.00 g |
| Fat: | 3.86 g |
| Sat. Fat: | 1.45 g |
| Cholesterol: | 22.67 mg |
| Sodium: | 13.60 mg |
| Fiber: | 0.00 g |
| PCF Ratio: | 47-0-53 |

**Exchange Approx.:**
1 Medium-Fat Meat

2 pounds (32 ounces) pork shoulder
1 teaspoon ground black pepper
1 teaspoon dried parsley
1 teaspoon Italian-style seasoning
1 teaspoon garlic powder
¾ teaspoon crushed anise seeds
⅛ teaspoon crushed red pepper flakes
½ teaspoon paprika
½ teaspoon instant minced onion flakes
1 teaspoon kosher **or** sea salt (optional)

Remove all fat from the meat. Cut the meat into cubes, put them in a food processor, and grind to desired consistency. Add the remaining ingredients and mix until well blended. You can put the sausage mixture in casings, but it works equally well broiled or grilled as patties.

## Simple (and Smart!) Substitutions

*Game meats—buffalo, venison, elk, moose—are low in fat, as are ground chicken or turkey. Substitute one of those meats for the pork in any of the sausage recipes in this chapter.*

# Italian Sweet Fennel Sausage

2 pounds (32 ounces) pork butt
½ teaspoon black pepper
1¼ teaspoons fennel seeds
¼ teaspoon cayenne pepper
2½ teaspoons crushed garlic

1 tablespoon sugar
1 teaspoon kosher **or** sea salt
  (optional)

1. Toast the fennel seeds and cayenne pepper in a nonstick skillet over medium heat, stirring constantly, until the seeds just begin to darken, about 2 minutes. Set aside.
2. Remove all fat from the meat. Cut the meat into cubes, put them in a food processor, and grind to desired consistency. Add the remaining ingredients and mix until well blended. You can put the sausage mixture in casings, but it works equally well broiled or grilled as patties.

### ℃ "Better the Second Day"

*Ideally, sausage is made the night before and refrigerated to allow the flavors to merge. Leftover sausage can be frozen for up to 3 months.*

| Yields about 2 pounds (32 ounces) Serving size: 1 ounce | |
|---|---|
| **Nutritional Analysis (per serving, without salt):** | |
| Calories: | 69.57 |
| Protein: | 7.73 g |
| Carbohydrate: | 0.47 g |
| Fat: | 3.86 g |
| Sat. Fat: | 1.45 g |
| Cholesterol: | 22.67 mg |
| Sodium: | 13.64 mg |
| Fiber: | 0.00 g |
| PCF Ratio: | 46-3-51 |
| **Exchange Approx.:** 1 Medium-Fat Meat | |

# Mock Chorizo 1

**Yields about 2 pounds**
**(32 ounces)**
**Serving size: 1 ounce**

### Nutritional Analysis
### (per serving, without salt):

| | |
|---|---|
| Calories: | 68.28 |
| Protein: | 7.73 g |
| Carbohydrate: | 0.17 g |
| Fat: | 3.86 g |
| Sat. Fat: | 1.45 g |
| Cholesterol: | 22.67 mg |
| Sodium: | 13.65 mg |
| Fiber: | 0.00 g |
| PCF Ratio: | 47-1-52 |

**Exchange Approx.:**
1 Medium-Fat Meat

*2 pounds (32 ounces) lean pork*
*4 tablespoons chili powder*
*¼ teaspoon ground cloves*
*2 tablespoons paprika*
*2½ teaspoons crushed fresh garlic*
*1 teaspoon crushed, dried oregano*
*3½ tablespoons cider vinegar*
*1 teaspoon kosher or sea salt (optional)*

1. Remove all fat from the meat. Cut the meat into cubes, put them in a food processor, and grind to desired consistency. Add the remaining ingredients and mix until well blended.
2. Tradition calls for aging this sausage in an airtight container in the refrigerator for 4 days before cooking. Leftover sausage can be stored in the freezer for up to 3 months.

### Break from Tradition

*Traditionally, chorizo is very high in fat. The chorizo recipes in this chapter are lower-fat alternatives. They make excellent replacements for adding flavor to recipes that call for bacon. In fact, 1 or 2 ounces of chorizo can replace an entire pound of bacon in cabbage, bean, or potato soup.*

# Mock Chorizo 2

1 pound (16 ounces) lean pork
2 tablespoons white wine vinegar
1 tablespoon dry sherry
2 teaspoons paprika
2 teaspoons chili powder
½ teaspoon dried oregano
¼ teaspoon ground cumin
½ teaspoon freshly ground
    black pepper
⅛ teaspoon ground cinnamon
⅛ teaspoon ground cloves
Pinch of ground coriander
Pinch of ground ginger
2 cloves garlic, crushed
Kosher **or** sea salt to taste
    (optional)

| Yields about 1 pound (16 ounces) Serving size: 1 ounce | |
| --- | --- |
| **Nutritional Analysis (per serving, without salt or soy sauce):** | |
| Calories: | 70.05 |
| Protein: | 7.75 g |
| Carbohydrate: | 0.37 g |
| Fat: | 3.86 g |
| Sat. Fat: | 1.45 g |
| Cholesterol: | 22.67 mg |
| Sodium: | 13.78 mg |
| Fiber: | 0.00 g |
| PCF Ratio: | 46-2-52 |
| **Exchange Approx.:** 1 Medium-Fat Meat | |

1. Remove all fat from the meat. Cut the meat into cubes, put them in a food processor, and grind to desired consistency. Add the remaining ingredients and mix until well blended.
2. Age the sausage in an airtight container in the refrigerator for 4 days. Leftover sausage can be stored in the freezer for up to 3 months.

**TIP:** *For a Chorizo stir-fry, consider decreasing the chili powder, adding some soy sauce or Bragg's Liquid Aminos, and increasing the garlic and ginger.*

# Mock Chorizo Moussaka

| Serves 4 |
| :---: |

**Nutritional Analysis (per serving):**

| | |
| :--- | ---: |
| Calories: | 244.31 |
| Protein: | 17.41 g |
| Carbohydrate: | 25.93 g |
| Fat: | 8.15 g |
| Sat. Fat: | 2.73 g |
| Cholesterol: | 110.88 mg |
| Sodium: | 132.11 mg |
| Fiber: | 4.08 g |
| PCF Ratio: | 28-42-30 |

**Exchange Approx.:**
1 Medium-Fat Meat,
1 Very Lean Meat,
½ Fat, 1½ Vegetables,
1 Starch

2 ounces Mock Chorizo
(see page 153)
2 cups peeled, seeded, and
chopped eggplant
2 cups peeled, seeded, and
chopped zucchini
4 small potatoes, peeled and
thinly sliced
2 eggs

4 tablespoons grated Parmesan
cheese, divided
1 cup nonfat cottage cheese
1 teaspoon Ener-G potato flour
2 teaspoons olive oil
1 teaspoon dried dill
1 teaspoon dried parsley
Pinch of nutmeg

1. Preheat oven to 350 degrees. Broil or grill the chorizo and set aside to drain on paper towels.
2. In a covered microwave-safe bowl, microwave the eggplant and zucchini on high for 5 minutes, or until they are steaming and just barely beginning to soften; drain and blot dry with paper towels. In a covered microwave-safe bowl, microwave the potatoes on high for 5 minutes. Set aside, covered, and allow the potatoes to steam.
3. In a bowl, beat the eggs with 2 tablespoons of the Parmesan cheese, stir in the eggplant and zucchini, and set aside.
4. Put the cottage cheese, potato flour, and the remaining Parmesan cheese in a blender or food processor and process until smooth.
5. To assemble the moussaka, treat a casserole dish with nonstick spray. Drain any moisture from the potatoes and pat dry with a paper towel, if necessary. Toss the potatoes with the olive oil and then layer them across the bottom of the casserole dish. Sprinkle the dill and parsley over the potatoes. Spread the vegetable-egg mixture over the top of the potatoes. Crumble the cooked chorizo over the top of the vegetables. Spread the cottage cheese mixture over the meat. Sprinkle nutmeg over the top of the casserole. Bake, uncovered, for 20 to 30 minutes, or until hot and bubbly.

# Rich Sausage Gravy

1 cup nonfat cottage cheese
1 cup Mock Cream
   (see page 42)
2 ounces Kovbasa
   (see page 149)

2 teaspoons olive oil
1 tablespoon flour
Salt and black pepper to taste
   (optional)

| Serves 4 | |
|---|---|
| **Nutritional Analysis (per serving, without salt):** | |
| Calories: | 120.86 |
| Protein: | 13.30 g |
| Carbohydrate: | 6.31 g |
| Fat: | 4.51 g |
| Sat. Fat: | 1.23 g |
| Cholesterol: | 16.32 mg |
| Sodium: | 56.18 mg |
| Fiber: | 0.05 g |
| PCF Ratio: | 45-21-34 |

**Exchange Approx.:**
1 Lean Meat,
½ Fat,
½ Skim Milk

1. In a blender or food processor, combine the cottage cheese and Mock Cream; process until smooth. Set aside.
2. In a nonstick skillet, fry the Kovbasa until done, breaking it into small pieces as you fry it. Add the olive oil and heat until sizzling. Stir in the flour, stirring constantly to create a roux. Gradually stir in some of the cottage cheese mixture, using the back of spatula or a whisk to blend it, stirring constantly to avoid "lumps." Once you have about ½ cup of the cottage cheese mixture blended into the roux, you can add the remaining amount.
3. Continue to cook, stirring constantly, until the mixture begins to steam. Lower the heat and allow the mixture to simmer (being careful that it doesn't come to a boil) until the gravy reaches the desired consistency.

# Slow-Cooker Pork with Plum Sauce

**Serves 4**

**Nutritional Analysis (per serving, with Bragg's Liquid Aminos):**

| | |
|---|---|
| Calories: | 125.08 |
| Protein: | 19.97 g |
| Carbohydrate: | 11.35 g |
| Fat: | 2.87 g |
| Sat. Fat: | 0.99 g |
| Cholesterol: | 35.72 mg |
| Sodium: | 147.84 mg |
| Fiber: | 0.00 g |
| PCF Ratio: | 42-37-21 |

**Exchange Approx.:**
2 Lean Meats,
½ Fruit

½ pound (8 ounces) cooked, shredded pork
1 clove garlic, crushed
½ teaspoon grated fresh ginger
⅛ cup apple juice
¼ teaspoon dry mustard

2 teaspoons Bragg's Liquid Aminos **or** soy sauce
⅛ teaspoon dried thyme
⅛ cup plum jam
½ teaspoon cornstarch

1. In a nonstick skillet treated with nonstick spray, stir-fry the pork, garlic, and ginger.
2. In a small bowl or measuring cup, combine the remaining ingredients to make a slurry; pour the mixture over the heated pork, mixing well. Cook over low to medium heat until the mixture thickens and the juice is absorbed into the pork.

# Warm Pork Salad

**Serves 2**

**Nutritional Analysis (per serving):**

| | |
|---|---|
| Calories: | 181.66 |
| Protein: | 14.13 g |
| Carbohydrate: | 24.59 g |
| Fat: | 3.51 g |
| Sat. Fat: | 1.08 g |
| Cholesterol: | 35.70 mg |
| Sodium: | 168.04 mg |
| Fiber: | 3.31 g |
| PCF Ratio: | 30-53-17 |

**Exchange Approx.:**
2 Lean Meats,
1 Fruit,
1 Vegetable

2 servings of Slow-Cooker Pork with Plum Sauce (see recipe on this page)
1 teaspoon cider vinegar
¼ teaspoon Dijon mustard
2 slices red onion

1 apple, peeled, cored, and sliced
2 cups coleslaw mix
4 drops toasted sesame oil
Dash of freshly ground black pepper

In a nonstick skillet treated with nonstick spray, stir-fry the leftover pork until warm. Add the vinegar and mustard, and mix until blended. Stir in the apple, onion, and coleslaw mix, then cover and cook for 2 minutes, or until the vegetables and apple just barely begin to soften. Serve warm, topping salads with two drops of the sesame oil and freshly ground black pepper.

# Cinnamon Grilled Pork Tenderloin

2 teaspoons Bragg's Liquid
   Aminos

2 teaspoons burgundy **or**
   red wine

1 teaspoon brown sugar

⅛ teaspoon honey

⅛ teaspoon garlic powder

⅛ teaspoon ground cinnamon

¼-pound (4-ounce) pork loin

| Serves 2 | |
|---|---|
| **Nutritional Analysis (per serving):** | |
| Calories: | 93.76 |
| Protein: | 13.4 g |
| Carbohydrate: | 11.44 g |
| Fat: | 3.59 g |
| Sat Fat: | 1.11 g |
| Cholesterol: | 33.45 mg |
| Sodium: | 387.05 mg |
| Fiber: | 0.00 g |
| PCF Ratio: | 56-11-33 |
| **Exchange Approx.:** | |
| 2 Lean Meats | |

Combine the first 6 ingredients in a large zip-top plastic bag. Add the roast and marinate in the refrigerator for at least 1 hour, or up to 6 hours. Grill tenderloins over hot coals until the thermometer reaches 160 degrees, turning while grilling. (Grilling time will depend on the thickness of the tenderloin. For example, a ¾" cut of pork grilled over medium-hot coals will take 12 to 14 minutes while a cut twice as thick, or a 1½" cut, can take more than half an hour.) Allow the meat to rest for up to 15 minutes, then slice thinly against the grain.

## Let It Set!

*Avoid the biggest cause of a dry roast! When you remove a roast from the oven, always allow it to rest for 10 minutes before you carve it. This allows the juices to redistribute through the roast (instead of draining out all over your cutting board).*

# Fruited Pork Loin Roast Casserole

| Serves 4 |
| --- |

**Nutritional Analysis (per serving):**

| | |
| --- | --- |
| Calories: | 169.78 |
| Protein: | 7.36 g |
| Carbohydrate: | 27.49 g |
| Fat: | 3.81 g |
| Sat. Fat: | 1.29 g |
| Cholesterol: | 18.99 mg |
| Sodium: | 32 mg |
| Fiber: | 2.82 g |
| PCF Ratio: | 17-63-20 |

**Exchange Approx.:**
1 Lean Meat,
1 Fruit,
1 Starch

*4 small Yukon Gold potatoes, peeled and sliced*
*2 (2-ounce) pieces trimmed boneless pork loin, pounded flat*
*1 apple, peeled, cored, and sliced*
*4 apricot halves*
*1 tablespoon chopped red onion **or** shallot*
*⅛ cup apple cider **or** apple juice*
*Optional seasonings to taste:*
*Olive oil*
*Parmesan cheese*
*Salt and freshly ground pepper*

1. Preheat oven to 350 degrees (325 degrees if using a glass casserole dish) and treat a casserole dish with nonstick spray.
2. Layer half of the potato slices across the bottom of the dish. Top with 1 piece of the flattened pork loin. Arrange the apple slices over the top of the loin and place the apricot halves on top of the apple. Sprinkle the red onion (or shallots) over the apricot and apples. Add the second flattened pork loin and layer the remaining potatoes atop the loin. Drizzle the apple cider (or apple juice) over the top of the casserole.
3. Cover and bake for 45 minutes to 1 hour, or until the potatoes are tender. Keep the casserole covered to let it set for 10 minutes after you remove it from the oven.

**TIP:** *To enhance the flavor of this dish, you can top it with the optional ingredients when it's served. Just be sure to make the appropriate Exchange Approximations adjustments if you do.*

 **Versatile Herbs**
*For a change of pace, you can substitute rosemary when thyme is called for in pork recipes.*

# White Wine and Lemon Pork Roast

1 clove garlic, crushed
½ cup dry white wine
1 tablespoon lemon juice
1 teaspoon olive oil
1 tablespoon minced red onion
   **or** shallots
¼ teaspoon dried thyme

⅛ teaspoon ground black
   pepper
½-pound (8-ounce) pork loin
   roast

| Serves 4 | |
|---|---|
| **Nutritional Analysis (per serving):** | |
| Calories: | 114.52 |
| Protein: | 12.29 g |
| Carbohydrate: | 1.13 g |
| Fat: | 4.35 g |
| Sat. Fat: | 1.26 g |
| Cholesterol: | 33.45 mg |
| Sodium: | 31.28 mg |
| Fiber: | 0.13 g |
| PCF Ratio: | 53-5-42 |

**Exchange Approx.:**
2 Lean Meats

1. Make the marinade by combining the first 7 ingredients in a heavy, freezer-style plastic bag. Add the roast and marinate in the refrigerator for an hour or overnight, according to taste. (Note: Pork loin is already tender, so you're marinating the meat to impart the flavors only.)
2. Preheat oven to 350 degrees. Remove meat from marinade and put on a nonstick spray–treated rack in a roasting pan. Roast for 20 to 30 minutes, or until the meat thermometer reads 150 to 170 degrees, depending on how well done you prefer it.

## Marmalade Marinade

Combine 1 teaspoon Dijon or stone-ground mustard, 1 tablespoon Smucker's Low-Sugar Orange Marmalade, 1 clove crushed garlic, and ¼ teaspoon dried thyme leaves. Marinate and prepare an ½-pound (8-ounce) pork loin as you would the White Wine and Lemon Pork Loin Roast. The Nutritional Analysis for a 2-ounce serving is: Calories: 89.52; Protein: 12.26 g; Carbohydrate: 1.90 g; Fat: 3.26 g; Sat. Fat: 1.11 g; Cholesterol: 33.45 mg; Sodium: 43.66 mg; Fiber: 0.09 g; PCF Ratio: 57-9-34. Exchange Approximations: 2 Lean Meats

# Pecan-Crusted Roast Pork Loin

| Serves 4 | |
|---|---|
| **Nutritional Analysis (per serving):** | |
| Calories: | 147.84 |
| Protein: | 12.88 g |
| Carbohydrate: | 2.39 g |
| Fat: | 9.69 g |
| Sat. Fat: | 1.72 g |
| Cholesterol: | 33.45 mg |
| Sodium: | 30.06 mg |
| Fiber: | 0.73 g |
| PCF Ratio: | 35-7-58 |

**Exchange Approx.:**
2 Lean Meats,
1 Fat

*1 teaspoon olive oil*
*1 clove garlic, crushed*
*1 teaspoon brown sugar*
*Thyme, sage, and pepper to taste (optional)*

*¼ cup chopped or ground pecans*
*½-pound (8-ounce) boneless pork loin roast*

1. Put the olive oil, crushed garlic, brown sugar, and seasonings (if using) in a heavy, freezer-style plastic bag. Work the bag until the ingredients are mixed. Add the roast and turn it in the bag to coat the meat. Marinate in the refrigerator for several hours or overnight.
2. Preheat oven to 400 degrees. Roll the pork loin in the chopped pecans and place it in a roasting pan. Make a tent of aluminum foil and arrange it over the pork loin, covering the nuts completely so that they won't char. Roast for 10 minutes, then lower the heat to 350 degrees. Continue to roast for another 8 to 15 minutes, or until the meat thermometer reads 150 to 170 degrees, depending on how well done you prefer it.

### Create a Celery Roasting Rack

*If you prefer to bake a loin roast in a casserole alongside potatoes and carrots, elevate the roast on 2 or 3 stalks of celery. The celery will absorb any fat that drains from the meat so that it's not absorbed by the other vegetables. Discard the celery.*

# Main Dish Pork and Beans

1 1/3 cups cooked pinto beans
2 tablespoons ketchup
1/4 teaspoon Dijon mustard
1/4 teaspoon dry mustard
1 teaspoon cider vinegar
4 tablespoons diced red onion
1 tablespoon 100 percent
   maple syrup

1 teaspoon brown sugar
1/4 pound (4 ounces) slow-
   cooked, shredded pork
1/8 cup (2 tablespoons) apple
   juice **or** cider

| Serves 4 | |
| --- | --- |
| **Nutritional Analysis (per serving):** | |
| Calories: | 153.41 |
| Protein: | 11.25 g |
| Carbohydrate: | 23.64 g |
| Fat: | 1.80 g |
| Sat. Fat: | 0.57 g |
| Cholesterol: | 17.86 mg |
| Sodium: | 145.79 mg |
| Fiber: | 5.22 g |
| PCF Ratio: | 29-61-10 |

**Exchange Approx.:**
2 Lean Meats,
1/2 Free,
1/2 Fruit/Misc. Carb.

1. Preheat oven to 350 degrees. In a casserole dish treated with nonstick spray, combine the first 8 ingredients. Layer the meat over the top of the bean mixture. Pour the apple juice (or cider) over the pork. Bake for 20 to 30 minutes, or until the mixture is well heated and bubbling. Stir well before serving.

TIP: *If you prefer thicker baked beans, after cooking, remove some of the beans and mash them. Stir them back into the dish.*

## Pork Broth

*For about 3 cups of broth, cook 1 pound lean pork shoulder or loin (cut into pieces) with 1 onion, 2 carrots, and 2 celery stalks (all chopped); 4 sprigs parsley, 6 peppercorns, 1/4 cup white wine, and 4 3/4 cups water in a slow-cooker. Use the high setting until mixture reaches a boil, then reduce heat to low. Allow to simmer overnight or up to 16 hours. Remove the pork, discard the vegetables, skim the fat, and freeze any broth you won't be using within a few days.*

# Ham and Artichoke Hearts Scalloped Potatoes

| | |
|---|---|
| 2 cups frozen artichoke hearts | ½ cup nonfat cottage cheese |
| 1 cup chopped onion | 1 teaspoon dried parsley |
| 4 small potatoes, thinly sliced | 1 teaspoon garlic powder |
| Sea salt and freshly ground black pepper to taste (optional) | ⅛ cup freshly grated Parmesan cheese |
| 1 tablespoon lemon juice | ¼ pound (4 ounces) lean ham, cubed |
| 1 tablespoon dry white wine | |
| 1 cup Mock Cream (see page 42) | 2 ounces Cheddar cheese, grated (to yield ½ cup) |

**Serves 4**

**Nutritional Analysis (per serving, without salt):**

| | |
|---|---|
| Calories: | 269.15 |
| Protein: | 21.49 g |
| Carbohydrate: | 30.65 g |
| Fat: | 7.58 g |
| Sat. Fat: | 4.14 g |
| Cholesterol: | 27.98 mg |
| Sodium: | 762.30 mg |
| Fiber: | 5.80 g |
| PCF Ratio: | 31-44-25 |

**Exchange Approx.:**
1½ Lean Meats,
½ High-Fat Meat,
1½ Vegetables,
1 Starch

1. Preheat oven to 300 degrees. Thaw the artichoke hearts and pat them dry with a paper towel. In a deep casserole dish treated with nonstick spray, layer the artichokes, onion, and potatoes, and lightly sprinkle salt and pepper over the top (if using).

2. In a food processor or blender, combine the lemon juice, wine, Mock Cream, cottage cheese, parsley, garlic powder, and Parmesan cheese, and process until smooth. Pour over the layered vegetables. Top with the ham. Cover the casserole dish (with a lid or foil) and bake for 35 to 40 minutes, or until the potatoes are cooked through.

3. Remove the cover and top with the Cheddar cheese. Return to the over for another 10 minutes, or until the cheese is melted and bubbly. Let rest 10 minutes before cutting.

TIP: *If you are on a sodium-restricted diet, use 4 ounces of 1 of the cooked sausage recipes in this chapter in place of the ham. Adjust the Exchange Approximations from 1 Lean Meat to 1 Medium-Fat Meat.*

## Simple Substitutions
*Artichoke hearts are expensive. You can substitute cabbage, broccoli, or cauliflower (or a mixture of all 3) for the artichokes.*

# Slow-Cooked Venison

*1lb. venison roast*
*1–2 tablespoons cider vinegar*

1. Put the venison into a ceramic-lined slow cooker, add enough water to cover, and add the vinegar; set on high. Once the mixture begins to boil, reduce temperature to low. Allow the meat to simmer for 8, or more, hours.
2. Drain the resulting broth from the meat and discard it. Remove any remaining fat from the meat and discard that as well. Weigh the meat and separate it into servings. The meat will keep for 1 or 2 days in the refrigerator, or freeze portions for use later.

## Use Quality Equipment

*Slow cookers with a ceramic interior maintain low temperatures better than do those with a metal cooking surface.*

| Yields about 1 pound Serving size: 1 ounce | |
|---|---|
| **Nutritional Analysis (per serving):** | |
| Calories: | 44.77 |
| Protein: | 8.56 g |
| Carbohydrate: | 0.00 g |
| Fat: | 0.90 g |
| Sat. Fat: | 0.35 g |
| Cholesterol: | 31.73 mg |
| Sodium: | 15.30 mg |
| Fiber: | 0.00 g |
| PCF Ratio: | 81-0-19 |
| **Exchange Approx.:** | |
| 1 Very Lean Meat | |

# Slow-Cooker Venison BBQ

| Serves 24 |
| :---: |

| Nutritional Analysis (per serving): ||
| :--- | ---: |
| Calories: | 58.68 |
| Protein: | 8.59 g |
| Carbohydrate: | 2.60 g |
| Fat: | 0.92 g |
| Sat. Fat: | 0.36 g |
| Cholesterol: | 31.73 mg |
| Sodium: | 92.36 mg |
| Fiber: | 0.02 g |
| PCF Ratio: | 65-20-16 |

**Exchange Approx.:**
1 Very Lean Meat,
1 Free Condiment

1½ pounds (24 ounces) Slow-Cooked Venison (see page 163)

1 cup water

½ cup dry white wine

½ cup Brooks Tangy Catsup

1 tablespoon red wine vinegar

1 tablespoon stone-ground mustard

1 tablespoon dried onion flakes

⅛ cup (2 tablespoons) Worcestershire sauce (see recipe for Homemade on page 40)

1 teaspoon dried minced garlic

1 teaspoon cracked black pepper

1 tablespoon brown sugar

Add the cooked venison to the slow cooker. Mix all the remaining ingredients together and pour over the venison. Add additional water, if necessary, to completely cover the meat. Set the slow cooker on high until the mixture begins to boil. Reduce heat to low and simmer for 2 or more hours. Adjust seasonings, if necessary.

 **Game Over**

*Instead of using the slow-cooker method to remove any gamy flavor from game meats, soak it in milk or tomato juice overnight. Drain the meat, and discard the soaking liquid.*

# Venison with
# Dried Cranberry Vinegar Sauce

⅛ cup (2 tablespoons) dried
    cranberries

1 tablespoon sugar

3 tablespoons water

⅛ cup (2 tablespoons) cham-
    pagne **or** white wine vinegar

2 teaspoons olive oil

1 tablespoon minced shallots **or**
    red onion

⅛ cup (2 tablespoons) dry
    red wine

1 teaspoon minced garlic

½ cup low-fat, reduced-sodium
    chicken broth

½ teaspoon cracked black pepper

½ pound (8 ounces) Slow-Cooked
    Venison (see page 163)

1 teaspoon cornstarch **or** potato
    flour

2 teaspoons butter

| Serves 4 |  |
| --- | --- |
| **Nutritional Analysis (per serving, without cornstarch or flour):** | |
| Calories: | 154.14 |
| Protein: | 17.48 g |
| Carbohydrate: | 4.36 g |
| Fat: | 6.05 g |
| Sat. Fat: | 2.23 g |
| Cholesterol: | 68.64 mg |
| Sodium: | 76.56 mg |
| Fiber: | 0.07 g |
| PCF Ratio: | 49-12-38 |

**Exchange Approx.:**
3 Very Low-Fat Meats,
1 Fat

1. Add the cranberries, sugar, water, and champagne (or vinegar) to a saucepan, and bring to a boil. Reduce the heat and simmer for 5 minutes. Remove from heat and transfer to a food processor or blender; process until the cranberries are chopped; it isn't necessary to purée because you want some cranberry "chunks" to remain. Set aside.

2. Pour the olive oil into a heated nonstick skillet; add the shallots and garlic, and sauté for 30 seconds. Deglaze the pan with the red wine, and cook, stirring occasionally, until the wine is reduced by half. Add the cranberry mixture and the chicken broth, and bring to a boil. Reduce the heat to medium-low, season with the pepper, add the venison, and simmer for 3 minutes, or until the meat is heated through.

3. Thicken the sauce, using a slurry of cornstarch or potato flour and 1 tablespoon of water; simmer until the sauce thickens. You'll need to cook the sauce a bit longer if you use cornstarch in order to remove the "starchy" taste. Remove from the heat, add the butter, and whisk to incorporate the butter into the sauce.

## Operate Your Appliances Safely

*When puréeing hot mixtures, leave the vent uncovered on your food processor. If using a blender, either remove the vent cover from the lid or leave the lid ajar so the steam can escape.*

# Easy Venison Stovetop Casserole

| Serves 4 | |
|---|---|
| **Nutritional Analysis (per serving):** | |
| Calories: | 227.47 |
| Protein: | 19.22 g |
| Carbohydrate: | 21.50 g |
| Fat: | 4.20 g |
| Sat. Fat: | 1.52 g |
| Cholesterol: | 66.06 mg |
| Sodium: | 251.23 mg |
| Fiber: | 2.90 g |
| PCF Ratio: | 38-43-19 |

**Exchange Approx.:**
2 Very Lean Meats,
1 Vegetable,
1 Fruit,
1 Fat

1 teaspoon olive oil
1 teaspoon butter
½ cup no-salt-added tomato purée
¾ cup dry red wine
2 tablespoons red currant jelly
¼ cup low-fat, reduced-sodium chicken broth
1 cup chopped **or** sliced sweet onion
1 cup thinly sliced carrots
½ pound (8 ounces) Slow-Cooked Venison (see page 163)

1 teaspoon arrowroot
1 tablespoon water
Freshly ground pepper to taste
⅛ cup (2 tablespoons) lemon juice
Optional garnish:
4 thin lemon slices
Fresh parsley sprigs

1. Heat the olive oil and butter in a deep, nonstick skillet. Add the tomato purée and sauté until brown. Add the red wine, red currant jelly, and chicken broth. Add the vegetables and venison, and stir to coat. Bring to a boil; reduce heat, cover, and simmer for 1 hour. Transfer the meat and vegetables to heated serving dish.

2. Mix the arrowroot with the water, and whisk it into the simmering pan juices to thicken. Season with pepper and stir in the lemon juice. Pour over the meat and vegetables. Garnish with lemon slices and parsley, if desired.

# Venison Liverwurst

1 (8" × 12") piece of
   unbleached muslin
1 pound (16 ounces) fresh
   pork liver
1 pound (16 ounces) lean
   venison, trimmed of any fat
1 large sweet white onion
   (about 1½ cups, finely diced)
3 tablespoons nonfat milk
   powder
2 teaspoons paprika

1 teaspoon freshly fine-ground
   white pepper
1½ teaspoons (or to taste)
   kosher **or** sea salt (optional)
1 teaspoon sugar
½ teaspoon marjoram
½ teaspoon finely ground
   coriander
¼ teaspoon mace
¼ teaspoon allspice
¼ teaspoon ground cardamom

| Yields 2 pounds (32 ounces) Serving size: 1 ounce | |
| --- | --- |
| **Nutritional Analysis (per serving, without salt):** | |
| Calories: | 58.57 |
| Protein: | 10.09 g |
| Carbohydrate: | 0.95 g |
| Fat: | 1.30 g |
| Sat. Fat: | 0.46 g |
| Cholesterol: | 78.23 mg |
| Sodium: | 31.66 mg |
| Fiber: | 0.00 g |
| PCF Ratio: | 72-7-21 |

**Exchange Approx.:**
½ Lean Meat,
½ Medium-Fat Meat

1. In place of casings, prepare the muslin: Fold the muslin in half length-wise and tightly stitch a seam across 1 of the short ends and continue along the open long side. The seam should be about an eighth of an inch from the edge of the material. Turn the muslin casing so that the stitching is on the inside. Set it aside until you are ready to stuff it.
2. Run the liver and venison through a meat grinder using the fine disk. (Alternatively, cut the meat into cubes and freeze for 20 minutes. Add the semi-frozen cubes to the bowl of your food processor and pulse until ground.) Mix well to combine the liver and venison. Transfer the ground meat to a bowl, sprinkle the remaining ingredients over the ground meat, and mix thoroughly.
3. Firmly pack the mixture into the muslin casing. (It's easier to get the meat packed to the bottom of the casing if you first fold the open end down over itself.) Secure the open end with a wire twist tie, butcher's twine, or cotton cord.
4. Bring enough water to a boil to cover the liverwurst in the muslin packet by 2 or 3 inches. Place a weight—such as a heavy plate—on it to keep it submerged. Bring the water to a boil, reduce the heat, and simmer for 3 hours. Transfer the muslin packet to a pan of ice water. When the liverwurst has cooled, refrigerate it overnight, and then remove the muslin casing. Slice into 1-ounce portions to serve. Liverwurst can be stored in the refrigerator for up to 10 days.

# CHAPTER 10
# *Pasta and Pizza*

| | |
|---|---|
| Quick Tomato Sauce | 170 |
| Basic Tomato Sauce | 171 |
| Uncooked Tomato Sauce | 172 |
| Fusion Lo Mein | 173 |
| Roasted Butternut Squash Pasta | 174 |
| Pasta with Artichokes | 175 |
| Pasta with Creamed Clam Sauce | 176 |
| Pasta with Tuna Alfredo Sauce | 177 |
| Pasta Fagioli | 178 |
| Macaroni Casserole | 179 |
| Bleu Cheese Pasta | 180 |

# Quick Tomato Sauce

| Serves 8 |
| --- |

### Nutritional Analysis
### (per serving, without salt):

| | |
| --- | --- |
| Calories: | 39.85 |
| Protein: | 1.01 g |
| Carbohydrate: | 5.51 g |
| Fat: | 2.07 g |
| Sat. Fat: | 0.28 g |
| Cholesterol: | 0.00 mg |
| Sodium: | 10.33 mg |
| Fiber: | 1.26 g |
| PCF Ratio: | 9-49-42 |

**Exchange Approx.:**
1 Vegetable,
½ Fat

2 pounds very ripe tomatoes
2 tablespoons extra-virgin olive oil
2 cloves garlic, minced
½ teaspoon ground cumin
2 large sprigs fresh thyme,
   **or** ½ teaspoon dried thyme
1 bay leaf
Kosher **or** sea salt and freshly
   ground black pepper to taste
   (optional)

3 tablespoons total of chopped
   fresh basil, oregano, tarragon, and parsley **or**
   cilantro; **or**, a combination of
   all the listed herbs according
   to taste. If using dried herbs,
   reduce the amount to
   1 tablespoon

1. Peel and seed the tomatoes; chop them with a knife or food processor.
2. Heat a large skillet and add the olive oil. Reduce the heat to low and sauté the garlic and cumin. Add the tomatoes, thyme, bay leaf, salt and pepper, if using. If you are using dried herbs, add them now. Simmer, uncovered, over medium heat for 8 to 10 minutes, stirring often; reduce the heat to maintain a simmer, if necessary. Simmer until the tomatoes are soft and the sauce has thickened. Discard the bay leaf and thyme sprigs. Adjust the seasoning to taste. If you are using fresh herbs, add them just before serving. This sauce is delicious served hot or cold.

 **Remember . . .**
*The addition of ¼ teaspoon of granulated sugar in tomato sauce helps cut the acidity of the tomatoes without affecting the Exchange Approximations for the recipe.*

# Basic Tomato Sauce

2 tablespoons olive oil
2 cups coarsely chopped
    yellow onion
½ cup sliced carrots
2 cloves garlic, minced
4 cups canned Italian plum
    tomatoes with juice
1 teaspoon dried oregano
1 teaspoon dried basil

¼ teaspoon sugar
Kosher **or** sea salt and freshly
    ground black pepper to
    taste (optional)
Dash of ground anise seed
    (optional)

**Yields about 5 cups**
**Serving size: ¼ cup**

| Nutritional Analysis (per serving, without salt): | |
|---|---|
| Calories: | 36.54 |
| Protein: | 0.86 g |
| Carbohydrate: | 5.49 g |
| Fat: | 1.60 g |
| Sat. Fat: | 0.22 g |
| Cholesterol: | 0.00 mg |
| Sodium: | 8.54 mg |
| Fiber: | 0.91 g |
| PCF Ratio: | 9-55-36 |

**Exchange Approx.:**
1½ Vegetables

Heat the olive oil in a large, deep skillet or saucepan over medium-high heat. Add the onions, carrots, and garlic; sauté until the onions are transparent. (For a richer-tasting sauce, allow the onions to caramelize or reach a light golden brown.) Purée the tomatoes in a food processor. Add the tomatoes, herbs, and sugar to the onion mixture along with the salt, pepper, and anise, if using. Simmer, partially covered, for 45 minutes. Process the sauce in the food processor again if you prefer a smoother sauce.

## Culinary Antacids

*Stir in a 2 teaspoons of Smucker's Low-Sugar Grape Jelly to tame hot chili or acidic sauce. You won't really notice the flavor of the jelly, and it will do a great job of reducing any tart, bitter, or acidic tastes in your sauce.*

# Uncooked Tomato Sauce

| Serves 4 |
|:---:|

| Nutritional Analysis (per serving, without salt): | |
|:---|:---:|
| Calories: | 94 |
| Protein: | 2.27 g |
| Carbohydrate: | 11.95 g |
| Fat: | 5.30 g |
| Sat. Fat: | 0.72 g |
| Cholesterol: | 0.00 mg |
| Sodium: | 21.84 mg |
| Fiber: | 2.89 g |
| PCF Ratio: | 9-46-46 |

**Exchange Approx.:**
2 Vegetables,
1 Fat

½ cup fresh basil leaves, divided

2 pounds firm ripe tomatoes, peeled, seeded, and chopped

2 cloves garlic, minced

4 tablespoons thinly sliced scallions (white and green parts)

2 tablespoons minced fresh parsley

4 teaspoons extra-virgin olive oil

1½ teaspoons red wine vinegar or lemon juice

¼ teaspoon sugar

Kosher or sea salt and freshly ground black pepper to taste (optional)

1. Chop half the basil leaves and set the rest aside until later.
2. In a large bowl combine the chopped basil, tomatoes, garlic, scallions, parsley, olive oil, and vinegar (or lemon juice). Let the mixture sit at room temperature for at least 4 hours, but no more than 6, then season with salt and pepper, if using. Garnish with the remaining basil.

### English Muffin Pizzas

*Top each half of an English muffin with your choice of tomato sauce. Add chopped, free-choice vegetables. Divide 1 ounce of grated mozzarella cheese between the muffin halves. Bake in a 400-degree oven until the cheese bubbles, and you have a meal with 2 Carbohydrate/Starch Exchanges and 1 Medium-Fat Meat Exchange, plus the Exchange Approximation for your choice of sauce.*

# Fusion Lo Mein

2 tablespoons rice vinegar

2 tablespoons thawed
  pineapple-orange juice

2 teaspoons minced shallots

2 teaspoons lemon juice

1 teaspoon cornstarch

1 teaspoon Worcestershire
  sauce (see recipe for
  Homemade on page 40)

1 teaspoon honey

2 cloves garlic, minced

1 teaspoon olive oil

$^3/_4$ cup chopped green onions

1 cup diagonally sliced ($^1/_4$-inch
  thick) carrots

1 cup julienned yellow bell
  pepper

1 cup julienned red bell pepper

3 cups small broccoli florets

1 cup fresh bean sprouts

1 $^1/_2$ cups cooked pasta

| Serves 6 | |
|---|---|
| **Nutritional Analysis (per serving):** | |
| Calories: | 126.06 |
| Protein: | 4.62 g |
| Carbohydrate: | 26.06 g |
| Fat: | 1.34 g |
| Sat. Fat: | 0.19 g |
| Cholesterol: | 0.00 mg |
| Sodium: | 35.29 mg |
| Fiber: | 4.18 g |
| PCF Ratio: | 14-77-9 |

**Exchange Approx.:**
1 Carb./Starch,
1 Vegetable,
½ Fruit

1. In a food processor or blender, combine the vinegar, juice concentrate, shallots, lemon juice, cornstarch, Worcestershire, honey, and garlic; process until smooth.

2. Heat a wok or large nonstick skillet coated with cooking spray over medium-high heat until hot, then add the olive oil. Add the onions and stir-fry for 1 minute. Add the carrots, bell peppers, and broccoli, and stir-fry for another minute. Cover the pan and cook for 2 more minutes. Add the vinegar mixture and the sprouts. Bring the mixture to a boil and cook, uncovered, for 30 seconds, stirring constantly. Add the cooked pasta and toss to mix.

# Roasted Butternut Squash Pasta

| Serves 4 |
| --- |

**Nutritional Analysis (per serving):**

| | |
| --- | --- |
| Calories: | 216.65 |
| Protein: | 5.23 g |
| Carbohydrate: | 39.81 g |
| Fat: | 5.18 g |
| Sat. Fat: | 0.71 g |
| Cholesterol: | 0.00 mg |
| Sodium: | 8.20 mg |
| Fiber: | 1.93 g |
| PCF Ratio: | 9-70-21 |

**Exchange Approx.:**
1 Starch
1 Carb./Starch,
1 Fat, ½ Vegetable

1 butternut squash
4 teaspoons extra-virgin olive
   oil
1 clove garlic, minced
1 cup chopped red onion
2 teaspoons red wine vinegar

¼ teaspoon dried oregano
2 cups cooked pasta
Freshly ground black pepper
   (optional)

1. Preheat oven to 400 degrees. Cut the squash in half and scoop out the seeds. Using nonstick spray, coat 1 side of each of 2 pieces of heavy-duty foil large enough to wrap the squash halves. Wrap the squash in the foil and place on a baking sheet; bake for 1 hour, or until tender.

2. Scoop out the baked squash flesh and discard the rind. Rough chop the squash. Add the olive oil, garlic, and onion to a nonstick skillet and sauté until the onion is transparent. (Alternatively, put the oil, garlic, and onion in a covered microwave-safe dish and microwave on high for 2 to 3 minutes.)

3. Remove pan from heat and stir in the vinegar and oregano. Add the squash and stir to coat it in the onion mixture. Add the pasta and toss to mix. Season with freshly ground black pepper, if desired.

TIP: *For added flavor, use roasted instead of raw garlic in this recipe. Roasting the garlic causes it to caramelize, adding a natural sweetness.*

# Pasta with Artichokes

1 (10-ounce) package frozen
   artichoke hearts
1¼ cups water
1 tablespoon lemon juice
4 teaspoons olive oil
¼ cup sun-dried tomatoes,
   packed in oil (drained and
   chopped)

2 cloves garlic, minced
¼ teaspoon red pepper flakes
2 teaspoons dried parsley
2 cups cooked pasta
¼ cup grated Parmesan cheese
Freshly ground black pepper to
   taste (optional)

| Serves 4 | |
|---|---|
| **Nutritional Analysis (per serving):** | |
| Calories: | 307.80 |
| Protein: | 9.75 g |
| Carbohydrate: | 46.66 g |
| Fat: | 9.23 g |
| Sat. Fat: | 1.74 g |
| Cholesterol: | 2.46 mg |
| Sodium: | 87.35 mg |
| Fiber: | 2.97 g |
| PCF Ratio: | 13-60-27 |

**Exchange Approx.:**
1 Medium-Fat Meat,
2 Vegetables,
1 Carb./Starch, 2 Fats

1. Cook the artichokes in the water and lemon juice according to package directions; drain, reserving ¼ cup of the liquid. Cool the artichokes, then cut into quarters. (Alternatively, you can decrease the amount of water to 3 tablespoons and add it with the artichokes and lemon juice to a covered microwave-safe dish. Microwave according to package directions; reserve all of the liquid. This results in a stronger lemon flavor, which compensates for the lack of salt in this recipe.)
2. Heat the olive oil in a nonstick skillet over medium heat. Add the garlic and sauté for 1 minute. Reduce heat to low and stir in the artichokes and tomatoes; simmer for 1 minute. Stir in the reserved artichoke liquid, red pepper flakes, and parsley; simmer for 5 minutes. Pour the artichoke sauce over the pasta in a large bowl; toss gently to coat. Sprinkle with cheese and top with pepper, if desired.

### Garlic Toast

*Large amounts of a butter- or olive oil–garlic mixture make garlic bread high in fat. For delicious results with only a touch of fat, spritz both sides of sliced bread with olive oil, and bake for 6 to 8 minutes in a 350-degree oven. Handling the toasted bread slices carefully, rub a cut garlic clove across the top of each slice. Nutritional Analysis and Exchange Approximations depend on the size and choice of bread slices; if done properly, each slice will have only a trace of fat.*

# Pasta with Creamed Clam Sauce

| Serves 4 | |
|---|---|

**Nutritional Analysis (per serving):**

| | |
|---|---|
| Calories: | 225.86 |
| Protein: | 14.68 g |
| Carbohydrate: | 23.65 g |
| Fat: | 7.46 g |
| Sat. Fat: | 1.96 g |
| Cholesterol: | 25.23 mg |
| Sodium: | 209.04 mg |
| Fiber: | 1.19 g |
| PCF Ratio: | 27-43-30 |

**Exchange Approx.:**
1 Lean Meat,
1 Carb./Starch,
1 Fat, ½ Skim Milk

1 (6½-ounce) can chopped clams
4 teaspoons olive oil
1 clove garlic, garlic
1 tablespoon dry white wine
 **or** dry vermouth
½ cup Mock Cream
 (see page 42)

¼ cup freshly grated Parmesan
 cheese
2 cups cooked pasta
Freshly ground black pepper to
 taste (optional)

1. Drain the canned clams and reserve the juice. Heat the olive oil in a large nonstick skillet. Add the garlic and sauté for 1 minute; stir in the clams and sauté for another minute. With a slotted spoon, transfer the clams to a bowl and cover to keep warm.
2. Add the wine (or vermouth) and reserved clam juice to the skillet, bring to a boil, and reduce by half. Lower the heat and add the Mock Cream and bring to serving temperature, being careful not to boil the cream. Stir in the Parmesan cheese and continue to heat the sauce for another minute, stirring constantly. Add the pasta and toss with the sauce. Divide into 4 equal servings and serve immediately, topped with freshly ground pepper, if desired.

# Pasta with Tuna Alfredo Sauce

1 cup nonfat cottage cheese
1 tablespoon skim milk
2 teaspoons olive oil
1 clove garlic, minced
2 (6-ounce) cans tuna packed
 in water, drained
⅛ cup (2 tablespoons) dry
 white wine

¼ cup freshly grated Parmesan
 cheese
2 cups cooked pasta
Freshly ground black pepper to
 taste (optional)

| Serves 4 | |
|---|---|
| **Nutritional Analysis (per serving):** | |
| Calories: | 278.46 |
| Protein: | 33.25 g |
| Carbohydrate: | 20.80 g |
| Fat: | 5.42 g |
| Sat. Fat: | 1.85 g |
| Cholesterol: | 32.10 mg |
| Sodium: | 400.90 mg |
| Fiber: | 1.19 g |
| PCF Ratio: | 50-31-18 |

**Exchange Approx.:**
1½ Very Lean Meats,
1½ Lean Meats,
1½ Carbs./Starches

1. Process the cottage cheese and skim milk together in a food processor or blender until smooth. Set aside.
2. Heat the olive oil in a large nonstick skillet. Add the garlic and sauté for 1 minute; stir in the tuna and sauté for another minute. Add the wine to the skillet and bring to a boil. Lower the heat and add the cottage cheese mixture and bring to serving temperature, being careful not to let it boil. Stir in the Parmesan cheese and continue to heat the sauce for 1 minute, stirring constantly. Add the pasta and toss with the sauce. Divide into 4 equal servings and serve immediately, topped with freshly ground pepper, if desired.

# Pasta Fagioli

| Serves 8 |
| --- |

| Nutritional Analysis (per serving): | |
| --- | --- |
| Calories: | 380.19 |
| Protein: | 20.37 g |
| Carbohydrate: | 57.48 g |
| Fat: | 7.52 g |
| Sat. Fat: | 1.82 g |
| Cholesterol: | 10.33 mg |
| Sodium: | 660.19 mg |
| Fiber: | 6.25 g |
| PCF Ratio: | 21-61-18 |

**Exchange Approx.:**
3 Lean Meats, ½ Vegetable,
2 Carbs./Starches,
1 Fat

1 (16-ounce) package ziti pasta
2 tablespoons olive oil
2 cloves garlic, minced
1½ cups sugar snap peas
1½ cups diced cooked extra-lean (4 percent) ham
1 (16-ounce) can cannellini beans, drained
¼ cup sun-dried tomatoes packed in oil, drained and chopped
1½ cups low-fat, reduced-sodium chicken broth
½ teaspoon kosher **or** sea salt
¼ teaspoon cracked black pepper
¼ cup grated Parmesan cheese

Cook the pasta as directed on the package. Meanwhile, heat a large skillet on medium and add the olive oil. Sauté the garlic for 2 minutes, being careful that it doesn't burn. Add the peas (thawed and drained, if you're using frozen) and stir-fry for about 3 minutes. Stir in the ham, beans, tomatoes, broth, salt and pepper, and simmer for 5 minutes. Toss the stir-fried bean mixture with the pasta and Parmesan cheese. (The ham in this dish makes it high in sodium, so consult your dietitian before including it in your menu plan if you are on a salt-restricted diet.)

## Little Bits
*Don't waste the unused tomato paste left in the can. Spoon out tablespoon-sized portions and place them on plastic wrap or in sandwich baggies. Seal the packages and store in the freezer. When you need tomato paste in a recipe, add the frozen paste directly to sauce; there is no need to defrost.*

# Macaroni Casserole

½ pound (8 ounces) ground
   turkey
1 cup chopped onion
⅛ cup (2 tablespoons)
   unsalted tomato paste
1 teaspoon dried parsley
¼ teaspoon cinnamon
Kosher **or** sea salt and black
   pepper to taste (optional)
1 cup skim milk

1 tablespoon Ener-G potato flour
2 cups cooked macaroni
4 ounces Cabot's 50 percent
   Light Cheddar Cheese,
   grated (to yield 1 cup)
1 recipe Mock Béchamel Sauce
   (see page 46)

| Serves 4 | |
| --- | --- |
| **Nutritional Analysis (per serving, without salt):** | |
| Calories: | 366.38 |
| Protein: | 28.76 g |
| Carbohydrate: | 37.08 g |
| Fat: | 12.09 g |
| Sat. Fat: | 5.45 g |
| Cholesterol: | 111.83 mg |
| Sodium: | 323.70 mg |
| Fiber: | 2.41 |
| PCF Ratio: | 31-40-29 |

**Exchange Approx.:**
3 Very Lean Meats,
1 Medium-Fat Meat,
1 Carb./Starch,
1 Skim Milk

1. Preheat oven to 350 degrees. Fry the ground turkey in a nonstick skillet; drain off any fat and pat the meat with paper towels. Add the onion and sauté with the ground turkey until transparent. Add the tomato paste and sauté until it starts to brown. Stir in the parsley, cinnamon, and salt and pepper, if using. Remove from heat and set aside.
2. Pour the milk in a bowl, add the potato flour, and whisk to mix. Stir in the macaroni and cheese.
3. Treat a 13" × 17" baking dish with nonstick spray. Pour half of the macaroni mixture into the pan. Spread the meat mixture over the macaroni. Add the rest of the macaroni, and top with the Béchamel Sauce. Bake for 1 hour.

# Bleu Cheese Pasta

| Serves 4 | |
|---|---|
| **Nutritional Analysis (per serving):** | |
| Calories: | 212.46 |
| Protein: | 12.10 g |
| Carbohydrate: | 20.74 g |
| Fat: | 8.75 g |
| Sat. Fat: | 4.26 g |
| Cholesterol: | 16.79 mg |
| Sodium: | 317.15 mg |
| Fiber: | 1.19 g |
| PCF Ratio: | 23-39-37 |

**Exchange Approx.:**
½ High Fat Meat,
½ Very Lean Meat,
½ Lean Meat,
1 Carb./Starch, ½ Fat

2 teaspoons olive oil
1 clove garlic, minced
½ cup nonfat cottage cheese
2 ounces crumbled bleu cheese
Skim milk (optional)
2 cups cooked pasta
¼ cup freshly grated Parmesan cheese
Freshly ground black pepper (optional)

Heat the olive oil in a large nonstick skillet. Add the garlic and sauté for a minute. Lower the heat, stir in the cottage cheese, and bring it to serving temperature. Add the bleu cheese and stir to combine; thin the sauce with a little skim milk, if necessary. Toss with the pasta and divide into 4 equal servings. Top each serving with a tablespoon of the Parmesan cheese and freshly ground black pepper, if desired.

## CHAPTER 11
# *Soups and Stews*

| | |
|---|---|
| Eggplant and Tomato Stew | 182 |
| Lentil Soup with Herbs and Lemon | 183 |
| Lentil-Vegetable Soup | 184 |
| Tomato-Vegetable Soup | 185 |
| Baked Beef Stew | 186 |
| Cold Roasted Red Pepper Soup | 187 |
| Nutty Greek Snapper Soup | 188 |
| Vegetable and Bean Chili | 189 |
| Rich and Creamy Sausage-Potato Soup | 190 |
| Chicken Corn Chowder | 191 |
| Smoked Mussel Chowder | 192 |
| Salmon Chowder | 193 |

# Eggplant and Tomato Stew

| Serves 4 | |
|---|---|
| **Nutritional Analysis (per serving):** | |
| Calories: | 135.02 |
| Protein: | 4.44 g |
| Carbohydrate: | 26.23 g |
| Fat: | 3.28 g |
| Sat. Fat: | 0.47 g |
| Cholesterol: | 0.00 mg |
| Sodium: | 22.36 mg |
| Fiber: | 8.56 g |
| PCF Ratio: | 12-69-19 |

**Exchange Approx.:**
½ Fat,
4 Vegetables

*2 eggplants, trimmed but left whole*
*2 teaspoons olive oil*
*1 medium-sized Spanish onion, chopped*
*1 teaspoon chopped garlic*
*2 cups cooked **or** canned unsalted tomatoes, chopped with liquid*

*Optional seasonings to taste:*
*1 teaspoon hot pepper sauce*
*Ketchup*
*Nonfat plain yogurt*
*Fresh parsley sprigs*

Preheat oven to 400 degrees. Roast the eggplants on a baking sheet until soft, about 45 minutes. Remove all the meat from the eggplants. In a large sauté pan, heat the oil, then sauté the onions and garlic. Add the eggplant and all the other ingredients, except the yogurt and parsley. Remove from heat and transfer the mixture to a food processor; pulse until it becomes creamy. Serve at room temperature, garnished with a dollop of yogurt and parsley, if desired.

## Too Salty?

*If a soup, sauce, or liquid is too salty, peel and place a raw potato in the pot. Use half of a potato for each quart of liquid. Simmer, and then discard the potato (which will have absorbed some of the salt).*

# Lentil Soup with Herbs and Lemon

1 cup lentils, soaked overnight
    in 1 cup water
6 cups low-fat, reduced-sodium
    chicken broth
1 carrot, sliced
1 stalk celery, sliced
1 yellow onion, thinly sliced
2 teaspoons olive oil
1 tablespoon dried tarragon

½ teaspoon dried oregano
Sea salt and black pepper to
    taste (optional)
1 tablespoon lemon juice
4 thin slices of lemon

| Serves 4 | |
| --- | --- |
| **Nutritional Analysis (per serving):** | |
| Calories: | 214.01 |
| Protein: | 14.91 g |
| Carbohydrate: | 34.12 g |
| Fat: | 2.89 g |
| Sat. Fat: | 0.40 g |
| Cholesterol: | 0.05 mg |
| Sodium: | 352.99 mg |
| Fiber: | 15.54 g |
| PCF Ratio: | 27-61-12 |

**Exchange Approx.:**
1 Lean Meat,
2 Starches,
1 Vegetable

1. Drain and rinse the lentils. Add the lentils and broth to a pot over medium heat and bring to a boil. Reduce the heat and simmer until tender, approximately 15 minutes. (If you did not presoak the lentils, increase the cooking time by about 15 more minutes).
2. While the lentils are cooking, sauté the carrot, celery, and onion in oil for 8 minutes, or until the onion is golden brown. Remove from heat and set aside.
3. When the lentils are tender, add the vegetables, herbs, and salt and pepper, if using; cook for 2 minutes. Stir in the lemon juice and ladle into 4 serving bowls; garnish with lemon slices.

## Believe It or Not!
*Put a fork at the bottom of the pan when you cook a pot of beans. The beans will cook in half the time.*

# Lentil-Vegetable Soup

| Serves 4 |
| :---: |

| Nutritional Analysis (per serving, with water): | |
| :--- | ---: |
| Calories: | 273.27 |
| Protein: | 16.45 g |
| Carbohydrate: | 52.69 g |
| Fat: | 0.95 g |
| Sat. Fat: | 0.16 g |
| Cholesterol: | 0.00 mg |
| Sodium: | 33.93 mg |
| Fiber: | 18.56 g |
| PCF Ratio: | 23-74-3 |

**Exchange Approx.:**
1 Very Lean Meat,
3 Starches,
1 Vegetable

*5 cups water **or** your choice of broth*
*1 medium-sized sweet potato, peeled and chopped*
*1 cup uncooked lentils*
*2 medium onions, chopped*
*¼ cup barley*
*2 tablespoons parsley flakes*
*2 carrots, sliced*
*1 celery stalk, chopped*
*2 teaspoons cumin (**or** any seasoning blend from Chapter 2)*

Combine all the ingredients in a soup pot and simmer until the lentils are soft, about 1 hour.

## Quick Lobster Bisque

*A combination of lobster broth, tomato paste, and seasonings, Minor's Lobster Base makes this "soup" a rich and satisfying soup course or snack. Microwave ½ cup water and 1 teaspoon lobster base for 1 minute on high. Stir until the base is dissolved. Add in ½ cup milk. If the soup cools too much, microwave at 70 percent power for another 15 to 30 seconds. Nutritional Analysis (per cup): 57 calories if it's made with skim milk; 68 calories if you use Mock Cream (see page 42). Allow ½ Skim Milk and 1 Free exchange for either version.*

# Tomato-Vegetable Soup

1 tablespoon olive oil
2 teaspoons minced garlic
²/₃ teaspoon cumin
2 carrots, chopped
2 stalks celery, diced
1 medium onion, chopped
²/₃ cup unsalted tomato paste
½ teaspoon red pepper flakes
2 cups canned, unsalted peeled
   tomatoes, with juice
²/₃ teaspoon chopped fresh
   oregano

3 cups low-fat, reduced-sodium
   chicken broth
3 cups fat-free beef broth
2 cups diced potatoes
2 cups shredded cabbage
½ cup green beans
½ cup fresh **or** frozen corn
   kernels
½ teaspoon freshly cracked
   black pepper
¼ cup lime juice **or** balsamic
   vinegar

| Serves 6 | |
|---|---|
| **Nutritional Analysis (per serving):** | |
| Calories: | 157.51 |
| Protein: | 4.99 g |
| Carbohydrate: | 31.21 g |
| Fat: | 3.14 g |
| Sat. Fat: | 0.44 g |
| Cholesterol: | 0.04 mg |
| Sodium: | 348.59 mg |
| Fiber: | 4.90 g |
| PCF Ratio: | 12-72-16 |

**Exchange Approx.:**
1½ Starches/Vegetables,
1 Vegetable

Heat the olive oil in a large stockpot and sauté the garlic, cumin, carrot, and celery for 1 minute; add the onion and cook until transparent. Stir in the tomato paste and sauté until it begins to brown. Add the remaining ingredients *except* for the lime juice (or vinegar). Bring to a boil, then reduce heat and simmer for 20 to 30 minutes, adding additional broth or water, if needed. Just before serving, add the lime juice or balsamic vinegar.

TIP: *It isn't necessary to follow the sauté suggestions at the beginning of this recipe, but the soup will taste much richer if you do. (Sodium content will vary depending upon the broths used.)*

### Easy Measures
*Consider freezing broth in an ice cube tray. Most ice cube tray sections hold ⅛ cup (2 tablespoons) of liquid. Once the broth is frozen, you can transfer the "cubes" to a freezer bag or container. This makes it easy to "measure" out the amount you'll need for recipes.*

# Baked Beef Stew

| Serves 4 |
| :---: |

| Nutritional Analysis (per serving): | |
| :--- | ---: |
| Calories: | 429.81 |
| Protein: | 31.25 g |
| Carbohydrate: | 61.28 g |
| Fat: | 7.33 g |
| Sat. Fat: | 2.17 g |
| Cholesterol: | 66.30 mg |
| Sodium: | 196.95 mg |
| Fiber: | 7.06 g |
| PCF Ratio: | 29-56-15 |

**Exchange Approx.:**
4 Lean Meats,
1 Starch/Vegetable,
1 Carb./Starch,
1 Vegetable

1 (12-ounce) can unsalted tomatoes, undrained
1 cup water
3 tablespoons quick-cooking tapioca
1 teaspoon sugar
1 pound lean beef stew meat, trimmed of all fat, cut into 1-inch pieces
4 medium carrots, cut into 1-inch chunks
4 small potatoes, peeled and quartered
4 celery stalks, cut into ¾-inch chunks
2 medium onions, chopped
2 slices whole-wheat bread, torn into cubes

Preheat oven to 375 degrees. In a large bowl, combine the tomatoes, water, tapioca, and sugar. Add all the remaining ingredients and mix well. Pour into a baking dish treated with nonstick spray. Cover and bake for 2 hours or until the meat and vegetables are tender.

### Flavor Saver

*If you discover that you've scorched a soup, don't stir it or scrape the bottom. Stirring is what distributes the burned flavor. Carefully pour the liquid into another pan. You should be able to salvage what remains. (If it still tastes slightly burnt, adding a little milk should remove that disagreeable flavor. For acidic soups, add some grape jelly.)*

# Cold Roasted Red Pepper Soup

1 teaspoon olive oil
½ cup chopped onion
3 roasted red bell peppers,
   seeded and chopped
   (see page 39)
3¼ cups low-fat, reduced-
   sodium chicken broth

½ cup nonfat plain yogurt
½ teaspoon sea salt (optional)
4 sprigs fresh basil (optional)

| Serves 4 |
| --- |

| Nutritional Analysis (per serving, without salt): | |
| --- | --- |
| Calories: | 73.00 |
| Protein: | 5.00 g |
| Carbohydrate: | 9.00 g |
| Fat: | 4.00 g |
| Sat. Fat: | 1.00 g |
| Cholesterol: | 3.00 mg |
| Sodium: | 404 mg |
| Fiber: | 3.08 g |
| PCF Ratio: | 21-39-40 |

**Exchange Approx.:**
½ Fat,
½ Starch

1. Heat a saucepan over medium-high heat. Add the olive oil and sauté the onion until transparent. Add the peppers and broth. Bring to a boil, then reduce the heat and simmer for 15 minutes. Remove from heat and purée in a blender or food processor until smooth.
2. Allow the soup to cool, then stir in the yogurt and the salt, if using; chill well in the refrigerator. Garnish the soup with fresh basil sprigs, if desired.

# Nutty Greek Snapper Soup

| Serves 4 |
|---|
| **Nutritional Analysis (per serving):** |

| | |
|---|---|
| Calories: | 309.00 |
| Protein: | 39.00 g |
| Carbohydrate: | 25.00 g |
| Fat: | 6.00 g |
| Sat. Fat: | 0.70 g |
| Cholesterol: | 46.00 mg |
| Sodium: | 240.00 mg |
| Fiber: | 2.41 g |
| PCF Ratio: | 50-33-17 |

**Exchange Approx.:**
4 Lean Meats,
1 Skim Milk,
1 Vegetable

1-pound (16-ounce) red snapper
   fillet
2 large cucumbers
4 green onions, chopped
3 tablespoons lime juice
4 cups nonfat plain yogurt
¼ cup chopped walnuts

1 cup, packed, mixed fresh
   parsley, basil, cilantro,
   arugula, and chives
Salt and pepper to taste (optional)
Herb sprigs, for garnish (optional)

1. Rinse the red snapper fillet and pat dry with paper towels. Broil the fillet until opaque through the thickest part, about 4 minutes on each side, depending on the thickness of the fillet. Let cool. (Alternatives would be to steam or poach the fillets.)

2. Peel and halve the cucumbers, then scoop out and discard the seeds; cut into roughly 1-inch pieces. Put half the cucumber with the green onions in the bowl of a food processor. Use the pulse button to coarsely chop; transfer to a large bowl. Add the remaining cucumber, yogurt, and herb leaves to the food processor and process until smooth and frothy. (Alternatively, you can grate the cucumbers, finely mince the green onion and herbs, and then stir them together with the yogurt in a large bowl.) Stir the lime juice into the soup and season with salt and pepper to taste, if using. Cover and refrigerate for at least 1 hour, or up to 8 hours; the longer the soup cools, the more the flavors will mellow.

3. While the soup cools, break the cooled red snapper fillet into large chunks, discarding the skin and any bones. Ladle the chilled soup into shallow bowls and add the red snapper. Sprinkle the chopped walnuts over the soup, garnish with herb sprigs, and serve.

TIP: *You can make this soup using leftover fish, or substitute halibut, cod, or sea bass for the snapper.*

# Vegetable and Bean Chili

4 teaspoons olive oil

2 cups chopped cooking onions

½ cup chopped green bell
   pepper

3 cloves garlic, chopped

1 small jalapeño pepper, finely
   chopped (Only include the
   seeds if you like the chili
   extra hot!)

1 tablespoon chili powder

1 teaspoon ground cumin

1 (28-ounce) can unsalted
   tomatoes, undrained

2 zucchini, peeled and chopped

2 (15-ounce) cans unsalted
   kidney beans, rinsed

1 tablespoon chopped semisweet chocolate

3 tablespoons chopped fresh
   cilantro

| Serves 8 | |
|---|---|
| **Nutritional Analysis (per serving):** | |
| Calories: | 205.17 |
| Protein: | 11.87 g |
| Carbohydrate: | 34.97 g |
| Fat: | 3.10 g |
| Sat. Fat: | 0.64 g |
| Cholesterol: | 0.05 mg |
| Sodium: | 156.12 mg |
| Fiber: | 12.57 g |
| PCF Ratio: | 22-65-13 |

**Exchange Approx.:**
1 Lean Meat,
2 Starches,
1 Vegetable

1. Heat a heavy pot over moderately high heat. Add the olive oil, onions, bell pepper, garlic, and jalapeño; sauté until the vegetables are softened, about 5 minutes. Add the chili powder and cumin, and sauté for 1 minute, stirring frequently to mix well.
2. Chop the tomatoes and add them, with their juice, and the zucchini. Bring to a boil; lower heat and simmer, partially covered, for 15 minutes, stirring occasionally. Stir in the beans and chocolate and simmer, stirring occasionally, for an additional 5 minutes, or until the beans are heated through and the chocolate is melted. Stir in the cilantro, and serve.

# Rich and Creamy Sausage-Potato Soup

| Serves 2 |
| :---: |

| Nutritional Analysis (per serving): | |
| :--- | ---: |
| Calories: | 326.26 |
| Protein: | 16.53 g |
| Carbohydrate: | 52.72 g |
| Fat: | 5.77 g |
| Sat. Fat: | 1.91 g |
| Cholesterol: | 18.68 mg |
| Sodium: | 258.90 mg |
| Fiber: | 3.08 g |
| PCF Ratio: | 20-64-16 |

**Exchange Approx.:**
1 Fat, ½ Medium-Fat Meat,
1 Starchy Vegetable,
1½ Skim Milks,
1 Vegetable

1  teaspoon olive oil
½ teaspoon butter
½ cup chopped onion, steamed
1 clove roasted garlic
    (see page 54)
1 ounce crumbled, cooked
    Chorizo (see page 152)
¼ teaspoon celery seed
2 Yukon gold potatoes, peeled
    and diced into 1-inch pieces
½ cup fat-free chicken broth

1 ½ cup Mock Cream
    (see page 42)
1 teaspoon white wine vinegar
1 teaspoon vanilla extract
Optional seasonings to taste:
    Fresh parsley
    Sea salt and freshly ground
        black pepper to taste

In a saucepan, heat the olive oil and butter over medium heat. Add the onion, roasted garlic, chorizo, celery seed, and potatoes; sauté until the mixture is heated. Add the chicken broth and bring the mixture to a boil. Cover the saucepan, reduce heat, and maintain simmer for 10 minutes, or until the potatoes are tender. Add the Mock Cream and heat. Remove pan from the burner and stir in the vinegar and vanilla.

### Skim the Fat

*You can remove fat from soups and stews by dropping ice cubes into the pot. The fat will cling to the cubes as you stir. Be sure to take out the cubes before they melt. Fat also clings to lettuce leaves; simply sweep them over the top of the soup. Discard ice cubes or leaves when you're done.*

# Chicken Corn Chowder

*1 pound boneless, skinless chicken breast, cut into chunks*
*1 medium onion, chopped*
*1 red bell pepper, diced*
*1 large potato, diced*
*2 (16-ounce) cans low-fat, reduced-sodium chicken broth*
*1 (8¾-ounce) can unsalted cream-style corn*

*½ cup all-purpose flour*
*2 cups skim milk*
*4 ounces Cheddar cheese, diced*
*½ teaspoon sea salt*
*Freshly ground pepper to taste*
*½ cup processed bacon bits*

| Serves 10 |
| --- |
| **Nutritional Analysis (per serving):** |

| | |
| --- | --- |
| Calories: | 193 |
| Protein: | 17.39 g |
| Carbohydrate: | 20.74 g |
| Fat: | 4.8 g |
| Sat. Fat: | 2.86 g |
| Cholesterol: | 39.18 mg |
| Sodium: | 155.07 mg |
| Fiber: | 1.61 g |
| PCF Ratio: | 22-36-42 |

**Exchange Approx.:**
1½ Very Lean Meats,
½ Starchy Vegetable,
1 Vegetable,
½ Skim Milk,
½ High-Fat Meat

1. Spray a large soup pot with nonstick cooking spray and heat on medium setting until hot. Add the chicken, onion, and bell pepper; sauté over medium heat until the chicken is browned and the vegetables are tender. Stir in the potatoes and broth, and bring to a boil. Reduce the heat and simmer, covered, for 20 minutes. Stir in the corn.
2. Blend the flour and milk in a bowl, then gradually stir it into the pot. Increase heat to medium and cook until the mixture comes to a boil, then reduce heat and simmer until soup is thickened, stirring constantly. Add the cheese and stir until it's melted and blended into the soup. Add the salt and pepper to taste, and sprinkle with bacon bits before serving.

**TIP:** *To trim down the fat in this recipe, use a reduced fat cheese, such as Cabot's 50 percent Light Cheddar.*

# Smoked Mussel Chowder

| Serves 6 | |
|---|---|
| **Nutritional Analysis (per serving):** | |
| Calories: | 272.74 |
| Protein: | 7.59 g |
| Carbohydrate: | 36.67 g |
| Fat: | 8.29 g |
| Sat. Fat: | 1.57 g |
| Cholesterol: | 20.63 mg |
| Sodium: | 578.79 mg |
| Fiber: | 3.28 g |
| PCF Ratio: | 12-58-30 |

**Exchange Approx.:**
1 Fat,
1 Lean Meat,
2 Vegetables/Starches,
1 Vegetable

2 tablespoons olive oil
1 medium onion, chopped
2 carrots, diced
2 stalks celery, diced
½ bulb fennel, diced
1 teaspoon chopped garlic
4 red potatoes, cut into ½-inch cubes
1 cup dry white wine
2½ cups clam juice
1 bay leaf
Pinch of cayenne pepper
½ teaspoon thyme
2 medium-sized white potatoes, peeled and quartered (to yield 2½ cups)
1 cup skim milk
4 ounces Ducktrap River smoked mussels
Sea salt and freshly ground black pepper to taste (optional)
Fresh parsley sprigs (optional)

1. Heat the olive oil in soup pot. Add the onions, carrots, celery, fennel, and garlic; gently sauté for 10 minutes. (Do not brown vegetables). Add the red potatoes, wine, clam juice, bay leaf, cayenne and thyme. Let the soup simmer until the potatoes are cooked.

2. In a separate pan of boiling water, cook the white potatoes until tender. Mash the potatoes by putting them through a potato ricer or into the bowl of a food processor along with some of the skim milk. Once the red potatoes in the chowder are tender, stir in the mashed potatoes, remaining milk, and mussels. Do not let the soup come to a boil. Salt and pepper to taste and serve garnish with parsley sprigs, if desired.

# Salmon Chowder

1 (7½-ounce) can unsalted
    salmon
2 teaspoons butter
1 medium onion, chopped
2 stalks celery, chopped
1 sweet green pepper, seeded
    and chopped
1 clove garlic, minced
4 carrots, peeled and diced
4 small potatoes, peeled and
    diced
1 cup fat-free chicken broth
1 cup water

½ teaspoon cracked black
    pepper
½ teaspoon dill seed
1 cup diced zucchini
1 cup Mock Cream (see page
    42)
1 (8¾-ounce) can unsalted
    cream-style corn
Freshly ground black pepper to
    taste
½ cup chopped fresh parsley
    (optional)

### Serves 4

**Nutritional Analysis
(per serving):**

| | |
|---|---|
| Calories: | 363.90 |
| Protein: | 20.44 g |
| Carbohydrate: | 61.27 g |
| Fat: | 5.67 g |
| Sat. Fat: | 2.20 g |
| Cholesterol: | 27.51 mg |
| Sodium: | 199.16 mg |
| Fiber: | 6.53 g |
| PCF Ratio: | 22-65-14 |

**Exchange Approx.:**
½ Fat,
2 Starches/Vegetables,
2 Lean Meats,
2 Vegetables,
½ Skim Milk

Drain and flake the salmon, discarding liquid. In large nonstick saucepan, melt the butter over medium heat; sauté the onion, celery, green pepper, garlic, and carrots, stirring often until the vegetables are tender, about 5 minutes. Add the potatoes, broth, water, pepper, and dill seed; bring to boil. Reduce heat, cover, and simmer for 20 minutes, or until the potatoes are tender. Add the zucchini; simmer, covered, for another 5 minutes. Add the salmon, Mock Cream, corn, and pepper. Cook over low heat just until heated through. Just before serving, add parsley, if desired.

# CHAPTER 12

# Side Salads

| | |
|---|---|
| Buttermilk Dressing | 196 |
| Bleu Cheese Dressing | 196 |
| Dijon Vinaigrette | 197 |
| Honey-Mustard Dressing | 197 |
| Tangy Lemon-Garlic Tomato Dressing | 198 |
| Cashew-Garlic Ranch Dressing | 198 |
| Lemon-Almond Dressing | 199 |
| Wilted Lettuce with a Healthier Difference | 200 |
| Greens in Garlic with Pasta | 201 |
| Green Bean and Mushroom Salad | 202 |
| White and Black Bean Salad | 203 |
| Broccoli-Cauliflower Slaw | 204 |
| Zesty Feta and Olive Salad | 205 |
| Avocado and Peach Salad | 206 |
| Orange-Avocado Slaw | 207 |
| Honey Dijon Tuna Salad | 207 |
| Spinach Salad with Apple-Avocado Dressing | 208 |
| Greek Pasta Salad | 209 |
| Bleu Cheese Pasta Salad | 210 |
| Taco Salad | 210 |
| Layered Salad | 211 |
| Golden Raisin Smoked Turkey Salad | 212 |

# Buttermilk Dressing

<table>
<tr><td colspan="2">Yields about ⅔ cup<br>Serving size: 1 tbs.</td></tr>
<tr><td colspan="2">Nutritional Analysis<br>(per serving, without salt):</td></tr>
<tr><td>Calories:</td><td>14.33</td></tr>
<tr><td>Protein:</td><td>0.89 g</td></tr>
<tr><td>Carbohydrate:</td><td>2.57 g</td></tr>
<tr><td>Fat:</td><td>0.07 g</td></tr>
<tr><td>Sat. Fat:</td><td>0.04 g</td></tr>
<tr><td>Cholesterol:</td><td>0.00 mg</td></tr>
<tr><td>Sodium:</td><td>18.15 mg</td></tr>
<tr><td>Fiber:</td><td>0.00 g</td></tr>
<tr><td>PCF Ratio:</td><td>25-71-5</td></tr>
<tr><td colspan="2">Exchange Approx.:<br>1 Free</td></tr>
</table>

½ cup plain nonfat yogurt
1 tablespoon buttermilk powder
1 teaspoon prepared mustard
¼ teaspoon cider vinegar
1 tablespoon light brown sugar

¼ teaspoon paprika
⅛ teaspoon hot red pepper
  (optional)
¼ teaspoon salt (optional)

The easiest way to make this fat-free dressing is to measure all the ingredients into a jar, then put the lid on the jar and shake it vigorously until it's mixed. Refrigerate any unused portions. May be kept in the refrigerator up to 3 days.

# Bleu Cheese Dressing

<table>
<tr><td colspan="2">Yields 6 tbs.<br>Serving size: 1 tbs.</td></tr>
<tr><td colspan="2">Nutritional Analysis<br>(per serving):</td></tr>
<tr><td>Calories:</td><td>23.58</td></tr>
<tr><td>Protein:</td><td>1.22 g</td></tr>
<tr><td>Carbohydrate:</td><td>1.35 g</td></tr>
<tr><td>Fat:</td><td>1.51 g</td></tr>
<tr><td>Sat. Fat:</td><td>0.57 g</td></tr>
<tr><td>Cholesterol:</td><td>2.66 mg</td></tr>
<tr><td>Sodium:</td><td>51.80 mg</td></tr>
<tr><td>Fiber:</td><td>0.00 g</td></tr>
<tr><td>PCF Ratio:</td><td>21-23-57</td></tr>
<tr><td colspan="2">Exchange Approx.:<br>½ Fat</td></tr>
</table>

2 tablespoons Mock Sour
  Cream (see page 43)
1 tablespoons cottage cheese
1 tablespoon Hellmann's or
  Best Foods Real Mayonnaise

½ teaspoon lemon juice
½ teaspoon honey
1 tablespoon, plus 2 teaspoons
  crumbled bleu cheese

Put the first 5 ingredients in a blender and process until smooth. Fold in the bleu cheese.

# Dijon Vinaigrette

1 tablespoon Dijon mustard
½ teaspoon sea salt
½ teaspoon freshly ground
    black pepper

1 tablespoons red wine vinegar
3 tablespoons virgin olive oil

Put all the ingredients in a small bowl and use a wire whisk or fork to mix.

| Yields about 5 tbs. Serving size: 1 tbs. | |
| --- | --- |
| **Nutritional Analysis (per serving):** | |
| Calories: | 74.00 |
| Protein: | 0.12 g |
| Carbohydrate: | 0.41 g |
| Fat: | 8.19 g |
| Sat. Fat: | 1.10 g |
| Cholesterol: | 0.00 mg |
| Sodium: | 266.18 mg |
| Fiber: | 0.10 g |
| PCF Ratio: | 1-2-97 |
| **Exchange Approx.:** 2 Fats | |

# Honey-Mustard Dressing

⅛ cup honey
1 clove garlic
2 tablespoons stone-ground
    mustard
1 tablespoon ground flaxseeds
1 teaspoon poppy seeds
1 tablespoon lemon juice

¼ cup flaxseed oil
1 tablespoon chopped fresh
    chives (**or** 1 teaspoon dried
    chives)
1 tablespoon toasted sesame
    seeds

Put all ingredients into a blender container or food processor and blend until smooth.

| Yields about ¾ cup Serving size: 1 tbs. | |
| --- | --- |
| **Nutritional Analysis (per serving):** | |
| Calories: | 53.56 |
| Protein: | 0.69 g |
| Carbohydrate: | 3.46 g |
| Fat: | 4.10 g |
| Sat. Fat: | 0.39 g |
| Cholesterol: | 0.00 mg |
| Sodium: | 24.82 mg |
| Fiber: | 0.74 g |
| PCF Ratio: | 5-26-69 |
| **Exchange Approx.:** 1 Fat | |

| Yields about ¾ cup Serving size: 1 tbs. | |
|---|---|
| **Nutritional Analysis (per serving):** | |
| Calories: | 7.37 |
| Protein: | 0.29 g |
| Carbohydrate: | 0.90 g |
| Fat: | 0.38 g |
| Sat. Fat: | 0.04 g |
| Cholesterol: | 0.00 mg |
| Sodium: | 1.14 mg |
| Fiber: | 0.38 g |
| PCF Ratio: | 14-44-42 |
| **Exchange Approx.:** ½ Free | |

# Tangy Lemon-Garlic Tomato Dressing

1 tablespoon ground flaxseeds
2 cloves garlic
⅛ cup cider vinegar
⅛ teaspoon freshly ground pepper
1 small tomato, chopped
¼ teaspoon celery seed
1 tablespoon lemon juice
¼ cup water

Place all ingredients in blender and blend until smooth.

## Friendly Fat and Fiber

*In addition to providing fiber, ground flaxseeds are rich sources of omega-3 and -6 essential fatty acids. The oil is low in saturated fat, and therefore a heart-healthy choice. Just remember that flaxseed oil must be refrigerated; otherwise it goes rancid.*

| Yields about ¾ cup Serving size: 1 tbs. | |
|---|---|
| **Nutritional Analysis (per serving):** | |
| Calories: | 20.77 |
| Protein: | 0.57 g |
| Carbohydrate: | 1.81 g |
| Fat: | 1.39 g |
| Sat. Fat: | 0.29 g |
| Cholesterol: | 0.14 mg |
| Sodium: | 13.57 mg |
| Fiber: | 0.12 g |
| PCF Ratio: | 10-33-57 |
| **Exchange Approx.:** ½ Fat | |

# Cashew-Garlic Ranch Dressing

¼ cup raw cashews
  (**or** ⅛ cup cashew butter without salt)
½ cup water
½ teaspoon stone-ground mustard
1½ tablespoons chili sauce
½ teaspoon horseradish
1 teaspoon Bragg's Liquid Aminos (**or** tamari sauce)
1 clove garlic
1½ teaspoon honey
⅛ teaspoon pepper

Process the cashews and water together in a blender or food processor until creamy. Add the remaining ingredients and mix well. Refrigerate for 30 minutes.

## Keeping Cashews

*Store raw cashews in the refrigerator; this preserves the healthy, but delicate, essential oils.*

# Lemon-Almond Dressing

¼ cup raw almonds
1 tablespoon lemon juice
¼ cup water
1 ½ teaspoons honey
¼ teaspoon lemon pepper
½ of a slice (1 inch in diameter) peeled ginger
¼ clove garlic

1 ½ teaspoons chopped, fresh chives (**or** ½ teaspoon dried chives)
1 ½ teaspoons chopped fresh sweet basil (**or** ½ teaspoon dried basil)

Put all the ingredients in a food processor or blender and process until smooth.

## Salad: Undressed

*Make a quick salad without dressing by mixing chopped celery, onion, and other vegetable choices such as cucumbers or zucchini. Add some of your favorite low-salt seasoning or toss the vegetables with some Bragg's Liquid Aminos or low-sodium soy sauce and serve over salad greens.*

**Yields about ⅔ cup
Serving size: 1 tbs.**

| Nutritional Analysis (per serving): | |
|---|---|
| Calories: | 24.49 |
| Protein: | 0.78 g |
| Carbohydrate: | 1.79 g |
| Fat: | 1.80 g |
| Sat. Fat: | 0.14 g |
| Cholesterol: | 0.00 mg |
| Sodium: | 0.15 mg |
| Fiber: | 0.45 g |
| PCF Ratio: | 12-27-61 |

**Exchange Approx.:**
½ Fat

# Wilted Lettuce
# with a Healthier Difference

| Serves 1 |
| --- |

| Nutritional Analysis (per serving): | |
| --- | --- |
| Calories: | 70.57 |
| Protein: | 1.56 g |
| Carbohydrate: | 6.50 g |
| Fat: | 4.83 g |
| Sat. Fat: | 0.55 g |
| Cholesterol: | 0.00 mg |
| Sodium: | 8.77 mg |
| Fiber: | 2.32 g |
| PCF Ratio: | 8-34-57 |

**Exchange Approx.:**
2 Free Vegetables,
1 Fat

½ teaspoon olive oil
¼ cup chopped red onion
1½ cups, tightly packed, loose-leaf lettuce
¼ teaspoon lemon juice **or** your choice of vinegar
½ teaspoon extra-virgin olive oil, walnut oil, **or** almond oil

Optional seasonings to taste:
   Dried herbs of your choice, such as thyme or parsley
Pinch of sugar
Pinch of toasted sesame seeds **or** grated Parmesan cheese

1. In a heated nonstick skillet treated with nonstick spray, add ½ teaspoon of the olive oil and all the red onion. Sauté until the onion is almost transparent, then add the greens. Sauté the greens until they're warmed and wilted.

2. In a salad bowl, whisk the lemon juice (or vinegar) with the ½ teaspoon of oil. Add the pinch of herbs and sugar, if using, and whisk into the oil mixture. Add the wilted greens to the bowl and toss with the dressing. Top the salad with a pinch of toasted sesame seeds or Parmesan cheese, if desired. Serve immediately.

### Adventuresome Additions
*Dried cranberries or other dried fruit, such as cherries or currants, are delicious in wilted lettuce dishes. The addition of diced apples or pineapple makes a perfect wilted greens accompaniment for pork. Have fun! Making necessary dietary changes isn't about learning a whole new way to cook. Adapting to a healthier new lifestyle is a chance to experiment.*

# Greens in Garlic with Pasta

2 teaspoons olive oil

4 cloves garlic, crushed

6 cups, tightly packed, loose-leaf greens (baby mustard, turnip, chard)

2 cups cooked pasta

2 teaspoons extra-virgin olive oil

¼ cup freshly grated Parmesan cheese

Salt and freshly ground black pepper to taste (optional)

| Serves 4 |
|---|

**Nutritional Analysis (per serving, without salt):**

| | |
|---|---|
| Calories: | 175.47 |
| Protein: | 7.60 g |
| Carbohydrate: | 25.56 g |
| Fat: | 5.00 g |
| Sat. Fat: | 0.72 g |
| Cholesterol: | 0.22 mg |
| Sodium: | 16.87 mg |
| Fiber: | 3.06 g |
| PCF Ratio: | 17-58-25 |

**Exchange Approx.:**
1 Free Vegetable,
1 Fat, 1 Starch,
½ Lean Meat

1. Place a sauté pan over medium heat. When the pan is hot, add the 2 teaspoons of olive oil and the crushed garlic. Cook, stirring frequently until golden brown (3–5 minutes), being careful not to burn the garlic, as that makes it bitter. Add the greens and sauté until they are coated in the garlic oil. Remove from heat.

2. In a large serving bowl, add the pasta, cooked greens, 2 teaspoons of extra-virgin olive oil, and Parmesan cheese; toss to mix. Serve immediately, and season as desired.

## Sweet or Salty?

*In most cases, when you add a pinch (less than ⅛ teaspoon) of sugar to a recipe, you can reduce the amount of salt without noticing a difference. Sugar acts as a flavor enhancer and magnifies the effect of the salt.*

# Green Bean and Mushroom Salad

| Serves 4 |
| :---: |
| **Nutritional Analysis (per serving):** |

| | |
| :--- | ---: |
| Calories: | 131.14 |
| Protein: | 2.35 g |
| Carbohydrate: | 9.14 g |
| Fat: | 10.44 g |
| Sat. Fat: | 1.43 g |
| Cholesterol: | 0.00 mg |
| Sodium: | 3.88 mg |
| Fiber: | 2.70 g |
| PCF Ratio: | 7-26-67 |

**Exchange Approx.:**
2 Fats,
2 Vegetables

*2 cups fresh, small green beans, ends trimmed*
*1½ cups sliced, fresh mushrooms*
*½ cup chopped red onion*
*3 tablespoons extra-virgin olive, canola, or corn oil*
*1 tablespoon balsamic or red wine vinegar*

*1 clove garlic, minced*
*½ teaspoon sea salt (optional)*
*¼ teaspoon freshly ground pepper (optional)*

1. Cook the green beans in a large pot of unsalted boiling water for 5 minutes. Drain the beans in a colander that you then immediately plunge into a bowl of ice water; this stops the cooking process and retains the bright green color of the beans.

2. Once the beans are cooled, drain and place in a large bowl. If you'll be serving the salad immediately, add the mushrooms and onions to the bowl and toss to mix. (Otherwise, as recommended earlier, chill the beans separately and add them to the salad immediately before serving.)

3. To make the dressing, combine the oil and vinegar in a small bowl. Whisk them together with the garlic and pour over the salad. Toss lightly and season with salt and pepper, if desired. Serve immediately.

# White and Black Bean Salad

1 cup finely chopped red onions

2 cloves garlic, minced

2 tablespoons olive oil **or** vegetable oil

⅓ cup red wine vinegar

¼ cup seeded and chopped red pepper

¼ cup seeded and chopped green pepper

2 tablespoons minced parsley

2 tablespoons granulated sugar

¼ teaspoon sea salt (optional)

¼ teaspoon pepper (optional)

1 (15-ounce) can Great Northern beans, rinsed and drained

1 (15-ounce) can black beans, rinsed and drained

Red and green pepper rings, for garnish

| Serves 8 | |
|---|---|
| **Nutritional Analysis (per serving):** | |
| Calories: | 165.22 |
| Protein: | 7.43 g |
| Carbohydrate: | 26.77 g |
| Fat: | 3.74 g |
| Sat. Fat: | 0.54 g |
| Cholesterol: | 0.00 mg |
| Sodium: | 207.82 mg |
| Fiber: | 6.76 g |
| PCF Ratio: | 17-63-20 |

**Exchange Approx.:**
1 Misc. Carb.,
1 Fat,
1 Starch

In a nonstick skillet over medium heat, sauté the onions and garlic in the oil until they're onions are just beginning to soften. Remove from the heat and allow to cool until warm. Stir the vinegar, peppers, parsley, and sugar into the onions and garlic. Pour the onion mixture over combined beans in a bowl and mix well. Season with salt and pepper, if desired, and garnish with pepper rings.

# Broccoli-Cauliflower Slaw

| Serves 8 |
|---|

| Nutritional Analysis (per serving): | |
|---|---|
| Calories: | 116.80 |
| Protein: | 5.77 g |
| Carbohydrate: | 13.16 g |
| Fat: | 5.43 g |
| Sat Fat: | 0.94 g |
| Cholesterol: | 0.00 mg |
| Sodium: | 45.54 mg |
| Fiber: | 1.25 g |
| PCF Ratio: | 19-42-39 |

**Exchange Approx.:**
1 Misc. Carb.,
1 Fat

4 cups raw broccoli flowerets
4 cups raw cauliflower
½ cup Hellmann's or Best
   Foods Real Mayonnaise
1 cup cottage cheese,
   1 percent fat

3 tablespoons tarragon vinegar
1 tablespoon balsamic vinegar
⅛ cup, packed, brown sugar
3 tablespoons red onion

Put the broccoli and cauliflower in a food processor and pulse-process to the consistency of shredded cabbage; pour into a bowl. Place the remaining ingredients in the food processor and process until smooth. Pour the resulting dressing over the broccoli-cauliflower mixture and stir. Chill until ready to serve.

**TIP:** *Substituting cottage cheese for some of the mayonnaise cuts the fat and calories in this recipe considerably. (You can cut them even more if you're able to tolerate nonfat cottage cheese and mayonnaise.)*

### Fresh Herb Conversions
*If you substitute dried herbs for the fresh ones called for in a recipe, only use ⅓ the amount.*

# Zesty Feta and Olive Salad

2 ounces crumbled feta
1 small red onion, diced
½ cup chopped celery
½ cup diced cucumber
1 clove garlic, minced
1 teaspoon lemon zest
1 teaspoon orange zest
1 cup halved, very small
    cherry tomatoes
½ cup mix of green and kala-
    mata olives, pitted and
    sliced
1 tablespoon extra-virgin olive oil

2 tablespoons minced fresh
    Italian parsley
2 teaspoons minced fresh
    oregano
1 teaspoon minced fresh mint
1 tablespoon minced fresh
    cilantro (optional)
Large romaine **or** butter lettuce
    leaves
Freshly ground black pepper

| Serves 4 | |
| --- | --- |
| **Nutritional Analysis (per serving):** | |
| Calories: | 108.63 |
| Protein: | 3.26 g |
| Carbohydrate: | 6.36 g |
| Fat: | 8.48 g |
| Sat. Fat: | 2.86 g |
| Cholesterol: | 12.62 mg |
| Sodium: | 326.57 mg |
| Fiber: | 1.96 g |
| PCF Ratio: | 11-22-66 |
| **Exchange Approx.:** 1 Vegetable, 2 Fats | |

Place the feta in a large bowl and add the onion, celery, cucumber, garlic, lemon zest, orange zest, cherry tomatoes, and olives; mix. Add the olive oil and fresh herbs and toss again. Arrange the lettuce leaves on 4 salad plates and spoon the feta salad on top. Top with freshly ground pepper, and serve.

# Avocado and Peach Salad

| Serves 4 |
|---|
| **Nutritional Analysis (per serving, without salt):** |
| Calories: 160.28 |
| Protein: 2.39 g |
| Carbohydrate: 15.07 g |
| Fat: 11.35 g |
| Sat. Fat: 1.72 g |
| Cholesterol: 0.00 mg |
| Sodium: 10.97 mg |
| Fiber: 4.44 g |
| PCF Ratio: 6-35-59 |
| **Exchange Approx.:** |
| 3 Fats, |
| 1 Free Vegetable, |
| ½ Fruit |

⅛ cup water
⅛ cup frozen orange juice
   concentrate
1 clove garlic, crushed
1 teaspoon rice wine vinegar
1 tablespoon extra-virgin olive oil
½ teaspoon vanilla
1½ cups, tightly packed, baby
   arugula
2 tablespoons tarragon leaves

1 avocado, peeled and diced
1 peach, peeled and diced
½ cup thinly sliced Vidalia
   onion
Kosher **or** Sea salt and freshly
   ground black pepper to
   taste (optional)

In a measuring cup, whisk the water, orange juice concentrate, garlic, vinegar, oil, and vanilla together until well mixed. Prepare the salad by arranging layers of the arugula and tarragon, then the avocado, peach, and onions, and then drizzle the salad with the orange juice vinaigrette. Season with salt and pepper, if desired, and serve.

### Experiment Sensibly
*When it comes to new herbs and spices, err on the side of caution. If you're not sure whether or not you like a seasoning, mix all of the other ingredients together and "test" a bite of the salad with a pinch of the herb or spice before you add it to the entire recipe.*

# Orange-Avocado Slaw

¼ cup orange juice
½ teaspoon curry powder
⅛ teaspoon ground cumin
¼ teaspoon sugar
1 teaspoon white wine vinegar
1 tablespoon olive oil

5 cups broccoli slaw mix
1 avocado, peeled and
    chopped
Sea salt and freshly ground
    black pepper to taste
    (optional)

In a bowl whisk together the orange juice, curry powder, cumin, sugar, and vinegar. Add the oil in a stream, whisking until emulsified. In a large bowl, toss the avocado with the slaw mix. Drizzle with the vinaigrette. Chill until ready to serve, and season with salt and pepper, if desired.

| Serves 10 | |
|---|---|
| **Nutritional Analysis (per serving, without salt):** | |
| Calories: | 59.87 |
| Protein: | 1.78 g |
| Carbohydrate: | 4.55 g |
| Fat: | 4.60 g |
| Sat. Fat: | 0.70 g |
| Cholesterol: | 0.00 mg |
| Sodium: | 14.01 mg |
| Fiber: | 2.34 g |
| PCF Ratio: | 11-27-62 |

**Exchange Approx.:**
1 Fat, ½ Free Vegetable

# Honey Dijon Tuna Salad

¼ cup tuna, canned in water,
    drained
½ cup diced celery
¼ cup diced onion
¼ cup seeded and diced red
    **or** green pepper
4 ounces (half of a small con-
    tainer) nonfat plain yogurt

1 teaspoon Dijon mustard
1 teaspoon lemon juice
¼ teaspoon honey
1 tablespoon raisins
1 cup, tightly packed, iceberg
    lettuce (**or** other salad
    greens)

1. Use a fork to flake the tuna into a bowl. Add all the other ingredients *except* the lettuce and mix well. Serve on lettuce or greens.
2. Alternate serving suggestion: Mix with ½ cup of chilled, cooked pasta before dressing the salad greens; adds 1 Starch Exchange choice.

| Serves 1 | |
|---|---|
| **Nutritional Analysis (per serving):** | |
| Calories: | 194.30 |
| Protein: | 22.42 g |
| Carbohydrate: | 24.43 g |
| Fat: | 1.34 g |
| Sat. Fat: | 0.25 g |
| Cholesterol: | 0.00 mg |
| Sodium: | 575.21 mg |
| Fiber: | 3.54 g |
| PCF Ratio: | 45-49-6 |

**Exchange Approx.:**
1 Lean Meat,
2 Vegetables,
½ Fruit, ½ Skim Milk

# Spinach Salad with
# Apple-Avocado Dressing

¼ cup unsweetened apple juice
1 teaspoon (**or** up to 1 tablespoon) cider vinegar
1 clove garlic, minced
1 teaspoon Bragg's Liquid Aminos **or** soy sauce
½ teaspoon Worcestershire sauce (see recipe for Homemade on page 40)
2 teaspoons olive oil
1 avocado, peeled and chopped
2½ cups, tightly packed, spinach and other salad greens
½ cup thinly sliced red onion
½ cup sliced radishes
½ cup bean sprouts

In a blender or food processor, combine the juice, vinegar (the amount of which will depend on how you like your dressing), garlic, Liquid Aminos (**or** soy sauce), Worcestershire, oil, and avocado; process until smooth. In a large bowl, toss the salad ingredients. Pour the dressing over the salad and toss again.

## Salads Don't Have to Be Fat Free

*Unless you're on a calorie-restricted diet, "fat free" may not be your best choice—consult your dietitian. Studies show that women who consume up to 41.7 grams of vegetable fat a day have up to a 22 percent less change of developing type 2 diabetes. Vegetable oils—combined with a diet rich in fish, fruits, vegetables, whole grains, and nuts—are much healthier than using those chemically created fat-free foods! This type of diet is not only heart-healthy, it's believed to prevent certain cancers, too. (Source: WebMD, ✎ http://my.webmd.com)*

# Greek Pasta Salad

1 tablespoon lemon juice
3 tablespoons olive oil
1 teaspoon dried oregano
1 teaspoon Dijon mustard
1 clove garlic, minced
2 cups cooked pasta
1 cup slivered, blanched
    almonds
1 cup sliced cucumber

1 cup diced fresh tomato
½ cup chopped red onion
½ cup Greek olives
2 ounces crumbled feta cheese
1½ cups romaine lettuce leaves

| Serves 4 | |
|---|---|
| **Nutritional Analysis (per serving):** | |
| Calories: | 419.81 |
| Protein: | 12.12 g |
| Carbohydrate: | 30.94 g |
| Fat: | 29.34 g |
| Sat. Fat: | 4.88 g |
| Cholesterol: | 12.62 mg |
| Sodium: | 312.38 mg |
| Fiber: | 6.05 g |
| PCF Ratio: | 11-28-61 |

**Exchange Approx.:**
1 Medium-Fat Meat,
1 Meat Substitute,
1 Free Vegetable,
1½ Starches, 4 Fats

In a large salad bowl, whisk the lemon juice together with the olive oil, oregano, mustard, and garlic. Cover and refrigerate for 1 hour, or up to 12 hours. Immediately before serving, toss the pasta with the almonds, cucumbers, tomatoes, red onions, olives, and feta cheese. Serve over the lettuce.

## Sweet and Savory Side Salad

*For 1 serving of an easy, versatile salad or a simple dressing over salad greens, mix ¾ cup shredded carrots, ¼ cup diced celery, 1 tablespoon raisins, and 1 teaspoon frozen pineapple juice concentrate. The Nutritional Analysis is: Calories: 31.00; Protein: 0.47 g; Carbohydrate: 7.64 g; Fat: 0.07 g; Sat. Fat: 0.01 g; Cholesterol: 0.00 mg; Sodium: 15.41 mg; Fiber: 1 g; PCF Ratio: 6-92-2. Exchange Approximations: ½ Fruit, 1 Free Vegetable, 1 Vegetable.*

# Bleu Cheese Pasta Salad

**Serves 4**

**Nutritional Analysis (per serving):**

| | |
|---|---|
| Calories: | 280.80 |
| Carbohydrate: | 23.72 g |
| Fat: | 11.04 g |
| Sat. Fat: | 4.58 g |
| Cholesterol: | 38.06 mg |
| Sodium: | 402.28 mg |
| Fiber: | 1.99 g |
| Protein: | 20.66 g |
| PCF Ratio: | 30-34-36 |

**Exchange Approx.:**
½ High Fat Meat,
1½ Very Lean Meats,
½ Lean Meat,
1 Carb./Starch, 1 Fat

*1 recipe Bleu Cheese Pasta (see page 180)*
*4 cups, tightly packed, salad greens*
*4 slices red onion*
*4 ounces thinly sliced **or** chopped chicken breast, broiled, grilled, **or** steamed*

*18 large black olives, sliced*
*Nonstarchy vegetables of your choice, such as sliced cucumbers, tomato, or zucchini to taste (optional)*

Prepare the Bleu Cheese Pasta (warm or chilled.) Divide the salad greens between 4 plates. Top each salad with a slice of red onion, the olives, 1 ounce of the chicken breast, and the free exchange vegetables of your choice, if desired. Top with the pasta.

# Taco Salad

**Serves 8**

**Nutritional Analysis (per serving):**

| | |
|---|---|
| Calories: | 426.45 |
| Protein: | 22.64 g |
| Carbohydrate: | 57.61 g |
| Fat: | 12.62 g |
| Sat. Fat: | 6.64 g |
| Cholesterol: | 29.79 mg |
| Sodium: | 379.78 mg |
| Fiber: | 13.22 g |
| PCF Ratio: | 21-53-26 |

**Exchange Approx.:**
1 Lean Meat,
1 High Fat Meat,
3 Starches, 2 Vegetables

*1 recipe Vegetable and Bean Chili (see page 189)*
*8 cups, tightly packed, salad greens*
*8 ounces Cheddar cheese, shredded (to yield 2 cups)*
*8 ounces nonfat corn chips*

*Nonstarchy free exchange vegetables of your choice, such as chopped celery, onion, or banana or jalapeno peppers (optional)*

Prepare the Vegetable and Bean Chili. Divide the salad greens between 8 large bowls. Top with the chili, Cheddar cheese, corn chips, and vegetables or peppers, if using.

# Layered Salad

¼ cup Hellmann's or Best
  Foods Real Mayonnaise
1¼ cups nonfat cottage cheese
½ cup nonfat plain yogurt
1 tablespoon apple cider
  vinegar **or** lemon juice
Pinch of sugar
6 cups shredded mixed lettuce
1½ cups diced celery
1½ cups chopped onion,
  any variety

1½ cups sliced carrots
1½ cups frozen green peas,
  thawed
6 ounces (2 percent fat or
  less) smoked turkey breast
6 ounces Cheddar cheese,
  shredded (to yield 1½ cups)

| Serves 6 | |
| --- | --- |
| **Nutritional Analysis (per serving):** | |
| Calories: | 286.45 |
| Protein: | 21.09 g |
| Carbohydrate: | 18.14 g |
| Fat: | 18.89 g |
| Sat. Fat: | 14.11 g |
| Cholesterol: | 48.51 mg |
| Sodium: | 521.05 mg |
| Fiber: | 4.24 g |
| PCF Ratio: | 26-22-52 |

**Exchange Approx.:**
1 High-Fat Meat,
1 Lean Meat,
1 Vegetable, 2 Fats

1. Combine the mayonnaise, cottage cheese, yogurt, vinegar (or lemon juice), and sugar in a food processor or blender; process until smooth. Set aside.
2. In a large salad bowl, layer the lettuce, celery, onion, carrots, peas, and turkey breast. Spread the mayonnaise mixture "dressing" over the top of the salad. Top with the shredded cheese.

## Yogurt-Mayo Sandwich Spread

*Spread a little flavor! Measure ½ teaspoon drained nonfat yogurt into a paper coffee filter. Twist to secure; drain over a cup or bowl in the refrigerator for at least 1 hour. In a small bowl, combine the drained yogurt with ½ teaspoon Hellmann's or Best Foods Real Mayonnaise. Use as you would mayonnaise. A 1-teaspoon serving has: Calories: 11.52; Protein: 0.23 g; Carbohydrate: 0.86 g; Fat: 0.82 g; Sat. Fat: 0.12 g; Cholesterol: 0.70 mg; Sodium: 20.11 mg; Fiber: 0.00 g; PCF Ratio: 8-29-63. Exchange Approximations: 1 Free Condiment.*

# Golden Raisin Smoked Turkey Salad

| Yields 4 generous-sized salads |
|---|

**Nutritional Analysis (per serving):**

| | |
|---|---|
| Calories: | 366.47 |
| Protein: | 20.84 g |
| Carbohydrate: | 61.04 g |
| Fat: | 7.84 g |
| Sat. Fat: | 1.51 g |
| Cholesterol: | 18.50 mg |
| Sodium: | 722.93 mg |
| Fiber: | 4.10 g |
| PCF Ratio: | 21-61-18 |

**Exchange Approx.:**
1 Very Lean Meat,
1 Lean Meat,
1½ Vegetables,
3 Fats, 1 Fruit,
1 Misc. Carb.

4 cups chopped broccoli
2 cup chopped cauliflower
3 shallots, chopped
1 ⅓ cups golden raisins
1 cup 1 percent cottage cheese
¼ cup Hellmann's or Best
  Foods Real Mayonnaise
¼ cup firm silken tofu
3 tablespoons tarragon vinegar
1 tablespoon balsamic vinegar
¼ cup brown sugar
¼ pound (4 ounces) smoked
  turkey breast, chopped
Freshly ground pepper
  (optional)
4 cups salad greens

Combine the broccoli, cauliflower, and shallots in a large bowl and stir in the raisins. In a blender or food processor, mix together the cottage cheese, mayonnaise, tofu, vinegars, brown sugar, and pepper until smooth. Toss the dressing over the broccoli, cauliflower, raisins, shallots, and turkey. Season with freshly ground pepper to taste. Chill until ready to serve, over salad greens.

**TIP:** *Because of the smoked turkey, this salad is high in sodium. If you're on a sodium-restricted diet, consider substituting regular cooked turkey or chicken breast. Punch up the flavor by adding 1 teaspoon of Bragg's Liquid Aminos or Homemade Worcestershire Sauce (see page 40).*

### Just How Bad Is Bacon?

*According to a Nutritional Analysis done by Cybersoft, Inc. (makers of the NutriBase 2001 software), when bacon is cooked until it's crisp—and drained to remove as much fat as possible, it still adds a whopping 731.52 calories! That comes out to about 39 grams of protein and 63 grams of fat, a third of which are from saturated fats (the bad guys).*

# CHAPTER 13
# Vegetables and Side Dishes

| | |
|---|---|
| Vegetable Broth | 214 |
| Layered Veggie Casserole | 215 |
| Creamy Polenta | 216 |
| Healthy Onion Rings | 216 |
| Oven-Baked Red Potatoes | 217 |
| Baked French Fries | 218 |
| Baked Potato Chips | 219 |
| Sweet Potato Crisps | 220 |
| Fluffy Buttermilk Mashed Potatoes | 220 |
| Roasted Garlic Mashed Potatoes | 221 |
| Corn Casserole | 222 |
| Gnocchi | 223 |

# Vegetable Broth

| Yields about 2½ quarts<br>Serving size: ¾ cup | |
|---|---|
| **Nutritional Analysis**<br>**(per serving):** | |
| Calories: | 9.83 |
| Protein: | 0.29 g |
| Carbohydrate: | 2.31 g |
| Fat: | 0.05 g |
| Sat. Fat: | 0.01 g |
| Cholesterol: | 0.00 mg |
| Sodium: | 8.33 mg |
| Fiber: | 0.57 g |
| PCF Ratio: | 11-85-4 |
| **Exchange Approx.:**<br>1 Free Vegetable | |

4 carrots, peeled and chopped
2 celery stalks and leaves, chopped
1 green bell pepper, seeded and chopped
2 medium zucchini, chopped
1 small onion, chopped
1 cup chopped fresh spinach
2 cups chopped leeks
½ cup chopped scallions
1 cup chopped green beans
1 cup chopped parsnips
2 bay leaves
2 cloves garlic, crushed
Sea salt and freshly ground black pepper (optional)
3 quarts water

1. Place all of the ingredients in a large pot and bring to a boil. Reduce the heat, cover the pan, and simmer for 30 minutes, or until vegetables are tender. Discard the bay leaf. Use a slotted spoon to transfer the vegetables to a different pot and mix them with some of the broth for "Free Exchange" vegetable soup. Freeze this mixture in single-serving containers to keep on hand for a quick, heat-in-the-microwave snack.
2. Strain the remaining vegetables from the broth, purée them in a blender or food processor, and return to the broth to add dietary fiber and add some body to the broth. Cool and freeze the broth until needed.

**TIP:** *If you strain the vegetables and discard them, a ½-cup serving size of the broth will have approximately 5 calories, and will still count as 1 Free Vegetable.*

## Perpetual Broth
*The easiest way to create vegetable broth is to keep a container in your freezer for saving the liquid from cooked vegetables. Vegetable broth makes a great addition to sauces, soups, and many other recipes. You can substitute it for meat broth in most recipes or use it instead of water for cooking pasta, rice, or other grains.*

# Layered Veggie Casserole

1 (10-ounce) package frozen
   mixed vegetables
½ cup diced onion
½ cup diced green pepper
1 cup unsalted tomato juice
⅛ teaspoon celery seed
⅛ teaspoon dried basil

⅛ teaspoon dried oregano
⅛ teaspoon dried parsley
¼ teaspoon garlic powder
3 tablespoons grated Parmesan
   cheese, divided

| Serves 4 |
| --- |
| **Nutritional Analysis (per serving):** |

| | |
| --- | --- |
| Calories: | 84.29 |
| Protein: | 4.50 g |
| Carbohydrate: | 15.51 g |
| Fat: | 1.35 g |
| Sat. Fat: | 0.75 g |
| Cholesterol: | 2.95 mg |
| Sodium: | 101.07 mg |
| Fiber: | 4.08 g |
| PCF Ratio: | 20-67-13 |

**Exchange Approx.:**
1 Vegetable,
1 Starch/Vegetable

1. Preheat oven to 350 degrees. Using a large casserole dish treated with nonstick spray, layer the frozen mixed vegetables, onion, and pepper. Mix the tomato juice with the seasonings and 2 tablespoons of the Parmesan cheese, and pour it over the vegetables. Cover and bake for 1 hour.

2. Uncover, sprinkle with remaining Parmesan cheese, and continue to bake for 10 minutes, or until the liquid thickens and the mixture bubbles.

## Season First

*When you ready vegetables for steaming them, add fresh or dried herbs, spices, sliced or diced onions, minced garlic, grated ginger, or just about any other seasoning you'd normally use. The seasonings will cook into the vegetables during steaming.*

# Creamy Polenta

| Serves 4 | |
|---|---|
| **Nutritional Analysis (per serving):** | |
| Calories: | 64.37 |
| Protein: | 5.84 g |
| Carbohydrate: | 9.17 g |
| Fat: | 0.46 g |
| Sat. Fat: | 0.16 g |
| Cholesterol: | 2.44 mg |
| Sodium: | 36.84 mg |
| Fiber: | 0.56 g |
| PCF Ratio: | 36-57-6 |
| **Exchange Approx.:** | |
| ½ Starch, | |
| ½ Skim Milk | |

*1 cup skim milk*
*½ cup nonfat cottage cheese*

*¼ cup yellow cornmeal*

Add the milk and cottage cheese to a blender and process until smooth. Pour the mixture into a nonstick, heavy saucepan. Over medium heat and stirring occasionally to prevent it from scorching, heat it until it begins to steam. Slowly stir in the cornmeal. Cook, stirring constantly, for 15 minutes.

# Healthy Onion Rings

| Serves 4 | |
|---|---|
| **Nutritional Analysis (per serving, without salt):** | |
| Calories: | 110.72 |
| Protein: | 4.39 g |
| Carbohydrate: | 22.16 g |
| Fat: | 0.53 g |
| Sat. Fat: | 0.11 g |
| Cholesterol: | 0.57 mg |
| Sodium: | 255.02 mg |
| Fiber: | 1.30 g |
| PCF Ratio: | 16-80-4 |
| **Exchange Approx.:** | |
| 1 Vegetable, | |
| 1 Carb./Starch | |

*1 cup yellow onion slices*
  *(¼-inch thick)*
*½ cup flour*
*½ cup nonfat plain yogurt*
*½ cup bread crumbs*

*Sea salt and freshly ground*
  *black pepper to taste*
  *(optional)*

1. Preheat oven to 350 degrees. Dredge the onion slices in the flour, shaking off any excess. Dip the onions in yogurt, then dredge them through the bread crumbs.
2. Prepare a baking sheet with nonstick cooking spray. Arrange the onion rings on the pan, and bake for 15 to 20 minutes. Place the onion rings under the broiler for an additional 2 minutes to brown them. Season with salt and pepper, if desired.

# Oven-Baked Red Potatoes

1 pound (16 ounces) small red
    potatoes, halved
¼ cup fresh lemon juice
1 teaspoon olive oil

1 teaspoon sea salt
¼ teaspoon freshly ground
    pepper

Preheat oven to 350 degrees. Arrange the potatoes in a 13" × 9" oven-proof casserole dish. Combine the remaining ingredients, and pour over the potatoes. Bake for 30 to 40 minutes, or until the potatoes are tender, turning 3 to 4 times to baste.

### Remember the Roasting "Rack"

*Use caution when roasting potatoes with meat. The potatoes will act like a sponge and soak up the fat. Your best option, of course, is to use lean cuts of meat and elevate the meat and vegetable out of the fat by putting them on a roasting rack within the pan. Or, make a "bridge" by elevating the meat on stalks of celery. Discard the celery that you've used to elevate the meat.*

| Serves 4 | |
| --- | --- |
| **Nutritional Analysis (per serving):** | |
| Calories: | 119.55 |
| Protein: | 2.29 g |
| Carbohydrate: | 25.85 g |
| Fat: | 1.24 g |
| Sat. Fat: | 0.18 g |
| Cholesterol: | 0.00 g |
| Sodium: | 587.25 mg |
| Fiber: | 1.80 g |
| PCF Ratio: | 7-84-9 |
| **Exchange Approx.:** 1 Starch/Vegetable | |

# Baked French Fries

| Serves 1 |
|:---:|

| Nutritional Analysis (per serving, without salt): | |
|:---|---:|
| Calories: | 118.88 |
| Protein: | 1.67 g |
| Carbohydrate: | 18.34 g |
| Fat: | 4.59 g |
| Sat. Fat: | 0.63 g |
| Cholesterol: | 0.00 mg |
| Sodium: | 4.25 mg |
| Fiber: | 1.28 g |
| PCF Ratio: | 5-60-34 |

**Exchange Approx.:**
1 Starch,
1 Fat

1 small white potato (3 ounces)
1 teaspoon olive oil

Sea salt and freshly ground
  black pepper to taste
  (optional)

1. Preheat oven to 400 degrees. Wash, peel, and slice the potatoes into French fry wedges. Wrap the slices in a paper towel to remove any excess moisture. "Oil" the potatoes by placing them into a plastic bag with the olive oil. Close the bag and shake the potatoes until they're evenly coated. Spread potatoes on a baking sheet treated with nonstick spray and bake for 5 to 10 minutes.
2. Remove the pan from the oven and quickly turn the potatoes. Return the pan to the oven and bake for another 10 to 15 minutes, depending on how crisp you prefer your fries. Season the potatoes with salt and pepper, if your diet allows for the additional sodium.

### Get a Head Start
*Speed up the time it takes to bake French fries! First, cook the potatoes in the microwave for 3 to 4 minutes in a covered microwave-safe dish. Allow potatoes to rest for at least a minute after removing the dish from the microwave. Dry potatoes with paper towels, if necessary. Arrange the potatoes on a nonstick spray–treated baking sheet. Spray the potatoes with flavored cooking spray or a few spritzes of olive oil and bake at 400 degrees for 5 to 8 minutes to crisp them.*

# Baked Potato Chips

*1 small white potato*
*(3 ounces)*
*1 teaspoon olive oil*

*Sea salt and freshly ground*
*black pepper to taste*
*(optional)*

| Serves 1 | |
|---|---|
| **Nutritional Analysis** **(per serving, without salt):** | |
| Calories: | 118.88 |
| Protein: | 1.67 g |
| Carbohydrate: | 18.34 g |
| Fat: | 4.59 g |
| Sat. Fat: | 0.63 g |
| Cholesterol: | 0.00 mg |
| Sodium: | 4.25 mg |
| Fiber: | 1.28 g |
| PCF Ratio: | 5-60-34 |
| **Exchange Approx.:** 1 Starch, 1 Fat | |

Preheat oven to 400 degrees. Wash, peel, and thinly slice the potatoes. Wrap the slices in a paper towel to remove any excess moisture. Spread the potatoes on a baking sheet treated with nonstick spray and spritz them with olive oil. Bake for 10 to 15 minutes, depending on how crisp you prefer your fries. Season the potatoes with salt and pepper, if your diet allows for the additional sodium.

TIP: *The Nutritional Allowance for this recipe allows for the teaspoon of olive oil. Even though you just spritz the potatoes with oil, remember that "chips" have more surface area than fries do.*

 **Fat-Cutting Alternatives**
*Eliminate the oil (and thus the Fat Exchange) in the Baked French Fries and Baked Potato Chips in this chapter by using butter-flavored or olive oil cooking spray instead.*

# Sweet Potato Crisps

| Serves 2 | |
|---|---|

**Nutritional Analysis (per serving, without salt):**

| | |
|---|---|
| Calories: | 89.24 |
| Protein: | 1.31 g |
| Carbohydrate: | 16.10 g |
| Fat: | 2.41 g |
| Sat. Fat: | 0.34 g |
| Cholesterol: | 0.00 mg |
| Sodium: | 7.30 mg |
| Fiber: | 8.94 g |
| PCF Ratio: | 6-70-24 |

**Exchange Approx.:**
1 Starch,
½ Fat

*1 small sweet potato **or** yam*
*1 teaspoon olive oil*

*Sea salt and freshly ground black pepper to taste (optional)*

1. Preheat oven to 400 degrees. Scrub the sweet potato or yam and pierce the flesh several times with a fork. Place on a microwave-safe plate and microwave for 5 minutes on high. Remove from the microwave and wrap the sweet potato in aluminum foil. Set aside for 5 minutes.
2. Remove the foil, peel the potato, and cut it into "French fries." Spread the fries on a baking sheet treated with nonstick spray and spritz with the olive oil. Bake for 10 to 15 minutes, or until crisp. There's a risk that sweet potato strips (French fries) will caramelize and burn. Check them often while cooking to ensure this doesn't occur; lower the oven temperature, if necessary. Season with salt and pepper, if desired.

# Fluffy Buttermilk Mashed Potatoes

| Serves 4 | |
|---|---|

**Nutritional Analysis (per serving, without salt):**

| | |
|---|---|
| Calories: | 97.13 |
| Protein: | 2.12 g |
| Carbohydrate: | 17.86 g |
| Fat: | 2.14 g |
| Sat. Fat: | 1.30 g |
| Cholesterol: | 5.71 mg |
| Sodium: | 19.72 mg |
| Fiber: | 1.53 g |
| PCF Ratio: | 9-72-19 |

**Exchange Approx.:**
1 Starch,
½ Fat

*¾ pound (12 ounces) peeled and boiled potatoes*
*¼ cup warm buttermilk*

*2 teaspoons unsalted butter*
*Sea salt and freshly ground black pepper to taste (optional)*

Place the potatoes in a large bowl and partially mash. Add the warm buttermilk and mix well, mashing the potatoes completely. Stir in the butter and salt and pepper (if using). (If you like your mashed potatoes creamy, add some of the potato water.)

# Roasted Garlic Mashed Potatoes

4 cloves roasted garlic
(for roasting instructions,
see "Dry-Roasted Garlic"
on page 54)
1 small onion, chopped
¾ pound (12 ounces) peeled,
cooked potatoes
2 cups cauliflower, steamed
and drained

¼ cup buttermilk
⅛ cup nonfat cottage cheese
2 teaspoons unsalted butter
Sea salt and freshly ground
black pepper to taste
(optional)

| Serves 4 | |
| --- | --- |
| **Nutritional Analysis (per serving, without salt):** | |
| Calories: | 126.30 |
| Protein: | 4.44 g |
| Carbohydrate: | 23.00 g |
| Fat: | 2.48 g |
| Sat. Fat: | 1.36 g |
| Cholesterol: | 6.02 mg |
| Sodium: | 30.56 mg |
| Fiber: | 3.48 g |
| PCF Ratio: | 13-70-17 |
| **Exchange Approx.:** | |
| 1 Starch, | |
| 1 Vegetable, | |
| ½ Fat | |

Combine all the ingredients and whip until fluffy. If the potatoes or cauliflower are overly moist, add the buttermilk gradually until the whipped mixture reaches the desired consistency. (Combining steamed cauliflower with the potatoes allows you to increase the portion size without significantly changing the flavor of the mashed potatoes.)

## Gravy Substitute

Instead of using gravy, sprinkle crumbled bleu cheese or grated Parmesan over mashed potatoes. Just remember that cheese is a Meat Exchange and adjust the Exchange Approximations for each serving accordingly.

# Corn Casserole

| Serves 2 | |
|---|---|
| **Nutritional Analysis (per serving):** | |
| Calories: | 187.89 |
| Protein: | 11.39 g |
| Carbohydrate: | 32.47 g |
| Fat: | 2.86 g |
| Sat. Fat: | 1.48 g |
| Cholesterol: | 9.95 mg |
| Sodium: | 132.71 mg |
| Fiber: | 2.44 g |
| PCF Ratio: | 23-65-13 |

**Exchange Approx.:**
1½ Starches,
1 Skim Milk,
½ Fat

1 tablespoon finely chopped onion
1 tablespoon finely chopped green **or** red bell pepper
1 cup frozen **or** fresh corn kernels
⅛ teaspoon ground mace
Dash ground white **or** black pepper
¾ cup skim milk
¼ cup nonfat dry milk
1 egg
1 teaspoon butter

1. Preheat oven to 325 degrees. In a medium-sized bowl, combine the onion, bell pepper, corn, mace, and pepper, and toss to mix.
2. In a blender, combine the skim milk, dry milk, egg, and butter, and process until mixed. Pour over the corn mixture and toss to mix. Pour the entire mixture into a glass casserole dish treated with non-stick spray. Bake for 1 hour, or until set.

### Special Spice Side Effects
*Ground mace or nutmeg can elevate blood pressure or cause an irregular heartbeat in some individuals. Check with your doctor or nutritionist before you add it to your diet.*

# Gnocchi

*1 cup boiled and mashed
    potatoes*
*1 egg*

*2 cups all-purpose **or** semolina
    flour*

| Serves 8 |
| --- |
| **Nutritional Analysis (per serving):** |

| | |
| --- | --- |
| Calories: | 138.72 |
| Protein: | 4.25 g |
| Carbohydrate: | 27.82 g |
| Fat: | 0.88 g |
| Sat. Fat: | 0.22 g |
| Cholesterol: | 23.38 mg |
| Sodium: | 8.53 mg |
| Fiber: | 1.19 g |
| PCF Ratio: | 12-82-6 |

**Exchange Approx.:**
1½ Starches

1. Combine the potato, flour, and egg in a large bowl. Knead until the dough forms a ball. The finished dough should be smooth, pliable, and slightly sticky. Shape 4 equal portions of the dough into long ropes, about ¾ inch in diameter. On a floured surface, cut the rope into ½-inch pieces. Press your thumb or forefinger into each piece to create an indentation. (Some gnocchi chefs also like to roll each piece with a fork to add a distinctive texture.)

2. Bring a large pot of water to a boil. Drop in the gnocchi, being careful that the amount you add doesn't stop the water from boiling. Cook for 3 to 5 minutes, or until the gnocchi rise to the top. Remove the gnocchi from water with a slotted spoon. Serve immediately, or, if you make it in batches, put finished gnocchi on a platter to be set in a warm oven.

**TIP:** *As a side dish, serve gnocchi with your favorite pasta sauce or dress it with a little olive oil and herbs or Parmesan cheese. (Be sure to add the extra Exchange Approximations if you do.)*

### Old Country Secrets

*Italian cooks sometimes toss each helping of gnocchi in a teaspoon of melted butter and sugar, then sprinkle it with cinnamon to serve it as a dessert. This adds 1 Fat Exchange and 1 Carb exchange to the Gnocchi recipe.*

# Aromatic Rice Flavor Suggestions

TO SPICE UP the flavor of 4 servings of cooked rice, try the following:

- **Green Rice:** Add ¼ cup each of chopped fresh parsley and chopped green onions (white and green parts).

- **Lemon-Parsley:** Add 2 tablespoons chopped parsley and 1 teaspoon grated lemon peel.

- **Orange-Cilantro:** Add 2 tablespoons chopped fresh cilantro and ½ teaspoon grated orange peel.

- **Asian:** Stir in two chopped green onions, a dash of soy sauce or Bragg's Liquid Aminos, and ¼ teaspoon toasted sesame oil.

∾

CHAPTER 14
# *Desserts*

| | |
|---|---|
| Individual Sponge Cakes | 226 |
| Glazed Carrot Cake | 227 |
| Linzertorte Muffins | 228 |
| Mock Whipped Cream | 229 |
| Date-Nut Roll | 230 |
| Chocolate Cheesecake Mousse | 230 |
| Chocolate Cheesecake Mousse II | 231 |
| Nonfat Whipped Milk Base | 232 |
| Orange Marmalade Cheesecake Mousse | 233 |
| Peanut Butter Pleaser | 233 |
| Whipped Lemon Cheesecake Mousse | 234 |
| Whipped Mocha Mousse | 234 |
| Carrot-Fruit Cup | 235 |
| Lucky Lemonade Gelatin | 235 |
| Faux Chocolate Bavarian Cream | 236 |
| Bubbly Berry Blast | 237 |
| Baked Pear Crisp | 238 |
| Nonfat Ice Cream or Smoothie Base | 239 |
| Mock Pumpkin Custard | 239 |
| Strawberry-Banana Sherbet | 240 |
| Bananas Foster | 241 |
| Almond Biscotti | 242 |
| Beanberry Blast | 242 |
| Apple Cookies with a Kick | 243 |
| Lemon Curd | 244 |
| Pineapple Upside-Down Cake | 245 |
| Whole-Grain Maple-Walnut Bread Pudding | 246 |
| Individual Apple-Blackberry Charlottes | 247 |

# Individual Sponge Cakes

1 cup flour
½ teaspoon salt
1 teaspoon baking powder
3 eggs
¾ cup granulated sugar
1 tablespoon lemon juice

6 tablespoons hot milk
½ teaspoon lemon zest (optional)

1. Preheat oven to 350 degrees. Mix together the flour, salt, and baking powder. In a food processor or mixing bowl, beat the eggs until fluffy and lemon colored. Add the sugar, lemon juice, and, if using, the lemon zest. Add the flour mixture; process only enough to blend. Add the hot milk and process until blended.
2. Pour into a 12-section muffin pan treated with nonstick spray. (Also works well as 24 mini-muffins.) If lining the muffin pan, use foil liners. Bake for 15 minutes, or until a toothpick inserted in the center of a cupcake comes out clean. The cakes will be golden brown and firm to the touch. Move the cupcakes to a rack to cool.

 **Snack Cakes**
*Use a pastry bag to "pump" some nonfat whipped topping or low-sugar jelly (or a mixture of the 2) into the center of the Individual Sponge Cakes, and you have a healthier, homemade snack cake alternative.*

# Glazed Carrot Cake

1½ cups unbleached all-purpose flour

1 teaspoon baking powder

1 teaspoon baking soda

1½ teaspoons cinnamon

¼ teaspoon ground cloves

¼ teaspoon ground allspice

⅛ teaspoon ground nutmeg

1 tablespoon sugar

⅛ cup (2 tablespoons) frozen, unsweetened apple juice concentrate

2 eggs

¼ cup water

2 tablespoons ground flaxseed

1 teaspoon vanilla

3 tablespoons nonfat plain yogurt

1 cup canned, unsweetened crushed pineapple, ¼ cup of liquid retained

1 cup finely shredded carrots

¼ cup seedless raisins

## Glaze

⅛ cup (2 tablespoons) frozen, unsweetened apple juice concentrate

1 tablespoon water

| Serves 9 | |
|---|---|
| **Nutritional Analysis (per serving):** | |
| Calories: | 148.63 |
| Protein: | 4.79 g |
| Carbohydrate: | 27.54 g |
| Fat: | 2.24 g |
| Sat. Fat: | 0.45 g |
| Cholesterol: | 41.73 mg |
| Sodium: | 220.39 mg |
| Fiber: | 2.06 g |
| PCF Ratio: | 13-74-13 |

**Exchange Approx.:**
1 Bread/Starch,
½ Vegetable,
1 Fruit

1. Preheat oven to 350 degrees. Sift together the dry ingredients and spices. Using a food processor or mixer, blend together the sugar, apple juice concentrate, and eggs until well mixed. Stir the water and ground flaxseed together in a small microwave-safe bowl and microwave on high for 30 seconds; stir. (Mixture should be the consistency of egg whites; if it hasn't thickened to that appearance, microwave at 15-second increments until it does.) Gradually beat into the egg mixture, along with the vanilla, yogurt, and the ¼ cup pineapple liquid. Stir in the dry ingredients. Fold the crushed pineapple (drained of any remaining juice), shredded carrots, and raisins.
2. Treat an 8-inch baking pan with nonstick spray. Spoon the mixture into the pan, then bake for 20 to 25 minutes. Allow the cake to cool slightly while you prepare the glaze.
3. Mix the apple juice concentrate and water until the concentrate is melted. (You can microwave the mixture for 15 to 20 seconds, if necessary.) Spread evenly over the cake.

# Linzertorte Muffins

| Yields 12 muffins Serving size: 1 muffin | |
|---|---|
| **Nutritional Analysis (per serving):** | |
| Calories: | 147.73 |
| Protein: | 3.59 g |
| Carbohydrate: | 29.53 g |
| Fat: | 1.70 g |
| Sat. Fat: | 0.27 g |
| Cholesterol: | 15.95 mg |
| Sodium: | 294.43 mg |
| Fiber: | 0.88 g |
| PCF Ratio: | 10-80-10 |
| **Exchange Approx.:** | |
| 1 Bread/Starch, 1 Fruit | |

¼ cup ground blanched hazelnuts (filberts)
2 cups unbleached all-purpose flour
2 teaspoons baking powder
½ teaspoon salt
1 teaspoon cinnamon
⅛ teaspoon ground allspice
⅛ teaspoon ground ginger
⅛ cup granulated sugar
¼ cup, firmly packed, brown sugar
½ cup applesauce
1 egg
1 teaspoon grated lemon peel
½ teaspoon vanilla
1 cup skim milk
12 teaspoons seedless black raspberry jam

1. Preheat oven to 400 degrees. Prepare the muffin pan by treating it with nonstick spray or use lining cups with cupcake papers. (Lighter Silverstone-coated muffin pans work fine, but dark nonstick pans are not recommended for these muffins.)

2. Pulse the filberts in a food processor until they are ground. Add all of the dry ingredients, including the spices, to the food processor with the filberts and pulse until everything is well mixed. Add the remaining ingredients *except* for the jam and process to mix. (If you're using a mixer, cream the egg, applesauce, and sugars. Mix in the milk and vanilla, then add the dry ingredients and lemon peel. Fold in the nuts.)

3. Spoon a tablespoonful of batter into each of the 12 muffin sections. Top the batter with a teaspoonful of seedless black raspberry jam per muffin, being careful that none of the jam touches the sides of the muffin pan. Evenly divide the remaining muffin batter between the 12 muffins, using it to top the jam. Gently spread the batter to cover the jam. Bake 15 to 20 minutes, or until lightly browned.

## Substitution Options

*Milk is an easy ingredient to substitute in baking. Fruit juice, rice milk, almond milk (or Ener-G NutQuik), or soy milk (or Ener-G SoyQuik) can be used 1 for 1, although such use will alter the Nutritional Analysis. Keep in mind that you can substitute water, but that may produce a blander-tasting baked product.*

# Mock Whipped Cream

1 envelope KNOX Unflavored
  Gelatine
¼ cup cold water
½ cup hot water
2 tablespoons almond oil
3 tablespoons powdered sugar

1 teaspoon vanilla
1 cup ice water
1¼ cups nonfat milk powder

| Yields 3½ cups<br>Serving size: 2 tbs. | |
|---|---|
| **Nutritional Analysis<br>(per serving):** | |
| Calories: | 23.68 |
| Protein: | 1.28 g |
| Carbohydrate: | 2.44 g |
| Fat: | 0.99 g |
| Sat. Fat: | 0.09 g |
| Cholesterol: | 0.55 mg |
| Sodium: | 17.21 mg |
| Fiber: | 0.00 g |
| PCF Ratio: | 21-41-38 |
| **Exchange Approx.:**<br>½ Fat | |

1. Allow the gelatin to soften in the cold water, then pour the mixture into a blender. Add the hot water and blend for 2 minutes until the gelatin is dissolved.
2. While continuing to blend the mixture, gradually add the almond oil and powdered sugar. Chill in the freezer for 15 minutes, or until the mixture is cool but hasn't yet begun to "set."
3. Using a hand mixer or whisk, add the ice water and nonfat milk powder to a chilled bowl and beat until peaks start to form. Add the gelatin mixture to the whipped milk and continuing to whip until stiffer peaks begin to form. This whipped topping will keep several days in the refrigerator. Whip again to reintroduce more air into the topping before serving.

TIP: *There is some fat in this recipe, but the use of vegetable oil reduces the Saturated Fat and Cholesterol Amounts considerably compared to making whipped cream using real cream.*

## Know Your Ingredients
*"Gelatine" is the name of the commercial "KNOX Unflavored Gelatine" product used to make gelatin. Although any unflavored gelatin will work, the nutritional analyses for all recipes are based on the Knox brand.*

# Date-Nut Roll

**Serves 12**

**Nutrient Analysis (per serving):**

| | |
|---|---|
| Calories: | 102.54 |
| Protein: | 1.74 g |
| Carbohydrate: | 17.52 g |
| Fat: | 3.23 g |
| Sat Fat: | 0.40 g |
| Cholesterol: | 0.09 mg |
| Sodium: | 95.43 mg |
| Fiber: | 1.27 g |
| PCF Ratio: | 7-66-27 |

**Exchange Approx.:**
1 Fat,
½ Bread/Starch,
½ Fruit

12 graham crackers
¼ cup finely chopped walnuts
12 dates, chopped

¼ cup Mock Whipped Cream
(see page 229)

Place graham crackers in a plastic bag and use a rolling pin to crush them or process into crumbs in a food processor. Mix the resulting graham cracker crumbs with the chopped walnuts and dates. Gently fold in the Mock Whipped Cream. Turn the mixture out onto a piece of aluminum foil (if you plan to freeze it) or onto plastic wrap (if you'll only be chilling it until you're ready to serve it). Shape the mixture into a log shape and wrap securely in the foil or plastic wrap. Chill for at least 4 hours before serving. Cut into 12 slices.

# Chocolate Cheesecake Mousse

**Serves 4**

**Nutritional Analysis (per serving):**

| | |
|---|---|
| Calories: | 83.41 |
| Protein: | 2.74 g |
| Carbohydrate: | 6.58 g |
| Fat: | 5.03 g |
| Sat. Fat: | 2.36 g |
| Cholesterol: | 8.60 mg |
| Sodium: | 47.17 mg |
| Fiber: | 0.19 g |
| PCF Ratio: | 13-32-55 |

**Exchange Approx.:**
½ Skim Milk,
1 Fat

¾ cup Mock Whipped Cream
(see page 229)
1 tablespoon semisweet chocolate chips

1 ounce cream cheese
1½ teaspoons cocoa
1 teaspoon vanilla

Put the chocolate chips and 1 tablespoon of the Mock Whipped Cream in a microwave-safe bowl and microwave on high for 15 seconds. Add the cream cheese to the bowl and microwave on high for another 15 seconds. Whip the mixture until it is well blended and the chocolate chips are melted. Stir in the cocoa and vanilla. Fold in the remaining Mock Whipped Cream. Chill until ready to serve.

# Chocolate Cheesecake Mousse II

4 ounces semisweet chocolate
   chips
1 recipe Nonfat Whipped Milk
   Base (see page 232)

4 ounces cream cheese, at
   room temperature
1 teaspoon vanilla

| Serves 12 | |
| --- | --- |
| **Nutritional Analysis (per serving):** | |
| Calories: | 104.40 |
| Protein: | 3.38 g |
| Carbohydrate: | 9.86 g |
| Fat: | 6.05 g |
| Sat. Fat: | 3.80 g |
| Cholesterol: | 11.26 mg |
| Sodium: | 53.76 mg |
| Fiber: | 0.00 g |
| PCF Ratio: | 13-37-51 |
| **Exchange Approx.:** 1 Skim Milk, ½ Fat | |

1. Put the chocolate chips in a microwave-safe bowl along with about ¼ cup of the Whipped Milk Base. Microwave on high for 20 seconds. Beat vigorously with a fork or whisk until the chocolate is melted and blended in with the milk. If necessary, microwave on high for another 5 to 10 seconds.

2. The mixture will be very warm at this point. Cut the cream cheese into several pieces, each about 1 tablespoon in size, and add it to the chocolate mixture. Beat vigorously until the cream cheese is blended into the chocolate. Add the vanilla and stir to mix. Pour the mixture into the remaining Whipped Milk Base, using a spatula to scrape the sides of the bowl. Chill for at least 1 hour before serving.

TIP: *To compensate for difference in whipped textures, this recipe uses more chocolate chips, so the calories per serving are higher than the recipe on page 230.*

# Nonfat Whipped Milk Base

| Yields about 3 cups | |
|---|---|
| **Nutritional Analysis (per recipe):** | |
| Calories: | 290.37 |
| Carbohydrate: | 42.40 g |
| Protein: | 28.22 g |
| Fat: | 0.69 g |
| Sat. Fat: | 0.44 g |
| Cholesterol: | 10.78 mg |
| Sodium: | 310.68 mg |
| Fiber: | 0.00 g |
| PCF Ratio: | 39-59-2 |
| **Exchange Approx.:** | |
| 2 Skim Milks, 1 Carb. | |

¼ cup nonfat milk powder
⅛ cup powdered sugar
1 cup chilled skim milk, divided

1½ envelopes KNOX Unflavored Gelatine

1. In a chilled bowl, combine the milk powder and sugar, and mix until well blended. Pour ¼ cup of the chilled skim milk and the gelatine into a blender; let sit for 1 or 2 minutes for the gelatin to soften.
2. In a microwave-safe container, heat the remaining skim milk until it almost reaches the boiling point, or about 30 to 45 seconds on high. Add the heated milk to the blender with the gelatine, and blend for 2 minutes, or until the gelatin is completely dissolved. Chill for 15 minutes or until the mixture is cool, but the gelatin hasn't yet begun to "set."
3. Using a hand mixer or a whisk, beat the mixture until it's doubled in size. (It won't form stiff peaks like whipped cream; however, you'll notice that it'll get a creamier white in color.) Chill until ready to use in one of the next desserts. If necessary, whip again immediately prior to folding in the other mousse ingredients.

TIP: *For best results, chill a glass bowl in the freezer for 1 hour for use in preparing this recipe.*

## Whipping Methods
*Because you don't need to whip the Whipped Milk Base until it reaches stiff peaks, you can use a blender or food processor; however, you won't be whipping as much air into the mixture if you do, so the serving sizes will be a bit smaller.*

# Orange Marmalade Cheesecake Mousse

⁷⁄₈ cup Mock Whipped Cream
(see page 229)
⅛ cup, plus 2 teaspoons
Smucker's Low-Sugar Orange
Marmalade

1 ounce cream cheese
1 teaspoon vanilla extract

In a microwave-safe bowl, heat the orange marmalade and cream cheese for 15 seconds. Whip until well blended. Gently fold in the Mock Whipped Cream and vanilla. Chill until ready to serve.

**Serves 4**

**Nutritional Analysis (per serving):**

| | |
|---|---|
| Calories: | 85.90 |
| Protein: | 2.78 g |
| Carbohydrate: | 8.59 g |
| Fat: | 4.22 g |
| Sat Fat: 1.71 g | |
| Cholesterol: | 8.74 mg |
| Sodium: | 51.14 mg |
| Fiber: | 0.00 g |
| PCF Ratio: | 13-41-46 |

**Exchange Approx.:**
½ Skim Milk,
½ Fat

# Peanut Butter Pleaser

⁷⁄₈ cups Mock Whipped Cream
(see page 229)
1 teaspoon vanilla extract

1 tablespoon, plus 1 teaspoon
unsalted, smooth peanut
butter

In a bowl, fold the peanut butter and vanilla into the Mock Whipped Cream until well blended. Chill until ready to serve.

**Serves 4**

**Nutritional Analysis (per serving):**

| | |
|---|---|
| Calories: | 76.13 |
| Protein: | 3.59 g |
| Carbohydrate: | 5.43 g |
| Fat: | 4.47 g |
| Sat Fat: | 0.71 g |
| Cholesterol: | 0.96 mg |
| Sodium: | 31.10 mg |
| Fiber: | 0.31 g |
| PCF Ratio: | 19-28-53 |

**Exchange Approx.:**
½ Skim Milk,
½ Fat

| Serves 10 | |
|---|---|
| **Nutritional Analysis (per serving):** | |
| Calories: | 80.63 |
| Protein: | 3.66 g |
| Carbohydrate: | 7.66 g |
| Fat: | 4.03 g |
| Sat. Fat: | 2.54 g |
| Cholesterol: | 13.51 mg |
| Sodium: | 64.55 mg |
| Fiber: | 0.01 g |
| PCF Ratio: | 18-38-44 |
| **Exchange Approx.:** | |
| 1 Skim Milk | |

# Whipped Lemon Cheesecake Mousse

*4 ounces cream cheese, room temperature*
*1 tablespoon lemon juice*
*1 teaspoon lemon zest*

*¼ cup powdered sugar*
*1 recipe Whipped Milk Base (see page 232)*

In a small bowl, combine the cream cheese, lemon juice and zest, and powdered sugar; using a fork or whisk, beat until well blended. Fold the mixture into the Whipped Milk Base. Chill for at least 1 hour before serving.

| Serves 10 | |
|---|---|
| **Nutritional Analysis (per serving):** | |
| Calories: | 82.11 |
| Protein: | 3.91 g |
| Carbohydrate: | 15.73 g |
| Fat: | 0.31 g |
| Sat. Fat: | 0.19 g |
| Cholesterol: | 1.07 mg |
| Sodium: | 36.51 mg |
| Fiber: | 0.62 g |
| PCF Ratio: | 19-77-3 |
| **Exchange Approx.:** | |
| 1 Skim Milk | |

# Whipped Mocha Mousse

*¼ cup cold water*
*1 envelope KNOX Unflavored Gelatine*
*¾ cup hot water*
*2 teaspoons instant espresso powder*

*½ cup sugar*
*¼ cup unsweetened cocoa*
*1½ teaspoons vanilla extract*
*1 recipe Whipped Milk Base (see page 232)*
*Ground cinnamon (optional)*

1. Pour the cold water into a blender and sprinkle the unflavored gelatin over it; let stand for 1 minute.
2. Add the hot water and instant espresso powder, and blend at low speed until the gelatin is completely dissolved. Add the sugar, cocoa, and vanilla; process at high speed until blended. Allow the mixture to cool to at least room temperature before folding it into the Whipped Milk Base. Chill until ready to serve.

# Carrot-Fruit Cup

1 tablespoon raisins
2 carrots, grated
1 apple, grated
1 tablespoon frozen apple juice
   concentrate

1 teaspoon cinnamon
Pinch of ginger
1 frozen banana, sliced

1. Soak the raisins overnight in a little more than enough water to cover them.
2. When you're ready to prepare the dessert, drain the water from the raisins and pour them into a bowl. Add the carrots and apple. Stir in the frozen apple juice concentrate and spices until blended. Add the banana slices and stir again. Chill until ready to serve.

**Serves 4**

**Nutritional Analysis (per serving):**

| | |
|---|---|
| Calories: | 69.41 |
| Protein: | 0.80 g |
| Carbohydrate: | 17.53 g |
| Fat: | 0.32 g |
| Sat. Fat: | 0.09 g |
| Cholesterol: | 0.00 mg |
| Sodium: | 13.43 mg |
| Fiber: | 2.49 g |
| PCF Ratio: | 4-92-4 |

**Exchange Approx.:**
1 Fruit,
½ Vegetable

# Lucky Lemonade Gelatin

1 envelope KNOX Unflavored
   Gelatine
¼ cup cold water
1½ cups hot water
¼ cup fresh lemon juice
   (**or** lime juice)

3 tablespoons Smucker's Low-
   Sugar Orange Marmalade
1 tablespoon sugar

In a blender container, soak the gelatin in the cold water for 2 minutes, then add the hot water and blend for about 2 minutes, or until the gelatin is dissolved. Add the juice, marmalade, and sugar, and blend until the sugar is dissolved. Pour into a dish or mold and refrigerate until set, about 3 hours, or longer.

**Serves 4**

**Nutritional Analysis (per serving):**

| | |
|---|---|
| Calories: | 40.91 |
| Protein: | 1.56 g |
| Carbohydrate: | 8.94 g |
| Fat: | 0.00 g |
| Sat. Fat: | 0.00 g |
| Cholesterol: | 0.00 mg |
| Sodium: | 3.93 mg |
| Fiber: | 0.06 g |
| PCF Ratio: | 15-85-0 |

**Exchange Approx.:**
1 Fruit

# Faux Chocolate Bavarian Cream

| Serves 4 | |
|---|---|
| **Nutritional Analysis (per serving):** | |
| Calories: | 78.61 |
| Protein: | 6.91 g |
| Carbohydrate: | 12.67 g |
| Fat: | 0.58 g |
| Sat. Fat: | 0.35 g |
| Cholesterol: | 2.76 mg |
| Sodium: | 79.45 mg |
| Fiber: | 0.90 g |
| PCF Ratio: | 33-61-6 |
| **Exchange Approx.:** | |
| 1 Skim Milk | |

1 envelope KNOX Unflavored
  Gelatine
⅛ cup cold water
1½ cups skim milk,
  plus 2 tablespoons
¼ cup nonfat milk powder

2 tablespoons unsweetened
  cocoa
4 teaspoons sugar
⅛ cup hot water

1. While you soak the gelatin in the cold water (for at least 3 minutes), heat the 1½ cups of skim milk in a saucepan over medium heat just until bubbles begin to form around the edge. Turn the heat as low as it will go, and add the milk powder, cocoa, and sugar; stir until they dissolve. Add the hot water to the gelatin, and stir until the gelatin dissolves. Add the gelatin to the milk mixture and stir well. Refrigerate until set, at least 3 hours.

2. Once the gelatin has set completely, put it in a blender with the remaining 2 tablespoons of skim milk. Blend until the mixture has a pudding-like consistency. If necessary, add more milk.

**TIP:** *This cream is best served right away, but if you have to wait, give it a quick blend just beforehand to mix in any ingredients that may have separated out.*

# Bubbly Berry Blast

2 envelopes KNOX Unflavored
  Gelatine
½ cup frozen, unsweetened
  apple juice concentrate
3 cups (24 ounces) unsweetened sparkling water

1 cup sliced strawberries
1 cup blueberries

| Serves 6 | |
|---|---|
| **Nutritional Analysis (per serving):** | |
| Calories: | 60.84 |
| Protein: | 2.41 g |
| Carbohydrate: | 12.94 g |
| Fat: | 0.26 g |
| Sat. Fat: | 0.02 g |
| Cholesterol: | 0.00 mg |
| Sodium: | 11.43 mg |
| Fiber: | 1.31 g |
| PCF Ratio: | 15-81-4 |
| **Exchange Approx.:** 1 Fruit | |

1. Mix the gelatin and apple juice in a small saucepan, stir, and let stand for 1 minute. Place the mixture over low heat and stir until completely dissolved, about 3 minutes. Cool slightly. (Alternatively, blend the gelatin and apple juice in a small, microwave-safe bowl, let stand 1 minute, and then microwave on high for 45 seconds; stir mixture until the gelatin is completely dissolved.) Stir in the sparkling water. Refrigerate until mixture begins to gel or is the consistency of unbeaten egg whites when stirred.
2. Fold the fruit into the partially thickened gelatin mixture. Pour into a 6-cup mold. Refrigerate for 4 hours, or until firm.

# Baked Pear Crisp

| Serves 4 |
| :---: |

### Nutritional Analysis (per serving):

| | |
| :--- | ---: |
| Calories: | 199.53 |
| Protein: | 1.49 g |
| Carbohydrate: | 42.27 g |
| Fat: | 3.51 g |
| Sat. Fat: | 1.90 g |
| Cholesterol: | 7.77 mg |
| Sodium: | 53.32 mg |
| Fiber: | 2.65 g |
| PCF Ratio: | 3-82-15 |

### Exchange Approx.:
1 Fruit,
1 Fat,
1 Carb./Sugar

2 pears
2 tablespoons frozen, unsweetened pineapple juice concentrate
1 teaspoon vanilla extract
1 teaspoon rum
1 tablespoon butter

⅛ cup Ener-G Brown Rice Flour
⅓ cup, firmly packed, brown sugar
½ cup oat bran flakes

1. Preheat oven to 375 degrees. Treat a 9" × 13" baking dish or large, flat casserole dish with nonstick cooking spray. Core and cut up the pears into the baking dish. (Except for any bruised spots; it's okay to leave the skins on.)

2. In a glass measuring cup, microwave the frozen juice concentrate for 1 minute. Stir in the vanilla and rum, then pour over the pears. Using the same measuring cup, microwave the butter 30-40 seconds until melted. Toss the remaining ingredients together in a bowl, being careful not to crush the cereal. Spread uniformly over the pears and dribble the melted butter over the top of the cereal. Bake for 35 minutes, or until the mixture is bubbling and the top is just beginning to brown. Serve hot or cold.

# Nonfat Ice Cream or Smoothie Base

¼ cup nonfat milk powder

1 cup skim milk

1 tablespoon lemon juice

2 tablespoons granulated sugar

Place all the ingredients in the blender and mix until well blended. Store in a covered container in the refrigerator until the expiration date shown on the milk carton.

| Serves 8 | |
| --- | --- |
| **Nutritional Analysis (per serving):** | |
| Calories: | 38.59 |
| Protein: | 2.58 g |
| Carbohydrate: | 6.91 g |
| Fat: | 0.11 g |
| Sat. Fat: | 0.07 g |
| Cholesterol: | 0.00 mg |
| Sodium: | 38.17 mg |
| Fiber: | 0.00 g |
| PCF Ratio: | 27-71-3 |

**Exchange Approx.:**
½ Carb./Sugar,
½ Skim Milk

# Mock Pumpkin Custard

1¾ cup cooked pinto beans, drained

1½ cup skim milk

⅜ cup nonfat dry milk

2 eggs

¼ teaspoon sea salt

⅛ cup granulated sugar

¼ cup, firmly packed, brown sugar

1¼ teaspoon ground cinnamon

½ teaspoon ground cloves

⅛ teaspoon ground ginger

Preheat oven to 375 degrees. Process all the ingredients in a food processor until puréed. Pour into a baking dish treated with nonstick spray. Bake for 30 minutes.

| Serves 8 | |
| --- | --- |
| **Nutritional Analysis (per serving):** | |
| Calories: | 142.04 |
| Protein: | 8.05 g |
| Carbohydrate: | 24.69 g |
| Fat: | 1.42 g |
| Sat. Fat: | 0.46 g |
| Cholesterol: | 48.77 mg |
| Sodium: | 143.99 mg |
| Fiber: | 3.22 g |
| PCF Ratio: | 22-69-9 |

**Exchange Approx.:**
1½ Breads,
½ Fat

# Strawberry-Banana Sherbet

| Serves 4 | |
|---|---|
| **Nutritional Analysis (per serving):** | |
| Calories: | 98.47 |
| Protein: | 3.49 g |
| Carbohydrate: | 21.59 g |
| Fat: | 0.46 g |
| Sat. Fat: | 0.15 g |
| Cholesterol: | 0.00 mg |
| Sodium: | 44.46 mg |
| Fiber: | 1.90 g |
| PCF Ratio: | 13-83-4 |

**Exchange Approx.:**
½ Skim Milk,
½ Fruit,
½ Carb.

1⅓ cup strawberries halves
2 tablespoons sugar
1 ripe (but not overly ripe) banana, mashed
1 tablespoon frozen orange juice concentrate
2 tablespoons water
1 tablespoon lemon juice
1 cup 1 percent milk
2 tablespoons nonfat milk powder

1. Sprinkle the sugar over the strawberries. Mash the strawberries with a fork, and allow a little time for the sugar to dissolve and draw the juice out of the strawberries, then combine all the ingredients in a blender or food processor and process to desired consistency. (Some people prefer chunks of fruit; others like a smoother sherbet.)
2. Pour the mixture into an ice-cream maker and freeze according to manufacturer's directions, or pour the mixture into ice cube trays or a covered container and freeze overnight.

**TIP:** *Although you could use 1 cup of the Whipped Milk Base (see page 232) in this recipe in place of the sugar and milk, the sugar helps draw the juice from the strawberries, so it enhances the flavor.*

# Bananas Foster

4 bananas, sliced
¼ cup apple juice concentrate
Grated zest of 1 orange
¼ cup fresh orange juice

1 tablespoon ground cinnamon
12 ounces nonfat frozen vanilla
   yogurt

Combine all the ingredients *except* the yogurt in a nonstick skillet, bring to a boil, and cook until the bananas are tender. Put 3 ounces of nonfat frozen vanilla yogurt in each dessert bowl or stemmed glass, and spoon the heated banana sauce over the top.

### ℰ Know Your Ingredients

*Overripe bananas are higher in sugar and therefore can adversely affect your blood glucose levels. You can freeze bananas in the skins until ready to use. Doing so makes them perfect additions for fruit smoothies or fruit cups. Remove them from the freezer and run a little water over the peel to remove any frost. Peel them using a paring knife and slice according to the recipe directions. Frozen bananas can be added directly to smoothie and other recipes.*

| Serves 4 | |
|---|---|
| **Nutritional Analysis (per serving):** | |
| Calories: | 220.00 |
| Protein: | 2.00 g |
| Carbohydrate: | 51.00 g |
| Fat: | 1.00 g |
| Sat. Fat: | 0.35 g |
| Cholesterol: | 0.00 mg |
| Sodium: | 43.00 mg |
| Fiber: | 4.00 g |
| PCF Ratio: | 4-92-4 |

**Exchange Approx.:**
2 ½ Fruits,
1 Skim Milk

# Almond Biscotti

| | |
|---|---|
| 1 cup sugar | 3½ cups all-purpose flour |
| ½ cup unsalted butter | 1 teaspoon baking powder |
| 1 tablespoon grated orange peel | ½ teaspoon sea salt |
| 2 eggs | ⅓ cup ground almonds |

1. Preheat oven to 350 degrees. Beat the sugar, butter, orange peel, and eggs in a small bowl. Mix together the flour, baking powder, and salt in a large bowl, and stir in the egg mixture and almonds. Shape half of the dough at a time into a rectangle 10" × 3" and place on an ungreased baking sheet. Bake about 20 minutes or until an inserted toothpick comes out clean.
2. Cool on the baking sheet for 15 minutes. Cut into ½-inch slices, and place cut-side down on baking sheet. Bake for another 15 minutes, or until crisp and light brown. Cool on a wire rack.

---

**Yields 42 cookies**
**Serving size: 1 cookie**

**Nutritional Analysis
(per serving):**

| | |
|---|---|
| Calories: | 86.00 |
| Protein: | 2.00 g |
| Carbohydrate: | 13.15 g |
| Fat: | 3.00 g |
| Sat. Fat: | 1.00 g |
| Cholesterol: | 9.00 mg |
| Sodium: | 65.00 mg |
| Fiber: | trace |
| PCF Ratio: | 8-60-32 |

**Exchange Approx.:**
½ Fat,
½ Bread/Starch

---

# Beanberry Blast

| | |
|---|---|
| 1 (15-ounce) can navy beans **or** Great Northern beans, drained and rinsed | 2 tablespoons honey |
| | 1½ teaspoons ground cinnamon |
| 1½ cups orange juice | ⅛ teaspoon ground nutmeg |
| 2 cups sliced strawberries | 6–8 ice cubes |

Process all the ingredients, *except* the ice cubes, in a blender until smooth. Add the ice cubes and blend until smooth. (If frozen strawberries are used, omit the ice cubes and thin with water, if necessary.) You can also prepare this the night before, mixing all of the ingredients except the ice. Add the ice cubes in the morning and process for an instant breakfast.

---

**Serves 4**

**Nutritional Analysis
(per serving):**

| | |
|---|---|
| Calories: | 207.00 |
| Protein: | 1.00 g |
| Carbohydrate: | 43.00 g |
| Fat: | 1.00 g |
| Sat. Fat: | 0.35 g |
| Cholesterol: | 0.00 mg |
| Sodium: | 245.00 mg |
| Fiber: | 2.00 g |
| PCF Ratio: | 1-43-1 |

**Exchange Approx.:**
1½ Fruits,
1½ Breads

# Apple Cookies with a Kick

1 tablespoon ground flaxseed
¼ cup water
¼ cup firmly packed brown sugar
⅛ cup granulated sugar
¾ cup cooked pinto beans, drained
⅓ cup unsweetened applesauce
2 teaspoons baking powder
⅛ teaspoon sea salt
1 teaspoon ground cinnamon
½ teaspoon ground nutmeg

¼ teaspoon ground cloves
¼ teaspoon ground allspice
1 cup Vita-Spelt white spelt flour
½ cup Vita-Spelt whole spelt flour
1 medium-sized golden delicious apple
1 cup sunflower seeds—dried, kernels (not roasted; unsalted)

| Yields 24 cookies Serving size: 1 cookie | |
|---|---|
| **Nutritional Analysis (per serving):** | |
| Calories: | 64.00 |
| Protein: | 2.00 g |
| Carbohydrate: | 12.00 g |
| Fat: | 1.30 g |
| Sat. Fat: | 0.13 g |
| Cholesterol: | 0.00 mg |
| Sodium: | 67.00 mg |
| Fiber: | 1.30 g |
| PCF Ratio: | 12-71-17 |
| **Exchange Approx.:** 1 Fruit | |

1. Preheat oven to 350 degrees. Put the flaxseed and water in a microwave-safe container; microwave on high for 15 seconds or until the mixture thickens and has the consistency of egg whites. Add the flaxseed mixture, sugars, beans, and applesauce to a mixing bowl and mix well.
2. Sift the dry ingredients together, then fold into the bean mixture. (Do not overmix; this will cause the muffins to become tough.)
3. Peel and chop the apple and fold it and the sunflower seeds into the batter. Drop by teaspoonful onto a baking sheet treated with nonstick spray. Bake for 12 to 18 minutes.

## Creative Substitutions
*Adding nuts and, of all things, beans to dessert recipes increases the amount of protein and fiber. Just because it's dessert doesn't mean it has to be all empty calories.*

# Lemon Curd

| Yields 1 1/8 cup<br>Serving size: 1 tbs. | |
|---|---|
| **Nutritional Analysis**<br>**(per serving):** | |
| Calories: | 35.84 |
| Protein: | 0.64 g |
| Carbohydrate: | 3.13 g |
| Fat: | 2.41 g |
| Sat. Fat: | 1.35 g |
| Cholesterol: | 25.95 mg |
| Sodium: | 15.09 mg |
| Fiber: | 0.01 g |
| PCF Ratio: | 7-34-59 |
| **Exchange Approx.:** | |
| ½ Fat, | |
| ½ Misc. Carb. | |

2 eggs
¼ cup sugar
⅛ teaspoon sea salt

¼ cup lemon juice
3 tablespoons butter

1. In a microwave-safe bowl, whip the eggs until fluffy. Gradually add the sugar, salt, and lemon juice, beating well. Add the butter. Microwave on high for 20 seconds to melt the butter; stir well. Rotate the bowl and microwave at 80 percent power for 1 minute.
2. Whip the lemon fluff, then microwave at 80 percent power for 20 seconds; whip again, rotate bowl, and repeat process 2 (or so) more times, whipping after each time it is microwaved. The mixture should coat the back of a spoon, and will thicken more as it cools.

TIP: *Pour through a fine strainer to remove any cooked egg solids that didn't get blended into the mixture.*

### Juicy Gelatin

*It's easy to make fruit juice gelatin. Add 1 tablespoon of powdered gelatin to ½ cup fruit juice. Allow to soften, then microwave on high for 30 seconds. Whisk to dissolve the gelatin, then stir in another 1 cup of fruit juice. (Kiwi fruit, mangoes, papaya, and pineapple juices won't work because they contain an enzyme that prevents gelling.) Refrigerate until set. Exchange Approximations will depend on the type of fruit juice you use and the size of the servings.*

# Pineapple Upside-Down Cake

1 tablespoon brown sugar
1 (8¼-ounce) can unsweetened,
   crushed pineapple in juice,
   (drained, juice reserved)
1 envelope KNOX Unflavored
   Gelatine
2 eggs
1 egg white
¾ cup granulated sugar

1 teaspoon vanilla
¾ cup all-purpose flour
1 teaspoon baking powder
¼ teaspoon salt

| Serves 8 | |
| --- | --- |
| **Nutritional Analysis (per serving):** | |
| Calories: | 138.00 |
| Protein: | 2.53 g |
| Carbohydrate: | 32.18 g |
| Fat: | 0.14 g |
| Sat. Fat: | 0.02 g |
| Cholesterol: | 0.00 g |
| Sodium: | 83.39 g |
| Fiber: | 0.56 mg |
| PCF Ratio: | 7-92-1 |
| **Exchange Approx.:** 1 Bread, 1 Fruit | |

1. Preheat oven to 375 degrees. Line a 9" × 1½" round baking pan with waxed paper and spray with nonstick cooking spray. Sprinkle the brown sugar on the waxed paper. Spread the crushed pineapple evenly in the bottom of the pan and sprinkle the gelatin over the top.
2. In a large bowl, beat the eggs and egg white until very thick. Gradually beat in the granulated sugar. Add enough water to the reserved pineapple juice to measure ⅓ cup; beat it into the egg mixture along with the vanilla.
3. In a separate bowl, mix together the flour, baking powder, and salt; gradually add it to the egg mixture, beating until the batter is smooth. Pour into pan. Bake about 25 to 30 minutes, or until an inserted toothpick comes out clean. Immediately loosen the cake from the edge of pan with a knife and invert the pan on a plate. Carefully remove the waxed paper and slice into 8 pieces.

# Whole-Grain Maple-Walnut Bread Pudding

| Serves 8 |
| --- |

| **Nutritional Analysis (per serving):** | |
| --- | --- |
| Calories: | 140.08 |
| Protein: | 5.63 g |
| Carbohydrate: | 18.15 g |
| Fat: | 5.17 g |
| Sat. Fat: | 1.33 g |
| Cholesterol: | 54.57 mg |
| Sodium: | 102.87 mg |
| Fiber: | 0.86 g |
| PCF Ratio: | 16-51-33 |

**Exchange Approx.:**
1 Starch,
1 Fat,
½ Misc. Carb.

1 cup skim milk
3/8 cup dry nonfat milk powder
2 teaspoons unsalted butter
2 eggs
1 teaspoon vanilla
3 tablespoons maple syrup
1 tablespoon brown sugar
4 ounces 7-Grain Bread (4 thick slices with crusts removed; see page 78)
¼ cup chopped walnuts
Pinch of sea salt (optional)

1. Preheat oven to 350 degrees. Put the first 7 ingredients in a food processor or blender and process until mixed. Tear the crustless bread into pieces and place in a mixing bowl. Pour the blended milk mixture over the bread, add the chopped walnuts, and toss to mix.
2. Pour the mixture into a nonstick spray–treated nonstick cake pan. Bake for 20 minutes (or until the egg is set). Cut into 8 pie-shaped wedges. Serve warm or chilled.

# Individual Apple-Blackberry Charlottes

6 Golden Delicious apples,
 peeled and sliced
3 tablespoons seedless blackberry jam or preserves
 (fruit-only, no sugar added)
1 tablespoon unsalted butter,
 at room temperature
12 sliced bread, crusts removed

⅛ cup (2 tablespoons) Mock
 Cream (see page 42)
1 egg
1 teaspoon vanilla
1 tablespoon powdered sugar

| Serves 6 | |
|---|---|
| **Nutritional Analysis (per serving):** | |
| Calories: | 169.84 |
| Protein: | 2.49 g |
| Carbohydrate: | 33.92 g |
| Fat: | 3.60 g |
| Sat. Fat: | 1.57 g |
| Cholesterol: | 36.59 mg |
| Sodium: | 80.09 mg |
| Fiber: | 4.00 g* |
| PCF Ratio: | 6-76-18 |

**Exchange Approx.:**
½ Fat,
1 Bread/Starch,
1 Fruit
* (even higher if you use
whole-grain bread)

1. Preheat oven to 350 degrees. Place the apples in a covered microwave-safe bowl and microwave on high until tender, about 5 minutes. Stir in the blackberry jam until the apples are well coated.

2. Prepare a 6-capacity, nonstick muffin tin (the kind used to make larger muffins) by spraying the bottom of each section with nonstick spray and coating the inside of each section with ½ teaspoon of the unsalted butter. Trim the bread so it's the same height as the depth of your muffin tin. Cut each slice into 3 strips.

3. In a small bowl, beat together the Mock Cream, egg, and vanilla. Dip each bread strip in the Mock Cream mixture. (Do not soak the bread in the mixture; you only want each strip lightly coated.) Leaving the bottom open, line the sides of each of the jumbo muffin-tin cups with 6 overlapping pieces of bread, pressing the bread against the butter-coated sides as you go.

4. Divide the apple mixture into each muffin tin section, ladling it in the center of the bread slices. Place the tins in the oven, and bake until the bread is golden brown on the outside, about 20 minutes.

5. Transfer the muffin pan to a wire rack to cool for 10 minutes. Unmold the charlottes by inverting onto a baking sheet or cutting board, then transfer each muffin to a dessert plate. Dust lightly with the powdered sugar.

# CHAPTER 15

# Snacks and Beverages

| | |
|---|---|
| Chocolate Candy Substitute | 250 |
| Honey Raisin Bars | 251 |
| Powdered Sugar–Coated Cocoa Cookies | 252 |
| No-Bake Chocolate–Peanut Butter Oatmeal Cookies | 253 |
| Tortilla Chips | 254 |
| Black Olive Mock Caviar | 254 |
| Snack Mix | 255 |
| Asian Popcorn | 256 |
| Zucchini with Cheese Spread | 258 |
| Toasted Pumpkin Seeds | 258 |
| Coffee-Spice Snack Cake | 259 |
| Creamy Fruit Cup | 260 |
| Sparkling Fruited Iced Tea | 261 |
| Minted Lemon Tea | 261 |
| Iced Ginger-Orange Green Tea | 262 |
| Hot Spiced Tea | 262 |
| Iced and Spiced Chai-Style Tea | 263 |
| Spiced Chai-Style Creamer Mix | 263 |
| Tangy Limeade | 264 |
| Frothy Orange Jewel | 265 |
| Orange-Pineapple Froth | 265 |
| Party Time Minted Raspberry Lemonade | 266 |
| Buttermilk Blush | 267 |
| Pineapple-Banana Blast | 267 |
| Peachy Ginger Ale | 268 |
| Fruit Frenzy Sparkler Concentrate | 269 |
| Strawberry Cooler | 269 |
| Nectarine Cocktail | 270 |
| Jam and Jelly Soft Drink Syrup | 270 |

# Chocolate Candy Substitute

**Yields 15–20 pieces**

**Nutritional Analysis (per serving):**

**Exchange Approx.:**
(for entire recipe, without dry milk):
1 Fruit,
1 Carb./Sugar,
1 Free Drink

1 tablespoon cocoa
1 tablespoon sugar
¾ cup fresh pineapple chunks

1–3 teaspoons nonfat dry milk (optional)

1. In a small bowl, mix the cocoa and sugar. Place waxed paper on a baking sheet. Dip each piece of pineapple in the cocoa-sugar mixture. (The choice on whether to coat only 1 side of the pineapple or all sides depends on whether or not you prefer a "dark, bittersweet chocolate" taste or a milder one. Add the dry milk powder to the mixture if you prefer a "milk chocolate" flavor.) Place each piece of pineapple on the waxed paper–covered baking sheet. Place the baking sheet in the freezer for several hours.
2. Once the pineapple is frozen, layer the pineapple "candies" on waxed paper in an airtight freezer container. Place a piece of aluminum foil over the top layer before you put on the lid, to prevent freezer burn.

**TIP:** *The Exchange Approximations given for this recipe is for the entire amount; however, it's intended to be used as a way to curb a candy craving. (You grab a frozen chunk from the freezer and eat it like candy.) Discuss this recipe with your dietitian to see how you can fit it into your meal plan.*

# Honey Raisin Bars

½ cup unbleached all-purpose
　flour
¼ teaspoon baking soda
⅛ teaspoon sea salt
¼ teaspoon cinnamon
¾ cup quick-cooking oatmeal
1 egg white, slightly beaten
2½ tablespoons sunflower oil

¼ cup honey
¼ cup skim milk
½ teaspoon vanilla
½ cup golden raisins

| Yields 18 bars | |
| --- | --- |
| **Nutritional Analysis (per serving):** | |
| Calories: | 71.23 |
| Protein: | 1.36 g |
| Carbohydrate: | 12.19 g |
| Fat: | 2.16 g |
| Sat. Fat: | 0.24 g |
| Cholesterol: | 0.06 mg |
| Sodium: | 39.31 mg |
| Fiber: | 0.62 g |
| PCF Ratio: | 7-66-26 |

**Exchange Approx.:**
½ Bread,
½ Misc. Carb.

1. Preheat oven to 350 degrees. Sift the flour, soda, salt, and cinnamon together into a bowl and stir in the oatmeal.

2. In another bowl, mix the slightly beaten egg whites with the oil, honey, milk, vanilla, and raisins. Add the flour mixture to liquid ingredients. Drop by teaspoon onto cookie sheets treated with nonstick spray. Bake for 12 to 15 minutes. (Longer baking time will result in crispier cookies.) Cool on a baking rack.

3. For cookie bars, spread the mixture in an even layer on a piece of parchment paper placed on the cookie sheet; bake for 15 to 18 minutes. Cool slightly, then use a sharp knife or pizza cutter to slice into 18 equal pieces (6 down, 3 across).

TIP: *If you like chewier cookies or need to cut the fat in your diet, you can substitute applesauce, plums, prunes, or mashed banana for the sunflower oil.*

# Powdered Sugar–Coated Cocoa Cookies

| Yields 24 cookies Serving size: 1 cookie | |
| --- | --- |
| **Nutritional Analysis (per serving, using plums packed in heavy syrup):** | |
| Calories: | 65.82 |
| Protein: | 0.88 g |
| Carbohydrate: | 13.78 g |
| Fat: | 1.36 g |
| Sat. Fat: | 0.73 g |
| Cholesterol: | 2.59 mg |
| Sodium: | 41.15 mg |
| Fiber: | 0.76 g |
| PCF Ratio: | 5-78-17 |
| **Exchange Approx.:** 1 Carb. | |

1 tablespoon ground flaxseed
2 tablespoons water **or** plum juice
2 tablespoons unsalted butter
3/8 cup cocoa powder
2/3 cup firmly packed brown sugar
1/2 teaspoon vanilla extract
1/4 cup mashed plums

2/3 cup white rice flour
1/3 cup Ener-G potato flour
1/2 teaspoon baking soda
1/8 teaspoon sea salt
1/4 cup powdered sugar
1/16 teaspoon ground black pepper (optional)

1. In a microwave-safe cup, combine the flaxseed with the water (or plum juice) and microwave on high for 15 to 30 seconds. Stir the mixture. (It should have the consistency of a thick egg white; this mixture is an egg substitute.)
2. Add the butter to a microwave-safe mixing bowl; microwave for 15 to 20 seconds, until the butter is melted. Add the cocoa and blend into the butter. Mix in the flaxseed mixture along with the brown sugar and vanilla.
3. Add mashed plums to the other ingredients. (If you wish to remove the plum skins, push the fruit through a mesh sieve. The skins add some fiber to the snack, but you may not like how they look. You can use a food processor to pulverize the plum skins.) Stir to combine. Blend in the flours, baking soda, and salt until a dough forms. Refrigerate for 1 or 2 hours, or until the mixture is firm enough to shape into balls.
4. Preheat oven to 350 degrees. Form a heaping teaspoon of the dough into a ball, roll it in powdered sugar, and place on an ungreased cookie sheet. Use the back of a fork to flatten each cookie. Bake cookies for 8 to 10 minutes or until firm. Cool completely on wire racks.

## Comparative Analysis

*Consider other substitutions, too. This analysis allows for all-purpose flour and plums canned in juice. The powdered sugar is omitted. Calories: 57.83; Protein: 0.92 g; Carbohydrate: 11.26 g; Fat: 1.37 g; Sat. Fat: 0.73 g; Cholesterol: 2.59 mg; Sodium: 41.15 mg; Fiber: 0.75 g; PCF Ratio: 6-74-20. Exchange Approximations: 1 Carb.*

# No-Bake Chocolate–Peanut Butter Oatmeal Cookies

2 tablespoons butter
¼ cup cocoa
½ cup granulated sugar
¼ cup Mock Cream (see page 42)
Dash of sea salt

1 teaspoon vanilla
1 tablespoon peanut butter
1½ cups oatmeal

| Serves 12 | |
|---|---|
| **Nutritional Analysis (per serving, with granulated sugar):** | |
| Calories: | 87.02 |
| Protein: | 1.66 g |
| Carbohydrate: | 13.39 g |
| Fat: | 3.14 g |
| Sat. Fat: | 1.49 g |
| Cholesterol: | 5.31 mg |
| Sodium: | 25.91 mg |
| Fiber: | 0.90 g |
| PCF Ratio: | 7-61-32 |
| **Exchange Approx.:** ½ Fat, 1 Bread | |

1. Add the butter to a deep, microwave-safe bowl and microwave on high for 20 to 30 seconds, or until the butter is melted. Add the cocoa and stir to blend. Stir in the sugar, Mock Cream, and salt. Microwave on high for 1 minute, 10 seconds to bring to a full boil. (Should you need to microwave the batter some more, do so in 10-second increments. You want a full boil, but because it will continue to cook for a while once it's removed from the microwave, heating it too long can cause the mixture to scorch.)
2. Add the vanilla and peanut butter and stir until mixed. Fold in the oatmeal. Drop by tablespoonful on waxed paper and allow to cool.

## Easy Graham Cracker Goodies

*A little of this rich peanut butter and cream cheese goes a long way. To make 4 treats, mix 1 teaspoon peanut butter, 1 teaspoon cream cheese, and 2 teaspoons powdered sugar until well blended. Divide between 6 whole graham crackers. Spread an equal amount of the icing on top of each graham cracker. Allow 3 open-faced squares per serving. The Analysis is: Calories: 145.65; Protein: 2.76 g; Carbohydrate: 23.22 g; Fat: 4.74 g; Sat. Fat: 1.08 g; Cholesterol: 1.83 mg; Sodium: 201.91 mg; Fiber: 1.1 g; PCF Ratio: 8-63-29. Exchange Approximations: 1 Bread, 1 Fat.*

# Tortilla Chips

**Serves 1**

**Nutritional Analysis
(per serving):**

**Exchange Approx.:**
1 Carb./Starch,
½ Fat

1 nonfat corn tortilla
Olive oil
Sea salt to taste (optional)

Seasoning blend of your
choice, to taste (see
Chapter 2 for recipes)

Preheat oven to 400 degrees. Spray both sides of the tortilla with olive oil.
Season lightly with sea salt or any season blend. Bake the tortillas on a
cookie sheet until crisp and beginning to brown, about 2 to 5 minutes,
depending on the thickness of the tortilla. Break the tortillas into large pieces.

TIP: *When you buy the tortillas, look for a brand made with only
cornmeal, water, and lime juice. Nutritional Analysis and Exchange
Approximations will depend on the brand of tortillas and the
amount of oil you use.*

# Black Olive Mock Caviar

**Yields 1¼ cups
Serving size: 1 tbs.**

**Nutritional Analysis
(per serving):**

| | |
|---|---|
| Calories: | 20.91 |
| Protein: | 0.14 g |
| Carbohydrate: | 1.24 g |
| Fat: | 1.63 g |
| Sat. Fat: | 0.10 g |
| Cholesterol: | 0.00 mg |
| Sodium: | 85.06 mg |
| Fiber: | 0.21 g |
| PCF Ratio: | 3-25-73 |

**Exchange Approx.:**
1 Free Condiment or
½ Fat

1 (5¾-ounce) can chopped
    black olives
1 (4-ounce) can chopped green
    chili peppers
1 cup diced fresh **or** canned
    (no salt added) tomato
2 tablespoons chopped green
    onions

1 clove garlic, minced
1 tablespoon extra-virgin
    olive oil
1 teaspoon red wine vinegar
Pinch of sugar
½ teaspoon freshly ground
    black pepper

In a medium-sized mixing bowl, mix together all the ingredients.
Cover, and chill overnight. Serve cold or at room temperature.

# Snack Mix

6 cups mixed cereal (such as a mixture of unsweetened bran, oat, rice, and wheat cereals)

1 cup mini bow-knot pretzels

⅔ cup dry-roasted peanuts

⅛ cup (2 tablespoons) butter, melted

⅛ cup (2 tablespoons) olive, canola, **or** peanut oil

1 tablespoon Worcestershire sauce (see recipe for Homemade on page 40)

¼ teaspoon garlic powder

Tabasco sauce **or** other liquid hot pepper sauce to taste (optional)

| Serves 16 Serving Size: ½ cup |
| --- |

| Nutritional Analysis (per serving, on average): | |
| --- | --- |
| Calories: | 125.00 |
| Protein: | 3.00 g |
| Carbohydrate | 16.00 g |
| Total Fat: | variable |
| Cholesterol: | 3.89 mg |
| Sodium: | 201.00 mg |
| Fiber: | 2.00 g |
| PCF Ratio: | variable |

**Exchange Approx.:**
1 Carb./Starch,
1 Fat

Preheat oven to 300 degrees. In a large bowl, combine the cereals, pretzels, and peanuts. In another bowl, combine the butter, oil, Worcestershire, garlic powder, and Tabasco (if using). Pour over the cereal mixture and toss to coat evenly. Spread the mixture on a large baking sheet and bake for 30 to 40 minutes, stirring every 10 minutes, until crisp and dry. Cool and store in an airtight container. Serve at room temperature.

TIP: *The nutritional analysis will depend on the type of fat and cereals used in the recipe, most notably regarding the PCF Ratio.*

## Microwave Popcorn—from Scratch

*To make "air-popped" popcorn in the microwave, add 1 cup of popcorn to a small brown paper bag. Fold down the top. Spray the bag with water (or wet your hand and tap water on each side and the bottom of the bag). Microwave on high for 3 minutes, or use the popcorn setting if your microwave has it.*

# Asian Popcorn

| Serves 1 | |
|---|---|
| **Nutritional Analysis (per serving):** | |
| Calories: | 128.78 |
| Protein: | 4.72 g |
| Carbohydrate | 26.01 g |
| Total Fat: | 1.34 g |
| Sat. Fat: | 0.18 g |
| Cholesterol: | 0.00 mg |
| Sodium: | 221.38 mg |
| Fiber: | 4.87 g |
| PCF Ratio: | 14-77-9 |

**Exchange Approx.:**
1 Carb./Starch,
1 Free Condiment

4 cups air-popped popcorn
1 teaspoon Bragg's Liquid Aminos **or** low-sodium soy sauce
2 teaspoons fresh lemon juice
1 teaspoon five-spice powder
¼ teaspoon ground coriander
¼ teaspoon garlic powder

1. Preheat oven to 250 degrees. Spread the popcorn on a nonstick cookie sheet and lightly coat with nonstick or butter-flavored cooking spray.
2. Mix together all the remaining ingredients. Drizzle the mixture over the popcorn and lightly toss to coat evenly. Bake for 5 minutes, toss the popcorn and rotate the pan, and then bake for an additional 5 minutes. Serve warm.

## Keeping Snacks in Stock

*Because there are no oils to go rancid, air-popped popcorn will keep for weeks if you store it in an airtight container. Pop up a large batch and keep some on hand for later. Then, depending on your mood, flavor it according to the suggestions in this section and you'll soon have a warm, healthy snack.*

# Mix It Up

POPCORN IS A GREAT SNACK. It's filling, it's good for you, and it's easy to prepare and keep on hand. Try the following varieties so you don't get bored. Preparation and Nutritional Analysis follow the Asian Popcorn recipe (see page 256).

## Dilled-Ranch Popcorn

½ teaspoon ranch-style
    dip mix
⅛ teaspoon dried dill
⅛ teaspoon onion powder
Pinch of dried lemon peel

## Mexican Popcorn

1 tablespoon dried Mexican
    spiced salad dressing mix
¼ teaspoon crushed dried
    oregano
¼ teaspoon crushed dried
    thyme
¼ teaspoon garlic powder

## Italian Spiced Popcorn

1 teaspoon dried Italian herbs
⅛ teaspoon cayenne pepper
1 teaspoon grated Parmesan
    cheese

## Pizza Popcorn

1 tablespoon Mrs. Dash
    Tomato Basil Garlic Blend
¼ teaspoon onion powder
1 tablespoon grated
    Parmesan cheese

# Zucchini with Cheese Spread

| Serves 8 | |
|---|---|
| **Nutritional Analysis (per serving):** | |
| Calories: | 38.00 |
| Protein: | 4.00 g |
| Carbohydrate: | 4.00 g |
| Fat: | trace |
| Sat. Fat: | trace |
| Cholesterol: | 2.00 mg |
| Sodium: | 140.00 mg |
| Fiber: | 2.00 g |
| PCF Ratio: | 42-43-15 |
| **Exchange Approx.:** | |
| 1 Vegetable, | |
| ½ Fat | |

*1 large green zucchini*
*⅓ cup softened fat-free cream cheese*
*¼ cup finely chopped red bell pepper*
*2 teaspoons dried parsley*
*¼ teaspoon onion powder*
*¼ teaspoon dried Italian seasoning*
*2 drops red pepper sauce*
*1 green onion, thinly sliced*

Peel the zucchini and cut it into ¼-inch slices. Mix together the remaining ingredients *except* the green onion until well blended. Spread 1–2 teaspoons of the cream cheese mixture onto each slice of zucchini and place on a serving platter. Sprinkle with green onion, cover, and refrigerate for 1 hour or until firm.

### Simple Substitutions

*Squash seeds are delicious when roasted, too. Serve them as snacks or as a garnish on soups or salads.*

# Toasted Pumpkin Seeds

| Serves 8 | |
|---|---|
| **Nutritional Analysis (per serving, without salt):** | |
| Calories: | 201.56 |
| Protein: | 8.47 g |
| Carbohydrate: | 6.14 g |
| Fat: | 17.51 g |
| Sat. Fat: | 3.22 g |
| Cholesterol: | 0.00 mg |
| Sodium: | 6.21 mg |
| Fiber: | 1.35 g |
| PCF Ratio: | 16-11-73 |
| **Exchange Approx.:** | |
| 1 Lean Meat, | |
| 3 Fats | |

*2 cups pumpkin seeds, scooped from a fresh pumpkin*
*Sea salt (optional)*
*1 tablespoons olive, peanut, **or** canola oil*

1. Rinse the pumpkin seeds, removing all pulp and strings. Spread the seeds in a single layer on a large baking sheet and let them air-dry for at least 3 hours.
2. Preheat oven to 375 degrees. Drizzle the oil over the seeds and lightly sprinkle with salt, if using. (Alternative method would be to put dried pumpkin seeds in a plastic bag and add the oil. Seal the bag and toss to mix the seeds with the oil.) Toss, then spread them out in a single layer. Bake for 15 to 20 minutes, until lightly browned and toasted. Stir the seeds occasionally during the baking to allow for even browning. Remove the hulls to eat.

# Coffee-Spice Snack Cake

1 cup honey
½ cup strong brewed coffee
1 tablespoon brandy
½ cup reduced-fat egg substitute
2 tablespoons olive oil
½ cup, firmly packed, brown
sugar
2 cups all-purpose flour

1 ½ teaspoons baking powder
1 ½ teaspoons baking soda
½ teaspoon salt
½ teaspoon ground cinnamon
¼ teaspoon ground ginger
⅛ teaspoon ground nutmeg
⅛ teaspoon ground cloves

| Serves 16 |  |
| --- | --- |
| **Nutritional Analysis (per serving):** | |
| Calories: | 172.00 |
| Protein: | 2.65 g |
| Carbohydrate: | 36.57 g |
| Fat: | 2.25 g |
| Sat. Fat: | 0.40 g |
| Cholesterol: | 0.22 mg |
| Sodium: | 137.11 mg |
| Fiber: | 0.47 g |
| PCF Ratio: | 6-83-11 |

**Exchange Approx.:**
2 Carbs./Starches,
½ Fat

1. Preheat oven to 325 degrees. Add the honey, coffee, and brandy to a bowl and mix well. Add the egg substitute, oil, and brown sugar, and beat until combined.
2. Sift together the flour, baking powder, baking soda, salt, and spices, and fold into the mixture. Pour the batter into a 9-inch-square baking dish treated with nonstick cooking spray. Bake for 50 to 60 minutes, or until an inserted toothpick comes out clean. Slice into 16 pieces.

# Creamy Fruit Cup

| Serves 1 | |
|---|---|
| **Nutritional Analysis (per serving, without additional applesauce or jelly):** | |
| Calories: | 128.62 |
| Protein: | 6.52 g |
| Carbohydrate: | 26.42 g |
| Fat: | 0.52 g |
| Sat. Fat: | 0.13 g |
| Cholesterol: | 0.00 mg |
| Sodium: | 89.23 mg |
| Fiber: | 1.99 g |
| PCF Ratio: | 19-77-3 |

**Exchange Approx.:**
½ Skim Milk,
1½ Fruits

4 ounces (half of a small container) nonfat plain yogurt
1 tablespoon unsweetened applesauce
1 teaspoon lemon juice
½ cup cubed fresh **or** frozen cantaloupe
¼ cup cubed or sliced apple
6 seedless red **or** green grapes
Lemon zest (optional)

Mix together the yogurt, applesauce, and lemon juice; drizzle over the mixed fruit. (If you prefer a sweeter dressing, you can add another tablespoon of applesauce or blend in 2 teaspoons of Smucker's Low-Sugar Apple Jelly without increasing the number of Fruit Exchanges; adjust the calorie count accordingly.) For a more zesty (and attractive!) dish, sprinkle lemon zest over the top of the dressing.

**TIP:** *Prepare the Creamy Fruit Cup for your lunchbox! If you do, keep the dressing and fruits in separate containers until you're ready to serve. To keep the lemon zest moist, you can mix it in with the dressing.*

 **Just Juice?**
*Fruit and fruit juice provide healthy nutrients, and, in most cases, fiber, too. That's the good news. The downside is they also convert quickly to glucose. For that reason, many people can only consume them as part of a meal, rather than alone as a snack.*

# Sparkling Fruited Iced Tea

3 cups decaffeinated tea
1 cup unsweetened orange juice
4 teaspoons fresh lemon juice
1 (12-ounce) can carbonated
    ginger ale

Seltzer water, Club Soda, **or**
    other unsweetened carbon-
    ated water

In a pitcher, mix together the tea, orange juice, and lemon juice. In tall, iced-tea glasses (16- to 20-ounce size), place 4 or 5 ice cubes. Pour the tea and juice mixture over the ice, then evenly divide the ginger ale between the glasses. Add carbonated water to finish filling the glasses. Stir to mix and serve.

| Serves 4 | |
| --- | --- |
| **Nutritional Analysis (per serving):** | |
| Calories: | 62.17 |
| Protein: | 0.44 g |
| Carbohydrate: | 15.64 g |
| Fat: | 0.04 g |
| Sat. Fat: | 0.01 g |
| Cholesterol: | 0.00 mg |
| Sodium: | 12.41 mg |
| Fiber: | 0.14 g |
| PCF Ratio: | 3-97-1 |
| **Exchange Approx.:** | |
| 1 Fruit | |

# Minted Lemon Tea

4 cups boiling water
4 tea bags
1 teaspoon chopped fresh mint
    **or** ¼ teaspoon dried mint
    flakes

Juice of 1 lemon (about 3–4
    teaspoons)
¼ cup (4 tablespoons) honey

In a ceramic or glass container, pour the boiling water over the tea bags and mint. Cover and allow to steep for 5 minutes. Add the lemon juice and honey. Stir until the honey is dissolved. Strain the mixture and divide between 4 mugs.

| Serves 4 | |
| --- | --- |
| **Nutritional Analysis (per serving):** | |
| Calories: | 67.48 |
| Protein: | 0.08 g |
| Carbohydrate: | 18.45 g |
| Fat: | 0.00 g |
| Sat. Fat: | 0.00 g |
| Cholesterol: | 0.00 mg |
| Sodium: | 8.00 mg |
| Fiber: | 0.06 g |
| PCF Ratio: | 0-100-0 |
| **Exchange Approx.:** | |
| 1 Carb./Sugar | |

# Iced Ginger-Orange Green Tea

| Serves 4 | |
|---|---|
| **Nutritional Analysis (per serving):** | |
| Calories: | 62.31 |
| Protein: | 0.97 g |
| Carbohydrate: | 14.51 g |
| Fat: | 0.29 g |
| Sat. Fat: | 0.05 g |
| Cholesterol: | 0.00 mg |
| Sodium: | 9.13 mg |
| Fiber: | 0.37 g |
| PCF Ratio: | 6-90-4 |
| **Exchange Approx.:** | |
| 1 Fruit | |

2 cups water
1 tablespoon coarsely chopped
   crystallized ginger
2 (1-inch) pieces orange zest

4 green tea bags
2 cups orange juice, chilled

In medium saucepan, bring the water to boil. In a ceramic container, pour the boiling water over the ginger and orange peel. Add tea bags; cover, and steep for 5 minutes. Remove the tea bags, ginger, and orange peel. Add the orange juice to the tea blend, and stir. Put ice cubes in 4 glasses, pour orange juice–tea blend over the ice, and serve.

### ℃ Monitor Your Exchanges
*If you add additional sweetener to any of the tea recipes, be sure to include that Exchange List choice as well, if applicable.*

# Hot Spiced Tea

| Serves 4 | |
|---|---|
| **Nutritional Analysis (per serving):** | |
| Calories: | 7.87 |
| Protein: | 0.11 g |
| Carbohydrate: | 2.04 g |
| Fat: | 0.02 g |
| Sat. Fat.: | 0.00 g |
| Cholesterol: | 0.00 mg |
| Sodium: | 2.87 mg |
| Fiber: | 0.00 g |
| PCF Ratio: | 5-93-2 |
| **Exchange Approx.:** | |
| ½ Free | |

2 tea bags
14 whole cloves
1 cinnamon stick
1 strip (about 3 inches) fresh
   orange zest

2 cups boiling water
¼ cup orange juice
1½ tablespoons lemon juice

Put the tea bags, spices, and orange peel in a ceramic or glass container and pour the boiling water over them; cover and allow to steep for 5 minutes. Strain the mixture. Stir in the orange and lemon juices; reheat if necessary. You can also chill it and serve over ice for a refreshing iced tea.

# Iced and Spiced Chai-Style Tea

2 cups skim milk
¼ cup honey (optional)
½ teaspoon ground cinnamon
¼ teaspoon ground ginger
⅛ teaspoon allspice

4 tea bags
2 cups chilled, unflavored,
    unsweetened carbonated
    water

In a medium saucepan, bring the milk just to boil. Stir in the remaining ingredients *except* for the carbonated water. Reduce heat to low and simmer, uncovered, for 3 minutes. Remove the tea bags and strain; chill. Serve over ice, adding an equal amount of the carbonated water to each serving.

**TIP:** *Alternative serving suggestion: This tea is also terrific when served warm in mugs; just replace the carbonated water with warm water.*

| Serves 4 | |
|---|---|
| **Nutritional Analysis (per serving):** | |
| Calories: | 107.56 |
| Protein: | 4.01 g |
| Carbohydrate: | 23.12 g |
| Fat: | 0.51 g |
| Sat. Fat.: | 0.29 g |
| Cholesterol: | 0.00 mg |
| Sodium: | 65.09 mg |
| Fiber: | 0.02 g |
| PCF Ratio: | 14-82-4 |
| **Exchange Approx.:** 1 Misc. Carb., ½ Skim Milk | |

# Spiced Chai-Style Creamer Mix

½ cup nonfat dry milk
1½ teaspoons cinnamon
¼ teaspoon nutmeg
¼ teaspoon ground cloves

½ teaspoon ginger
¼ teaspoon allspice
¼ cup sugar

Combine all the ingredients in a lidded jar and shake to mix. Store in a cool, dry place. Because this recipe uses noninstant nonfat milk, it must be stirred into hot liquid. For iced tea, you can mix in the "creamer" using a blender.

| Yields 15 tsp.s Serving size: 1 tbs. | |
|---|---|
| **Nutritional Analysis (per serving):** | |
| Calories: | 86.08 |
| Protein: | 4.40 g |
| Carbohydrate: | 17.17 g |
| Fat: | 0.19 g |
| Sat. Fat: | 0.10 g |
| Cholesterol: | 0.00 mg |
| Sodium: | 64.92 mg |
| Fiber: | 0.00 g |
| PCF Ratio: | 20-78-2 |
| **Exchange Approx.:** 1 Misc. Carb. | |

# Tangy Limeade

**Serves 8**

**Nutritional Analysis
(per serving, without salt):**

| | |
|---|---|
| Calories: | 63.45 |
| Protein: | 0.35 g |
| Carbohydrate: | 17.78 g |
| Fat: | 0.10 g |
| Sat. Fat: | 0.01 g |
| Cholesterol: | 0.00 mg |
| Sodium: | 1.13 mg |
| Fiber: | 1.41 g |
| PCF Ratio: | 2-97-1 |

**Exchange Approx.:**
1 Misc. Carb.

6 fresh limes
½ cup granulated sugar
2½ cups water
½ teaspoon salt (optional)

12 ice cubes (**or** 1½ cups cold water)

1. Roll the limes on a cutting board using hard pressure to loosen the flesh and release the juice easily. Cut the limes in half juice them, minus any seeds and the pith. Place the rinds in a non-corrosive metal or glass container, cover with the sugar, and set aside.
2. Bring the water to boil and then pour it over the lime juice, rinds, and sugar mixture. Allow the mixture to steep for 5 to 10 minutes, depending on your taste. (Two minutes is sufficient for an intense lime flavor; 10 minutes will have a hint of bitterness. If you prefer a sweeter limeade, omit the rinds and steep the mixture with the juice and pulp.)
3. If you're using the optional salt, add it now and stir thoroughly. Strain the warm liquid. Add ice cubes and stir until the ice is melted. Serve over additional ice cubes.

## Carbonated Limeade

*To make a concentrate that can be stored in the refrigerator for up to 3 days, reduce the boiling water to 1 cup in the Limeade recipe. In a glass, combine 3 tablespoons of the concentrate with enough seltzer water or club soda to fill an 8- to 12-ounce glass. Remember that more carbonated water will produce a weaker-tasting beverage. Exchange Approximations: 1 Misc. Carb, ½ Fruit.*

# Frothy Orange Jewel

*¼ cup fresh orange juice*
*1 cup skim milk*
*1½ teaspoon powdered sugar*

*½ teaspoon vanilla*
*1–2 ice cubes (optional)*

Combine all the ingredients in a blender and process until mixed.
Serve in a frosted glass. If you don't have fresh orange juice on hand,
you can substitute 1 tablespoon frozen orange juice concentrate and
3 tablespoons of water.

| Serves 1 | |
| --- | --- |
| **Nutritional Analysis (per serving):** | |
| Calories: | 135.26 |
| Protein: | 8.79 g |
| Carbohydrate: | 22.58 g |
| Fat: | 0.57 g |
| Sat. Fat: | 0.30 g |
| Cholesterol: | 4.90 mg |
| Sodium: | 128.25 mg |
| Fiber: | 0.12 g |
| PCF Ratio: | 27-69-4 |
| **Exchange Approx.:** | |
| 1 Fruit, | |
| 1 Skim Milk | |

# Orange-Pineapple Froth

*1 tablespoon frozen orange
    juice concentrate*
*1 tablespoon frozen pineapple
    juice concentrate*

*1 cup skim milk*
*½ cup chilled water*
*½ teaspoon vanilla*

Combine all the ingredients in a blender container and process until
mixed. Serve in a chilled glass.

| Serves 1 | |
| --- | --- |
| **Nutritional Analysis (per serving):** | |
| Calories: | 152.52 |
| Protein: | 9.03 g |
| Carbohydrate: | 26.90 g |
| Fat: | 0.50 g |
| Sat. Fat: | 0.29 g |
| Cholesterol: | 4.90 mg |
| Sodium: | 128.75 mg |
| Fiber: | 0.27 g |
| PCF Ratio: | 24-73-3 |
| **Exchange Approx.:** | |
| 2 Fruits, | |
| 1 Skim Milk | |

# Party Time
# Minted Raspberry Lemonade

**Yields about 4 quarts**

| Nutritional Analysis (per serving): | |
|---|---|
| Calories: | 117.02 |
| Protein: | 0.33 g |
| Carbohydrate: | 31.43 g |
| Fat: | 0.06 g |
| Sat. Fat: | 0.00 g |
| Cholesterol: | 0.00 mg |
| Sodium: | 0.86 mg |
| Fiber: | 0.94 g |
| PCF Ratio: | 1-99-0 |

**Exchange Approx.:**
½ Fruit,
1 Misc. Carb.

1 cup raspberries
3 cups freshly squeezed lemon juice (12 to 15 lemons)
1½ cups sugar
12 cups water

1 tablespoon finely chopped fresh mint (**or** 1 teaspoon dried mint)

Mash the raspberries and press through a sieve to remove the seeds. Add the raspberries and other ingredients to a gallon container and stir until the sugar is dissolved. Serve chilled or over ice. (This beverage has both ½ Fruit and 1 Carb (Sugar). Be sure to consult your dietitian if you have problems with fruit juice or sugar raising your blood glucose levels.)

## Bubbly Touch-of-Fruit Taste Drink
*Another soft drink option is to pour a cup of chilled, unsweetened club soda or seltzer over fresh or frozen fruit. The fruit imparts subtle flavor and sweetness to the beverage and when your drink is gone, you can eat the fruit for dessert. Nutritional Analysis depends on the chosen fruit, but for any choice, the Exchange Approximation is: ½ Fruit.*

# Buttermilk Blush

½ cup chilled tomato juice **or**
   ½ cup chilled vegetable
   juice
½ cup cold buttermilk

½ teaspoon fresh lemon juice
Dash of Tabasco sauce
   (optional)

Combine all the ingredients in a blender and process until mixed. Serve in a chilled glass.

| Serves 1 | |
| --- | --- |
| **Nutritional Analysis** **(per serving):** | |
| Calories: | 70.79 |
| Protein: | 4.99 g |
| Carbohydrate: | 11.23 g |
| Fat: | 1.15 g |
| Sat. Fat: | 0.68 g |
| Cholesterol: | 4.29 mg |
| Sodium: | 140.68 mg |
| Fiber: | 0.98 g |
| PCF Ratio: | 27-60-14 |

**Exchange Approx.:**
½ Skim Milk,
1 Vegetable

# Pineapple-Banana Blast

¼ frozen banana, sliced
1 tablespoon frozen pineapple
   juice concentrate

3 tablespoons water
½ cup buttermilk

Combine all the ingredients in a blender and process until mixed. Serve in a chilled glass.

| Serves 1 | |
| --- | --- |
| **Nutritional Analysis** **(per serving):** | |
| Calories: | 109.14 |
| Protein: | 4.61 g |
| Carbohydrate: | 20.76 g |
| Fat: | 1.24 g |
| Sat. Fat: | 0.73 g |
| Cholesterol: | 4.29 mg |
| Sodium: | 129.42 mg |
| Fiber: | 0.83 g |
| PCF Ratio: | 16-74-10 |

**Exchange Approx.:**
1 Fruit,
½ Skim Milk

# Peachy Ginger Ale

| Serves 4 |
|:---:|

| Nutritional Analysis (per serving): | |
|:---|---:|
| Calories: | 43.49 |
| Protein: | 0.29 g |
| Carbohydrate: | 11.21 g |
| Fat: | 0.04 g |
| Sat. Fat: | 0.01 g |
| Cholesterol: | 0.00 mg |
| Sodium: | 2.82 mg |
| Fiber: | 0.81 g |
| PCF Ratio: | 3-97-1 |

**Exchange Approx.:**
½ Fruit,
½ Misc. Carb.

*1 large peach*
*⅛ cup brown sugar*
*2 teaspoons minced fresh ginger*
*⅛ cup water*

*Unsweetened club soda, seltzer water, **or** carbonated water*

1. Peel the peach and cut into 10 slices. Place 8 slices on a tray and set in the freezer. Put the remaining 2 slices of peach in a bowl and mash with a fork. Add the brown sugar and mash it in with the peach; set aside.
2. In a microwave-safe container, mix the minced ginger with the water and microwave on high for 2 minutes. Cover the container and allow the mixture to steep for 5 minutes. Strain the ginger water (to remove the ginger) over the peach-brown sugar mixture. Stir until the brown sugar is completely dissolved.
3. Remove the peach slices from freezer and put 2 slices in each of 4 (12-ounce) glasses. Divide the ginger-peach mixture between the glasses. Pour the unsweetened carbonated water over the frozen fruit, and stir. Serve with an iced-tea spoon, and enjoy the fruit for dessert.

## Unbelievable Fact

*There are 9 teaspoons of sugar in a 12-ounce can of regular soft drink. (Source: American Diabetes Association, www.diabetes.org)*

# Fruit Frenzy Sparkler Concentrate

1 cup peeled, seeded, and
    chopped peach **or** papaya
1 cup peeled and cubed fresh
    pineapple
1 teaspoon peeled and grated
    fresh ginger

1 cup orange juice
1 cup frozen banana slices
Unsweetened club soda, seltzer
    water, **or** carbonated water

Place all the ingredients in a food processor and process until smooth. To serve, pour ½ cup of the concentrate over ice in a 12- to 16-ounce glass. Complete filling the glass with carbonated water.

| Serves 8 | |
| --- | --- |
| **Nutritional Analysis (per serving):** | |
| Calories: | 53.26 |
| Protein: | 0.69 g |
| Carbohydrate: | 13.25 g |
| Fat: | 0.26 g |
| Sat. Fat: | 0.05 g |
| Cholesterol: | 0.00 mg |
| Sodium: | 0.76 mg |
| Fiber: | 1.32 g |
| PCF Ratio: | 5-91-4 |
| **Exchange Approx.:** 1 Fruit | |

# Strawberry Cooler

½ cup frozen strawberries
¼ cup apple juice

Sparkling water

In a large tumbler, combine ½ cup frozen strawberries. Pour ¼ cup apple juice over the strawberries, and finish filling the glass with the sparkling water. Stir, and serve with an iced-tea spoon; eat the fruit at the end of your meal for dessert.

| Serves 1 ?? | |
| --- | --- |
| **Nutritional Analysis (per serving):** | |
| Calories: | 51.94 |
| Protein: | 0.50 g |
| Carbohydrate: | 12.58 g |
| Fat: | 0.35 g |
| Sat. Fat: | 0.03 g |
| Cholesterol: | 0.00 mg |
| Sodium: | 2.62 mg |
| Fiber: | 1.81 g |
| PCF Ratio: | 4-91-6 |
| **Exchange Approx.:** 1 Fruit | |

# Nectarine Cocktail

| Serves 4 | |
|---|---|
| **Nutritional Analysis (per serving):** | |
| Calories: | 108.67 |
| Protein: | 4.69 g |
| Carbohydrate: | 20.57 g |
| Fat: | 1.39 g |
| Sat. Fat: | 0.71 g |
| Cholesterol: | 4.29 mg |
| Sodium: | 131.18 mg |
| Fiber: | 1.09 g |
| PCF Ratio: | 17-72-11 |
| **Exchange Approx.:** | |
| 1 Fruit, | |
| ½ Skim Milk | |

2 cups buttermilk  
2 large, chilled nectarines  
⅛ cup brown sugar

Combine 2 cups buttermilk, 2 large, chilled nectarines, peeled and cut into pieces, and ⅛ cup brown sugar in a blender and process until the nectarines are puréed. Serve in a chilled glass.

# Jam and Jelly Soft Drink Syrup

| Serves 1 |
|---|
| **Nutritional Analysis (per serving):** |
| **Exchange Approx.:** |
| 1 Free |

2 teaspoons "Free Exchange" jam or jelly  
1 tablespoon water  
Ice cubes  
Carbonated water  
Your choice of fruit

Microwave 2 teaspoons "Free Exchange" jam or jelly and 1 tablespoon water on high for 30 seconds to 1 minute; stir. Put ice cubes in a 12- to 16-ounce glass. Pour the "syrup" over the ice, and fill the glass with carbonated water. The Nutritional Analysis depends on the fruit you choose.

# *Resources*

As you learn to accept and adjust to changes in your lifestyle, you may have more questions, or want to find additional information about diabetes. The following resources provide a wealth of information regarding diabetes in general, as well as diets, forums, and frequently asked questions.

# Diabetes Resources

### ASK THE DIETITIAN

✐ *www.dietitian.com*
Joanne Larsen, MS, RD, LD maintains this site. Post specific diet-related questions or read the answers to questions from other visitors.

### AMERICAN DIABETES ASSOCIATION

✐ *www.diabetes.org*
This site, maintained by the recognized authority on diabetes, the American Diabetes Association, is dedicated to providing up-to-date information regarding medications and diabetes research findings.

### DIABETIC GOURMET MAGAZINE

✐ *www.diabeticgourmet.com*
Articles, recipes, and resources dedicated to healthy cooking techniques.

### DIABETES LIFESTYLES

✐ *www.diabeteslifestyles.com*
A diabetes resource that includes articles about how to cope with how diabetes affects your life.

### DIABETES STATION

✐ *www.diabetesstation.org*
Information about living with diabetes, including a special Teens 'n' Kids Program section.

### INTERNATIONAL DIABETES FEDERATION

✐ *www.idf.org*
A global advocate for people with diabetes and their health-care providers in official relations with the World Health Organization (WHO) and the Pan American Health Organization (PAHO).

## JOSLIN DIABETES CENTER

✍ *www.joslin.harvard.edu*

This informational site includes online courses on an overview of diabetes and another on type 2 diabetes and the role of various medications in treating this form of the disease.

# Online Sources for Gourmet Ingredients and Equipment

The quality of the foods you prepare is based on the quality of the ingredients you use. That's elementary. The equipment you use can make a difference, too. Even if you don't have a gourmet grocery or cooking supply store nearby, you don't have to forego using sherry vinegar or chestnuts or truffle oil or any other out-of-the-ordinary ingredient or product you've been wanting to try. Chances are you can order it online through one of these sites:

### CHEF'S CATALOG

✍ *www.chefscatalog.com*

### CHRISTINE AND ROB'S

"America's Gourmet Breakfast Company"

✍ *www.christineandrobs.com*

### COUNTRY LIFE NATURAL FOODS

✍ *www.clnf.org*

### EARTHY DELIGHTS

✍ *www.earthy.com*

### FLORENTYNA'S FRESH PASTA FACTORY

✍ *www.florentynaspasta.com*

### H&H BAGELS
*www.hhbagels.com*

### LOBSTER GRAM
*www.livelob.com*

### KALYX.COM
*www.kalyx.com*

### MEXGROCER.COM
*www.mexgrocer.com*

### MONTANA ORGANIC FARMS, INC.
(Organic meats)
*www.mtorganicfarms.com*

### ORGANIC VALLEY FAMILY OF FARMS
(Has nutritional analysis information
online for their meats)
*www.organicvalley.com*

### RUSS & DAUGHTERS
*www.russanddaughters.com*

### SEATTLE'S FINEST EXOTIC MEATS
*www.exoticmeats.com*

### SUR LA TABLE
*www.surlatable.com*

### VERMONT NATURAL MEATS
*www.naturalmeat.com*

## APPENDIX B

# *Food Exchange Lists*

Because Food Exchange Lists can be an important part of arriving at individualized meal plans, this chapter covers many of the common foods found on such lists.

Please remember that the information contained in this book is not intended as medical advice. Consult your dietitian with any questions or details regarding the diet he or she has designed specifically for you. The information in this chapter is intended as a general guide only.

---

### KEY

† = 3 grams or more of fiber per serving

‡ = High in sodium; if more than one serving is eaten, these foods have 400mg or more of sodium.

1 Carbohydrate Exchange List choice = 15 g carbohydrate

1 Protein Exchange List choice = 7 g protein

1 Milk Exchange List choice = 12 g carbohydrate and 8 g of protein

1 Fat Exchange List choice = 5 g fat

---

# STARCHES AND BREAD

These are the foods found on the bottom tier of the food pyramid. Each exchange in this category contains about 15 grams of carbohydrates, 3 grams of protein, and a trace of fat for a total of 80 calories. Serving sizes may vary. A general rule is that ½ cup of cooked cereal, grain, or pasta equals one exchange and 1 ounce of a bread product is 1 serving. Those foods within this category that contain 3 grams or more of fiber are identified using a "+" symbol.

## Bread

| FOOD | AMOUNT |
| --- | --- |
| Bagel | ½ (1 ounce) |
| Bread sticks, crisp, 4 in. long × ½ in. | 2 (⅔ ounces) |
| Bun, hotdog or hamburger | ½ (1 ounce) |
| Croutons, low fat | 1 cup |
| English muffin | ½ |
| Pita, 6 in. across | ½ |
| Plain roll, small | 1 (1 ounce) |
| Raisin, unfrosted | 1 slice |
| Rye†, pumpernickel | 1 slice (1 ounce) |
| Tortilla, 6 in. across | 1 |
| White (including French, Italian) | 1 slice (1 ounce) |
| Whole wheat | 1 slice |

## Cereals and Pasta

| FOOD | AMOUNT |
| --- | --- |
| Bran cereals†, concentrated 100% Bran | ⅔ cup |
| All Bran | ⅓ cup |
| All-Bran with extra fiber | 1 cup |
| Bran Buds | ⅓ cup |
| Bran Chex | ½ cup |
| Fiber One | ⅔ cup |
| Multi-Bran Chex | ⅓ cup |
| Bran cereals†, flaked 40% bran flakes | ½ cup |
| Fortified Oat Flakes | ⅓ cup |
| Nutri-Grain | ½ cup |
| Bulgur, cooked | ½ cup |
| Cereals, most ready-to-eat, unsweetened, plain | ¾ cup |
| Cheerios† | 1 cup |
| Cooked cereals | ½ cup |
| Cornflakes | ¾ cup |
| Frosted Flakes | ¼ cup |
| Grape Nuts | 3 tablespoons |
| Grits, cooked | ½ cup |
| Kix | 1 cup |
| Life | ½ cup |
| Pasta, cooked | ½ cup |
| Puffed cereal, rice or wheat | 1 ½ cups |
| Rice Krispies | ⅔ cup |
| Shredded wheat, biscuit | 1 cup |
| Shredded wheat, spoon size | ½ cup |
| Shredded Wheat and Bran† | ½ cup |
| Special K | 1 cup |

## Cereals and Pasta (continued)

| FOOD | AMOUNT |
|---|---|
| Total | 3/4 cup |
| Wheat Chex† | 1/2 cup |
| Wheaties† | 2/3 cup |

## Grains

| FOOD | AMOUNT |
|---|---|
| Barley, cooked | 1/3 cup |
| Buckwheat, cooked | 1/2 cup |
| Bulgar, cooked | 1/3 cup |
| Cornmeal, dry | 2 1/2 tablespoons |
| Cornstarch | 2 tablespoons |
| Couscous, cooked | 1/3 cup |
| Flour | 3 tablespoons |
| Kasha, cooked | 1/3 cup |
| Millet, dry | 3 tablespoons |
| Oat bran, cooked | 1/4 cup |
| Quinoa, cooked | 1/3 cup |
| Rice, white or brown, cooked | 1/3 cup |
| Rice, wild, cooked | 1/2 cup |
| Wheat berries, cooked | 2/3 cup |
| Wheat germ† | 1/4 cup |
| (1 carb and 1 low-fat protein) | |

## Crackers and Snacks

| FOOD | AMOUNT |
|---|---|
| Animal crackers | 8 |
| Cheese Nips, reduced fat | 22 |
| Club, reduced fat | 6 |

## Crackers and Snacks (continued)

| FOOD | AMOUNT |
|---|---|
| Finn Crisp | 4 |
| Graham crackers, (2 1/2 in. square) | 3 |
| Matzoh | 1 (3/4 ounce) |
| Matzoh with bran | 1 (3/4 ounce) |
| Manischewitz whole wheat matzoh crackers | 7 |
| Melba toast, rectangles | 5 |
| Melba toast, rounds | 10 |
| Mr. Phipps pretzel chips‡ | 12 |
| Orville Redenbacher Smart Pop! popcorn | 4 cups |
| Popcorn, air-popped, no fat added | 4 cups |
| Pretzels‡ | 3/4 ounce |
| Rye crisp, 2 in. × 3 1/2 in. | 4 |
| Saltine-type crackers‡ | 6 |
| Snack-Well's, fat-free, cheddar‡ | 24 |
| Snack-Well's, fat-free, cracked pepper | 8 |
| Snack-Well's, fat-free, wheat | 6 |
| Town House, reduced fat‡ | 8 |
| Triscuits, reduced fat‡ | 8 |
| Wasa Golden Rye | 2 |
| Wasa Hearty Rye | 2 |
| Wasa Lite | 2 |

## Dried Beans, Lentils, and Peas

Note: All portions given are for cooked amounts.

| FOOD | AMOUNT |
| --- | --- |
| Baked beans† | ¼ cup |
| Beans†, white | ⅓ cup |
| Chickpeas† | ⅓ cup |
| Garbanzo beans† | ⅓ cup |
| Kidney beans† | ⅓ cup |
| Lentils† | ⅓ cup |
| Lima beans† | ½ cup |
| Navy beans† | ⅓ cup |
| Peas†, black-eyed | ⅓ cup |
| Peas†, split | ⅓ cup |
| Pinto beans† | ⅓ cup |

## Starchy Vegetables

| FOOD | AMOUNT |
| --- | --- |
| Corn† | ½ cup |
| Corn on the cob†, 6 in. long | 1 |
| Lima beans† | ½ cup |
| Mixed vegetables, with corn or peas | ⅔ cup |
| Peas†, green (canned or frozen) | ½ cup |
| Plantain† | ½ cup |
| Potato, baked or boiled | 1 small (3 ounce) |
| Potato, mashed | ½ cup |
| Pumpkin | ¾ cup |
| Squash, winter (acorn, butternut) | ¾ cup |
| Yam, sweet potato | ⅓ cup |

## Starches and Breads Prepared with Fat

These count as 1 starch/bread plus 1 fat choice:

| FOOD | AMOUNT |
| --- | --- |
| Biscuit, 2 ½ in. across | 1 |
| Chow mein noodles | ½ cup |
| Corn bread, 2-in. cube | 1 (2 ounce) |
| Crackers: | |
| Arrowroot | 4 |
| Butter cracker‡, round | 7 |
| Butter cracker‡, rectangle | 6 |
| Cheese Nips‡ | 20 |
| Cheez-It‡ | 27 |
| Club‡ | 6 |
| Combos‡ | 1 ounce |
| Escort‡ | 5 |
| Lorna Doone | 3 |
| Meal Mates‡ | 5 |
| Oyster‡ | 24 |
| Peanut butter crackers‡ | 3 |
| Pepperidge Farm Bordeaux cookies | 3 |
| Pepperidge Farm Goldfish‡ | 36 |
| Popcorn, microwave light | 4 cups |
| Ritz‡ | 7 |
| Sociables‡ | 9 |
| Stella D'oro Sesame Breadsticks | 2 |
| Sunshine HiHo‡ | 6 |
| Teddy Grahams | 15 |
| Tidbits‡ | 21 |
| Triscuits‡ | 5 |

## Starches and Breads
## Prepared with Fat (continued)

| FOOD | AMOUNT |
|------|--------|
| Crackers: (continued) | |
| Town House‡ | 6 |
| Vanilla Wafers | 6 |
| Wasa Breakfast crispbread | 2 |
| Wasa Fiber Plus crispbread | 4 |
| Wasa Sesame crispbread | 2 |
| Waverly Wafers‡ | 2 |
| Wheat Thins, reduced fat‡ | 13 |
| French fries | |
| (2 in. to 3 ½ in. long) | 10 (1 ½ ounce) |
| Muffin, plain, small | 1 |
| Pancake, 4 in. across | 2 |
| Stuffing, bread (prepared) | ¼ cup |
| Taco shell, 6 in. across | 2 |
| Waffle, 4 ½ in. square | 1 |

## Vegetable Exchange List

Cooked or steamed serving.

| FOOD | AMOUNT |
|------|--------|
| Artichoke | ½ medium |
| Asparagus | 1 cup |
| Bamboo shoots | 1 cup |
| Bean sprouts | ½ cup |
| Beet greens | ½ cup |
| Beets | ½ cup |
| Broccoli | ½ cup |
| Brussels sprouts | ½ cup |

# VEGETABLES

Vegetables fall within the second tier of the food pyramid. Each vegetable serving is calculated to contain 5 grams of carbohydrates, 2 grams of protein, between 2 to 3 grams of fiber, and 25 calories. Vegetables are a good source of vitamins and minerals. Fresh or frozen vegetables are preferred because of their higher vitamin and mineral content; however, canned vegetables are also acceptable, with the preference being for the low-sodium or salt-free varieties. As a general rule, one Vegetable Exchange is usually equal to ½ cup cooked, 1 cup raw, or ½ cup juice.

Not all vegetables are found on the Vegetable Exchange List. Starchy vegetables such as corn, peas, and potatoes are a part of the Starches and Bread Exchange List. Vegetables with fewer than ten calories per serving are found on the Free Food Exchange List.

## Vegetable Exchange List (continued)

| FOOD | AMOUNT |
|------|--------|
| Cabbage | 1 cup |
| Carrots | ½ cup |
| Cauliflower | ½ cup |
| Celery | 1 cup |
| Collard greens | 1 cup |
| Eggplant | ½ cup |
| Fennel leaf | 1 cup |

## Vegetable Exchange List (continued)

| FOOD | AMOUNT |
| --- | --- |
| Green beans | 1 cup |
| Green pepper | 1 cup |
| Kale | ½ cup |
| Kohlrabi | ½ cup |
| Leeks | ½ cup |
| Mushrooms, fresh | 1 cup |
| Mustard greens | 1 cup |
| Okra | ½ cup |
| Onions | ½ cup |
| Pea pods | ½ cup |
| Radishes | 1 cup |
| Red pepper | 1 cup |
| Rutabaga | ½ cup |
| Sauerkraut‡ | ½ cup |
| Spaghetti sauce, jar | ¼ cup |
| Spaghetti squash | ½ cup |
| Spinach | ½ cup |
| Summer squash | 1 cup |
| Tomato | 1 medium |
| Tomato, canned‡ | ½ cup |
| Tomato, paste‡ | 1 ½ tablespoons |
| Tomato sauce, canned‡ | ⅓ cup |
| Tomato/vegetable juice‡ | ½ cup |
| Turnip greens | 1 cup |
| Turnips | ½ cup |
| Water chestnuts | 6 whole or ½ cup |
| Wax beans | ½ cup |
| Zucchini | 1 cup |

## FRUITS

One Fruit Exchange has about 15 grams of carbohydrates, which totals 60 calories. The serving sizes for fruits vary considerably, so consult the list. Also, note that portion amounts are given for fruit that is dried, fresh, frozen, or canned packed in its own juice with no sugar added.

## Fresh, Frozen, and Unsweetened Canned Fruit

| FOOD | AMOUNT |
| --- | --- |
| Apple, raw, 2 in. across | 1 |
| Apple, dried | 4 rings |
| Applesauce, unsweetened | ½ cup |
| Apricots, canned, 4 halves | ½ cup |
| Apricots, dried | 7 halves |
| Apricots, fresh | 4 medium |
| Banana, 9 in. long | ½ |
| Banana flakes or chips | 3 tablespoons |
| Blackberries, raw | ¾ cup |
| Blueberries†, raw | ¾ cup |
| Boysenberries | 1 cup |
| Canned fruit, unless otherwise stated | ½ cup |
| Cantaloupe, 5 in. across | ⅓ |
| Cantaloupe, cubes | 1 cup |
| Casaba, 7 in. across | 1/6 melon |
| Casaba, cubed | 1 ⅓ cups |
| Cherries, large, raw | 12 whole |
| Cherries, canned | ½ cup |

## Fresh, Frozen, and Unsweetened Canned Fruit (continued)

| FOOD | AMOUNT |
| --- | --- |
| Cherries, dried (no sugar added) | 2 tablespoons |
| Cranberries, dried (no sugar added) | 2 tablespoons |
| Currants | 2 tablespoons |
| Dates | 3 |
| Fig, dried | 1 |
| Figs, fresh, 2 in. across | 2 |
| Fruit cocktail, canned | 1/2 cup |
| Grapefruit, medium | 1/2 |
| Grapefruit, sections | 3/4 cup |
| Grapes, small | 15 |
| Guavas | 1 1/2 small |
| Honeydew melon, medium | 1/8 |
| Honeydew melon, cubes | 1 cup |
| Kiwi, large | 1 |
| Kumquats | 5 medium |
| Loquats, fresh | 12 |
| Lychees, dried or fresh | 10 |
| Mandarin oranges | 3/4 cup |
| Mango, small | 1/2 |
| Nectarine, 2 1/2 in. across | 1 |
| Orange, 3 in. across | 1 |
| Papaya, fresh 3 1/2 in. across | 1/2 |
| Papaya, fresh, cubed | 1 cup |
| Peach, 2 3/4 in. across | 1 peach or 3/4 cup |
| Peaches, canned | 2 halves or 1 cup |
| Peach, fresh, 2 1/2 in. across | 1 |
| Pear | 1 small |
| Pears, canned | 2 halves or 1/2 cup |

## Fresh, Frozen, and Unsweetened Canned Fruit (continued)

| FOOD | AMOUNT |
| --- | --- |
| Persimmon, medium, native | 2 |
| Pineapple, raw | 3/4 cup |
| Pineapple, canned | 1/3 cup |
| Plantain, cooked | 1/3 cup |
| Plum, raw, 2 in. across | 2 |
| Pomegranate† | 1/2 |
| Prunes, dried, medium | 3 |
| Raisins | 2 tablespoons |
| Raspberries†, raw | 1 cup |
| Strawberries†, raw, whole | 1 1/3 cups |
| Tangerine, 2 1/2 in. across | 2 |
| Watermelon, cubes | 1 1/4 cups |

## Dried Fruit†

| FOOD | AMOUNT |
| --- | --- |
| †Apples | 4 rings |
| †Apricots | 7 halves |
| Dates, medium | 2 1/2 |
| †Figs | 1 1/2 |
| †Prunes, medium | 3 |
| Raisins | 2 tablespoon |

## Fruit Juice

| FOOD | AMOUNT |
| --- | --- |
| Apple cider | 1/2 cup |
| Apple juice, unsweetened | 1/2 cup |
| Cranapple juice, unsweetened | 3/8 cup |
| Cranberry juice cocktail | 1/3 cup |
| Cranberry juice, low-calorie | 1 1/8 cup |
| Cranberry juice, unsweetened | 1/2 cup |

## Fruit Juice (continued)

| FOOD | AMOUNT |
|------|--------|
| Grapefruit juice | ½ cup |
| Grape juice | ⅜ cup |
| Orange juice | ½ cup |
| Pineapple juice | ½ cup |
| Prune juice | ⅜ cup |

## MILK

Milk servings are usually marked at 1 cup or 8 ounces. Like meats, Milk Exchange Lists are divided into categories depending on the fat content of the choices. Each Milk Exchange has about 12 grams of carbohydrate and 8 grams of protein; however, the calories in each exchange will vary according to the fat content.

### Skim or Very Lowfat Milk

| FOOD | AMOUNT |
|------|--------|
| ½% milk | 1 cup |
| 1% milk | 1 cup |
| Buttermilk, lowfat or 1% | 1 cup |
| Nonfat milk, dry | ⅓ cup |
| Skim milk | 1 cup |
| Skim milk, evaporated | ½ cup |
| Yogurt, plain nonfat | 8 ounces |

### Lowfat Milk

| FOOD | AMOUNT |
|------|--------|
| 2% milk | 1 cup |
| Yogurt, plain low-fat with added nonfat milk solids | 8 ounces |

## Whole Milk

The whole-milk group has much more fat per serving than the skim and low-fat groups. Whole milk has more than 3 ¼% butterfat, so you should limit your choices from this group as much as possible.

| | |
|------|--------|
| Whole milk | 1 cup |
| Whole milk, evaporated | ½ cup |
| Yogurt, plain whole milk | 8 ounces |

## MEATS

Each serving of meat or meat substitute has about 7 grams of protein. As shown in the tables below, the Meats Exchange Lists are divided depending on the fat content of the meat or meat substitute choice. (See Chapter 5 for suggestions on the healthiest ways to prepare meats.)

Make your selections from the lean and medium-fat meat, poultry, and fish choices in your meal plan as much as possible. This helps you keep the fat intake in your diet low, which may help decrease your risk for heart disease. Remember that the meats in the high-fat group have more saturated fat, cholesterol, and calories, so you should consult with your dietician as to whether or not your diet should include any meats from that group. When they are permitted, most dieticians recommend limiting your choices from the high-fat group to a maximum of three times per week.

Meats and meat substitutes that have 400 milligrams or more of sodium per exchange are indicated with the "‡" symbol.

| EXCHANGE | CARBOHYDRATE | PROTEIN (g) | FAT(g) | CALORIES |
|---|---|---|---|---|
| Very Lean Meats | 0 | 7 | 0-1 | 35 |
| Lean Meats | 0 | 7 | 3 | 55 |
| Medium-Fat | 0 | 7 | 5 | 75 |
| High-Fat | 0 | 7 | 8 | 100 |

Meats Exchange List portions generally are one ounce of cooked meat (using the 4 ounces of raw meat results in 3 ounces of cooked meat standard). Beef, pork, fish, poultry, cheese, eggs, and, when they're used as meat substitutes, dried beans, legumes, and some nuts fall within the Meats Exchange Lists categories. Because the calorie counts vary so widely (as does the cholesterol and saturated fat content), your dietician will advise from which lists you are to choose your selections.

## Very Lean Meats (and Meat Substitutes)

Meats in this category are usually the reduced-fat varieties, like Healthy Choice and contain 4 percent or fewer of the calories from fat, which unless otherwise noted below are at 1 ounce per Food Exchange List portion. Name brand foods come and go, with new ones introduced regularly that phase out others. Check product labels or with your dietician to ascertain which products currently fall within this category.

One choice provides about 35 to 45 calories, 7 grams of protein, no carbohydrates, and 0 to 2 grams of fat.

## Very Lean Meats (and Meat Substitutes) (continued)

| FOOD | AMOUNT |
|---|---|
| Buffalo | 1 ounce |
| Chicken, white meat, skinless | 1 ounce |
| Cornish hen, white meat, skinless | 1 ounce |
| Cottage cheese, fat-free or 1% | ¼ cup |
| Ricotta, 100% fat-free‡ | 1 ounce |
| Egg substitute, plain (if less than 40 calories per serving) | ¼ cup |
| Fish and seafood, fresh or frozen, cooked: clams, cod, crab, flounder, haddock, halibut, imitation crabmeat, lobster, scallops, shrimp, trout, tuna (in water) | 2 ounces |
| Ostrich | 1 ounce |
| Turkey, ground, 93-99% fat-free | 1 ounce |
| Turkey, white meat, skinless | 1 ounce |
| Turkey sausage, 97% fat-free‡ | 1 ounce |
| Venison | 1 ounce |

## Lean Meats
## (and Meat Substitutes)

One choice provides about 55 calories, 7 grams of protein, no carbohydrates, and 3 grams of fat.

| FOOD | AMOUNT |
|------|--------|
| 95% fat-free luncheon meat | 1 ounce |
| Beef, USDA Good or Choice grades of lean beef such as: | |
|   Chipped beef‡ | 1 ounce |
|   Flank steak | 1 ounce |
|   Round steak | 1 ounce |
|   Sirloin steak | 1 ounce |
|   Tenderloin | 1 ounce |
| Clams, fresh or canned in water‡ | 2 ounces |
| Cottage cheese, any variety | ¼ cup |
| Crab | 2 ounces |
| Diet cheese‡ (with fewer than 55 calories per ounce) | 1 ounce |
| Duck, without skin | 1 ounce |
| Egg substitutes (with fewer than 55 calories per ¼ cup) | ¼ cup |
| Egg whites | 3 |
| Fish, all fresh and frozen catfish, salmon, and other "fattier" fish | 1 ounce |
| Goose, without skin | 1 ounce |
| Grated Parmesan | 2 tablespoons |
| Herring, uncreamed or smoked | 1 ounce |
| Lobster | 2 ounces |

## Lean Meats
## (and Meat Substitutes) (continued)

| FOOD | AMOUNT |
|------|--------|
| Oysters | 6 medium |
| Pheasant (without skin) | 1 ounce |
| Pork, lean cuts such as: | |
|   Boiled ham‡ | 1 ounce |
|   Canadian bacon‡ | 1 ounce |
|   Canned ham‡ | 1 ounce |
|   Cured ham‡ | 1 ounce |
|   Fresh ham | 1 ounce |
|   Tenderloin | 1 ounce |
| Poultry: | |
|   Chicken, dark meat, without skin | 1 ounce |
|   Cornish game hen, dark meat, without skin | 1 ounce |
|   Turkey, dark meat, without skin | 1 ounce |
| Rabbit | 1 ounce |
| Sardines, canned | 2 medium |
| Scallops | 2 ounces |
| Shrimp | 2 ounces |
| Squirrel | 1 ounce |
| Tofu | 3 ounces |
| Veal, all cuts are lean except for veal cutlets (ground or cubed) | 1 ounce |
| Venison | 1 ounce |

## Medium-Fat Meats (and Meat Substitutes)

One choice provides about 75 calories, 7 grams of protein, no carbohydrates, and 5 grams of fat.

| FOOD | AMOUNT |
| --- | --- |
| 86% fat-free luncheon meat‡ | 1 ounce |
| Most beef products, such as: | |
| Chuck roast | 1 ounce |
| Cubed steak | 1 ounce |
| Ground beef | 1 ounce |
| Meat loaf | 1 ounce |
| Porterhouse steak | 1 ounce |
| Rib roast | 1 ounce |
| Rump roast | 1 ounce |
| T-bone steak | 1 ounce |
| Skim or part-skim milk cheeses, such as: | |
| Diet cheeses‡ (with 56–80 calories per ounce) | 1 ounce |
| Mozzarella | 1 ounce |
| Ricotta | ¼ cup |
| Egg (high in cholesterol, so limit to 3 per week) | 1 |
| Egg substitutes (with 56–80 calories per ¼ cup) | ¼ cup |
| Heart (high in cholesterol) | 1 ounce |
| Kidney (high in cholesterol) | 1 ounce |

## Medium-Fat Meats (and Meat Substitutes) (continued)

| FOOD | AMOUNT |
| --- | --- |
| Most lamb products, such as: | |
| Chops | 1 ounce |
| Leg | 1 ounce |
| Roast | 1 ounce |
| Liver (high in cholesterol) | 1 ounce |
| Parmesan cheese‡ | 3 tablespoons |
| Most pork products, such as: | |
| Chops | 1 ounce |
| Loin roast | 1 ounce |
| Boston butt | 1 ounce |
| Cutlets | 1 ounce |
| Chicken (with skin) | 1 ounce |
| Duck, domestic, well drained of fat | 1 ounce |
| Goose, domestic, well drained of fat | 1 ounce |
| Ground turkey | 1 ounce |
| Romano cheese | 3 tablespoons |
| Sweetbreads (high in cholesterol) | 1 ounce |
| Tofu (2 ½" × 2¾" × 1") | 4 ounce |
| Tuna‡, canned in oil and drained | ¼ cup |
| Salmon‡, canned | ¼ cup |
| Veal cutlet, ground or cubed, unbreaded | 1 ounce |

## High-Fat Meats
## (and Meat Substitutes)

Remember, these items are high in saturated fat, cholesterol, and calories, and should be eaten only three or fewer times per week.

One choice provides about 100 calories, 7 grams of protein, no carbohydrates, and 8 grams of fat. One exchange choice is equal to any one of the following items:

| FOOD | AMOUNT |
| --- | --- |
| Most USDA Prime cuts of beef | 1 ounce |
| Beef‡, corned | 1 ounce |
| Ribs, beef | 1 ounce |
| Bologna‡ | 1 ounce |
| Cheese, all regular cheese‡: | |
| American | 1 ounce |
| Bleu | 1 ounce |
| Cheddar | 1 ounce |
| Monterey | 1 ounce |
| Swiss | 1 ounce |
| Fish, fried | 1 ounce |
| Hotdog‡: | |
| Chicken, 10/pound | 1 frank |
| Turkey, 10/pound | 1 frank |
| Lamb, ground | 1 ounce |
| Peanut butter | |
| (contains unsaturated fat) | 1 tablespoon |
| Pimiento loaf‡ | 1 ounce |
| Pork chop | 1 ounce |

## High-Fat Meats
## (and Meat Substitutes) (continued)

| FOOD | AMOUNT |
| --- | --- |
| Pork, ground | 1 ounce |
| Spareribs | 1 ounce |
| Steak | 1 ounce |
| Salami‡ | 1 ounce |
| Sausage‡: | |
| Bratwurst‡ | 1 ounce |
| Italian | 1 ounce |
| Knockwurst, smoked | 1 ounce |
| Polish | 1 ounce |
| Pork sausage‡ (patty or link) | 1 ounce |

Counts as one high-fat meat **plus** one fat exchange:

| | |
| --- | --- |
| Hotdog‡ — beef, pork, or combination, 400 mg or more of sodium per exchange, 10/pound | 1 frank |

## FATS

Each Fats Exchange List serving will contain about 5 grams of fat and 45 calories. Fats are found in margarine, butter, oils, nuts, meat fat, and dairy products. Saturated fat amounts and sodium content can vary considerably, depending on the choice. Most dieticians recommend polyunsaturated or mono-unsaturated fats whenever possible.

## Unsaturated Fats

| FOOD | AMOUNT |
|---|---|
| Almonds, dry roasted | 6 |
| Avocado | ⅛ medium |
| Cashews, dry roasted | 1 tablespoon or 6 |
| Cooking oil (corn, cottonseed, safflower, soybean, sunflower, olive, peanut) | 1 teaspoon |
| Hazelnuts (filberts) | 5 |
| Macadamia nuts | 3 |
| Margarine | 1 teaspoon |
| Margarine, diet‡ | 1 tablespoon |
| Mayonnaise | 1 teaspoon |
| Mayonnaise, reduced-calorie‡ | 1 tablespoon |
| Olives, black‡ | 9 large |
| Olives, green‡ | 10 large |
| Other nuts | 1 tablespoon |
| Peanuts, large | 10 |
| Peanuts, small | 20 |
| Pecans | 4 halves |
| Pine nuts | 1 tablespoon |
| Pistachio | 12 |
| Pumpkin seeds | 2 teaspoons |
| Salad dressing, all varieties, regular | 1 tablespoon |
| Salad dressing, mayonnaise-type reduced-calorie | 1 tablespoon |
| Salad dressing, mayonnaise-type regular | 2 teaspoons |
| Salad dressing, reduced-calorie‡ (2 tablespoons of low-calorie dressing is a free food) | 2 tablespoons |

## Unsaturated Fats (continued)

| FOOD | AMOUNT |
|---|---|
| Sesame seeds | 1 tablespoon |
| Sunflower seeds, without shells | 1 tablespoon |
| Tahini | 2 teaspoons |
| Walnuts | 4 halves |

## Saturated Fats

| FOOD | AMOUNT |
|---|---|
| Bacon‡ | 1 slice |
| Butter | 1 teaspoon |
| Butter, whipped | 2 teaspoons |
| Chitterlings | ½ ounces |
| Coconut, shredded | 2 tablespoons |
| Coffee whitener, liquid | 2 tablespoon |
| Coffee whitener, powder | 4 tablespoon |
| Cream, heavy | 1 tablespoon |
| Cream (light, coffee, table) | 2 tablespoons |
| Cream, sour | 2 tablespoon |
| Cream, whipping | 1 tablespoon |
| Cream cheese | 1 tablespoon |
| Salt pork‡ | ¼ ounce |

## FREE FOODS

A free food is any food or drink that contains less than 20 calories per serving. Unless a serving size is specified, you can eat as much as you want of those foods. You are limited to eating two or three servings per day of those foods with a specific serving size.

### Free Drinks

| FOOD | AMOUNT |
|---|---|
| Bouillon or canned broth without fat‡ | |
| Bouillon, low-sodium | |
| Broth, low-sodium | |
| Carbonated drinks, sugar-free | |
| Carbonated water | |
| Club soda | |
| Cocoa powder, unsweetened | 1 tablespoon |
| Coffee | |
| Drink mixes, sugar-free | |
| Tea | |
| Tonic water, sugar-free | |

### Free Fruits and Vegetables

| FOOD | AMOUNT |
|---|---|
| Cranberries, unsweetened | (½ cup) |
| Rhubarb, unsweetened | (½ cup) |

### Vegetables (1 cup raw)

Alfalfa sprouts

Cabbage

Celery

Chinese cabbage†

Cucumber

Endive

Escarole

Green onion

Hot peppers

Lettuce

Mushrooms

Parsley

Pickles, unsweetened‡

Pimento

Radishes

Romaine

Salad Greens

Spinach

Watercress

Zucchini†

### Free Sweets

| FOOD | AMOUNT |
|---|---|
| Candy, hard, sugar-free | |
| Gelatin, sugar-free | |
| Gum, sugar-free | |
| Jam/jelly, low sugar | 2 teaspoons |
| Jam/jelly, sugar-free | 2 teaspoons |
| Pancake syrup, sugar-free | 1–2 tablespoons |
| Sugar substitutes (saccharin, aspartame. Splenda) | |
| Whipped topping | 2 tablespoons |

## Free Condiments

| FOOD | AMOUNT |
|------|--------|
| Catsup | 1 tablespoon |
| Horseradish | |
| Mustard | |
| Nonstick pan spray | |
| Pickles, dill, unsweetened‡ | |
| Salad dressing, low-calorie | 2 tablespoons |
| Taco sauce | 1 tablespoon |
| Vinegar | |

## Free Seasonings

Seasonings can be very helpful in making foods taste better, but be careful of how much sodium you use. Read labels to help you choose seasonings that do not contain sodium or salt.

Basil

Celery seeds

Chili powder

Chives

Cinnamon

Curry

Dill

Garlic

Garlic powder

Herbs

Hot pepper sauce

Lemon

Lemon juice

Lemon pepper

Lime

Lime juice

## Free Seasonings (continued)

Mint

Onion powder

Oregano

Paprika

Pepper

Pimiento

Soy sauce, low sodium ("lite")

Soy sauce‡

Spices

Wine, ¼ cup used in cooking

Worcestershire sauce‡

## Free Flavoring Extracts

Almond

Butter

Lemon

Peppermint

Vanilla

Walnut

## Meat Substitute Protein Foods

Note: Foods on this list equal 1 Protein (0 g carb, 7 g protein, 0–5 g fat) Food Exchange List serving.

| FOOD | AMOUNT |
|------|--------|
| Egg substitute | ¼ cup |
| Soy cheese | 1 ounce |
| Tofu, firm | ½ cup (4 ounces) |

## Beans Used as a Meat Substitute

| FOOD | AMOUNT | EXCHANGES |
|------|--------|-----------|
| Dried beans† | 1 cup, cooked | 1 lean meat, 2 starches |
| Dried lentils† | 1 cup, cooked | 1 lean meat, 2 starches |
| Dried peas† | 1 cup, cooked | 1 lean meat, 2 starches |

## Nuts and Seeds Used as a Meat Substitute

Note: Foods on this list equal 1 Protein and 2 or 3 Fat (0 g carb, 7 g protein, 10–15 g fat) Food Exchange List serving. Consult product label to determine the fat content for your choice.

| FOOD | AMOUNT |
|------|--------|
| Almonds | ¼ cup |
| Pecans | ¼ cup |
| Peanuts | ¼ cup |
| Pine nuts | 2 tablespoons |
| Pignolias | 2 tablespoons |
| Pistachios | ¼ cup (1 ounce) |
| Pumpkin seeds | ¼ cup |
| Sesame seeds | ¼ cup |
| Squash seeds | ¼ cup |
| Sunflower seeds | ¼ cup |
| Walnuts | 16–20 halves |

## COMBINATION FOODS

Food is often mixed together in various combinations that do not fit into only one exchange list. Each of the recipes in this book gives the Exchange List Exchanges for that dish. The following is included as a list of average Exchange List values for some typical combination foods. Ask your dietitian for information about these or any other combination of foods you'd like to eat.

## Fat Foods Used as a Meat Substitute

Note: Foods on this list equal 1 Fat (0 g carb, 5 g fat) Food Exchange List serving.

| FOOD | AMOUNT | EXCHANGES |
|------|--------|-----------|
| Almond butter | 1 tablespoon | 2 fat |
| Cashew butter | 1 tablespoon | 2 fat |
| Flax seed oil | 1 teaspoon | 1 fat |
| Peanut oil | 1 teaspoon | 1 fat |
| Sesame butter | 1 tablespoon | 2 fat |

## FOODS FOR SPECIAL TREATS

These foods, despite their sugar or fat content, are intended to be added to your meal plan in moderate amounts, as long as your dietician agrees and if despite consuming them, you can still maintain blood-glucose control. Your dietitian can also advise how often you can eat these foods. Because these special treats are concentrated sources of carbohydrate, the portion sizes are very small.

## Combo Foods

| FOOD | AMOUNT | EXCHANGES |
|------|--------|-----------|
| Bean soup†‡ | 1 cup (8 ounces) | 1 lean meat, 1 starch, 1 vegetable |
| Casserole, homemade | 1 cup (8 ounces) | 2 medium-fat meat, 2 starches, 1 fat |
| Cheese pizza‡, thin crust | ¼ of a 15-ounce size pizza or a 10" pizza | 1 medium-fat meat, 2 starches, 1 fat |
| Chili with beans, commercial†‡ | 1 cup (8 ounces) | 2 medium-fat meat, 2 starches, 2 fats |
| Chow mein†‡ (without noodles or rice) | 2 cups (16 ounces) | 2 lean meat, 1 starch, 2 vegetable |
| Chunky soup, all varieties‡ | 10¾-ounce can | 1 medium-fat meat, 1 starch, 1 vegetable |
| Cream soup‡ (made with water) | 1 cup (8 ounces) | 1 starch, 1 fat |
| Macaroni and cheese‡ | 1 cup (8 ounces) | 1 medium-fat meat, 2 starches, 2 fats |
| Spaghetti and meatballs, canned‡ | 1 cup (8 ounces) | 1 medium-fat meat, 1 fat, 2 starches |
| Sugar-free pudding (made with skim milk) | ½ cup | 1 starch |
| Vegetable soup‡ | 1 cup (8 ounces) | 1 starch |

## Foods for Special Treats

| FOOD | AMOUNT | EXCHANGES |
|------|--------|-----------|
| Angel-food cake | 1/12 cake | 2 starches |
| Cake, no icing | 1/12 cake (3-in. square) | 2 starches, 2 fats |
| Cookies | 2 small (1 3/4 in. across) | 2 starches, 1 fat |
| Frozen fruit yogurt | 1/3 cup | 1 starch |
| Gingersnaps | 3 | 1 starch |
| Granola | 1/4 cup | 1 starch, 1 fat |
| Granola bars | 1 small | 1 starch, 1 fat |
| Ice cream, any flavor | 1/2 cup | 1 starch, 2 fats |
| Ice milk, any flavor | 1/2 cup | 1 starch, 1 fat |
| Sherbet, any flavor | 1/4 cup | 1 starch |
| Snack chips‡, all varieties | 1 ounce | 1 starch, 2 fats |
| Vanilla wafers | 6 small | 1 starch, 2 fats |

## Miscellaneous Foods

| FOOD | AMOUNT | FOOD GROUP | CARBOHYDRATE GRAMS | CALORIES |
|------|--------|-----------|--------------------|----------|
| Jam, regular | 1 tablespoon | 1 carbohydrate | 13 g | 80 |
| Jelly, regular | 1 tablespoon | 1 carbohydrate | 13 g | 80 |
| Honey, regular | 1 tablespoon | 1 carbohydrate | 13 g | 80 |
| Sugar | 1 tablespoon | 1 carbohydrate | 12 g | 46 |
| Syrup, light | 2 tablespoons | 1 carbohydrate | 13 g | 80 |
| Syrup, regular | 2 tablespoons | 2 carbohydrate | 27 g | 160 |
| Yogurt, regular with fruit | 1 cup | 3 carbohydrate | 45 g | 240 |

## Other Special Foods

| FOOD | AMOUNT | EXCHANGES |
|------|--------|-----------|
| Brewer's yeast | 3 tablespoons | 1 bread |
| Carob flour | 1/8 cup | 1 bread |
| Kefir | 1 cup | 1 milk and 1 fat |
| Miso | 3 tablespoons | 1 bread and 1/2 lean meat |

## Other Special Foods (continued)

| FOOD | AMOUNT | EXCHANGES |
|------|--------|-----------|
| Sea vegetables, cooked | ½ cup | 1 vegetable |
| Soy flour | ¼ cup | 1 lean meat plus ½ bread |
| Soy grits, raw | ⅛ cup | 1 lean meat |
| Soy milk | 1 cup | 1 milk and 1 fat |
| Tahini | 1 teaspoon | 1 fat |
| Tempeh | 4 ounces | 1 bread and 2 protein |
| Wheat germ | 1 tablespoon | ½ bread |

## MEASURING FOODS

Portion control is an important part of implementing a diet based on the Food Exchange Lists. This helps ensure that you eat the right serving sizes of food. Liquids and some solid foods (such as tuna, cottage cheese, and canned fruits) can be measured using a measuring cup. Measuring spoons are useful to guarantee correct amounts for foods used in smaller portions, like oil, salad dressing, and peanut butter. A scale can be very useful for measuring almost anything, especially meat, poultry, and fish.

Similar to manner how professional chefs cook, you will eventually learn how to estimate food amounts. Until then, it can be useful to remember that a cup is about equal in size to an average woman's closed fist. A thumb is about the size of a tablespoon or a one-ounce portion of cheese. The tip of the thumb equals about a teaspoon, a useful gauge when trying to determine how much butter to add to your bread or dressing to add to a salad when you're dining out and don't have measuring spoons available.

Many raw foods will weigh less after they are cooked. This is especially true for most meats. On the other hand, starches often swell during cooking, so a small amount of uncooked starch results in a much larger amount of cooked food. Some examples of those changes are:

| STARCH GROUP | UNCOOKED | COOKED |
|--------------|----------|--------|
| Cream of wheat | 2 level tablespoon | ½ cup |
| Dried beans | 3 tablespoons | ⅓ cup |

| STARCH GROUP | UNCOOKED | COOKED |
|---|---|---|
| Dried peas | 3 tablespoons | ⅓ cup |
| Grits | 3 level tablespoon | ½ cup |
| Lentils | 2 tablespoons | ⅓ cup |
| Macaroni | ¼ cup | ½ cup |
| Noodles | ⅓ cup | ½ cup |
| Oatmeal | 3 level tablespoons | ½ cup |
| Rice | 2 level tablespoons | ⅓ cup |
| Spaghetti | ¼ cup | ½ cup |
| **MEAT GROUP** | **UNCOOKED** | **COOKED** |
| Chicken | 1 small drumstick | 1 ounce |
| Chicken | ½ chicken breast | 3 ounce |
| Hamburger | 4 ounces | 3 ounces |

## READING FOOD LABELS

Labels like "dietetic" or "diabetic" don't necessarily mean a food is a healthy choice. Such words on a food label usually just mean that an ingredient has been changed or replaced. It can mean the food has less salt, less fat, or, in the case of "diabetic," less or no sugar. It does not guarantee that the food is sugar-free or calorie-free. Some sugar-free foods can still be very high in fat. Some dietetic foods are useful because those that contain 20 calories or less per serving may be chosen as your three free foods per day. Other times, a reduction in one ingredient, such as fat, is compensated by an increase in the amount of sodium in the food. That's why, when making food purchase selections, it's important that you consider all aspects of the food label. (It's also why it often proves to be easier-and less expensive-to cook from scratch rather than relying on a diet of processed, packaged foods.)

| CALORIES | 1,200 | 1,500 | 1,800 | 2,000 | 2,200 |
|---|---|---|---|---|---|
| Starches and Bread | 5 | 8 | 10 | 11 | 13 |
| Meats | 4 | 5 | 7 | 8 | 8 |
| Vegetables | 2 | 3 | 3 | 4 | 4 |
| Fruits | 3 | 3 | 3 | 3 | 3 |
| Fats | 2 | 3 | 3 | 4 | 5 |
| Milk | 2 | 2 | 2 | 2 | 2 |

# Index

## A

Alcohol consumption, 8–9
Almonds
  about: fat in, 30
  Almond Biscotti, 242
  Almond Honey Mustard, 59
  Almond Spread, 31
  Asian Gingered Almonds, 30
  Baked Red Snapper Almandine, 131
  Baked Snapper with Orange-Rice
    Dressing, 132
  Cinnamon Nut Butter, 55
  Greek Pasta Salad, 209
  Lemon-Almond Dressing, 199
  Spicy Almond Dip, 55
  Zesty Almond Spread, 59
Aloha Ham Microwave Casserole, 97
*American Diabetes Association Guide*
  *to Healthy Restaurant Eating, The*
  (Warshaw), 7
Angelic Buttermilk Batter Biscuits, 82
Another Healthy "Fried" Chicken, 106
Appetizers
  Almond Honey Mustard, 59
  Bean Dip, 57
  Cinnamon Nut Butter, 55
  Cucumber Slices with Smoke Salmon
    Cream, 52
  Easy Olive Spread, 61
Dipping Sauce, 37
  Flaxseed Oil-Fortified Salsa Dip, 53
  French Onion Soup Dip, 56
  Garbanzo Dip, 58
  Garlic and Feta Cheese Dip, 54
  Gluten-Free Sesame Seed Crackers, 63
  Herbed Cheese Spread, 58
  Horseradish Dip, 57
  Lemon Tahini Vegetable Dip, 53
  Mushroom Caviar, 62
  Onion Dip, 56
  Smoked Mussel Spread, 60
  Spicy Almond Dip, 55

Zesty Almond Spread, 59
Apples/apple juice
  Apple Cookies with a Kick, 243
  Carrot-Fruit Cup, 235
  Cranberry-Raisin Chutney, 33
  Creamy Fruit Cup, 260
  Fruited Pork Loin Roast Casserole, 158
  Individual Apple-Blackberry
    Charlottes, 247
  Spinach Salad with Apple-Avocado
    Dressing, 208
Apricots
  Fruited Pork Loin Roast Casserole, 158
  Overnight Oatmeal, 70
  Roasted Red Pepper and Plum
    Sauce, 38
Aquaculture, 127
Artichokes
  about: substitutes for, 162
  Ham and Artichoke Hearts Scalloped
    Potatoes, 162
  Pasta with Artichokes, 175
Asian-style dishes
  Asian Gingered Almonds, 30
  Asian Popcorn, 256
  Asian-Style Fish Cakes, 125
  *see also* Stir-fried dishes
Avocadoes
  Avocado and Peach Salad, 206
  Avocado-Corn Salsa, 36
  Orange-Avocado Slaw, 207
  Spinach Salad with Apple-Avocado
    Dressing, 208

## B

Bacon, about: 212
Baked dishes
  Baked Beef Stew, 186
  Baked Bread Crumb–Crusted Fish
    with Lemon, 130
  Baked French Fries, 218

Baked Orange Roughy with Spicy
  Plum Sauce, 134
Baked Pear Crisp, 238
Baked Potato Chips, 219
Baked Red Snapper Almandine, 131
Baked Snapper with Orange-Rice
  Dressing, 132
Bananas
  about: freezing, 241
  Bananas Foster, 241
  Carrot-Fruit Cup, 235
  Cranberry-Raisin Chutney, 33
  Fruit Frenzy Sparkler Concentrate, 269
  Pineapple-Banana Blast, 267
  Strawberry-Banana Sherbet, 240
Barbeque
  Barbecue Spice Blend, 48
  Slow-Cooker Venison BBQ, 164
Basic Tomato Sauce, 171
Basil
  about: preserving fresh, 41
  Pesto Sauce, 41
  Uncooked Tomato Sauce, 172
Beans
  about: cooking, 183; servings per day,
    3
  Apple Cookies with a Kick, 243
  Beanberry Blast, 242
  Bean Dip, 57
  Chicken and Green Bean Stovetop
    Casserole, 112
  Garbanzo Dip, 58
  Green Bean and Mushroom Salad,
    202
  Lentil Soup with Herbs and Lemon,
    183
  Lentil-Vegetable Soup, 184
  Main Dish Pork and Beans, 161
  Marmalade-Black Bean Salsa, 34
  Mock Pumpkin Custard, 239
  Pasta Fagioli, 178
  Pineapple–Black Bean Sauce, 119

Scallops and Shrimp with White
    Bean Sauce, 137
Tomato-Vegetable Soup, 185
Vegetable and Bean Chili, 188
Vegetable Broth, 214
White and Black Bean Salad, 203
Bean sprouts
    Fusion Lo Mein, 173
Béchamel Sauce, mock, 46
Beef
    Baked Beef Stew, 186
    Beef Broth: Easy Slow-Cooker
        Method, 146
    Kielbasa, 149
    Kovbasa (Ukrainian Kielbasa), 149
    Single-Serving Beef (Almost)
        Stroganoff, 99
    Single-Serving Unstuffed Cabbage and
        Green Peppers, 101
    Stovetop Grilled Beef Loin, 147
    Ultimate Grilled Cheeseburger
        Sandwich, 148
Berries
    Beanberry Blast, 242
    Berry Puff Pancakes, 67
    Bubbly Berry Blast, 237
    Fruit Salsa, 34
    Individual Apple-Blackberry
        Charlottes, 247
    Linzertorte Muffins, 228
    Party Time Minted Raspberry
        Lemonade, 266
    Strawberry-Banana Sherbet, 240
    Strawberry Cooler, 269
    Strawberry Spoon Sweet, 35
Beverages
    Buttermilk Blush, 267
    Frothy Orange Jewel, 265
    Fruit Frenzy Sparkler Concentrate, 269
    Hot Spiced Tea, 262
    Iced and Spiced Chai-Style Tea, 263
    Iced Ginger-Orange Green Tea, 262
    Jam and Jelly Soft Drink Syrup, 270
    Minted Lemon Tea, 261
    Nectarine Cocktail, 270
    Orange-Pineapple Froth, 265
    Party Time Minted Raspberry
        Lemonade, 266
    Peachy Ginger Ale, 268

Pineapple-Banana Blast, 267
Sparkling Fruited Iced Tea, 261
Spiced Chai-Style Creamer Mix, 263
Strawberry Cooler, 269
Tangy Limeade, 264
Biscotti, almond, 242
Biscuits. *See* Breads
Black beans
    Marmalade–Black Bean Salsa, 34
Blackberries
    Fruit Salsa, 34
    Individual Apple-Blackberry
        Charlottes, 247
Black Olive Mock Caviar, 254
Bleu cheese
    Bleu Cheese Dressing, 196
    Bleu Cheese Pasta, 180
    Bleu Cheese Pasta Salad, 210
Blueberries
    Bubbly Berry Blast, 237
Bragg's Liquid Aminos, 57
Brandy, substitute for, 9
Breads
    about: slicing, 75; sponge process, 76
    Angelic Buttermilk Batter Biscuits, 82
    Basic White Bread, 74
    Bread Machine White Bread, 77
    Cheddar Cornbread, 78
    Cinnamon Raisin Bread, 75
    Cottage Cheese Bread, 79
    Hawaiian-Style Bread, 80
    Honey Oat Bran Bread, 77
    Milk Biscuits, 81
    Orange Date Bread, 84
    7-Grain Bread, 78
    Whole-Wheat Bread, 76
    Zucchini Bread, 83
Breakfast
    about: importance of, 6
    Berry Puff Pancakes, 67
    Buckwheat Pancakes, 66
    Buttermilk Pancakes, 68
    Egg Clouds on Toast, 71
    Egg White Pancakes, 66
    Eggs Benedict Redux, 69
    Fruit Smoothie, 69
    Overnight Oatmeal, 70
    Sweet Potato Flour Crêpes, 68
    Tofu Smoothie, 70

Broccoli
    Broccoli-Cauliflower Slaw, 204
    Chicken and Broccoli Casserole, 111
    Chicken and Mushroom Rice
        Casserole, 95
    Fusion Lo Mein, 173
    Orange-Avocado Slaw, 207
    Single-Serving Salmon Scramble, 100
    Stir-Fried Ginger Scallops with
        Vegetables, 136
Broth
    about: freezing, 185
    Perpetual Vegetable Broth, 214
    Pork Broth, 161
    Vegetable Broth, 214
    *see also* Soups and stews
Brunch. *See* Breakfast
Bubbly Berry Blast, 237
Buckwheat Pancakes, 66
Butter
    as *monter*, 20
    substitutes for, 81
Buttermilk
    Angelic Buttermilk Batter Biscuits, 82
    Buttermilk Blush, 267
    Buttermilk Dressing, 196
    Buttermilk Pancakes, 68
    Buttermilk Ranch Chicken Salad, 107
    Fluffy Buttermilk Mashed Potatoes, 220
    Roasted Garlic Mashed Potatoes, 221
Butternut squash
    Roasted Butternut Squash Pasta, 174

**C**

Cabbage
    Italian Ground Turkey Casserole,
        96–97
    Piccalilli, 32
    Single-Serving Beef (Almost)
        Stroganoff, 99
    Single-Serving Unstuffed Cabbage and
        Green Peppers, 101
    Tomato-Vegetable Soup, 185
Cajun Spice Blend, 48
Cakes. *See* Desserts
Canola oil, 22
Cantaloupe
    Creamy Fruit Cup, 260
    Fruit Salsa, 34

Carbohydrates
  fiber and, 11
  function of, 11, 18
Caribbean Spice Blend, 48
Carrots
  Baked Beef Stew, 186
  Basic Tomato Sauce, 171
  Carrot-Fruit Cup, 235
  Chicken à la King, 111
  Fusion Lo Mein, 173
  Glazed Carrot Cake, 227
  Layered Salad, 211
  Lentil-Vegetable Soup, 184
  Salmon Chowder, 193
  Smoked Mussel Chowder, 192
  Tomato-Vegetable Soup, 185
  Vegetable Broth, 214
Cashews
  about: storing, 198
  Cashew-Garlic Ranch Dressing, 198
Casseroles
  Aloha Ham Microwave Casserole, 97
  Chicken and Broccoli Casserole, 111
  Chicken and Green Bean Stovetop
    Casserole, 112
  Chicken and Mushroom Rice
    Casserole, 95
  Corn Casserole, 222
  Easy Venison Stovetop Casserole, 166
  Fruited Pork Loin Roast Casserole, 158
  Ham and Artichoke Hearts Scalloped
    Potatoes, 162
  Italian Ground Turkey Casserole, 96–97
  Layered Veggie Casserole, 215
  Macaroni Casserole, 179
  Shrimp Microwave Casserole, 98
  Single-Serving Beef (Almost)
    Stroganoff, 99
  Single-Serving Salmon Scramble, 100
  Single-Serving Smoked Turkey
    Casserole, 100
  Single-Serving Unstuffed Cabbage and
    Green Peppers, 101
  Thanksgiving Feast: Turkey Casserole
    in a Pumpkin, 115
  Traditional Stovetop Tuna-Noodle
    Casserole, 94
Catfish
  Asian-Style Fish Cakes, 125

  Crunchy "Fried" Catfish Fillets, 133
  Mock Sour Cream Baked Catfish, 129
Cauliflower
  Broccoli-Cauliflower Slaw, 204
  Golden Raisin Smoked Turkey Salad,
    212
  Mock Cauliflower Sauce, 47
  Piccalilli, 32
  Roasted Garlic Mashed Potatoes, 221
Caviar (mock)
  Black Olive Mock Caviar, 254
  Mushroom Caviar, 62
Celery
  about: as roasting rack, 20, 160
  Baked Beef Stew, 186
  Condensed Cream of Celery Soup, 89
  Lentil-Vegetable Soup, 184
  Salmon Chowder, 193
  Smoked Mussel Chowder, 192
  Tomato-Vegetable Soup, 185
  Vegetable Broth, 214
Celiac disease(CD), 25–26
Chai. See Beverages
Cheese
  Bleu Cheese Dressing, 196
  Bleu Cheese Pasta, 180
  Bleu Cheese Pasta Salad, 210
  Cheddar Cornbread, 78
  Chicken Corn Chowder, 191
  Condensed Cheese Soup, 91
  Italian Ground Turkey Casserole, 96–97
  Layered Salad, 211
  Macaroni Casserole, 179
  Taco Salad, 210
  Ultimate Grilled Cheeseburger
    Sandwich, 148
Chicken
  about: fat in skin, 106
  Another Healthy "Fried" Chicken, 106
  Bleu Cheese Pasta Salad, 210
  Buttermilk Ranch Chicken Salad, 107
  Chicken à la King, 111
  Chicken and Broccoli Casserole, 111
  Chicken and Green Bean Stovetop
    Casserole, 112
  Chicken and Mushroom Rice
    Casserole, 95
  Chicken Broth: Easy Slow-Cooker
    Method, 104

  Chicken Corn Chowder, 191
  Chicken Pasta with Herb Sauce, 113
  Chicken Thighs Cacciatore, 114
  Condensed Cream of Chicken Soup,
    Minor's Base Method, 88
  Easy Chicken Paprikash, 110
  Herbed Chicken and Brown Rice
    Dinner, 109
  Molded Chicken Salad, 108
  Oven-Fried Chicken Thighs, 105
  Walnut Chicken with Plum Sauce, 109
Chocolate
  Chocolate Candy Substitute, 250
  Chocolate Cheesecake Mousse, 230
  Chocolate Cheesecake Mousse II, 231
  Faux Chocolate Bavarian Cream, 236
  Whipped Mocha Mousse, 234
Cholesterol, 13–15
Chorizo
  Mock Chorizo 1, 152
  Mock Chorizo 2, 153
  Mock Chorizo Moussaka, 154
Chowders. See Soups and stews
Christmas Colors with Yogurt Sauce, 120
Chutney
  Cranberry-Raisin Chutney, 33
Cinnamon
  Cinnamon Grilled Pork Tenderloin, 157
  Cinnamon Nut Butter, 55
  Cinnamon Raisin Bread, 75
Clams
  Pasta with Creamed Clam Sauce, 176
Coconut oil, 13, 14
Cod
  Fish Pie, 144
  A Taste of Italy Baked Fish, 131
Coffee liqueur, substitute for, 9
Coffee-Spice Snack Cake, 259
Cold Roasted Red Pepper Soup, 187
Condensed soups. See Soups and stews
Cooking equipment
  baking pans, 80
  slow cookers, 163
  sources of, 273–274
Cooking techniques
  baking, 228
  condensed soup preparation, 92–93
  frying, 21–22
  gluten-free, 25–27

grilling, 116
meat handling, 119
microwaving, 25
microwaving popcorn from scratch, 255
mixing oil and vinegar, 31
recipe modification, 19–22
reducing acidity, 171
reducing broth, 104
roasting bones, 146
roasting garlic, 54
roasting meat, 157
roasting peppers, 39
roasting vegetables, 128
sautéing, 62
steaming, 24
stir-frying, 24
thickening dips, 56
toasting nuts and seeds, 30
whipping, 232
Corn
    Avocado-Corn Salsa, 36
    Chicken Corn Chowder, 191
    Corn Casserole, 222
    Pepper and Corn Relish, 33
    Tomato-Vegetable Soup, 185
Cornbread
    Cheddar Cornbread, 78
Cottage Cheese Bread, 79
Country Spice Blend, 48
Crab Cakes with Sesame Crust, 127
Cranberries
    Cranberry-Raisin Chutney, 33
    Cranberry-Turkey Sausage, 118
    Venison with Dried Cranberry
       Vinegar Sauce, 165
Cream, mock, 42
Creamy Fruit Cup, 260
Creamy Polenta, 216
Creamy Shrimp Pie with Rice Crust, 128
Crunchy "Fried" Catfish Fillets, 133
Cucumber
    Cucumber Slices with Smoke Salmon
       Cream, 52
    Greek Pasta Salad, 209
    Nutty Greek Snapper Soup, 188
    Piccalilli, 32

**D**

Dairy, servings per day, 3

Dates
    Date-Nut Roll, 230
    Orange Date Bread, 84
Desserts
    Almond Biscotti, 242
    Apple Cookies with a Kick, 243
    Baked Pear Crisp, 238
    Bananas Foster, 241
    Beanberry Blast, 242
    Bubbly Berry Blast, 237
    Carrot-Fruit Cup, 235
    Chocolate Cheesecake Mousse, 230
    Chocolate Cheesecake Mousse II, 231
    Date-Nut Roll, 230
    Faux Chocolate Bavarian Cream, 236
    Glazed Carrot Cake, 227
    Individual Apple-Blackberry
       Charlottes, 247
    Individual Sponge Cakes, 226
    Lemon Curd, 244
    Linzertorte Muffins, 228
    Lucky Lemonade Gelatin, 235
    Mock Pumpkin Custard, 239
    Mock Whipped Cream, 229
    Nonfat Ice Cream or Smoothie Base,
       239
    Nonfat Whipped Milk Base, 232
    Orange Marmalade Cheesecake
       Mousse, 233
    Peanut Butter Pleaser, 233
    Pineapple Upside-Down Cake, 245
    Strawberry-Banana Sherbet, 240
    Whipped Lemon Cheesecake Mousse,
       234
    Whipped Mocha Mousse, 234
    Whole-Grain Maple-Walnut Bread
       Pudding, 246
    *see also* Snacks
Diabetes management, 1–27
    alcohol consumption, 8–9
    creative cooking, 23–25
    food labels, 16–18
    gluten-free foods, 25–27
    as lifestyle, not diet, 2–5
    nutrition basics, 3, 10–16
    recipe modifications, 19–13
    in restaurants, 5–7
    sugars, 18
Dijon Vinaigrette, 197

Dilled-Ranch Popcorn, 257
Dips. *See* Appetizers
Dressings. *See* Salad dressings

**E**

Easy Chicken Paprikash, 110
Easy Graham Cracker Goodies, 253
Easy Olive Spread, 61
Easy Venison Stovetop Casserole, 166
Eggplant
    Eggplant and Tomato Stew, 182
    Mock Chorizo Moussaka, 154
Eggs
    about: cholesterol in, 14
    Egg Clouds on Toast, 71
    Egg White Pancakes, 66
    Eggs Benedict Redux, 69
Equipment. *See* Cooking equipment
Exercise, 5

**F**

"Fat-free," used on labels, 17
Fat-Free Roux, 44
Fats
    good fats, 30
    health issues, 208
    need for, 11, 13
    recipe modification, 19–22
    removing from drippings, 20
    removing from soups, 190
    in salad dressings, 12–13
    servings per day, 3
    types of, 13–15
Faux Chocolate Bavarian Cream, 236
Fennel
    Smoked Mussel Chowder, 192
Feta cheese
    Garlic and Feta Cheese Dip, 54
    Greek Pasta Salad, 209
    Zesty Feta and Olive Salad, 205
Fiber
    blood glucose and, 11
    recipe modification, 22–23
    water and, 4, 11
Fish. *See* Seafood and fish
Flaxseed
    about: health benefits, 53, 198
    Flaxseed Oil-Fortified Salsa Dip, 53
    Honey-Mustard Dressing, 197

Lemon Tahini Vegetable Dip, 53
Salsa with a Kick, 36
Tangy Lemon-Garlic Tomato Dressing, 198
Flours
    gluten-free, 27
    potato flour, 56
Fluffy Buttermilk Mashed Potatoes, 221
"Free," used on labels, 17
French Fries, baked, 218
French Onion Soup Dip, 56
French Spice Blend, 49
Frothy Orange Jewel, 265
Fruits
    about: glucose, 260; infusion of, 130; in salads, 200; servings per day, 3
    Avocado and Peach Salad, 206
    Cranberry-Raisin Chutney, 33
    Creamy Fruit Cup, 260
    Fruited Pork Loin Roast Casserole, 158
    Fruit Frenzy Sparkler Concentrate, 269
    Fruit Salsa, 34
    Fruit Smoothie, 69
    Gingered Peach Sauce, 42
    Lemon-Almond Dressing, 199
    Lemon Curd, 244
    Lemon Tahini Vegetable Dip, 53
    Lentil Soup with Herbs and Lemon, 183
    Minted Lemon Tea, 261
    Party Time Minted Raspberry Lemonade, 266
    Peachy Ginger Ale, 268
    White Wine and Lemon Pork Roast, 159
    see also Berries
Fusion Lo Mein, 173

G
Garbanzo Dip, 58
Garlic
    about: dry roasting, 54; on breads, 175
    Cashew-Garlic Ranch Dressing, 198
    Garlic and Feta Cheese Dip, 54
    Greens in Garlic with Pasta, 201
    Roasted Garlic Mashed Potatoes, 221
Gelatin
    about: commercial brands, 229; with fruit juice, 244
    Lucky Lemonade Gelatin, 235

Gingered Peach Sauce, 42
Glazed Carrot Cake, 227
Gluten-free foods
    about: 25–27
    Gluten-Free Sesame Seed Crackers, 63
Gnocchi, 223
Golden Raisin Smoked Turkey Salad, 212
Graham crackers
    Easy Graham Cracker Goodies, 253
Grains, servings per day, 3
Grapes
    Creamy Fruit Cup, 260
Gravies
    about: substitutes for, 221
    Rich Sausage Gravy, 155
Greek Pasta Salad, 209
Green beans. See Beans
Greens. See Salads

H
Halibut
    Baked Bread Crumb–Crusted Fish with Lemon, 130
Ham
    Aloha Ham Microwave Casserole, 97
    Ham and Artichoke Hearts Scalloped Potatoes, 162
    Pasta Fagioli, 178
Hawaiian-Style Bread, 80
Hazelnuts
    Linzertorte Muffins, 228
Healthy Onion Rings, 216
Herbs
    about: drying, 48; in rice dishes, 224; using dried for fresh, 204
    Basic Tomato Sauce, 171
    Herbed Cheese Spread, 58
    Herbed Chicken and Brown Rice Dinner, 109
    Herbs de Provence, 49
    Lentil Soup with Herbs and Lemon, 183
    Nutty Greek Snapper Soup, 188
    Quick Tomato Sauce, 170
    see also Spice blends
Hollandaise Sauce, mock, 40
Homemade Worcestershire Sauce, 40
Honey
    Honey and Cider Glaze for Baked Chicken, 121

Honey Dijon Tuna Salad, 207
Honey-Mustard Dressing, 197
Honey Oat Bran Bread, 77
Honey Raisin Bars, 251
Horseradish
    Horseradish Dip, 57
    Horseradish Mustard, 31
Hot Spiced Tea, 262

I
Iced tea. See Beverages
Individual Apple-Blackberry Charlottes, 247
Individual Sponge Cakes, 226
Italian-style dishes
    Italian Ground Turkey Casserole, 96–97
    Italian Sausage, 150
    Italian Spice Blend, 49
    Italian Spiced Popcorn, 257
    Italian Sweet Fennel Sausage, 151

J
Jam and Jelly Soft Drink Syrup, 270
Jones, Michelle, 7
Journal, importance of keeping, 4

K
Kattau, Sally, 2
Kielbasa, 149
    Kovbasa (Ukrainian Kielbasa), 149

L
Labels, 16–18
Lactose-free bread, 78
Layered Salad, 211
Layered Veggie Casserole, 215
Leeks
    Vegetable Broth, 214
Lemons/lemon juice
    about: infusion of, 130
    Lemon-Almond Dressing, 199
    Lemon Curd, 244
    Lemon Tahini Vegetable Dip, 53
    Lentil Soup with Herbs and Lemon, 183
    Minted Lemon Tea, 261
    Party Time Minted Raspberry Lemonade, 266
    White Wine and Lemon Pork Roast, 159

Lentils
    Lentil Soup with Herbs and Lemon, 183
    Lentil-Vegetable Soup, 184
Limes
    Tangy Limeade, 264
Linzertorte Muffins, 228
Liverwurst, venison, 167
Lobster Bisque, 184
Lo mein, fusion, 173
Low-fat food, defined, 13
Lucky Lemonade Gelatin, 235

**M**

Macaroni Casserole, 179
Mace, about: 222
Madeira Sauce, 45
Main dishes. *See* Casseroles; Chicken;
    Meats; Turkey
Marmalade
    Marmalade–Black Bean Salsa, 34
    Marmalade Marinade, 159
Meats
    about: removing gamy flavor, 164;
        servings per day, 3
    Aloha Ham Microwave Casserole, 97
    Beef Broth: Easy Slow-Cooker
        Method, 146
    Cinnamon Grilled Pork Tenderloin, 157
    Easy Venison Stovetop Casserole, 166
    Fruited Pork Loin Roast Casserole, 158
    Ham and Artichoke Hearts Scalloped
        Potatoes, 162
    Italian Sausage, 150
    Italian Sweet Fennel Sausage, 151
    Kielbasa, 149
    Kovbasa (Ukrainian Kielbasa), 149
    Main Dish Pork and Beans, 161
    Mock Chorizo 1, 152
    Mock Chorizo 2, 153
    Mock Chorizo Moussaka, 154
    Pecan-Crusted Roast Pork Loin, 160
    Rich Sausage Gravy, 155
    Single-Serving Beef (Almost)
        Stroganoff, 99
    Single-Serving Unstuffed Cabbage and
        Green Peppers, 101
    Slow-Cooked Venison, 163
    Slow-Cooker Pork with Plum Sauce, 156
    Slow-Cooker Venison BBQ, 164

Stovetop Grilled Beef Loin, 147
Ultimate Grilled Cheeseburger
    Sandwich, 148
Venison Liverwurst, 167
Venison with Dried Cranberry
    Vinegar Sauce, 165
Warm Pork Salad, 156
White Wine and Lemon Pork Roast, 159
Medication, for diabetes, 5
Mediterranean Spice Blend, 49
Mexican Popcorn, 257
Middle Eastern Spice Blend, 49
Milk Biscuits, 81
Minted Lemon Tea, 261
Mock dishes
    Black Olive Mock Caviar, 254
    Faux Chocolate Bavarian Cream, 236
    Mock Béchamel Sauce, 46
    Mock Cauliflower Sauce, 47
    Mock Chorizo 1, 152
    Mock Chorizo 2, 153
    Mock Chorizo Moussaka, 154
    Mock Cream, 42
    Mock Hollandaise Sauce, 40
    Mock Pumpkin Custard, 239
    Mock Sour Cream, 43
    Mock Sour Cream Baked Catfish, 129
    Mock Whipped Cream, 229
    Mock White Sauce, 43
    Mushroom Caviar, 62
Molded Chicken Salad, 108
Monounsaturated fats, 14
Mousse
    Chocolate Cheesecake Mousse, 230
    Chocolate Cheesecake Mousse II, 231
    Orange Marmalade Cheesecake
        Mousse, 233
    Whipped Lemon Cheesecake Mousse,
        234
Muffins, linzertorte, 228
Mushrooms
    Chicken à la King, 111
    Chicken and Green Bean Stovetop
        Casserole, 112
    Chicken and Mushroom Rice
        Casserole, 95
    Chicken Pasta with Herb Sauce, 113
    Condensed Cream of Mushroom
        Soup, 87

Easy Chicken Paprikash, 110
Green Bean and Mushroom Salad, 202
Italian Ground Turkey Casserole, 96–97
Mushroom Caviar, 62
Shrimp Microwave Casserole, 98
Smoked Mussels Cream Sauce with
    Pasta, 140
Turkey Mushroom Burgers, 117
Mussels
    Smoked Mussels and Pasta, 138
    Smoked Mussels Cream Sauce with
        Pasta, 140
    Smoked Mussel Spread, 60
    Smoked Mussels Scramble, 141

**N**

Nectarine Cocktail, 270
No-Bake Chocolate–Peanut Butter
    Oatmeal Cookies, 253
Nonfat foods
    about: 13
    Nonfat Ice Cream or Smoothie Base,
        239
    Nonfat Whipped Milk Base, 232
"No sugar added," used on labels, 17
Nutmeg, about: 222
Nuts
    about: storing, 198; toasting, 58
    Cashew-Garlic Ranch Dressing, 198
    Date-Nut Roll, 230
    Linzertorte Muffins, 228
    Nut butter, 68
    Nutty Greek Snapper Soup, 188
    Pasta and Smoked Trout with Lemon
        Pesto, 139
    Pesto Sauce, 41
    Walnut Chicken with Plum Sauce, 109
    Whole-Grain Maple-Walnut Bread
        Pudding, 246
    Zucchini Bread, 83

**O**

Oats
    Honey Oat Bran Bread, 77
    Overnight Oatmeal, 70
Oils
    adding to vinegar, 31
    as fat, 13
    types of, 22

*see also* Fats
Old Bay Seasoning Blend, 50
Olive oil
  about: 22
  on toasted bread, 148
Olives
  Black Olive Mock Caviar, 254
  Bleu Cheese Pasta Salad, 210
  Easy Olive Spread, 61
  Greek Pasta Salad, 209
  Shrimp Microwave Casserole, 98
  Zesty Feta and Olive Salad, 205
Onions
  about: sautéing, 62
  French Onion Soup Dip, 56
  Healthy Onion Rings, 216
  Onion Dip, 56
  Sweet Onion–Baked Yellowtail
    Snapper, 135
Orange liqueur, substitute for, 9
Orange Marmalade Cheesecake Mousse,
  233
Orange roughy
  Baked Orange Roughy with Spicy
    Plum Sauce, 134
Oranges/orange juice
  Frothy Orange Jewel, 265
  Fruit Frenzy Sparkler Concentrate, 269
  Iced Ginger-Orange Green Tea, 262
  Orange-Avocado Slaw, 207
  Orange Date Bread, 84
  Orange-Pineapple Froth, 265
  Sparkling Fruited Iced Tea, 261
Oven-Baked Potatoes, 217
Oven-Fried Chicken Thighs, 105
Overnight Oatmeal, 70

**P**
Pacific Rim Spice Blend, 50
Palm oil, 13, 14
Pancakes
  about: alternate toppings, 66
  Berry Puff Pancakes, 67
  Buckwheat Pancakes, 66
  Buttermilk Pancakes, 68
  Egg White Pancakes, 66
Parsnips
  Vegetable Broth, 214
Partially hydrogenated vegetable oil, 15

Party Time Minted Raspberry
    Lemonade, 266
Pasta
  Basic Tomato Sauce, 171
  Bleu Cheese Pasta, 180
  Chicken Pasta with Herb Sauce, 113
  Chicken Thighs Cacciatore, 114
  Fusion Lo Mein, 173
  Greek Pasta Salad, 209
  Greens in Garlic with Pasta, 201
  Macaroni Casserole, 179
  Pasta and Smoked Trout with Lemon
    Pesto, 139
  Pasta Fagioli, 178
  Pasta with Artichokes, 175
  Pasta with Creamed Clam Sauce, 176
  Pasta with Tuna Alfredo Sauce, 177
  Quick Tomato Sauce, 170
  Roasted Butternut Squash Pasta, 174
  Smoked Mussels Cream Sauce with
    Pasta, 140
  Uncooked Tomato Sauce, 172
PCF Ratio, defined, 13
Peaches
  Avocado and Peach Salad, 206
  Cranberry-Raisin Chutney, 33
  Fruit Frenzy Sparkler Concentrate, 269
  Gingered Peach Sauce, 42
  Peachy Ginger Ale, 268
Peanut butter
  Easy Graham Cracker Goodies, 253
  No-Bake Chocolate–Peanut Butter
    Oatmeal Cookies, 253
  Peanut Butter Pleaser, 233
Pears
  Baked Pear Crisp, 238
Peas
  Layered Salad, 211
Pecan-Crusted Roast Pork Loin, 160
Peppers, banana or jalapeño
  Asian-Style Fish Cakes, 125
  Avocado-Corn Salsa, 36
  Black Olive Mock Caviar, 254
  Fruit Salsa, 34
  Pepper and Corn Relish, 33
  Pineapple–Black Bean Sauce, 119
  Vegetable and Bean Chili, 188
Peppers, bell
  about: roasting, 39

Chicken Corn Chowder, 191
Christmas Colors with Yogurt Sauce,
  120
Cold Roasted Red Pepper Soup, 187
Corn Casserole, 222
Fruit Salsa, 34
Fusion Lo Mein, 173
Marmalade–Black Bean Salsa, 34
Piccalilli, 32
Pineapple–Black Bean Sauce, 119
Pineapple-Chili Salsa, 35
Roasted Red Pepper and Plum
  Sauce, 38
Shrimp Microwave Casserole, 98
Smoked Shrimp Sandwich Filling, 142
Vegetable and Bean Chili, 189
Vegetable Broth, 214
"Percentage daily allowance," used on
  labels, 16
Pesto Sauce, 41
Piccalilli, 32
Pineapples/pineapple juice
  Aloha Ham Microwave Casserole, 97
  Chocolate Candy Substitute, 250
  Fruit Frenzy Sparkler Concentrate, 269
  Fusion Lo Mein, 173
  Glazed Carrot Cake, 227
  Hawaiian-Style Bread, 80
  Orange-Pineapple Froth, 265
  Pineapple–Black Bean Sauce, 119
  Pineapple-Banana Blast, 267
  Pineapple-Chili Salsa, 35
  Pineapple Upside-Down Cake, 245
Pine nuts
  Pasta and Smoked Trout with Lemon
    Pesto, 139
  Pesto Sauce, 41
Pizza
  English Muffin Pizza, 172
  Pizza Popcorn, 257
  *see also* Pasta
Plums
  Baked Orange Roughy with Spicy
    Plum Sauce, 134
  Plum Sauce, 37
  Powdered Sugar–Coated Cocoa
    Cookies, 252
  Roasted Red Pepper and Plum
    Sauce, 38

Slow-Cooker Pork with Plum Sauce, 156
Polenta, creamy, 216
Polyunsaturated fats, 15
Popcorn
    about: microwaving from scratch, 255;
        storing, 256
    Asian Popcorn, 256
    Dilled-Ranch Popcorn, 257
    Italian Spiced Popcorn, 257
    Mexican Popcorn, 257
    Pizza Popcorn, 257
Pork
    Cinnamon Grilled Pork Tenderloin, 157
    Fruited Pork Loin Roast Casserole, 158
    Italian Sausage, 150
    Italian Sweet Fennel Sausage, 151
    Kielbasa, 149
    Kovbasa (Ukrainian Kielbasa), 149
    Main Dish Pork and Beans, 161
    Mock Chorizo 1, 152
    Mock Chorizo 2, 153
    Pecan-Crusted Roast Pork Loin, 160
    Pork Broth, 161
    Slow-Cooker Pork with Plum Sauce, 156
    Venison Liverwurst, 167
    Warm Pork Salad, 156
    White Wine and Lemon Pork Roast, 159
Potatoes
    about: absorbing salt with, 182;
        roasting, 217
    Baked Beef Stew, 186
    Baked French Fries, 218
    Baked Potato Chips, 219
    Chicken Corn Chowder, 191
    Condensed Cream of Potato Soup, 89
    Fruited Pork Loin Roast Casserole, 158
    Ham and Artichoke Hearts Scalloped
        Potatoes, 162
    Mock Chorizo Moussaka, 154
    Oven-Baked Potatoes, 217
    Rich and Creamy Sausage-Potato
        Soup, 190
    Roasted Garlic Mashed Potatoes, 221
    Salmon Chowder, 193
    Smoked Mussel Chowder, 192
    Sweet Potato Crisps, 220
    Tomato-Vegetable Soup, 185
    see also Sweet potatoes
Potato flour, substitutes for, 87

Poultry. See Chicken; Turkey
Powdered Sugar–Coated Cocoa Cookies,
    252
Proteins, about: 10
Pumpkin
    Mock Pumpkin Custard, 239
    Thanksgiving Feast: Turkey Casserole
        in a Pumpkin, 115
    Toasted Pumpkin Seeds, 258

Q
Quesadillas
    Smoked Shrimp and Cheese
        Quesadillas, 143
Quick Tomato Sauce, 170

R
Raisins
    Cinnamon Raisin Bread, 75
    Cranberry-Raisin Chutney, 33
    Golden Raisin Smoked Turkey Salad,
        212
    Honey Raisin Bars, 251
Raspberries
    Linzertorte Muffins, 228
    Party Time Minted Raspberry
        Lemonade, 266
"Reduced," used on labels, 17
Rice
    about: herbs in, 224
    Aloha Ham Microwave Casserole, 97
    Baked Snapper with Orange-Rice
        Dressing, 132
    Chicken and Green Bean Stovetop
        Casserole, 112
    Chicken and Mushroom Rice
        Casserole, 95
    Creamy Shrimp Pie with Rice Crust,
        128
    Herbed Chicken and Brown Rice
        Dinner, 109
Rich and Creamy Sausage-Potato Soup, 190
Rich Sausage Gravy, 155
Roasted Butternut Squash Pasta, 174
Roasted Garlic Mashed Potatoes, 221
Roasted Red Pepper and Plum Sauce, 38
Roux, fat-free, 44
Rum, substitute for, 9

S
Salad dressings
    about: fat content, 12–13
    Bleu Cheese Dressing, 196
    Buttermilk Dressing, 196
    Cashew-Garlic Ranch Dressing, 198
    Dijon Vinaigrette, 197
    Honey-Mustard Dressing, 197
    Lemon-Almond Dressing, 199
    Tangy Lemon-Garlic Tomato Dressing,
        198
Salads
    about: undressed, 199
    Avocado and Peach Salad, 206
    Bleu Cheese Pasta Salad, 210
    Broccoli-Cauliflower Slaw, 204
    Golden Raisin Smoked Turkey Salad,
        212
    Greek Pasta Salad, 209
    Green Bean and Mushroom Salad, 202
    Greens in Garlic with Pasta, 201
    Honey Dijon Tuna Salad, 207
    Layered Salad, 211
    Orange-Avocado Slaw, 207
    Spinach Salad with Apple-Avocado
        Dressing, 208
    Sweet and Savory Side Salad, 209
    Taco Salad, 210
    White and Black Bean Salad, 203
    Wilted Lettuce with a Healthier
        Difference, 200
    Zesty Feta and Olive Salad, 205
    see also Salad dressings
Salmon
    Cucumber Slices with Smoke Salmon
        Cream, 52
    Eggs Benedict Redux, 69
    Salmon Chowder, 193
    Salmon Patties, 126
    Single-Serving Salmon Scramble, 100
    Slow-Roasted Salmon, 126
    Smoked Salmon Cream Sauce, 142
Salsa. See Appetizers; Sauces
Salt. See Sodium
Saturated fats, 14
Sauces
    Almond Spread, 31
    Asian Gingered Almonds, 30
    Avocado-Corn Salsa, 36

Cranberry-Raisin Chutney, 33
Dipping Sauce, 37
Fat-Free Roux, 44
Fruit Salsa, 34
Gingered Peach Sauce, 42
Homemade Worcestershire Sauce, 40
Horseradish Mustard, 31
Madeira Sauce, 45
Marmalade–Black Bean Salsa, 34
Mock Béchamel Sauce, 46
Mock Cauliflower Sauce, 47
Mock Cream, 42
Mock White Sauce, 43
Pepper and Corn Relish, 33
Pesto Sauce, 41
Piccalilli, 32
Pineapple-Chili Salsa, 35
Plum Sauce, 37
Roasted Red Pepper and Plum
    Sauce, 38
Salsa with a Kick, 36
Smoked Salmon Cream Sauce, 142
Speedy Sauce, 38
Strawberry Spoon Sweet, 35
Toasted Sesame Seeds, 30
Sausage
    Italian Sausage, 150
    Italian Sweet Fennel Sausage, 151
    Rich and Creamy Sausage-Potato
        Soup, 190
    Rich Sausage Gravy, 155
Scallops
    Scallops and Shrimp with White
        Bean Sauce, 137
    Stir-Fried Ginger Scallops with
        Vegetables, 136
Seafood and fish
    about: handling fish, 124; herb blend
        for, 49
    Asian-Style Fish Cakes, 125
    Baked Bread Crumb–Crusted Fish
        with Lemon, 130
    Baked Orange Roughy with Spicy
        Plum Sauce, 134
    Baked Red Snapper Almandine, 131
    Baked Snapper with Orange-Rice
        Dressing, 132
    Crab Cakes with Sesame Crust, 127
    Creamy Shrimp Pie with Rice Crust, 128

Crunchy "Fried" Catfish Fillets, 133
Cucumber Slices with Smoke Salmon
    Cream, 52
Eggs Benedict Redux, 69
Fish Pie, 144
Fish Stock, 124
Honey Dijon Tuna Salad, 207
Lobster Bisque, 184
Mock Sour Cream Baked Catfish, 129
Nutty Greek Snapper Soup, 188
Pasta and Smoked Trout with Lemon
    Pesto, 139
Pasta with Creamed Clam Sauce, 176
Pasta with Tuna Alfredo Sauce, 177
Salmon Chowder, 193
Salmon Patties, 126
Scallops and Shrimp with White
    Bean Sauce, 137
Shrimp Microwave Casserole, 98
Single-Serving Salmon Scramble, 100
Slow-Roasted Salmon, 126
Smoked Mussels and Pasta, 138
Smoked Mussels Cream Sauce with
    Pasta, 140
Smoked Mussels Scramble, 141
Smoked Salmon Cream Sauce, 142
Smoked Shrimp in Cheese
    Quesadillas, 143
Smoked Shrimp Sandwich Filling, 142
Stir-Fried Ginger Scallops with
    Vegetables, 136
Sweet Onion–Baked Yellowtail
    Snapper, 135
Taste of Italy Baked Fish, 131
Traditional Stovetop Tuna-Noodle
    Casserole, 94
Seasonings
    Horseradish Mustard, 31
    Old Bay Seasoning, 50
    Texas Seasoning, 50
    Toasted Almond Seasonings, 31
    see also Spice blends
Seaweed, 125
Seeds
    about: health benefits, 53, 198;
        toasting, 30
    Apple Cookies with a Kick, 243
    Cinnamon Nut Butter, 55
    Crab Cakes with Sesame Crust, 127

Flaxseed Oil-Fortified Salsa Dip, 53
Gluten-Free Sesame Seed Crackers, 63
Honey-Mustard Dressing, 197
Lemon Tahini Vegetable Dip, 53
Salsa with a Kick, 36
Tangy Lemon-Garlic Tomato Dressing,
    198
Toasted Pumpkin Seeds, 258
Toasted Sesame Seeds, 30
Sesame seeds
    Cinnamon Nut Butter, 55
    Crab Cakes with Sesame Crust, 127
    Gluten-Free Sesame Seed Crackers, 63
    Honey-Mustard Dressing, 197
    Lemon Tahini Vegetable Dip, 53
    Toasted Sesame Seeds, 30
7-Grain Bread, 78
Shrimp
    Creamy Shrimp Pie with Rice Crust,
        128
    Scallops and Shrimp with White
        Bean Sauce, 137
    Shrimp Microwave Casserole, 98
    Smoked Shrimp and Cheese
        Quesadillas, 143
    Smoked Shrimp Sandwich Filling, 142
Side dishes. See Potatoes; Vegetables
Single-serving dishes
    Beef (Almost) Stroganoff, 99
    Salmon Scramble, 100
    Smoked Turkey, 100
    Unstuffed Cabbage and Green
        Peppers, 101
Slow-cooked dishes
    Chicken Broth: Easy Slow-Cooker
        Method, 104
    Slow-Cooked Venison, 163
    Slow-Cooker Pork with Plum Sauce,
        156
    Slow-Cooker Venison BBQ, 164
    Slow-Roasted Salmon, 126
Smoked-style dishes
    Smoked Mussel Chowder, 192
    Smoked Mussels and Pasta, 138
    Smoked Mussel Spread, 60
    Smoked Mussels Scramble, 141
    Smoked Salmon Cream Sauce, 142
    Smoked Shrimp in Cheese
        Quesadillas, 143

Smoked Shrimp Sandwich Filling, 142
Snacks
  about: as part of diet, 4; having
    handy, 6
  Asian Popcorn, 256
  Black Olive Mock Caviar, 254
  Chocolate Candy Substitute, 250
  Coffee-Spice Snack Cake, 259
  Creamy Fruit Cup, 260
  Honey Raisin Bars, 251
  No-Bake Chocolate–Peanut Butter
    Oatmeal Cookies, 253
  Powdered Sugar–Coated Cocoa
    Cookies, 252
  Snack Mix, 255
  Toasted Pumpkin Seeds, 258
  Tortilla Chips, 254
  Zucchini with Cheese Spread, 258
  see also Desserts
Snapper
  Baked Red Snapper Almandine, 131
  Baked Snapper with Orange-Rice
    Dressing, 132
  Nutty Greek Snapper Soup, 188
  Sweet Onion–Baked Yellowtail
    Snapper, 135
Sodium, 15–16
  in bread, 79
  recipe modification, 23
  reducing in seafood, 143
  in soup, 86
  soy sauce and, 57
Sonoran Spice Blend, 50
Soups and stews
  about: condensed commercial, 86;
    handling of scorched, 186;
    preparation methods, 92–93
  Baked Beef Stew, 186
  Chicken Corn Chowder, 191
  Cold Roasted Red Pepper Soup, 187
  Condensed Cheese Soup, 91
  Condensed Cream of Celery Soup, 89
  Condensed Cream of Chicken Soup,
    Minor's Base Method, 88
  Condensed Cream of Mushroom
    Soup, 87
  Condensed Cream of Potato Soup, 89
  Condensed Tomato Soup, 90
  Eggplant and Tomato Stew, 182

Lentil Soup with Herbs and Lemon,
  183
Lentil-Vegetable Soup, 184
Lobster Bisque, 184
Nutty Greek Snapper Soup, 188
Rich and Creamy Sausage-Potato
  Soup, 190
Salmon Chowder, 193
Smoked Mussel Chowder, 192
Tomato-Vegetable Soup, 185
Vegetable and Bean Chili, 189
see also Broth
Sour cream, mock, 43
  Mock Sour Cream Baked Catfish, 129
Spaghetti. See Pasta
Sparkling Fruited Iced Tea, 261
Spice blends
  Barbecue Blend, 48
  Cajun Blend, 48
  Caribbean Blend, 48
  Country Blend, 48
  Fish and Seafood Herbs, 49
  French Blend, 49
  Herbs de Provence, 49
  Italian Blend, 49
  Mediterranean Blend, 49
  Middle Eastern Blend, 49
  Old Bay Seasoning, 50
  Pacific Rim Blend, 50
  Sonoran Blend, 50
  Stuffing Blend, 50
  Texas Seasoning, 50
  see also Seasonings
Spiced Chai-Style Creamer Mix, 263
Spice Tea Chicken Marinade, 121
Spicy Almond Dip, 55
Spinach
  Spinach Salad with Apple-Avocado
    Dressing, 208
  Vegetable Broth, 214
Sponge cakes, individual, 226
Spreads. See Appetizers
Stews. See Soups and stews
Stir-fried dishes
  Mock Chorizo 2, 153
  Stir-Fried Ginger Scallops with
    Vegetables, 136
Stovetop Grilled Beef Loin, 147
Stovetop Real Turkey Breast, 116

Strawberries
  Beanberry Blast, 242
  Bubbly Berry Blast, 237
  Strawberry-Banana Sherbet, 240
  Strawberry Cooler, 269
  Strawberry Spoon Sweet, 35
Stuffing Spice Blend, 50
Sugars
  in bread, 82
  on food labels, 18
  recipe modification, 19
  with salt, 201
  servings per day, 3
  in soft drinks, 268
  in tomato sauce, 170
Sunflower seeds
  Apple Cookies with a Kick, 243
  Cinnamon Nut Butter, 55
Sweet and Savory Side Salad, 209
Sweet Onion–Baked Yellowtail Snapper, 135
Sweet potatoes
  Lentil-Vegetable Soup, 184
  Sweet Potato Crisps, 220
  Sweet Potato Flour Crêpes, 68

**T**
Taco Salad, 210
Tahini. See Sesame seeds
Tangy Lemon-Garlic Tomato Dressing, 198
Tangy Limeade, 264
Taste of Italy Baked Fish, 131
Tea. See Beverages
Texas Seasoning Blend, 50
Thanksgiving Feast: Turkey Casserole in
  a Pumpkin, 115
Toasted Pumpkin Seeds, 258
Toasted Sesame Seeds, 30
Tofu
  about: in salad dressings, 12–13
  Golden Raisin Smoked Turkey Salad, 212
  Tofu Smoothie, 70
Tomatoes
  about: saving leftover paste, 178
  Baked Beef Stew, 186
  Basic Tomato Sauce, 171
  Black Olive Mock Caviar, 254
  Condensed Tomato Soup, 90
  Eggplant and Tomato Stew, 182
  Greek Pasta Salad, 209

Italian Ground Turkey Casserole, 96–97
Pasta Fagioli, 178
Pasta with Artichokes, 175
Piccalilli, 32
Quick Tomato Sauce, 170
Salsa with a Kick, 36
Tangy Lemon-Garlic Tomato Dressing, 198
Tomato-Vegetable Soup, 185
Uncooked Tomato Sauce, 172
Vegetable and Bean Chili, 188
Tortillas
    Smoked Shrimp and Cheese Quesadillas, 143
    Tortilla Chips, 254
Traditional Stovetop Tuna-Noodle Casserole, 94
Transfatty acids, 15
Trout
    Fish Pie, 144
    Pasta and Smoked Trout with Lemon Pesto, 139
Tuna
    Honey Dijon Tuna Salad, 207
    Pasta with Tuna Alfredo Sauce, 177
    Traditional Stovetop Tuna-Noodle Casserole, 94
Turkey
    Christmas Colors with Yogurt Sauce, 120
    Cranberry-Turkey Sausage, 118
    Golden Raisin Smoked Turkey Salad, 212
    Honey and Cider Glaze for Baked Chicken, 121
    Italian Ground Turkey Casserole, 96–97
    Layered Salad, 211
    Macaroni Casserole, 179
    Pineapple–Black Bean Sauce, 119
    Single-Serving Smoked Turkey Casserole, 100
    Stovetop Real Turkey Breast, 116
    Thanksgiving Feast: Turkey Casserole in a Pumpkin, 115
    Turkey Mushroom Burgers, 117

U

Ultimate Grilled Cheeseburger Sandwich, 148

Uncooked Tomato Sauce, 172
Unsaturated fats, 13, 14

V

Vegetables
    about: protein in, 10; seasoning of, 215; servings per day, 3
    Avocado-Corn Salsa, 36
    Broccoli-Cauliflower Slaw, 204
    Carrot-Fruit Cup, 235
    Chicken and Broccoli Casserole, 111
    Chicken Corn Chowder, 191
    Chicken and Mushroom Rice Casserole, 95
    Condensed Cream of Celery Soup, 89
    Corn Casserole, 222
    Creamy Polenta, 216
    Eggplant and Tomato Stew, 182
    Fusion Lo Mein, 173
    Gnocchi, 223
    Golden Raisin Smoked Turkey Salad, 212
    Healthy Onion Rings, 216
    Italian Ground Turkey Casserole, 96–97
    Layered Salad, 211
    Layered Veggie Casserole, 215
    Lentil-Vegetable Soup, 184
    Mock Cauliflower Sauce, 47
    Mock Chorizo Moussaka, 154
    Orange-Avocado Slaw, 207
    Piccalilli, 32
    Single-Serving Beef (Almost) Stroganoff, 99
    Single-Serving Salmon Scramble, 100
    Single-Serving Unstuffed Cabbage and Green Peppers, 101
    Spinach Salad with Apple-Avocado Dressing, 208
    Stir-Fried Ginger Scallops with Vegetables, 136
    Sweet Potato Crisps, 220
    Sweet Potato Flour Crêpes, 68
    Tomato-Vegetable Soup, 185
    Vegetable and Bean Chili, 189
    Vegetable Broth, 214
    see also Beans; Peppers; Potatoes; Tomatoes
Venison
    Easy Venison Stovetop Casserole, 166

Slow-Cooked Venison, 163
Slow-Cooker Venison BBQ, 164
Venison with Dried Cranberry Vinegar Sauce, 165
Vinaigrette, Dijon, 197

W

Walnuts
    Date-Nut Roll, 230
    Nutty Greek Snapper Soup, 188
    Walnut Chicken with Plum Sauce, 109
    Whole-Grain Maple-Walnut Bread Pudding, 246
    Zucchini Bread, 83
Warm Pork Salad, 156
Warshaw, Hope S., 7
Water, 4
Whipped cream, mock, 229
Whipped Lemon Cheesecake Mousse, 234
Whipped Mocha Mousse, 234
White and Black Bean Salad, 203
White sauce, mock, 43
White Wine and Lemon Pork Roast, 159
Whole-Grain Maple-Walnut Bread Pudding, 246
Whole-Wheat Bread, 76
Wilted Lettuce with a Healthier Difference, 200
Wine, substitute for, 9
Worcestershire Sauce, 40

Y

Yogurt
    Christmas Colors with Yogurt Sauce, 120
    Yogurt-Mayo Sandwich Spread, 211

Z

Zesty Almond Spread, 59
Zesty Feta and Olive Salad, 205
Zucchini
    Mock Chorizo Moussaka, 154
    Salmon Chowder, 193
    Vegetable and Bean Chili, 188
    Vegetable Broth, 214
    Zucchini Bread, 83
    Zucchini with Cheese Spread, 258

# The EVERYTHING Series!

## BUSINESS & PERSONAL FINANCE

Everything® Accounting Book
Everything® Budgeting Book
Everything® Business Planning Book
Everything® Coaching and Mentoring Book
Everything® Fundraising Book
Everything® Get Out of Debt Book
Everything® Grant Writing Book
**Everything® Guide to Personal Finance for Single Mothers**
Everything® Home-Based Business Book, 2nd Ed.
Everything® Homebuying Book, 2nd Ed.
Everything® Homeselling Book, 2nd Ed.
**Everything® Improve Your Credit Book**
Everything® Investing Book, 2nd Ed.
Everything® Landlording Book
Everything® Leadership Book
Everything® Managing People Book, 2nd Ed.
Everything® Negotiating Book
Everything® Online Auctions Book
Everything® Online Business Book
Everything® Personal Finance Book
Everything® Personal Finance in Your 20s and 30s Book
Everything® Project Management Book
Everything® Real Estate Investing Book
**Everything® Retirement Planning Book**
Everything® Robert's Rules Book, $7.95
Everything® Selling Book
Everything® Start Your Own Business Book, 2nd Ed.
Everything® Wills & Estate Planning Book

## COOKING

Everything® Barbecue Cookbook
Everything® Bartender's Book, $9.95
**Everything® Cheese Book**
Everything® Chinese Cookbook
Everything® Classic Recipes Book
Everything® Cocktail Parties and Drinks Book
Everything® College Cookbook
Everything® Cooking for Baby and Toddler Book
Everything® Cooking for Two Cookbook
Everything® Diabetes Cookbook
Everything® Easy Gourmet Cookbook
Everything® Fondue Cookbook
Everything® Fondue Party Book
Everything® Gluten-Free Cookbook
Everything® Glycemic Index Cookbook
Everything® Grilling Cookbook

Everything® Healthy Meals in Minutes Cookbook
Everything® Holiday Cookbook
Everything® Indian Cookbook
Everything® Italian Cookbook
Everything® Low-Carb Cookbook
Everything® Low-Fat High-Flavor Cookbook
Everything® Low-Salt Cookbook
Everything® Meals for a Month Cookbook
Everything® Mediterranean Cookbook
Everything® Mexican Cookbook
**Everything® No Trans Fat Cookbook**
Everything® One-Pot Cookbook
**Everything® Pizza Cookbook**
Everything® Quick and Easy 30-Minute, 5-Ingredient Cookbook
Everything® Quick Meals Cookbook
Everything® Slow Cooker Cookbook
Everything® Slow Cooking for a Crowd Cookbook
Everything® Soup Cookbook
**Everything® Stir-Fry Cookbook**
Everything® Tex-Mex Cookbook
Everything® Thai Cookbook
Everything® Vegetarian Cookbook
Everything® Wild Game Cookbook
Everything® Wine Book, 2nd Ed.

## GAMES

Everything® 15-Minute Sudoku Book, $9.95
Everything® 30-Minute Sudoku Book, $9.95
Everything® Blackjack Strategy Book
Everything® Brain Strain Book, $9.95
Everything® Bridge Book
Everything® Card Games Book
Everything® Card Tricks Book, $9.95
Everything® Casino Gambling Book, 2nd Ed.
Everything® Chess Basics Book
Everything® Craps Strategy Book
Everything® Crossword and Puzzle Book
Everything® Crossword Challenge Book
**Everything® Crosswords for the Beach Book, $9.95**
Everything® Cryptograms Book, $9.95
Everything® Easy Crosswords Book
Everything® Easy Kakuro Book, $9.95
**Everything® Easy Large Print Crosswords Book**
Everything® Games Book, 2nd Ed.
Everything® Giant Sudoku Book, $9.95
Everything® Kakuro Challenge Book, $9.95
Everything® Large-Print Crossword Challenge Book

Everything® Large-Print Crosswords Book
Everything® Lateral Thinking Puzzles Book, $9.9
Everything® Mazes Book
**Everything® Movie Crosswords Book, $9.95**
**Everything® Online Poker Book, $12.95**
Everything® Pencil Puzzles Book, $9.95
Everything® Poker Strategy Book
Everything® Pool & Billiards Book
**Everything® Sports Crosswords Book, $9.9**
Everything® Test Your IQ Book, $9.95
Everything® Texas Hold 'Em Book, $9.95
Everything® Travel Crosswords Book, $9.95
Everything® Word Games Challenge Book
**Everything® Word Scramble Book**
Everything® Word Search Book

## HEALTH

Everything® Alzheimer's Book
Everything® Diabetes Book
Everything® Health Guide to Adult Bipolar Disorder
Everything® Health Guide to Controlling Anxiety
Everything® Health Guide to Fibromyalgia
**Everything® Health Guide to Postpartum Care**
Everything® Health Guide to Thyroid Disease
Everything® Hypnosis Book
Everything® Low Cholesterol Book
Everything® Massage Book
Everything® Menopause Book
Everything® Nutrition Book
Everything® Reflexology Book
Everything® Stress Management Book

## HISTORY

Everything® American Government Book
**Everything® American History Book, 2nd Ed.**
Everything® Civil War Book
Everything® Freemasons Book
Everything® Irish History & Heritage Book
Everything® Middle East Book

## HOBBIES

Everything® Candlemaking Book
Everything® Cartooning Book
Everything® Coin Collecting Book
Everything® Drawing Book
Everything® Family Tree Book, 2nd Ed.
Everything® Knitting Book
Everything® Knots Book
Everything® Photography Book

Everything® Quilting Book
Everything® Scrapbooking Book
Everything® Sewing Book
**Everything® Soapmaking Book, 2nd Ed.**
Everything® Woodworking Book

## HOME IMPROVEMENT

Everything® Feng Shui Book
Everything® Feng Shui Decluttering Book, $9.95
Everything® Fix-It Book
Everything® Home Decorating Book
Everything® Home Storage Solutions Book
Everything® Homebuilding Book
Everything® Organize Your Home Book

## KIDS' BOOKS

**All titles are $7.95**

Everything® Kids' Animal Puzzle & Activity Book
Everything® Kids' Baseball Book, 4th Ed.
Everything® Kids' Bible Trivia Book
Everything® Kids' Bugs Book
Everything® Kids' Cars and Trucks Puzzle
   & Activity Book
Everything® Kids' Christmas Puzzle
   & Activity Book
Everything® Kids' Cookbook
Everything® Kids' Crazy Puzzles Book
Everything® Kids' Dinosaurs Book
Everything® Kids' First Spanish Puzzle and
   Activity Book
**Everything® Kids' Gross Cookbook**
Everything® Kids' Gross Hidden Pictures Book
Everything® Kids' Gross Jokes Book
Everything® Kids' Gross Mazes Book
Everything® Kids' Gross Puzzle and
   Activity Book
Everything® Kids' Halloween Puzzle
   & Activity Book
Everything® Kids' Hidden Pictures Book
Everything® Kids' Horses Book
Everything® Kids' Joke Book
Everything® Kids' Knock Knock Book
Everything® Kids' Learning Spanish Book
Everything® Kids' Math Puzzles Book
Everything® Kids' Mazes Book
Everything® Kids' Money Book
Everything® Kids' Nature Book
Everything® Kids' Pirates Puzzle and Activity Book
**Everything® Kids' Presidents Book**
Everything® Kids' Princess Puzzle and Activity Book
Everything® Kids' Puzzle Book
Everything® Kids' Riddles & Brain Teasers Book
Everything® Kids' Science Experiments Book
Everything® Kids' Sharks Book
Everything® Kids' Soccer Book
**Everything® Kids' States Book**
Everything® Kids' Travel Activity Book

## KIDS' STORY BOOKS

Everything® Fairy Tales Book

## LANGUAGE

Everything® Conversational Japanese Book with
   CD, $19.95
Everything® French Grammar Book
Everything® French Phrase Book, $9.95
Everything® French Verb Book, $9.95
Everything® German Practice Book with CD,
   $19.95
Everything® Inglés Book
**Everything® Intermediate Spanish Book with
   CD, $19.95**
**Everything® Learning Brazilian Portuguese
   Book with CD, $19.95**
Everything® Learning French Book
Everything® Learning German Book
Everything® Learning Italian Book
Everything® Learning Latin Book
**Everything® Learning Spanish Book with
   CD, 2nd Edition, $19.95**
Everything® Russian Practice Book with CD, $19.95
Everything® Sign Language Book
Everything® Spanish Grammar Book
Everything® Spanish Phrase Book, $9.95
Everything® Spanish Practice Book
   with CD, $19.95
Everything® Spanish Verb Book, $9.95
Everything® Speaking Mandarin Chinese Book
   with CD, $19.95

## MUSIC

Everything® Drums Book with CD, $19.95
**Everything® Guitar Book with CD, 2nd
   Edition, $19.95**
Everything® Guitar Chords Book with CD, $19.95
Everything® Home Recording Book
Everything® Music Theory Book with CD, $19.95
Everything® Reading Music Book with CD, $19.95
Everything® Rock & Blues Guitar Book
   with CD, $19.95
**Everything® Rock and Blues Piano Book
   with CD, $19.95**
Everything® Songwriting Book

## NEW AGE

Everything® Astrology Book, 2nd Ed.
Everything® Birthday Personology Book
Everything® Dreams Book, 2nd Ed.
Everything® Love Signs Book, $9.95
Everything® Numerology Book
Everything® Paganism Book
Everything® Palmistry Book
Everything® Psychic Book
Everything® Reiki Book

Everything® Sex Signs Book, $9.95
Everything® Tarot Book, 2nd Ed.
**Everything® Toltec Wisdom Book**
Everything® Wicca and Witchcraft Book

## PARENTING

Everything® Baby Names Book, 2nd Ed.
Everything® Baby Shower Book
Everything® Baby's First Year Book
Everything® Birthing Book
Everything® Breastfeeding Book
Everything® Father-to-Be Book
Everything® Father's First Year Book
Everything® Get Ready for Baby Book
Everything® Get Your Baby to Sleep Book, $9.95
Everything® Getting Pregnant Book
Everything® Guide to Raising a One-Year-Old
Everything® Guide to Raising a Two-Year-Old
Everything® Homeschooling Book
Everything® Mother's First Year Book
**Everything® Parent's Guide to Childhood
   Illnesses**
Everything® Parent's Guide to Children
   and Divorce
Everything® Parent's Guide to Children
   with ADD/ADHD
Everything® Parent's Guide to Children
   with Asperger's Syndrome
Everything® Parent's Guide to Children
   with Autism
Everything® Parent's Guide to Children with
   Bipolar Disorder
**Everything® Parent's Guide to Children with
   Depression**
Everything® Parent's Guide to Children
   with Dyslexia
**Everything® Parent's Guide to Children with
   Juvenile Diabetes**
Everything® Parent's Guide to Positive Discipline
Everything® Parent's Guide to Raising a
   Successful Child
Everything® Parent's Guide to Raising Boys
**Everything® Parent's Guide to Raising Girls**
Everything® Parent's Guide to Raising Siblings
Everything® Parent's Guide to Sensory
   Integration Disorder
Everything® Parent's Guide to Tantrums
Everything® Parent's Guide to the Strong-Willed
   Child
Everything® Parenting a Teenager Book
Everything® Potty Training Book, $9.95
**Everything® Pregnancy Book, 3rd Ed.**
Everything® Pregnancy Fitness Book
Everything® Pregnancy Nutrition Book
Everything® Pregnancy Organizer, 2nd Ed., $16.95
Everything® Toddler Activities Book
Everything® Toddler Book

Everything® Tween Book
Everything® Twins, Triplets, and More Book

## PETS

Everything® Aquarium Book
Everything® Boxer Book
Everything® Cat Book, 2nd Ed.
Everything® Chihuahua Book
Everything® Dachshund Book
Everything® Dog Book
Everything® Dog Health Book
**Everything® Dog Obedience Book**
Everything® Dog Owner's Organizer, $16.95
Everything® Dog Training and Tricks Book
Everything® German Shepherd Book
Everything® Golden Retriever Book
Everything® Horse Book
Everything® Horse Care Book
Everything® Horseback Riding Book
Everything® Labrador Retriever Book
Everything® Poodle Book
Everything® Pug Book
Everything® Puppy Book
Everything® Rottweiler Book
Everything® Small Dogs Book
Everything® Tropical Fish Book
Everything® Yorkshire Terrier Book

## REFERENCE

**Everything® American Presidents Book**
Everything® Blogging Book
Everything® Build Your Vocabulary Book
Everything® Car Care Book
Everything® Classical Mythology Book
Everything® Da Vinci Book
Everything® Divorce Book
Everything® Einstein Book
**Everything® Enneagram Book**
Everything® Etiquette Book, 2nd Ed.
Everything® Inventions and Patents Book
Everything® Mafia Book
Everything® Philosophy Book
**Everything® Pirates Book**
Everything® Psychology Book

## RELIGION

Everything® Angels Book
Everything® Bible Book
Everything® Buddhism Book
Everything® Catholicism Book
Everything® Christianity Book
**Everything® Gnostic Gospels Book**
Everything® History of the Bible Book
Everything® Jesus Book

Everything® Jewish History & Heritage Book
Everything® Judaism Book
Everything® Kabbalah Book
Everything® Koran Book
Everything® Mary Book
Everything® Mary Magdalene Book
Everything® Prayer Book
**Everything® Saints Book, 2nd Ed.**
Everything® Torah Book
Everything® Understanding Islam Book
Everything® World's Religions Book
Everything® Zen Book

## SCHOOL & CAREERS

Everything® Alternative Careers Book
Everything® Career Tests Book
Everything® College Major Test Book
Everything® College Survival Book, 2nd Ed.
Everything® Cover Letter Book, 2nd Ed.
Everything® Filmmaking Book
**Everything® Get-a-Job Book, 2nd Ed.**
Everything® Guide to Being a Paralegal
**Everything® Guide to Being a Personal
   Trainer**
Everything® Guide to Being a Real Estate
   Agent
Everything® Guide to Being a Sales Rep
Everything® Guide to Careers in Health Care
Everything® Guide to Careers in Law
   Enforcement
Everything® Guide to Government Jobs
Everything® Guide to Starting and Running
   a Restaurant
Everything® Job Interview Book
Everything® New Nurse Book
Everything® New Teacher Book
Everything® Paying for College Book
Everything® Practice Interview Book
Everything® Resume Book, 2nd Ed.
Everything® Study Book

## SELF-HELP

Everything® Dating Book, 2nd Ed.
Everything® Great Sex Book
Everything® Self-Esteem Book
**Everything® Tantric Sex Book**

## SPORTS & FITNESS

Everything® Easy Fitness Book
Everything® Running Book
Everything® Weight Training Book

## TRAVEL

Everything® Family Guide to Cruise Vacations
Everything® Family Guide to Hawaii
Everything® Family Guide to Las Vegas, 2nd Ed.
Everything® Family Guide to Mexico
Everything® Family Guide to New York City,
   2nd Ed.
Everything® Family Guide to RV Travel &
   Campgrounds
Everything® Family Guide to the Caribbean
Everything® Family Guide to the Walt Disney
   World Resort®, Universal Studios®,
   and Greater Orlando, 4th Ed.
Everything® Family Guide to Timeshares
**Everything® Family Guide to Washington
   D.C., 2nd Ed.**

## WEDDINGS

Everything® Bachelorette Party Book, $9.95
Everything® Bridesmaid Book, $9.95
Everything® Destination Wedding Book
Everything® Elopement Book, $9.95
Everything® Father of the Bride Book, $9.95
Everything® Groom Book, $9.95
Everything® Mother of the Bride Book, $9.95
Everything® Outdoor Wedding Book
Everything® Wedding Book, 3rd Ed.
Everything® Wedding Checklist, $9.95
Everything® Wedding Etiquette Book, $9.95
Everything® Wedding Organizer, 2nd Ed., $16.95
Everything® Wedding Shower Book, $9.95
Everything® Wedding Vows Book, $9.95
Everything® Wedding Workout Book
Everything® Weddings on a Budget Book, $9.95

## WRITING

Everything® Creative Writing Book
Everything® Get Published Book, 2nd Ed.
Everything® Grammar and Style Book
**Everything® Guide to Magazine Writing**
Everything® Guide to Writing a Book Proposal
Everything® Guide to Writing a Novel
Everything® Guide to Writing Children's Books
**Everything® Guide to Writing Copy**
Everything® Guide to Writing Research Papers
Everything® Screenwriting Book
Everything® Writing Poetry Book
Everything® Writing Well Book

---

Available wherever books are sold! To order, call 800-258-0929, or visit us at *www.everything.com*.
Everything® and everything.com® are registered trademarks of F+W Publications, Inc.
Bolded titles are new additions to the series.
All Everything® books are priced at $12.95 or $14.95, unless otherwise stated. Prices subject to change without notice.